Rethinking
the
Western
Tradition

*The volumes in this series
seek to address the present debate
over the Western tradition
by reprinting key works of
that tradition along with essays
that evaluate each text from
different perspectives.*

On Heroes, Hero-Worship, and the Heroic in History

THOMAS CARLYLE

Edited by

David R. Sorensen and Brent E. Kinser

with essays by

Sara Atwood

Owen Dudley Edwards

Christopher Harvie

Brent E. Kinser

Terence James Reed

David R. Sorensen

Beverly Taylor

Yale

UNIVERSITY PRESS

New Haven and London

Yale University Press books may be purchased in quantity for educational, business, or
promotional use. For information, please e-mail sales.press@yale.edu (U.S. office) or
sales@yaleup.co.uk (U.K. office).

Set in Times Roman type by Keystone Typesetting, Inc.
Printed in the United States of America.

Library of Congress Cataloging-in-Publication Data
On heroes, hero-worship, and the heroic in history / Thomas Carlyle ; edited by
David R. Sorensen and Brent E. Kinser ; with essays by Sara Atwood,
Owen Dudley Edwards, Christopher Harvie, Brent E. Kinser, Terence James Reed,
David R. Sorensen, Beverly Taylor.
Pages cm — (Rethinking the Western tradition)
Includes bibliographical references and index.
ISBN 978-0-300-14860-2 (pbk.)
1. Heroes. 2. Hero worship. I. Sorensen, David R., 1953– editor of compilation.
II. Kinser, Brent E., editor of compilation. III. Carlyle, Thomas, 1795–1881.
On heroes, hero-worship, and the heroic in history.
PR4426.A2S67 2013
824'.8 — dc23
2012045115

A catalogue record for this book is available from the British Library.

This paper meets the requirements of ANSI/NISO Z39.48-1992 (Permanence of Paper).

For Fielding, DeLaura, and apRoberts

"Flowing Light-Fountains"

Contents

Introduction

DAVID R. SORENSEN

The other sect (to which I belong) . . . look upon hero-worship as no better than any other idolatry, and upon the attitude of mind of the hero-worshipper as essentially immoral.
> —T. H. Huxley to Charles Kingsley, 8 Nov. 1866, concerning charges of criminality against Governor John Eyre of Jamaica;
> *Life and Letters* 1:304

"My dear young friend," said Mustapha Mond, "civilization has absolutely no need of nobility or heroism. These things are symptoms of political inefficiency. In a properly organized society like ours, nobody has any opportunities for being noble or heroic."
> —Aldous Huxley, *Brave New World* (1932) 161

In a striking example of what Thomas Carlyle called a "conflux of two Eternities" ("Signs of the Times" [1829], *Works* 27:59), the fate of *On Heroes, Hero-Worship, and the Heroic in History* (1841) has closely paralleled that of his own reputation in the twenty-first century. Today neither Carlyle nor his book is widely known among students of English literature. However unfairly, both have been tarnished by their association with the authoritarian and totalitarian personality cults that brought European civilization to the brink of destruction in World War II and that left what Michael Burleigh has called a "dystopian stain" (xi) on the historical record. Renowned in the early Victorian period as the indomitable opponent of mechanistic social engineering, Carlyle later became implicated in its worst excesses. Significantly, in *Culture and Society* (1958) — the boldest and most successful attempt to revive Carlyle's standing as a prophet — Raymond Williams referred to *Heroes and Hero-Worship* as a turning point in the author's career, signaling his "steady withdrawal from genuinely social thinking into the preoccupations with personal power" (83).

Carlyle's contemporaries themselves were equally dismayed by the direction his thinking took in the wake of this "withdrawal." His notorious slurs on Africans, Jews, Irish Catholics, and Poles, his equivocal support of the Confederacy in the American Civil War, his adulation of Prussian militarism, and his defense of Governor John Eyre's brutal suppression of the Jamaican revolt in 1866 offended those who had been moved by his earlier polemics against laissez-faire economics and his tenacious prosecution of the "Condition of England" question. His reputation reached its nadir in early 1945, when in his diary Joseph Goebbels cited Carlyle's *History of Frederick the Great* (1858–65) as Adolf Hitler's chief source of solace during his final months in the Berlin bunker. Never again was the "Sage of Chelsea" readily identified with the cause of common humanity. Like the Prussian state that he revered, Carlyle, the prophet recognized by Williams as "qualified to become the most important social thinker of his century" (76), effectively ceased to exist as an intellectual force in the years after the war.

Hero-worship itself has followed a similar downward trajectory. The trend began in the period following the "Great War" — the war that was to have prevented World War II and all other wars — when what Paul Fussell called the "static world" of Victorian morality, with its seemingly "permanent and reliable" (21) abstractions, began to unravel as the enormity of the conflict became apparent. Later in the century, in the wake of the catastrophic experiments in human transformation that traumatized societies as politically and culturally diverse as China, Cambodia, Germany, Iraq, Libya, North Korea, Romania, and the Soviet Union in the twentieth century — experiments conducted to exalt the supreme wisdom of transcendent leaders — skepticism toward heroic avatars became more deeply entrenched in Western thought. Summarizing this consensus at the outset of a new millennium, Lucy Hughes-Hallett argued that the "notion of the hero — that some men are born special — is radically inegalitarian. It can open the way for tyranny." She goes on to point out that hero-worship "allows worshippers to abnegate responsibility, looking to the great man for salvation or for fulfilment that they should more properly be working to accomplish for themselves" (3). To those who complained about the triviality of modern life, Hughes-Hallett bluntly responded that the dominance of popular culture was a necessary consequence of a more democratic society. Modern "triviality," however dispiriting, was far less hazardous to the body politic than the "desperation that prompts people to crave a champion, a protector, or a redeemer and, having identified one, to offer him their worship" (2).

Despite the influential efforts of philosophers such as Hannah Arendt and John Rawls to enshrine equality as the highest social good by arguing for the inherent dignity of all human beings, dissenters continue to press the

case for heroic distinction. Robert Faulkner, a shrewd proponent of Aristotelian "magnanimity," has recently contended that "the new liberalism's
antipathy to superior statesmen and to human excellence is peculiarly zealous, parochial, and antiphilosophic" (210). But his argument is unlikely to
gain much traction in the digital age. To a younger generation obsessively
attuned to the Internet, blogging, Facebook, and Twitter, heroes are increasingly defined by extrinsic rather than intrinsic factors. In his essay
"From Hero to Celebrity" (1987), Daniel Boorstin traced the origins of this
shift to the period of what he termed the "Graphic Revolution" in the
1850s, when technological changes began to privilege image over print and
accelerated "the means of fabricating well-knownness" (285). Heroes
could be created instantly for the sake of a mass market that conflated
distinction and popularity. Boorstin cautioned, "Celebrity-worship and
hero-worship should not be confused. Yet we confuse them every day, and
by doing so we come dangerously close to depriving ourselves of all real
models. . . . We come closer to degrading all fame into notoriety" (ix). This
personalization of heroes has coincided with the postmodernist urge to
"interrogate" the lives of exceptional individuals and to unmask the as-
sumptions of power and hierarchy concealed by their apparent altruism and
self-sacrifice. Biographers and historians are encouraged to unearth secrets
that will compromise grand narratives and alert the public to the slipperi-
ness of all heroic discourse. As one exasperated advocate of heroes, Peter
Gibbon, has complained, "What role is left for the hero when the culture
would rather be titillated than inspired and prefers gossip to gospel?" (xviii)
    Always alive to the ironies of history, Carlyle would have responded to
this debate by reminding his audience that too much can be made of the
novelty of the present. In the public lectures that he delivered in the spring
of 1840, he too voiced alarm at the eviscerated state of hero-worship, which
had degenerated into what he had earlier called "Puffery and Quackery"
(*Sartor* 11). Yet he did not believe that the phenomenon Boorstin would
label the "Graphic Revolution" was necessarily inimical to the growth of
genuine hero-worship. Influential in the campaign to establish national
portrait galleries in London and Edinburgh, Carlyle regarded truthful and
accurate images of the human face as the surest means to arouse popular
veneration for great men and women. What mattered to him most, though,
were the internal qualities of heroism. In an important sense, his public
lectures marked the culmination of a fruitful period of reflection on the
topic, which he had explored from literary, historical, and political perspectives. These writings were united by his conviction that industrialization
had contributed to a dehumanization of social life. For him, the ubiquitous

mechanization of life had leveled moral distinctions, numbed individual initiative, and harnessed human potential to the exigencies of production and consumption.

In his first important attempt at social commentary, "Signs of the Times" (1829), Carlyle noticed that society's drift toward efficiency and uniformity had penetrated to the deepest layers of the human psyche: "For the same habit regulates not our modes of action alone, but our modes of thought and feeling. Men are grown mechanical in head and in heart, as well as in hand. They have lost faith in individual endeavour, and in natural force, of any kind.... Their whole efforts, attachments, opinions, turn on mechanism, and are of a mechanical character" (*Works* 27:62–63). Even in his early commentary, however, Carlyle was not promoting an escape to some idyllic past. He acknowledged the contribution that technology had made "and [was] still making, to the physical power of mankind; how much better fed, clothed, lodged and, in all outward respects, accommodated men now are." But above all, Carlyle recognized that the cost to humanity of these "wonderful accessions" (*Works* 27:60) was far steeper than the advocates of progress were prepared to admit. Beneath the surface of an English society that many radicals treated as a petri dish for Utilitarian reform, Carlyle discerned widespread demoralization and indifference to any aims beyond simple material advancement. In his early major works — *Sartor Resartus* (1833–34), *The French Revolution* (1837), and *Chartism* (1839) — he identified the crisis of his age as spiritual in origin. Diogenes Teufelsdröckh, the hero of *Sartor Resartus,* experiences "sorrows" that spring from his crisis of faith and from his dread of the dominant "Mechanical Profit-and-Loss Philosophies, with the sick ophthalmia and hallucination they had brought on" (123). Not coincidentally, his ecstatic vision of "Natural Supernaturalism" (*Sartor* book 3, ch. 8) is accompanied by an awakening reverence for the "Godlike . . . revealed in his fellow-man." It is through heroes that the Professor realizes his own heroic possibilities. Hero-worship itself constitutes for Teufelsdröckh "the corner-stone of living rock, whereon all Politics for the remotest time may stand secure" (185).

In *The French Revolution* Carlyle extended this analysis, insisting that the upheaval in France was not merely economic. Startling all sides in the debate and anticipating the later analyses of Jules Michelet and Alexis de Tocqueville, he treated the Revolution as a miraculous manifestation of suppressed spirituality, the electric reverberations of which continued to be felt worldwide. He refused to accept the Burkean Tory view that Jacobin ideology was a "drunken delirium" (Burke 142) or the Benthamite Liberal estimate that the Revolution itself was an unfortunate phase in a necessary

transition to democracy, individualism, and laissez-faire. The defining element of the French "Political Evangel" was its appeal to a purified future,
which was celebrated and sanctified in popular public rituals, symbols, and
liturgies. In his 1906 edition of Carlyle's history, John Holland Rose co-
gently defined Carlyle's achievement: "[He] asserted that no visible and
finite object had ever spurred men on to truly great and far-reaching movements. Only the invisible and the infinite could do that" (1:xiv). The Revolution brought a new abstraction to the stage of history — "the masses" — an
inchoate and unknown entity. In his history Carlyle had striven to re-create
them as flesh-and-blood realities, endowed with individual as well as collective aspirations. For him they were the true heroes of the Revolution, and it
was their predicament that had compelled him to fathom the meaning and
purport of the cataclysm. Nonetheless, Carlyle was profoundly disturbed by
the violent and chaotic direction that the Revolution eventually took, with its
bloody "self-devourment" in Thermidor and the protracted violence and
warfare of the Napoleonic period. The fiery "Consummation of Sansculottism" (*Works* 4:243) had revealed the terrible discrepancy between the popular demand for leadership and the paucity of worthy candidates. One after
another the leaders of the Revolution — Mirabeau, Danton, Marat, and
Robespierre — were first Pantheonized as heroes and then de-Pantheonized
as traitors by the volatile populace.

It was symptomatic of this frenzied epoch that the leader who emerged
as the savior of France — one whom Carlyle classified in *Heroes and Hero-
Worship* as "our last Great Man" (195) — eventually crowned himself emperor. Napoleon's destiny was intimately linked to that of France. Remarks
Carlyle, "He believed too much in the *Dupeability* of men; saw no fact
deeper in man than Hunger and this! He was mistaken." Yet the nation that
he misled continued to follow him until his defeat. To a degree, his cult of
invincibility mirrored their own fantasies of power: "Alas, in all of us this
charlatan-element exists; and *might* be developed, were the temptation
strong enough" (194). Ironically, in the same month that Carlyle delivered
his lectures, May 1840, Louis Philippe's government had requested the
exhumation and return of Bonaparte's body to France. In an extravagant
ceremony in Paris on 15 December 1840 — memorably satirized by Carlyle's friend William Makepeace Thackeray in "The Second Funeral of
Napoleon" (1841) — Napoleon's corpse was reinterred at Les Invalides in
Paris. The event provided a vital backdrop to Carlyle's lectures, confirming
his view that hero-worship was now synonymous with theatricality and
chimeras.

Surveying the "Condition of England" on the eve of the "hungry forties," Carlyle was convinced that the country would suffer its own French Revolution, and that in its reincarnation this cataclysm might prove to be even more destructive and catastrophic than its predecessor. In *Chartism* (1839) he delivered a withering indictment of the country's "*Laissez-faire*" culture as a response to Liberal reformers who argued that a greater distribution of wealth through the operation of a free market would enlarge the domain of personal choice, enrich opportunity, and achieve the Benthamite dictum by securing the "greatest happiness of the greatest number." On the contrary, Carlyle declared, the triumph of this doctrine had ensured that all social bonds other than those dictated by "*Cash Payment* . . . the universal sole nexus of man to man" (*Works* 29:162) were disregarded. The vast majority of the population lived without guidance or inspiration, sullenly surviving while political economists trumpeted the social and economic advantages of obeying the ineluctable laws of supply and demand. Either a new type of hero would arise to restore the human relations that had created Britain, Carlyle predicted, or the society itself would disintegrate in a violent bloodbath.

Carlyle had concluded that the ruthlessly incontrovertible logic of the marketplace had shrunk people's faith in themselves and their peers. Everywhere, Carlyle asserted, a "sense for the true and false" was absent. Victorian Britain marked "the heyday of Imposture; of Semblance recognising itself, and getting itself recognised, for Substances" (*Works* 29:151). In reaction to the crisis, radicals championed the panacea of Democracy, but from Carlyle's vantage point, this weak if noisy attempt at egalitarianism represented "the consummation of No-government and *Laissez-faire*," and though necessary "and natural for our Europe at present," it was hardly a substitute for "government by the wisest" (29:159). He was determined to consider his topic from a vantage point beyond the political and philosophical orthodoxies of his time. Political debate in England was shackled by sloganeering. Himself under the pressure of monetary necessity, Carlyle began to plan a series of lectures on heroes. From the beginning he was determined to counter the propensity to reduce all human interaction to a calculus of pleasure, and he was equally keen to eschew any labels that his audience may have been tempted to attach either to him or to his ideas. The syllabus for his six lectures, to be delivered at 17 Edward Street, Portman Square, between 5 and 27 May 1840, specified that he would explore heroes and hero-worship in relation to history. The title, "On Heroes, Hero-Worship, and the Heroic in Human History" (Tarr, *Bibliography* 90), which he maintained with the exception of the word "Human" for the book version in 1841, was meant to emphasize the variability of his subject, "a thing

forever changing . . . different in each age, difficult to do well in any age"
(52). Heroes both shaped and were shaped by their times, and neither dimension could be ignored in assessing their influence. It required time, distance,
patience, and discrimination to determine the impact that they wielded on
their age.

Firmly holding to his historical conception of heroes, Carlyle sought to
look beyond the dominant "ists" and "isms" of the present, but he had no
intention of ignoring them. His primary goal was to challenge the prevailing Benthamite philosophy, which gave priority to rational self-interest as a
means of promoting an efficient, orderly, regulated, and therefore "happy"
society. In his *Deontology; or the Science of Morality* (1834), Bentham had
singled out hero-worship as the most retrograde of social doctrines: "Of all
that is pernicious in admiration, the admiration of heroes is the most pernicious; and how delusions should have made us admire what virtue should
teach us to hate and loathe, is among the saddest evidences of human
weakness and folly" (2:254). What was required, Bentham insisted, was a
study of heroes that exposed the fallacies of traditional conceptions and that
demanded definitions that were consistent with Utilitarian ethics: "In the
better and happier epoch, the wise and the good will be busied in hurling
into oblivion, or dragging forth, for exposure to universal ignominy and
obloquy, many of the deeds we deem heroic; while the true fame and the
perdurable glories will be gathered round the creators and diffusers of
happiness" (2:256). This call for Utilitarian heroes — answered later in the
century by Samuel Smiles in his best-selling series of biographies of successful Victorian inventors and entrepreneurs — prompted Carlyle to address the topic in starkly contrary terms.

In his lectures he undermined Bentham by lauding the negative value of
Utilitarianism: "[His] creed . . . seems . . . comparatively worthy of praise. It
is a determinate being what all the world, in a cowardly half-and-half manner, was tending to be" (*Heroes* 145). Utilitarianism boldly and unequivo-
cally diagnosed the fallen state of Victorian hero-worship and the shallow-
ness and hypocrisy of the religious attitude that sponsored it. Inevitably, an
era in which religion was confused with doctrinal "Respectability" was also
one in which economic success became the sole criterion of inward strength.
Carlyle congratulated Bentham for his trenchant analysis of contemporary
ethics and spirituality. Utilitarianism "was a laying down of cant; a saying to
oneself: 'Well, then, this world is a dead ironic machine, the god of it Gravitation and selfish Hunger; let us see what, by checking and balancing . . . can
be made of it!' " In contrast to those who were vainly striving to restore the
"old clothes" of Christianity — Carlyle had in mind the Tractarians and John

Henry Newman's biographical panegyrics on English saints — Benthamism "has something complete, manful, in such fearless committal of itself to what it finds true." Yet in their "laying down of cant," the Utilitarians had neglected to notice their own brand of hypocrisy. Their heroism, according to Carlyle, was "an *eyeless*" sort because their science denied the possibility of acts of altruism or of conscience, reducing all behavior to a "wretched love of Pleasure, fear of Pain" (145).

Carlyle rightly gauged that many of the Liberals in his audience were uneasy about the social and spiritual repercussions of Bentham's philosophy. He deliberately tried to provoke further discomfort among them with his witheringly backhanded endorsement of Bentham's "Steam-engine" (*Heroes* 75) dogma. In particular, he knew that his acolyte John Stuart Mill — their friendship would not survive Carlyle's reactionary turn in the 1840s — shared many of his own reservations about the soullessness of the "felicific calculus" mapped out by Bentham in the fourth chapter of *An Introduction to the Principles of Morals and Legislation* (1789). In his essay on Bentham in 1838, Mill had remarked, "Man is never recognised by him as a being capable of pursuing spiritual perfection as an end; of desiring for its own sake, the conformity of his own character to his standard of excellence, without hope of good or fear of evil from other source than his own inward consciousness." Bentham not only underestimated "the moral part of man's nature," Mill contended, he also overlooked "the pursuit of any other ideal end for its own sake" (*CWM* 10:95). Long after his breach with Carlyle, Mill continued to acknowledge the importance of heroes. In *On Liberty* (1859) he conceded that "when the opinions of masses of merely average men are everywhere become or becoming the dominant power, the counterpoise and corrective to that tendency would be, the more and more pronounced individuality of those who stand on the higher eminences of thought." Though Mill condemned "the strong man of genius for forcibly seizing on the government of the world and making it do his bidding in spite of itself," he steadfastly affirmed the benefits of "exceptional individuals . . . acting differently from the mass" (*CWM* 18:269).

In important ways, Mill's effort to preserve hero-worship in liberal culture was influenced by Carlyle, who in his lectures attributed the "*spiritual paralysis*" (*Heroes* 143) of his era to the superficiality of its ethos. By default, Benthamite Utilitarianism had become the reigning philosophy of the day because of the enervated state of Victorian Christianity. Not coincidentally, the first four lectures — on the hero as divinity, as prophet, as poet, and as priest — highlighted the "organic filaments" that linked nobleness of character to a dynamic "religiosity" (55). Carlyle distinguished the heroes of this class — Odin, Mahomet, Dante, Shakespeare, Luther, and Knox — by their personal "radiance" (100) rather than by their acquisitiveness or their lust for fame. The basis of their strength resided in their deep and abiding comprehension of the divinity of creation, the "emblem of the Godlike." This divine awareness was the primal "Fact" of their existence, releasing them from doubt, checking their worldly ambitions, and imbuing them with the courage to seek the truth about themselves and their relation to God. Each conducted his search in a different historical environment, yet Carlyle traced the "perennial fibre" of their quest to their mutual recognition that "every object has a divine beauty in it" (27). Gifted with the intellectual power to penetrate the subterfuges of life — for Carlyle, heroism was pre-eminently a mental endowment — they won trust and loyalty by the integrity of their aims and the sincerity of their motives. In this respect their achievement was not simply personal but collective. Carlyle asked, "Does not every true man feel that he is himself made higher by doing reverence to what is really above him?" (31). What defined this group of premodern heroes was their ability to awaken heroic instincts in others, and to channel these toward the comprehension and the realization of order, hierarchy, harmony, beauty, and justice.

Rejecting the miraculous aspects of the doctrinal Christ, Carlyle sought to realign Christianity with the mythmaking energies that were common to all great religions, which "have all had a truth in them, or men would not have taken them up" (*Heroes* 23). As one religion among many for Carlyle, Christianity represented the highest stage of a vast historical spiritual evolution whereby humankind advanced to a fuller revelation of its own infinite capacities. Heroes uniquely possessed the vision to transform this potential into good works. In this respect Jesus, "the greatest of all Heroes" (28) was the descendant of Odin and Mahomet. As Ruth apRoberts has acutely remarked, Carlyle's lectures were informed by his conviction that "the sacred and the secular are one," and that his taking a " 'god' as a hero is in itself a bold step and clear statement against supernaturalism" (*Ancient Dialect* 78). This secularization of divinity was also part of Carlyle's nimble strategy to expose the parochialism of the debates generated by the Oxford Movement. Inhibited by dogmatic "Quackery" (*Heroes* 23), Victorian Christians were invited by Carlyle to revitalize their faith by exploring their ancestral ties to paganism and even to Islam. In his first two lectures he elevates both religions on the grounds of their vigorous idealism and "rude greatness of soul" (46). At the core of Odin's creed was a yearning to overcome fear by cultivating "valour." This desire was the path to godliness, and his people "thought . . . him a Divinity for telling it them." In releasing them from mental bondage, in Carlyle's view, Odin fired the Norse with a "longing only to become articulate, to go on articulating ever farther!" (44).

For Carlyle, Mahomet exerted a similar impact on his followers. Though lacking finesse and culture in Carlyle's mind, he evinced a fierce intelligence and a "bursting earnestness" (*Heroes* 75). Like all of his premodern heroes, Mahomet's strength of mind and purpose originated in his acceptance that "we must *submit* to God" (61), the fount of all law and morality. For Carlyle's Mahomet, this "Annihilation of Self" (62) was in no way indicative of intellectual surrender. On the contrary, submission was the first step to freedom conceived as "Duty," a freedom "to be earned by faith and welldoing, by valiant action, and a divine patience which is still more valiant." Carlyle conceived of Islam as a continuation of "Scandinavian Paganism," with a "truly celestial element superadded to that" and also as "a kind of Christianity" with "a genuine element of what is spiritually highest looking through it." From both creeds, Carlyle's version of Islam derived a robustness of mind and spirit that contrasted favorably with Benthamite Utilitarianism, a servile and abject philosophy that reduced "this God's-world to a dead Hay-balance for weighing hay and thistles on, pleasures and pains on." Carlyle remained convinced that no dimmer view of human possibility existed than this mechanistic anathema, which could only measure the worth of religion in relation to Bentham's grand assertion: "conduciveness or repugnancy to the greatest human happiness" (*Deontology* 1:127). Juxtaposed with Mahomet, Bentham emerges as an apt symbol of the bankruptcy of the present. Carlyle proclaims, "If you ask me which gives . . . the beggarlier and falser view of Man and his Destinies in this Universe, I will answer, It is not Mahomet! — " (*Heroes* 75).

What the prophets were to morality, so too were the poets to beauty. Through Dante and Shakespeare, "these two provinces run into one another" (*Heroes* 79), nourishing a broader and richer understanding between them. With the ascendancy of science, divinity and prophecy migrated into fresh forms of heroic expression. Dante and Shakespeare each spoke in a "world-voice" (94), addressing two distinct yet complementary psychological currents in European history. The Italian poet "was sent into our world to embody musically the Religion of the Middle Ages, the Religion of our Modern Europe, its Inner Life." Conversely, for Carlyle, Shakespeare "embodies for us the Outer Life of our Europe as developed then, its chivalries, courtesies, humours, ambitions, what practical way of thinking, acting, looking at the world, men then had" (93). Fulfilling their roles as catalysts, the poets promoted in their writing an extension of sympathy and an increase of insight. Carlyle's reading of Dante's allegory of the "soul of Christianity" (61) re-created the moment of transition from paganism to Christianity, when the sensuous reception of the "Operations of Nature" yielded to a more refined perception of the centrality of "the Law of Human duty, the Moral Law of Man" (91) in human relations.

Shakespeare's work reflects the grandeur of his intellect. Indeed, for Carlyle he remains "the greatest of Intellects" (*Heroes* 98). Throughout his disquisition on the Bard, Carlyle comments on the liberality and the suppleness of Shakespeare's judgment, and the manner in which he combines these in his art. The "Force which dwells in him, is essentially one and indivisible," Carlyle observes: "what we call imagination, fancy, understanding, and so forth, are but different powers of the same Power of Insight, all indissolubly connected with each other, physiognomically related" (97). Shakespeare performed the noblest function of a hero by liberating the European mind from the fetters of "narrow superstition, harsh asceticism, intolerance, fanatical fierceness [and] perversion" (100–101). If Dante exemplified "Middle-Age Catholicism" (94), Shakespeare went further by transforming himself into a "melodious Priest of a *true* Catholicism, the 'Universal Church' of the Future and of all times" (100). Through the power of his song, he transported spirituality to more expansive regions, where laughter and wisdom were compatible sides of an unfettered mental equilibrium. Among Carlyle's heroes, Shakespeare stands out because he stubbornly resisted the temptation of factional prophecy: "Was it not perhaps far better that this Shakspeare, every way an unconscious man, was *conscious* of no Heavenly message? He did not feel, like Mahomet, because he saw into those internal Splendours, that he specially was the 'Prophet of God:' . . . was he not greater than Mahomet in that? Greater" (101).

Significantly, Carlyle here regarded the Reformation and the Puritan Revolution as movements that retarded the free play of thought and imagination that Dante and Shakespeare had initiated; his attitudes would soon change as his contempt for the "ballot-box, parliamentary eloquence, voting, [and] constitution-building" (*Heroes* 162) sharpened. Carlyle portrayed his heroic priests, Martin Luther and John Knox, as iconoclasts whose dogged hostility to idolatry narrowed their mental horizons. They belonged to the second act of a world-historical upheaval that began with Mahomet and culminated with the French Revolution. It was essentially a regenerative process, yet it was one that was necessary to the emergence of "Truth and Reality in opposition to Falsehood and Semblance." Carlyle candidly acknowledged that Protestantism, at least on first impressions, was "entirely destructive to this that we call Hero-worship." Yet the destructive tenor of

Protestantism, however narrow and rigid, promised a "new genuine sovereignty and order" that was rooted in rigorous self-inquiry and "private judgment" (110). Luther's achievement was to wrest spiritual authority from abstract "Idols" and to lodge it in the heart and conscience of the believer. The creator of the Lutheran Bible was, like Shakespeare, "a great Thinker" (121) whose character combined rugged honesty with piercing intelligence. Knox too had "a good honest intellectual talent, no transcendent one," but when set against Luther, he was a "narrow, inconsiderable man" (128). Still, Knox's life mission extended beyond the borders of his native country: "The Puritanism of Scotland became that of England, of New England. A tumult in the High Church of Edinburgh spread into a universal battle and struggle over all these realms; — there came out, after fifty years struggling, what we all call the '*Glorious* Revolution,' a *Habeas-Corpus* Act, Free Parliaments, and much else!" (126). It was irrelevant for Carlyle that Knox's triumph was posthumous, for the same could have been said of Odin, Mahomet, Dante, and Shakespeare. That Knox's distinct Scottish identity lived after his death in the pages of his country's philosophy, literature, science, art, and poetry was a sure proof of his heroic stature.

From the discussion of the hero as priest and the compulsion of theocracy, Carlyle proceeded to his fifth lecture, "The Hero as Man of Letters." This transition was a carefully designed move, one meant to highlight a leitmotif — the hero as an exemplary thinker and activist — that had been implicit in each of the previous lectures. Carlyle was ready to declare that a fresh reservoir of spiritual authority had emerged in the nineteenth century that radically altered the way in which beliefs could be transmitted. The creation of cheap printing served as a lectern to a new priestcraft: "The writers of Newspapers, Pamphlets, Poems, Books, these *are* the real working effective Church of a modern century." Carlyle himself was an eminent member of this clerisy, and in his role as lecturer to a wealthy and influential audience in Portman Square, he demonstrated the prestige of this "recognised Union of our Priests or Prophets" (*Heroes* 138). It was a vocation available to all and free of the adhesions of class or privilege: "It matters not what rank he has, what revenues or garnitures: the requisite thing is, that he have a tongue which others will listen to; this and nothing more is requisite." Trading in the currency of ideas, the authority of writers transcended that of kings. Democracy itself, Carlyle argued, was the inevitable offspring of the print revolution: "Literature is our Parliament . . . Printing, which comes necessarily out of Writing[,] . . . is equivalent to Democracy: invent Writing, Democracy is inevitable" (139). As the French Revolution had emphatically shown, kings who ignored this "Church" did so at their peril.

Yet Carlyle was too honest a historian to overlook the ominous impediments that men of letters confronted in seeking to speak the truth. With some
reluctance, he conceded that the careers of Samuel Johnson, Jean-Jacques
Rousseau, and Robert Burns were dominated by failure and humiliation.
The "galling conditions" under which they lived prevented them from "unfold[ing] themselves into clearness, victorious interpretation of that 'Divine
Idea,' " which the German philosopher Fichte had set as the supreme goal of
their craft. These men "were not heroic bringers of the light, but heroic
seekers of it," and what Carlyle proposed to exhibit was their "*Tombs*"
(*Heroes* 135) rather than their triumphs. This shift in tone from the possibilities of literary utterance to the squalid reality of literary life haunted Carlyle
personally and professionally, and the stylistic tergiversations of the lecture
vividly evoked his own anxieties. On the one hand, the ennobling aspects of
"ugly Poverty" (141) are evident in his descriptions of the heroic exertions
of Johnson, Rousseau, and Burns. On the other, their "unregulated" struggle
condemned them to brutal drudgery and opprobrium, with "Johnson languishing inactive in garrets, . . . Burns dying brokenhearted as a Gauger, . . .
Rousseau driven into mad exasperation, kindling French Revolutions by his
paradoxes" (140). Carlyle had not yet lost hope in the prospect of "Men of
Letters" as "Governors," with the "man of intellect at the top of affairs."
But he was not prepared to speculate as to how this change could be effected
in the present circumstances, in which "large masses of mankind, in every
society of our Europe, are no longer capable of living at all by the things
which have been" (143). Still uncertain about his own prospects as a writer,
Carlyle feared to make predictions about the future of his profession.

In his final lecture, "The Hero as King. Cromwell, Napoleon: Modern
Revolutionism," Carlyle explored "the last phasis of Heroism" (*Heroes*
168). The two commanders he chose both rose to prominence by restoring
order from chaos. Cromwell and Napoleon were called upon to redirect just
expressions of revolt toward constructive purposes. Puritanism and Sansculottism, according to Carlyle, originated in a common animus, the popular
refusal to tolerate government founded on duplicity: "It has been the soul of
all just revolts among men. Not *Hunger* alone produced even the French
Revolution; no, but the feeling of the insupportable all pervading *Falsehood*
which had now embodied itself in Hunger, in universal material Scarcity and
Nonentity, and thereby become *indisputably* false in the eyes of all" (172).
Cromwell's attempt to govern in accordance with God's truth — "let us go by
what actually *is* God's Truth" (191) — was an act for which English historians never forgave him. Painted as a schemer, a hypocrite, and a coarse
"Tartuffe," Cromwell had occupied "a place of ignominy, accusation, black-

ness and disgrace" (170, 190). For Carlyle, his fate mirrored the fate of hero-worship in England. Cromwell's heroic quest to create order out of anarchy by making "Christ's Law, the Right and the True . . . the Law of this land" (188) was doomed from the outset, yet he persevered, selflessly and without any hope of reward or vindication. Reviled by Puritans and Royalists alike, he was left in the impossible position of being unable to resign, since his departure would occasion the return of Charles Stuart and the cavaliers. Carlyle noted ruefully, "This Prime Minister could *retire* no-whither except into his tomb" (190). But Carlyle hoped that by his efforts as a lecturer, the Protector would be rescued from contumely and resurrected as a hero. Cromwell possessed an undeniable spark of divinity. It was there for his audience to see, if they were willing to see it.

If Napoleon lacked the moral stature of Cromwell, Carlyle submitted, then it was because of the epoch he inhabited. He "had to begin not out of the Puritan Bible, but out of poor Sceptical *Encyclopédies,*" and his "blamable ambition" partook of the self-promotion that characterized a period in which the distinction between "Quack" and "Hero" was often negligible (*Heroes* 191). His "faith" amounted to the shrewd recognition that "Democracy" was an "insuppressible Fact," and that its watchword— "*La carrière ouverte aux talens*" (192)—now belonged permanently to the vocabulary of European political life. Napoleon had no illusions about the difficulties involved in applying this principle. His first task was to "bridle in that great devouring, self-devouring French Revolution; to *tame* it, so that its intrinsic purpose can be made good, that it may become *organic,* and be able to live among other organisms and *formed* things, not as a wasting destruction alone." To a remarkable extent, Napoleon was successful, yet for Carlyle, his victory also marked his downfall. Bonaparte's effort to drape himself in the symbols and vestments of "the old false Feudalities which he once saw clearly to be false" betrayed the "charlatan-element" that had always lurked in his character. Carlyle contended that Napoleon created a personal cult, and behind the "paltry patchwork of theatrical paper-mantles, tinsel and mummery" (193), he employed violence to glorify himself. But might disguised as right could not last, and Napoleon discovered that "Injustice pays itself with frightful compound interest." For Carlyle, the act that disclosed the emperor's essential iniquity—his murder of the German bookseller Palm—tainted his heroic credentials. Yet this heinous piece of "tyrannous murderous injustice" fomented a rage that "burnt deep into the hearts of men, it and the like of it; suppressed fire flashed in the eyes of men, as they thought of it—waiting their day! Which day *came:* Germany rose round him" (194). Appropriately, his brutal viola-

tion of the domain of the new "Union" — letters and literature — sparked a
counterreaction that even Napoleon could not quell.

Carlyle's final lecture revealed the contradictory impulses in his outlook
that gradually drove him to more extremist positions. Whereas his paean to
the "great savage *Baresark*" (*Heroes* 171) Cromwell identified him with
dictatorship and despots, his prescient condemnation of Napoleon's tyranni-
cal "upholstery" (192) offered a sterling example of his political acumen.
Blair Worden has shrewdly observed that between 1839 and 1845, "Carlyle's theory of hero-worship, which always had its authoritarian streak, was
taken over by it." Heroes no longer incarnated the truth because they were
"the best . . . representatives of the societies that have produced them."
Instead, "[t]hey have become not representatives but enforcers" (140). This
tendency, never easy to pinpoint because of Carlyle's slippery resistance
to labels, became more pronounced as his disillusionment with Anglo-
American liberalism grew. Paradoxically, in his own century *Heroes and
Hero-Worship* exerted a deeper influence on radicals than on reactionaries,
exhorting them to pursue their aims through social activism. The range of his
impact accommodated a disparate array of revolutionaries, nationalists,
socialists, liberals, feminists, and socialists, including Elizabeth Barrett
Browning, Charles Gavan Duffy, Ralph Waldo Emerson, Friedrich Engels,
Margaret Fuller, Alexander Herzen, Geraldine Jewsbury, Karl Marx, Giuseppe Mazzini, John Mitchel, William Morris, John Ruskin, Henry David
Thoreau, Walt Whitman, and Oscar Wilde. The core of the book's appeal
resided in Carlyle's powerful feeling of solidarity with his heroes. Commented Thoreau in 1847, "There is a sympathy, not with mere fames, and
formless, incredible things, but with kindred men — not transiently, but life-
long he has walked with them" (10:125).

In the twenty-first century, Carlyle is unlikely to attract such an eclectic
range of "living light-fountain[s]" (*Heroes* 21). Permanently under suspicion of conflating might with right, his famous retort that "right is the eternal
symbol of might" (Froude, *Life in London* 2:422) rang hollow in the aftermath
of the totalitarian nightmares of the twentieth century. In his memorable response to Carlyle's apologia, the great Dutch historian and concentration-
camp survivor Pieter Geyl (1887–1966) commented, "The reply leaves me
completely unconvinced. In both phrases the emphasis falls on the indispensable connection between the two concepts" (48). Geyl rightly cautioned
that Carlyle's connections to the violent ideologies of the Nazis and the
Bolsheviks should neither be underestimated nor exaggerated. What Geyl
referred to as the "tragedy" (54) of Carlyle's life — his denigration of the
powers of intellect and reasoning that had once formed the bedrock of the

heroic personality — was not without a redemptive element. Numerous heroes of the twentieth century, among them Anna Akhmatova, Winston Churchill, Mohandas Gandhi, Vasily Grossman, Václav Havel, Martin Luther King, Rosa Luxemburg, Nelson Mandela, Osip Mandelstam, George Orwell, Franklin Delano Roosevelt, and Alexander Solzhenitsyn — pursued paths that frequently fulfilled Carlylean notions of the heroic. By their words and their actions, they inspired others to transcend self-interest in a wider battle against injustice and falsehood.

However much he tried to disown his affinities with progressive opinion, Carlyle played a central part in shaping liberalism's response to industrialization. Of Carlyle's friend and disciple, Charles Dickens, Orwell wrote in 1939 that he possessed "the face of a man who is always fighting against something, but who fights in the open and is not frightened, the face of a man who is *generously angry* — in other words, of a nineteenth-century liberal, a free intelligence, a type hated with equal hatred by all the smelly little orthodoxies which are now contending for our souls" (75). In no small way, the man who had inspired this "type" of character was Carlyle, whose heroes incarnated "generous anger," "fierce intelligence," and stout resistance to "smelly little orthodoxies." The pattern of heroic virtue that he illuminated in his lectures continues to be relevant to the civic life of twenty-first century society. In his recent plea for Western conventions of heroism to be revised, the distinguished ethicist Andrew Michael Flescher unwittingly paid tribute to the enduring relevance of *On Heroes and Hero-Worship*. According to Flescher's new formulation, "heroes are . . . oriented towards the communal. They see themselves as connected to and responsible for those around them. They likely do this because they remember what it was like to be merely ordinary, for they were not *born* heroic but became so gradually, over time. For these reasons, an investigation into the nature of heroes ought not to begin by attempting to locate an essential 'heroic' core from the outset, but by examining the circumstances that surround heroes' historical background and rearing" (110). Carlyle himself would surely have been heartened by such calls for an urgent reconsideration of heroes and hero-worship. They confirm his indomitable conviction that through these "flowing light-fountains," we "enter deeply . . . into the secret of Mankind's ways and vitalest interests in this world" (*Heroes* 21, 195).

A Note on the Text

The text for this edition of Carlyle's *Heroes, Hero-Worship, and the Heroic in History* is the first edition, published by James Fraser and entered into the *Stationers' Record* in London on 17 June 1841 (see Tarr, *Bibliography* 88–90). Although the first edition contains a few errors, it is the closest version to the manuscript that Carlyle prepared for publication from June to September 1840. The editors of the present edition used a copy of the first edition owned by the late Kenneth J. Fielding and provided to them by its current owner, David Southern — to whom the editors express immense gratitude — as the exemplar for establishing this text. Typographical errors in the text, most of which were corrected in later editions (in which new errors inevitably appeared), are noted by [*sic*], and errors of fact are corrected in the Glossary, which is intended to serve as a starting point for further exploration and a resource for recalling Carlyle's many allusions and citations. The definitive scholarly edition of *Heroes* remains the Strouse Edition, edited by Michael K. Goldberg, with text established by Goldberg, Joel J. Brattin, and Mark Engel (Berkeley: University of California Press, 1993). As in the case of any serious study of Carlyle's *Heroes,* the Strouse Edition served as an invaluable resource for the editors of and contributors to the present edition. Page references for quotations from *Heroes* are to the present edition.

On Heroes,
Hero-Worship,
and the Heroic
in History

LECTURE I.

[TUESDAY, 5TH MAY, 1840.]

The Hero as Divinity. Odin. Paganism: Scandinavian Mythology.

We have undertaken to discourse here for a little on Great Men, their manner of appearance in our world's business, how they have shaped themselves in the world's history, what ideas men formed of them, what work they did; — on Heroes, namely, and on their reception and performance; what I call Hero-worship and the Heroic in human affairs. Too evidently this is a large topic; deserving quite other treatment than we can expect to give it at present. A large topic; indeed, an illimitable one; wide as Universal History itself. For, as I take it, Universal History, the history of what man has accomplished in this world, is at bottom the History of the Great Men who have worked here. They were the leaders of men, these great ones; the modellers, patterns, and in a wide sense creators, of whatsoever the general mass of men contrived to do or to attain; all things that we see standing accomplished in the world are properly the outer material result, the practical realisation and embodiment, of Thoughts that dwelt in the Great Men sent into the world: the soul of the whole world's history, it may justly be considered, were the history of these. Too clearly it is a topic we shall do no justice to in this place!

One comfort is, that Great Men, taken up in any way, are profitable company. We cannot look, however imperfectly, upon a great man, without gaining something by him. He is the living light-fountain, which it is good and pleasant to be near. The light which enlightens, which has enlightened the darkness of the world: and this not as a kindled lamp only, but rather as a natural luminary shining by the gift of Heaven; a flowing light-fountain, as I say, of native original insight, of manhood and heroic nobleness; — in whose radiance all souls feel that it is well with them. On any terms whatsoever, you will not grudge to wander in such neighbourhood for a while. These Six classes of Heroes, chosen out of widely distant countries and epochs, and in mere external figure differing altogether, ought, if we look faithfully at them, to illustrate several things for us. Could we see *them* well, we should get some glimpses into the very marrow of the world's history.

How happy, could I but, in any measure, in such times as these, make manifest to you the meanings of Heroism; the divine relation (for I may well call it such) which in all times unites a Great Man to other men; and thus, as it were, not exhaust my subject, but so much as break ground on it! At all events, I must make the attempt.

It is well said, in every sense, that a man's religion is the chief fact with regard to him. A man's, or a nation of men's. By religion I do not mean here the church-creed which he professes, the articles of faith which he will sign and, in words or otherwise, assert; not this wholly, in many cases not this at all. We see men of all kinds of professed creeds attain to almost all degrees of worth or worthlessness under each or any of them. This is not what I call religion, this profession and assertion; which is often only a profession and assertion from the outworks of the man, from the mere argumentative region of him, if even so deep as that. But the thing a man does practically believe (and this is often enough *without* asserting it even to himself, much less to others); the thing a man does practically lay to heart, and know for certain, concerning his vital relations to this mysterious Universe, and his duty and destiny there, that is in all cases the primary thing for him, and creatively determines all the rest. That is his *religion;* or, it may be, his mere scepticism and *no-religion:* the manner it is in which he feels himself to be spiritually related to the Unseen World or No-world; and I say, if you tell me what that is, you tell me to a very great extent what the man is, what the kind of things he will do is. Of a man or of a nation we inquire, therefore, first of all, What religion they had? Was it Heathenism, — plurality of gods, mere sensuous representation of this Mystery of Life, and for chief recognised element therein Physical Force? Was it Christianism; faith in an Invisible, not as real only, but as the only reality; Time, through every meanest moment of it, resting on Eternity; Pagan empire of Force displaced by a nobler supremacy, that of Holiness? Was it Scepticism, uncertainty and inquiry whether there was an Unseen World, any Mystery of Life except a mad one; — doubt as to all this, or perhaps unbelief and flat denial? Answering of this question is giving us the soul of the history of the man or nation. The thoughts they had were the parents of the actions they did; their feelings were parents of their thoughts: it was the unseen spiritual in them that determined the outward and actual; — their religion, as I say, was the great fact about them. In these Discourses, limited as we are, it will be good to direct our survey chiefly to that religious phasis of the matter. That once known well, all is known. We have chosen as the first Hero in our series, Odin the central figure of Scandinavian Paganism; an emblem to us of a most extensive province of things. Let us look, for a little, at the Hero as Divinity, the oldest primary form of Heroism.

Surely it seems a very strange-looking thing this Paganism; almost inconceivable to us in these days. A bewildering, inextricable jungle of delusions, confusions, falsehoods, and absurdities, covering the whole field of life there. A thing that fills us with astonishment, almost, if it were possible, with incredulity, — for truly it is not easy to understand that sane men could ever calmly, with their eyes open, believe and live by such a set of doctrines. That men should have worshipped their poor fellow-man as a God, and not him only, but stocks and stones, and all manner of animate and inanimate objects; and fashioned for themselves such a distracted chaos of hallucinations by way of Theory of the Universe: all this looks like an incredible fable. Nevertheless it is a clear fact that they did it. Such hideous inextricable jungle of misworships, misbeliefs, men, made as we are, did actually hold by, and live at home in. This is strange. Yes, we may pause in sorrow and silence over the depths of darkness that are in man; if we rejoice in the heights of purer vision he has attained to. Such things were and are in man; in all men; in us too.

Some speculators have a short way of accounting for the Pagan religion: mere quackery, priestcraft, and dupery, say they; no sane man ever did believe it, — merely contrived to persuade other men, not worthy of the name of sane, to believe it! It will be often our duty of hypothesis about men's doings and history; and I here, on the very threshold, protest against it in reference to Paganism, and to all other *isms* by which man has ever for a length of time striven to walk in this world. They have all had a truth in them, or men would not have taken them up. Quackery and dupery do abound; in religions, above all in the more advanced decaying stages of religions, they have fearfully abounded: but quackery was never the originating influence in such things; it was not the health and life of such things, but their disease, the sure precursor of their being about to die! Let us never forget this. It seems to me a most mournful hypothesis, that of quackery giving birth to any faith even in savage men. Quackery gives birth to nothing; gives death to all. We shall not see into the true heart of anything, if we look merely at the quackeries of it; if we do not reject the quackeries altogether; as mere diseases, corruptions, with which our and all men's sole duty is to have done with them, to sweep them out of our thoughts as out of our practice. Man everywhere is the born enemy of lies. I find Grand Lamaism itself to have a kind of truth in it. Read the candid, clear-sighted, rather sceptical Hamilton's *Travels* into that country, and see. They have their belief, these poor Thibet people, that Providence sends down always an Incarnation of Himself into every generation. At bottom some belief in a kind of Pope! At bottom still better, belief that there is a *Greatest* Man; that *he* is discoverable; that, once discovered, we ought to treat him with an obedience which knows no bounds! This is the truth of Grand Lamaism; the 'discoverability' is the only error here. The Thibet Priests have methods of their own of discovering what Man is Greatest, fit to be supreme over them. Bad methods: but are they so much worse than our methods, — of understanding him to be always the eldest-born of a certain genealogy? Alas, it is a difficult thing to find good methods for! —— We shall begin to have a chance of understanding Paganism, when we first admit that to its followers it was, at one time, earnestly true. Let us consider it very certain that men did believe in Paganism; men with open eyes, sound senses, men made altogether like ourselves; that we, had we been there, should have believed in it. Ask now, What Paganism could have been?

Another theory, somewhat more respectable, attributes such things to Allegory. It was a play of poetic minds, say these theorists; a shadowing forth, in allegorical fable, in personification, and visual form, of what such poetic minds had known and felt of this Universe. Which agrees, add they, with a primary law of human nature, still everywhere observably at work, though in less important things, That what a man feels intensely, he struggles to speak out of him, to see represented before him in visual shape, and as if with a kind of life and historical reality in it. Now doubtless there is such a law, and it is one of the deepest in human nature; neither need we doubt that it did operate fundamentally in this business. The hypothesis which ascribes Paganism wholly or mostly to this agency, I call a little more respectable; but I cannot yet call it the true hypothesis. Think, would *we* believe, and take with us as our life-guidance, an allegory, a poetic sport? Not sport but earnest is what we should require. It is a most earnest thing to be alive in this world; to die is not sport for a man. Man's life never was a sport to him; it was a stern reality, altogether a serious matter to be alive! I find, therefore, that though these Allegory-theorists are on the way towards truth in this matter, they have not reached it either. Pagan Religion is indeed an Allegory, a Symbol of what men felt and knew about the Universe; and all Religions are Symbols of that, altering always as that alters: but it seems to me a radical perversion, and even *in*version, of the business, to put that forward as the origin and moving cause, when it was rather the result and termination. To get beautiful allegories, a perfect poetic symbol, was not the want of men; but to know what they were to believe about this Universe, what course they were to steer in it; what, in this mysterious Life of theirs, they had to hope and to fear, to do and to forbear doing. The *Pilgrim's*

Progress is an Allegory, and a beautiful, just and serious one; but consider whether Bunyan's Allegory could have *preceded* the Faith it symbolizes! The Faith had to be already there, standing believed by everybody; — of which the Allegory could *then* become a shadow; and, with all its seriousness, we may say a *sportful* shadow, a mere play of the Fancy, in comparison with that awful Fact and scientific certainty, which it poetically strives to emblem. The Allegory is the product of the certainty, not the producer of it; not in Bunyan's nor in any other case. For Paganism, therefore, we have still to inquire, Whence came that scientific certainty, the parent of such a bewildered heap of allegories, errors and confusions? How was it, what was it?

Surely it were a foolish attempt to pretend 'explaining,' in this place, or in any place, such a phenomenon as that far-distant distracted cloudy imbroglio of Paganism, — more like a cloudfield, than a distant continent of firm-land and facts! It is no longer a reality, yet it was one. We ought to understand that this seeming cloudfield was once a reality; that not poetic allegory, least of all that dupery and deception was the origin of it. Men, I say, never did believe idle songs, never risked their soul's life on allegories: men, in all times, especially in early earnest times, have had an instinct for detecting quacks, for detesting quacks. Let us try if, leaving out both the quack-theory and the allegory one, and listening with affectionate attention to that far-off confused rumour of the Pagan ages, we cannot ascertain so much as this at least, That there was a kind of fact at the heart of them; that they too were not mendacious and distracted, but in their own poor way true and sane!

You remember that fancy of Aristotle's, of a man who had grown to maturity in some dark distance, and were [*sic*] brought on a sudden into the upper air to see the sun rise. What would his wonder be, says the Philosopher, his rapt astonishment at the sight we daily witness with indifference! With the free open sense of a child, yet with the ripe faculty of a man, his whole heart would be kindled by that sight, he would discern it well to be Godlike, his soul would fall down in worship before it. Now, just such a childlike greatness was in the primitive nations. The first Pagan Thinker among rude men, the first man that began to think, was precisely this childman of Aristotle. Simple, open as a child, yet with the depth and strength of a man. Nature had as yet no name to him; he had not yet united under a name the infinite variety of sights, sounds, shapes and motions, which we now collectively name Universe, Nature, or the like, — and so with a name dismiss it from us. To the wild deep-hearted man all was yet new, unveiled under names or formulas; it stood naked, flashing in on him there, beautiful, awful, unspeakable. Nature was to this man, what to the Thinker and Prophet it forever is, *preter*natural. This green flowery rock-built earth, the trees, the mountains, rivers, many-sounding seas; — that great deep sea of azure that swims overhead; the winds sweeping through it; the black cloud fashioning itself together, now pouring out fire, now hail and rain: what *is* it? Ay, what? At bottom we do not yet know; we can never know at all. It is not by our superior insight that we escape the difficulty; it is by our superior levity, our inattention, our *want* of insight. It is by *not* thinking that we cease to wonder at it. Hardened round us, encasing wholly every notion we form, is a wrappage of traditions, hearsays, mere *words*. We call that fire of the black thundercloud 'electricity,' and lecture learnedly about it, and grind the like of it out of glass and silk: but *what* is it? What made it? Whence comes it? Whither goes it? Science has done much for us; but it is a poor science that would hide from us the great deep sacred infinitude of Nescience, whither we can never penetrate, on which all science swims as a mere superficial film. This world, after all our science and sciences, is still a miracle; wonderful, inscrutable, *magical* and more, to whosoever will *think* of it.

That great mystery of Time, were there no other; the illimitable, silent, never-resting thing called Time, rolling, rushing on, swift, silent, like an all-embracing ocean-tide, on which we and all the Universe swim like exhalations, like apparitions which *are*, and then *are not:* this is forever very literally a miracle; a thing to strike us dumb, — for we have no word to speak about it. This Universe, ah me! — what could the wild man know of it; what can we yet know? That it is a Force, and thousandfold Complexity of Forces; a Force which is *not we*. That is all; it is not we, it is altogether different from *us*. Force, Force, everywhere Force; we ourselves a mysterious Force in the centre of that. 'There is not a leaf rotting on the highway but has Force in it: how else could it rot?' Nay surely, to the Atheistic Thinker, if such a one were possible, it must be a miracle too, this huge illimitable whirlwind of Force, which envelopes us here; never-resting whirlwind, high as Immensity, old as Eternity. What is it? God's Creation, the religious people answer; it is the Almighty God's! Atheistic science babbles poorly of it, with scientific nomenclatures, experiments and what not, as if it were a poor dead thing, to be bottled up in Leyden jars, and sold over counters: but the natural sense of man, in all times, if he will honestly apply his sense, proclaims it to be a living thing, — ah, an unspeakable, godlike thing; towards which the best attitude for us, after never so much science, is awe, devout prostration and humility of soul; worship if not in words, then in silence.

But now I remark farther: What in such a time as ours it requires a Prophet or Poet to teach us, namely, the stripping off of those poor undevout wrappages, nomenclatures and scientific hearsays, — this, the ancient earnest soul, as yet unencumbered with these things, did for itself. The world, which is now divine only to the gifted, was then divine to whosoever would turn his eye upon it. He stood bare before it face to face. 'All was Godlike or God:' — Jean Paul still finds it so; the giant Jean Paul, who has power to escape out of hearsays: but then there were no hearsays. Canopus shining down over the desert, with its blue diamond brightness (that wild blue spirit-like brightness, far brighter than we ever witness here), would pierce into the heart of the wild Ishmaelitish man, whom it was guiding through the solitary waste there. To his wild heart, with all feelings in it, with no *speech* for any feeling, it might seem a little eye, that Canopus, glancing out on him from the great deep Eternity; revealing the inner Splendour to him. Cannot we understand how these men *worshipped* Canopus; became what we call Sabeans, worshipping the stars? Such is to me the secret of all forms of Paganism. Worship is transcendent wonder; wonder for which there is now no limit or measure; that is worship. To these primeval men, all things and everything they saw exist beside them were an emblem of the Godlike, of some God.

And look what perennial fibre of truth was in that. To us also, through every star, through every blade of grass, is not a God made visible, if we will open our minds and eyes? We do not worship in that way now: but is it not reckoned still a merit, proof of what we call a 'poetic nature,' that we recognise how every object has a divine beauty in it; how every object still verily is 'a window through which we may look into infinitude itself?' He that can discern the loveliness of things, we call him Poet, Painter, Man of Genius, gifted, loveable. These poor Sabeans did even what he does, — in their own fashion. That they did it, in what fashion soever, was a merit: better than what the entirely stupid man did, what the horse and camel did, — namely, nothing!

But now if all things whatsoever that we look upon are emblems to us of the Highest God, I add that more so than any of them is man such an emblem. You have heard of St. Chrysostom's celebrated saying, in reference to the Shekinah, or Ark of Testimony, visible Revelation of God, among the Hebrews: "The true Shekinah is Man!" Yes, it is even so: this is no vain phrase; it is veritably so. The essence of our being, the mystery in us that calls itself "I," — ah, what words have we for such things? — is a breath of Heaven; the Highest Being reveals himself in man. This body, these faculties, this life of ours, is it not all as a vesture for that Unnamed? 'There is but one temple in the Universe,' says the devout Novalis, 'and that is the Body of Man. Nothing is holier than that high form. Bending before men is a reverence done to this Revelation in the Flesh. We touch Heaven when we lay our hand on a human body!' This sounds much like a mere flourish of rhetoric; but it is not so. If well meditated, it will turn out to be a scientific fact; the expression, in such words as can be had, of the actual truth of the thing. *We* are the miracle of miracles, — the great inscrutable mystery of God. We cannot understand it, we know not how to speak of it; but we may feel and know, if we like, that it is verily so.

Well; these truths were once more readily felt than now. The young generations of the world, who had in them the freshness of young children, and yet the depth of earnest men, who did not think that they had finished off all things in Heaven and Earth by merely giving them scientific names, but had to gaze direct at them there, with awe and wonder: they felt better what of divinity is in man and Nature; — they, without being mad, could *worship* Nature, and man more than anything else in Nature. Worship, that is, as I said above, admire without limit: this, in the full use of their faculties, with all sincerity of heart, they could do. I consider Hero-worship to be the grand modifying element in that ancient system of thought. What I called the perplexed jungle of Paganism sprang, we may say, out of many roots: every admiration, adoration of a star or natural object, was a root or fibre of a root; but Hero-worship is the deepest root of all; the tap-root, from which in a great degree all the rest were nourished and grown.

And now if worship even of a star had some meaning in it, how much more might that of a Hero! Worship of a Hero is transcendent admiration of a Great Man. I say great men are still admirable; I say there is, at bottom, nothing else admirable! No nobler feeling than this of admiration for one higher than himself dwells in the breast of man. It is to this hour, and at all hours, the vivifying influence in man's life. Religion I find stand [*sic*] upon it; not Paganism only, but far higher and truer religions, — all religion hitherto known. Hero-worship, heartfelt prostrate admiration, submission, burning, boundless, for a noblest godlike Form of Man, — is not that the germ of Christianity itself? The greatest of all Heroes is One — whom we do not name here! Let sacred silence meditate that sacred matter; you will find it the ultimate perfection of a principle extant throughout man's whole history on earth.

Or coming into lower, less *un*speakable provinces, is not all Loyalty akin to religious Faith also? Faith is loyalty to some inspired Teacher, some spiritual Hero. And what therefore is loyalty proper, the life-breath of all society, but an effluence of Hero-worship, submissive admiration for the truly great? Society is founded on Hero-worship. All dignities of rank, on which human association rests, are what we may call a *Hero*archy (Government of Heroes), — or a Hierarchy, for it is 'sacred' enough withal! The Duke means *Dux*, Leader; King is *Kön-ning*, *Kan-ning*, Man that *knows* or *cans*. Society everywhere is some representation, not *in*supportably inaccurate, of a graduated Worship of Heroes; — reverence and obedience done to men really great and wise. Not *in*supportably inaccurate, I say! They are all as bank-notes, these social dignitaries, all representing gold; — and several of them, alas, always are *forged* notes. We can do with some forged false notes; with a good many even: but not with all, or the most of them forged! No: there have to come revolutions then; cries of Democracy, Liberty and Equality, and I know not what: — the notes being all false, and no gold to be had for *them*, people take to crying in their despair that there is no gold, that there never was any! — 'Gold,' Hero-worship, *is* nevertheless, as it was always and everywhere, and cannot cease till man himself ceases.

I am well aware that in these days Hero-worship, the thing I call Hero-worship, professes to have gone out, and finally ceased. This, for reasons which it will be worth while some time to inquire into, is an age that as it were denies the existence of great men; denies the desirableness of great men. Shew our critics a great man, a Luther for example, they begin to what they call 'account' for him; not to worship him, but take the dimensions of him, — and bring him out to be a little kind of man! He was the 'creature of the Time,' they say; the Time called him forth, the Time did everything, he nothing — but what we the little critic could have done too! This seems to me but melancholy work. The Time call forth? Alas, we have known Times *call* loudly enough for their great man; but not find him when they called! He was not there; Providence had not sent him; the Time, *calling* its loudest, had to go down to confusion and wreck because he would not come when called. For if we will think of it, no Time need have gone to ruin, could it have *found* a man great enough, a man wise and good enough: wisdom to discern truly what the Time wanted, valour to lead it on the right road thither; these are the salvation of any Time. But I liken common languid Times, with their unbelief, distress, perplexity, with their languid doubting characters and embarrassed circumstances, impotently crumbling down into ever worse distress towards final ruin; — all this I liken to dry dead fuel, waiting for the lightning out of Heaven that shall kindle it. The great man, with his free force direct out of God's own hand, is the lightning. His word is the wise healing word which all can believe in. All blazes round him now, when he has once struck on it, into fire like his own. The dry mouldering sticks are thought to have called him forth. They did want him greatly; but as to calling him forth — ! — Those are critics of small vision, I think, who cry: "See, is it not the sticks that made the fire?" No sadder proof can be given by a man of his own littleness than disbelief in great men. There is no sadder symptom of a generation than such general blindness to the spiritual lightning, with faith only in the heap of barren dead fuel. It is the last consummation of unbelief. In all epochs of the world's history, we shall find the Great Man to have been the indispensable saviour of his epoch; — the lightning, without which the fuel never would have burnt. The History of the World, I said already, was the Biography of Great Men.

Such small critics do what they can to promote unbelief and universal spiritual paralysis; but happily they cannot always completely succeed. In all times it is possible for a man to arise great enough to feel that they and their doctrines are chimeras and cobwebs. And what is notable, in no time whatever can they entirely eradicate out of living men's hearts a certain altogether peculiar reverence for Great Men; genuine admiration, loyalty, adoration, however dim and perverted it may be. Hero-worship endures forever while man endures. Boswell venerates his Johnson, right truly even in the Eighteenth century. The unbelieving French believe in their Voltaire; and burst out round him into very curious Hero-worship, in that last act of his life, when they 'stifle him under roses.' It has always seemed to me extremely curious this of Voltaire. Truly, if Christianity be the highest instance of Hero-worship, then we may find here in Voltairism one of the lowest! He whose life was that of a kind of Antichrist, does again on this side exhibit a curious contrast. No people ever were so little prone to admire at all as those French of Voltaire. *Persiflage* was the character of their whole mind; adoration had nowhere a place in it. Yet see! The old man of Ferney comes up to Paris; an old, tottering, infirm man of eighty-four years. They feel that he too is a kind of Hero; that he has spent his life in opposing error and injustice, delivering Calases, unmasking hypocrites in high places; — in short that *he* too, though in a strange way, has fought like a valiant man. They feel withal that, if *persiflage* be the great thing, there never was such a *persifleur*. He is the realized ideal of every one of them; the thing they are all wanting to be; of all Frenchmen the most French. *He* is properly their god, — such god as they are fit for. Accordingly all persons, from the Queen Antoinette to the Douanier at the Porte St. Denis, do they not worship him? People of quality disguise themselves as tavern-waiters. The Maitre de Poste, with a broad oath, orders his Postilion: "*Va bon train;* thou art driving M. de Voltaire." At Paris his carriage is 'the nucleus of a comet, whose train fills whole streets.' The ladies pluck a hair or two from his fur, to keep it as a sacred relic. There was nothing highest, beautifullest, noblest in all France, that did not feel this man to be higher, beautifuller, nobler.

Yes, from Norse Odin to English Samuel Johnson, from the divine Founder of Christianity to the withered Pontiff of Encyclopedism, in all times and places, the Hero has been worshipped. It will ever be so. We all love great men; love, venerate and bow down submissive before great men: nay can we honestly bow down to anything else? Ah, does not every true man feel that he is himself made higher by doing reverence to what is really above him? No nobler or more blessed feeling dwells in man's heart. And to me it is very cheering to consider that no sceptical logic, or general triviality, insincerity and aridity of any Time and its influences can destroy this noble inborn loyalty and worship that is in man. In times of unbelief, which soon have to become times of revolution, much down-rushing, sorrowful decay and ruin is visible to everybody. For myself in these days, I seem to see in this indestructibility of Hero-worship the everlasting adamant lower than which the confused wreck of revolutionary things cannot fall. The confused wreck of things, crumbling and even crashing and tumbling all round us in these revolutionary ages, will get down so far; *no* farther. It is an eternal corner-stone, from which they can begin to build themselves up again. That man, in some sense or other, worships Heroes; that we all of us reverence and must ever reverence Great Men: this is, to me, the living rock amid all rushings down whatsoever; — the one fixed point in modern revolutionary history, otherwise as if bottomless and shoreless.

So much of truth, only under an ancient obsolete vesture, but the spirit of it still true, do I find in the Paganism of old nations. Nature is still divine, the revelation of the workings of God; the Hero is still worshipable: this, under poor cramped incipient forms, is what all Pagan religions have struggled, as they could, to set forth. I think Scandinavian Paganism, to us here, is more interesting than any other. It is, for one thing, the latest; it continued in these regions of Europe till the eleventh century; eight hundred years ago the Norwegians were still worshippers of Odin. It is interesting also as the creed of our fathers; the men whose blood still runs in our veins, whom doubtless we still resemble in so many ways, — strange: they did believe that, while we believe so differently. Let us look a little at this poor Norse creed, for many reasons. We have tolerable means to do it; for there is another point of interest in these Scandinavian mythologies: that they have been preserved so well.

In that strange island Iceland, — burst up, the geologists say, by fire from the bottom of the sea; a wild land of barrenness and lava; swallowed many months of every year in black tempests, yet with a wild gleaming beauty in summer-time; towering up there, stern and grim, in the North Ocean; with its snow-jokuls, roaring geysers, sulphur pools and horrid volcanic chasms, like the waste chaotic battle-field of Frost and Fire; — where of all places we least looked for Literature or written memorials, the record of these things was written down. On the seabord of this wild land is a rim of grassy country, where cattle can subsist, and men by means of them and of what the sea yields; and it seems they were poetic men these, men who had deep thoughts in them, and uttered musically their thoughts. Much would be lost had Iceland not been burst up from the sea, not been discovered by the Northmen! The old Norse Poets were many of them natives of Iceland.

Sæmund, one of the early Christian Priests there, who perhaps had a lingering fondness for Paganism, collected certain of their old Pagan songs, just about becoming obsolete then, — Poems or Chaunts of a mythic, prophetic, mostly all of a religious character: this is what Norse critics call the *Elder* or Poetic *Edda*. *Edda*, a word of uncertain etymology, is thought to signify *Ancestress*. Snorro Sturleson, an Iceland gentleman, an extremely notable personage, educated by this Sæmund's grandson, took in hand next, near a century afterwards, to put together, among several other books he wrote, a kind of Prose Synopsis of the whole Mythology; elucidated by new fragments of traditionary verse. A work constructed really with great ingenuity, native talent, what one might call unconscious art; altogether a perspicuous clear work, pleasant reading still: this is the *Younger* or Prose *Edda*. By these and the numerous other *Sagas*, mostly Icelandic, with the commentaries, Icelandic or not, which go on zealously in the North to this day, it is possible to gain some direct insight even yet; and see that old Norse system of Belief, as it were, face to face. Let us forget that it is erroneous Religion; let us look at it as old Thought, and try if we cannot sympathise with it somewhat.

The primary characteristic of this old Northland Mythology I find to be Impersonation of the visible workings of Nature. Earnest simple recognition of the workings of Physical Nature, as a thing wholly miraculous, stupendous and divine. What we now lecture of as Science, they wondered at, and fell down in awe before, as Religion. The dark hostile Powers of Nature they figure to themselves as '*Jötuns*,' Giants, huge shaggy beings of a demonic character. Frost, Fire, Sea-tempest; these are Jötuns. The friendly Powers again, as Summer-heat, the Sun, are Gods. The empire of this Universe is divided between these two; they dwell apart, in perennial internecine feud.

The Gods dwell above in Asgard, the Garden of the Asen or Divinities; Jötunheim, a distant dark chaotic land, is the Home of the Jötuns.

Curious all this; and not idle or inane, if we will look at the foundation of it! The power of *Fire*, or *Flame*, for instance, which we designate by some trivial chemical name, thereby hiding from ourselves the essential character of wonder that dwells in it as in all things, is with these old Northmen, Loke, a most swift subtle *Demon*, of the brood of the Jötuns. The savages of the Ladrones Islands too (say some Spanish voyagers) thought Fire, which they never had seen before, was a devil or god, that bit you sharply when you touched it, and lived there upon dry wood. From us too, no Chemistry, if it had not Stupidity to help it, would hide that Flame is a wonder. What *is* Flame? — *Frost* the old Norse Seer discerns to be a monstrous Hoary Jötun, the Giant *Thrym*, *Hrym;* or *Rime*, the old word now nearly obsolete here, but still used in Scotland to signify hoar-frost. *Rime* was not then as now a dead chemical thing, but a living Jötun or Devil; the monstrous Jötun *Rime* drove home his Horses at night, sat 'combing their manes,' — which Horses were *Hail-Clouds*, or fleet *Frost-winds*. His Cows — No, not his, but a kinsman's, the Giant Hymir's Cows are *Ice-bergs:* this Hymir 'looks at the rocks' with his devil-eye, and they *split* in the glance of it.

Thunder was not then mere Electricity, vitreous or resinous; it was the God Donner (Thunder) or Thor, — God also of beneficent Summer-heat. The thunder was his wrath; the gathering of the black clouds is the drawing down of Thor's angry brows; the fire-bolt bursting out of Heaven is the all-rending Hammer flung from the hand of Thor: he urges his loud chariot over the mountain-tops, — that is the peal: wrathful he 'blows in his red beard;' that is the rustling stormblast before the thunder begin. Balder again, the White God, the beautiful, the just and benignant (whom the early Christian Missionaries found to resemble Christ), is the Sun, — beautifullest of visible things; wondrous too, and divine still, after all our Astronomies and Almanacs! But perhaps the notablest god we hear tell of is one of whom Grimm the German Etymologist finds trace: the God *Wünsch*, or Wish. The God *Wish;* who could give us all that we *wished!* Is not this the sincerest and yet rudest voice of the spirit of man? The *rudest* ideal that man ever formed; which still shews itself in the latest forms of our spiritual culture. Higher considerations have to teach us that the God *Wish* is not the true God.

Of the other Gods or Jötuns I will mention only for etymology's sake, that Sea-tempest is the Jötun *Aegir*, a very dangerous Jötun; — and now to this day, on our river Trent, as I learn, the Nottingham bargemen, when the River is in a certain flooded state (a kind of backwater, or eddying swirl it has, very dangerous to them), call it *Eager;* they cry out, "Have a care, there is the *Eager* coming!" Curious; that word surviving, like the peak of a submerged world! The *oldest* Nottingham bargemen had believed in the God Aegir. Indeed our English blood too in good part is Danish, Norse; or rather, at bottom, Danish and Norse and Saxon have no distinction, except a superficial one, — as of Heathen and Christian, or the like. But all over our Island we are mingled largely with Danes proper, — from the incessant invasions there were: and this, of course, in a greater proportion along the east coast; and greatest of all, as I find, in the North Country. From the Humber upwards, all over Scotland, the speech of the common people is still in a singular degree Icelandic; its Germanism has still a peculiar Norse tinge. They too are 'Normans,' Northmen, — if that be any great beauty! —

Of the chief god, Odin, we shall speak by and by. Mark at present so much; what the essence of Scandinavian and indeed of all Paganism is: a recognition of the forces of Nature as godlike, stupendous, personal Agencies, — as Gods and Demons. Not inconceivable to us. It is the infant Thought of man opening itself, with awe and wonder, on this ever-stupendous Universe. To me there is in the Norse System something very genuine, very great and manlike. A broad simplicity, rusticity, so very different from the light gracefulness of the old Greek Paganism, distinguishes this Scandinavian System. It is Thought; the genuine Thought of deep, rude, earnest minds, fairly opened to the things about them; a face-to-face and heart-to-heart inspection of the things, — the first characteristic of all good Thought in all times. Not graceful lightness, half-sport, as in the Greek Paganism; a certain homely truthfulness and rustic strength, a great rude sincerity, discloses itself here. It is strange, after our beautiful Apollo statues and clear smiling mythuses, to come down upon the Norse Gods 'brewing ale' to hold their feast with Aegir, the Sea-Jötun; sending out Thor to get the cauldron for them in the Jötun country; Thor, after many adventures, clapping the Pot on his head, like a huge hat, and walking off with it, — quite lost in it, the ears of the Pot reaching down to his heels! A kind of vacant hugeness, large awkward gianthood, characterises that Norse System; enormous force, as yet altogether untutored, stalking helpless with large uncertain strides. Consider only their primary mythus of the Creation. The Gods, having got the Giant Ymer slain, a Giant made by 'warm winds' and much confused work out of the conflict of Frost and Fire, — determined on constructing a world with him. His blood made the Sea; his flesh was the Land, the Rocks his bones; of his eyebrows they formed Asgard their Gods'-dwelling; his scull was the great blue vault of Immensity, and the brains of it became the Clouds. What a Hyper-Brobdignagian business! Untamed Thought, great, giantlike, enormous; —

to be tamed in due time into the compact greatness, not giantlike, but godlike and stronger than gianthood, of the Shakspeares, the Goethes! — Spiritually as well as bodily these men are our progenitors.

I like, too, that representation they have of the Tree Igdrasil. All Life is figured by them as a Tree. Igdrasil, the Ash-tree of Existence, has its roots deep down in the kingdoms of Hela or Death; its trunk reaches up heaven-high, spreads its boughs over the whole Universe: it is the Tree of Existence. At the foot of it, in the Death-kingdom, sit Three *Nornas*, Fates, — the Past, Present, Future; watering its roots from the Sacred Well. Its 'boughs,' with their buddings and disleafings, — events, things suffered, things done, catastrophes, — stretch through all lands and times. Is not every leaf of it a biography, every fibre there an act or word? Its boughs are Histories of Nations. The rustle of it is the noise of Human Existence, onwards from of old. It grows there, the breath of Human Passion rustling through it; — or stormtost, the stormwind howling through it like the voice of all the gods. It is Igdrasil, the Tree of Existence. It is the past, the present, and the future; what was done, what is doing, what will be done; 'the infinite conjugation of the verb *To do*.' Considering how human things circulate, each inextricably in communion with all, — how the word I speak to you today is borrowed, not from Ulfila the Moesogoth only, but from all men since the first man began to speak, — I find no similitude so true as this of a Tree. Beautiful; altogether beautiful and great. The '*Machine* of the Universe,' — alas, do but think of that in contrast!

Well, it is strange enough this old Norse view of Nature; different enough from what we believe of Nature. Whence it specially came, one would not like to be compelled to say very minutely! One thing we may say: It came from the thoughts of Norse men; — from the thought, above all, of the *first* Norse man who had an original power of thinking. The First Norse 'man of genius,' as we should call him! Innumerable men had passed by, across this Universe, with a dumb vague wonder, such as the very animals may feel; or with a painful, fruitlessly inquiring wonder, such as men only feel; — till the great Thinker came, the *original* man, the Seer; whose shaped spoken Thought awakes the slumbering capability of all into Thought. It is ever the way with the Thinker, the spiritual Hero. What he says, all men were not far from saying, were longing to say. The Thoughts of all start up, as from painful enchanted sleep, round his Thought; answering to it, Yes, even so! Joyful to men as the dawning of day from night; — *is* it not, indeed, the awakening for them from no-being into being, from death into life? We still honour such a man; call him Poet, Genius, and so forth: but to these wild men he was a very magician, a worker of miraculous unexpected blessing for them; a Prophet, a God! — Thought once awakened does not again slumber; unfolds itself into a System of Thought; grows, in man after man, generation after generation, — till its full stature is reached, and *such* System of Thought can grow no farther, but must give place to another.

For the Norse people, the Man now named Odin, and Chief Norse God, we fancy, was such a man. A Teacher, and Captain of soul and of body; a Hero, of worth *im*measurable; admiration for whom, transcending the known bounds, became adoration. Has he not the power of articulate Thinking; and many other powers, as yet miraculous? So, with boundless gratitude, would the rude Norse heart feel. Has he not solved for them the Sphinx-enigma of this Universe; given assurance to them of their own destiny there. By him they know now what they have to do here, what to look for hereafter. Existence has become articulate, melodious by him; he first has made Life alive! — We may call this Odin the origin of Norse Mythology: Odin, or whatever name the First Norse Thinker bore while he was a man among men. His view of the Universe once promulgated, a like view starts into being in all minds; grows, keeps ever growing, while it continues credible there. In all minds it lay written, but invisibly, as in sympathetic ink; at his word it starts into visibility in all. Nay, in every epoch of the world, the great event, parent of all others, is it not the arrival of a Thinker in the world! —

One other thing we must not forget; it will explain, a little, the confusion of these Norse Eddas. They are not one coherent System of Thought; but properly the *summation* of several successive systems. All this of the old Norse Belief which is flung out for us, in one level of distance in the Edda, like a Picture painted on the same canvass, does not at all stand so in the reality. It stands rather at all manner of distances and depths, of successive generations since the Belief first began. All Scandinavian thinkers, since the first of them, contributed to that Scandinavian System of Thought; in ever new elaboration and addition, it is the combined work of them all. What history it had, how it changed from shape to shape, by one thinker's contribution after another, till it got to the full final shape we see it under in the *Edda*, no man will now ever know: *its* Councils of Trebisond, Councils of Trent, Athanasiuses, Dantes, Luthers, are sunk without echo in the dark night! Only that it had such a history we can all know. Wheresoever a thinker appeared, there in the thing he thought of was a contribution, accession, a change or revolution made. Alas, the grandest 'revolution' of all, the one made by the man Odin himself, is not this too sunk for us like the rest! Of Odin what history? Strange rather to reflect that he *had* a history! That this Odin, in his wild Norse vesture, with his wild beard and eyes, his rude Norse speech and ways, was a man like us; with our sorrows, joys, with our limbs, features; — intrinsically all one as we; and did such a work! But the work, much of it, has perished; the worker, all to the name. "Wednesday," men will say tomorrow; Odin's day! Of Odin there exists no history: no document of it; no guess about it worth repeating.

Snorro indeed, in the quietest manner, almost in a brief business style, writes down, in his *Heimskringla*, how Odin was a heroic Prince, in the Black-Sea region, with Twelve Peers, and a great people straitened for room. How he led these *Asen* (Asiatics) of his out of Asia; settled them in the North parts of Europe, by warlike conquest; invented Letters, Poetry and so forth, — and came by and by to be worshipped as Chief God by these Scandinavians, his Twelve Peers made into Twelve Sons of his own, Gods like himself: Snorro has no doubt of this. Saxo Grammaticus, a very curious Northman of that same century, is still more unhesitating; scruples not to find out a historical fact in every individual mythus, and writes it down as a terrestrial event in Denmark or elsewhere. Torfæus, learned and cautious, some centuries later, assigns by calculation a *date* for it: Odin, he says, came into Europe about the Year 70 before Christ. Of all which, as grounded on mere uncertainties, found to be untenable now, I need say nothing. Far, very far beyond the Year 70! Odin's date, adventures, whole terrestrial history, figure and environment, are sunk from us forever into unknown thousands of years.

Nay Grimm, the German Antiquary, goes so far as to deny that any man Odin ever existed. He proves it by etymology. The word *Wuotan*, which is the original form of *Odin*, a word spread, as name of their chief Divinity, over all the Teutonic Nations everywhere; this word, which connects itself, according to Grimm, with the Latin *vadere*, with the English *wade* and such like, — means primarily *Movement*, Source of Movement, Power; and is the fit name of the highest god, not of any man. The word signifies Divinity, he says, among the old Saxon, German and all Teutonic Nations; the adjectives formed from it all signify *divine*, *supreme*, or something pertaining to the chief god. Like enough! We must bow to Grimm in matters etymological. Let us consider it fixed that *Wuotan* means *Wading*, force of *Movement*. And now still, what hinders it from being the name of a Heroic Man and *Mover*, as well as of a god? As for the adjectives, and words formed from it, — did not the Spaniards in their universal admiration for Lope, get into the habit of saying 'a Lope flower,' 'a Lope *dama*,' if the flower or woman were of surpassing beauty? Had this lasted, *Lope* would have grown, in Spain, to be an adjective signifying *godlike* also. Indeed Adam Smith, in his *Essay on Language*, surmises that all adjectives whatsoever were formed precisely in that way: some very green thing, chiefly notable for its green-ness, got the appellative name *Green*, and then the next thing remarkable for that quality, a tree for instance, was named the *green* tree, — as we still say 'the *steam* coach,' 'four-horse coach,' or the like. All primary adjec-tives, according to Smith, were formed in this way; were at first substan-tives and things. We cannot annihilate a man for etymologies like that! Surely there was a First Teacher and Captain; surely there must have been an Odin, palpable to the sense at one time; no adjective, but a real Hero of flesh and blood! The voice of all tradition, history or echo of history, agrees with all that thought will teach one about it, to assure us of this.

How the man Odin came to be considered a *god*, the chief god? — that surely is a question which nobody would wish to dogmatise upon. I have said, his people knew no *limits* to their admiration of him; they had as yet no scale to measure admiration by. Fancy your own generous heart's-love of some greatest man expanding till it *transcended* all bounds, till it filled and overflowed the whole field of your thought! Or what if this man Odin, — since a great deep soul, with the afflatus and mysterious tide of vision and impulse rushing on him he knows not whence, is ever an enigma, a kind of terror and wonder to himself, — should have felt that perhaps *he* was divine; that *he* was some effluence of the 'Wuotan,' '*Movement*,' Supreme Power and Divinity, of whom to his rapt vision all Nature was the awful Flame-image; that some effluence of *Wuotan* dwelt here in him! He was not neces-sarily false; he was but mistaken, speaking the truest he knew. A great soul, any sincere soul, knows not *what* he is, — alternates between the highest height and the lowest depth; can, of all things, the least measure — Himself! What others take him for, and what he guesses that he may be; these two items strangely act on one another, help to determine one another. With all men reverently admiring him; with his own wild soul full of noble ardours and affections, of whirlwind chaotic darkness and glorious new light; a divine Universe bursting all into godlike beauty round him, and no man to whom the like ever had befallen, what could he think himself to be? "Wuo-tan?" All men answered, "Wuotan!" —

And then consider what mere Time will do in such cases; how if a man was great while living, he becomes tenfold greater when dead. What an enormous *camera-obscura* magnifier is Tradition! How a thing grows in the human Memory, in the human Imagination, when love, worship and all that lies in the human Heart, is there to encourage it. And in the darkness, in the entire ignorance; without date or document, no book, no Arundel-marble; only here and there some dumb monumental cairn. Why, in thirty or forty years, were there no books, any great man would grow *mythic*, the contem-

poraries, who had seen him, being once all dead. And in three hundred
years, and in three thousand years — ! — To attempt *theorising* on such matters would profit little: they are matters which refuse to be *theoremed* and
diagramed; which Logic ought to know that she *cannot* speak of. Enough
for us to discern, far in the uttermost distance, some gleam as of a small real
light shining in the centre of that enormous camera-obscura image; to discern that the centre of it all was not a madness and nothing, but a sanity and
something.

This light, kindled in the great dark vortex of the Norse Mind, dark but
living, waiting only for light: this is to me the centre of the whole. How such
light will then shine out, and with wondrous thousandfold expansion spread
itself, in forms and colours, depends not on *it*, so much as on the National
Mind recipient of it. The colours and forms of your light will be those of the
cut-glass it has to shine through. — Curious to think how, for every man, any
the truest fact is modelled by the nature of the man! I said, The earnest man,
speaking to his brother men, must always have stated what seemed to him a
fact, a real Appearance of Nature. But the way in which such Appearance or
fact shaped itself, — what sort of *fact* it became for him, — was and is modified by his own laws of thinking; deep, subtle, but universal, ever-operating
laws. The world of Nature, for every man, is the Fantasy of Himself; this
world is the multiplex 'Image of his own Dream.' Who knows to what
unnameable subtleties of spiritual law all these Pagan Fables owe their
shape! The number *Twelve*, divisiblest of all, which could be halved, quar-
tered, parted into three, into six, the most remarkable number, — this was
enough to determine the *Signs of the Zodiac*, the number of Odin's *Sons*,
and innumerable other Twelves. Any vague rumour of number had a tendency to settle itself into Twelve. So with regard to every other matter. And
quite unconsciously too, — with no notion of building up 'Allegories!' But
the fresh clear glance of those First Ages would be prompt in discerning the
secret relations of things, and wholly open to obey these. Schiller finds in
the *Cestus of Venus* an everlasting æsthetic truth as to the nature of all
Beauty; curious: — but he is careful not to insinuate that the old Greek
Mythists had any notion of lecturing about the 'Philosophy of Criticism!' —
— On the whole, we must leave those boundless regions. Cannot we conceive that Odin was a reality? Error indeed, error enough: but sheer falsehood, idle fables, allegory aforethought, — we will not believe that our
Fathers believed in these.

Odin's *Runes* are a significant feature of him. Runes, and the miracles of
'magic' he worked by them, make a great feature in tradition. Runes are the

Scandinavian Alphabet; suppose Odin to have been the inventor of Letters, as well as 'magic,' among that people! It is the greatest invention man has ever made, this of marking down the unseen thought that is in him by written characters. It is a kind of second speech, almost as miraculous as the first. You remember the astonishment and incredulity of Atahualpa the Peruvian King; how he made the Spanish Soldier who was guarding him scratch *Dios* on his thumb-nail, that he might try the next soldier with it, to ascertain whether such a miracle was possible. If Odin brought Letters among his people, he might work magic enough!

Writing by Runes has some air of being original among the Norsemen; not a Phenician Alphabet, but a native Scandinavian one. Snorro tells us farther that Odin invented Poetry; the music of human speech, as well as that miraculous runic marking of it. Transport yourselves into the early childhood of nations; the first beautiful morning-light of our Europe, when all yet lay in fresh young radiance as of a great sunrise, and our Europe was first beginning to think, to be! Wonder, hope; infinite radiance of hope and wonder, as of a young child's thoughts, in the hearts of these strong men! Strong sons of Nature; and here was not only a wild Captain and Fighter; discerning with his wild flashing eyes what to do, with his wild lion-heart daring and doing it; but a Poet too, all that we mean by a Poet, Prophet, great devout Thinker and Inventor, — as the truly Great Man ever is. A Hero is a Hero at all points; in the soul and thought of him first of all. This Odin, in his rude semi-articulate way, had a word to speak. A great heart laid open to take in this great Universe, and man's Life here, and utter a great word about it. A Hero, as I say, in his own rude manner; a wise, gifted, noble-hearted man. And now, if we still admire such a man beyond all others, what must these wild Norse souls, first awakened into thinking, have made of him! To them, as yet without names for it, he was noble and noblest; Hero, Prophet, God; *Wuotan*, the greatest of all. Thought is Thought, howsoever it speak or spell itself. Intrinsically, I conjecture, this Odin must have been of the same sort of stuff as the greatest kind of men. A great thought in the wild deep heart of him! The rough words he articulated, are they not the rudimental roots of those English words we still use? He worked so, in that obscure element. But he was as a *light* kindled in it; a light of Intellect, rude Nobleness of heart, the only light we have yet; a Hero, as I say: and he had to shine there, and make his obscure element a little lighter, — as is still the task of us all.

We will fancy him to be the Type-Northman; the finest Teuton whom that race had yet produced. The rude Norse heart burst up into *boundless* admiration round him; into adoration. He is as a root of so many great things; the fruit of him is found growing, from deep thousands of years, over the whole field of Teutonic Life. Our own Wednesday, as I said, is it not still Odin's day? Wednesbury, Wansborough, Wanstead, Wandsworth: Odin grew into England too, these are still leaves from that root! He was the Chief God to all the Teutonic Peoples: their Pattern Norseman, in such way did *they* admire their Pattern Northman; that was the fortune he had in the world.

Thus if the man Odin himself have vanished utterly, there is this huge Shadow of him which still projects itself over the whole History of his People. For this Odin once admitted to be God, we can understand well that the whole Scandinavian Scheme of Nature, or dim No-scheme, whatever it might before have been, would now begin to develope itself altogether differently, and grow thenceforth in a new manner. What this Odin saw into, and taught with his runes and his rhymes, the whole Teutonic People laid to heart and carried forward. His way of thought became their way of thought: — such, under new conditions, is the history of every great thinker still. In gigantic confused lineaments, like some enormous camera-obscura shadow thrown upwards from the dead deeps of the Past, and covering the whole Northern Heaven, is not that Scandinavian Mythology in some sort the Portraiture of this man Odin? The gigantic image of *his* natural face, legible or not legible there, expanded and confused in that manner! Ah, Thought, I say, is always Thought. No great man lives in vain. The History of the world is but the Biography of great men.

To me there is something very touching in this primeval figure of Heroism; in such artless, helpless, but hearty entire reception of a Hero by his fellow-men. Never so helpless in shape, it is the noblest of feelings, and a feeling in some shape or other perennial as man himself. If I could shew in any measure, what I feel deeply for a long time now, That it is the vital element of manhood, the soul of man's history here in our world, — it would be the chief use of this discoursing at present. We do not now call our great men Gods, nor admire *without* limit; ah no, *with* limit enough! But if we have no great men, or do not admire at all, — that were a still worse case.

This poor Scandinavian Hero-worship, that whole Norse way of looking at the Universe, and adjusting oneself there, has an indestructible merit for us. A rude childlike way of recognising the divineness of Nature, the divineness of Man; most rude, yet heartfelt, robust, giantlike; betokening what a giant of a man this child would yet grow to! It was a truth, and is none. Is it not as the half-dumb stifled voice of the long-buried generations of our own Fathers, calling out of the depths of ages to us, in whose veins their blood still runs: "This then, this is what *we* made of the world: this is all the image and notion we could form to ourselves of this great mystery of a Life and Universe. Despise it not. You are raised high above it, to large free scope of vision; but you too are not yet at the top. No, your notion too, so much enlarged, is but a partial, imperfect one; that matter is a thing no man will ever, in time or out of time, comprehend; after thousands of years of ever-new expansion, man will find himself but struggling to comprehend again a part of it: the thing is larger than man, not to be comprehended by him; an Infinite thing!"

The essence of the Scandinavian, as indeed of all Pagan Mythologies, we found to be recognition of the divineness of Nature; sincere communion of man with the mysterious invisible Powers visibly seen at work in the world round him. This, I should say, is more sincerely done in the Scandinavian than in any Mythology I know. Sincerity is the great characteristic of it. Superior sincerity (far superior) consoles us for the total want of old Grecian grace. Sincerity, I think, is better than grace. I feel that these old Northmen were looking into Nature with open eye and soul: most earnest, honest; childlike, and yet manlike; with a greathearted simplicity and depth and freshness, in a true, loving, admiring, unfearing way. A right valiant, true old race of men. Such recognition of Nature one finds to be the chief element of Paganism: recognition of Man, and his Moral Duty, though this too is not wanting, comes to be the chief element only in purer forms of religion. Here, indeed, is a great distinction and epoch in Human Beliefs; a great landmark in the religious development of Mankind. Man first puts himself in relation with Nature and her Powers, wonders and worships over those; not till a later epoch does he discern that all Power is Moral, that the grand point is the distinction for him of Good and Evil, of *Thou shalt* and *Thou shalt not*.

With regard to all these fabulous delineations in the *Edda*, I will remark, moreover, as indeed was already hinted, that most probably they must have been of much newer date; most probably, even from the first, were comparatively idle for the old Norsemen, and as it were a kind of Poetic sport. Allegory and Poetic Delineation, as I said above, cannot be religious Faith; the Faith itself must first be there, then Allegory enough will gather round it, as the fit body round its soul. The Norse Faith, I can well suppose, like other Faiths, was most active while it lay mainly in the silent state, and had not yet much to say about itself, still less to sing.

Among those shadowy *Edda* matters, amid all that fantastic congeries of assertions, and traditions, in their musical Mythologies, the main practical belief a man could have was probably not much more than this: of the *valkyrs* and the *Hall of Odin;* of an inflexible *Destiny*, and that the one thing needful for a man was *to be brave*. The *Valkyrs* are Choosers of the Slain; a Destiny inexorable, which it is useless trying to bend or soften, has appointed who is to be slain: this was a fundamental point for the Norse believer; — as indeed it is for all earnest men everywhere, for a Mahomet, a Luther, for a Napoleon too. It lies at the basis this for every such man; it is the woof out of which his whole system of thought is woven. The *Valkyrs;* and then that these *Choosers* lead the brave to a heavenly *Hall of Odin;* only the base and slavish being thrust elsewhither, into the realms of Hela the Death-goddess: I take this to have been the soul of the whole Norse Belief. They understood in their heart that it was indispensable to be brave; that Odin would have no favour for them, but despise and thrust them out, if they were not brave. Consider too whether there is not something in this! It is an everlasting duty, valid in our day as in that, the duty of being brave. *Valour* is still *value*. The first duty for a man is still that of subduing *Fear*. We must get rid of Fear; we cannot act at all till then. A man's acts are slavish, not true but specious; his very thoughts are false, he thinks too as a slave and coward, till he have got Fear under his feet. Odin's creed, if we disentangle the real kernel of it, is true to this hour. A man shall and must be valiant; he must march forward, and quit himself like a man, — trusting imperturbably in the appointment and *choice* of the upper Powers; and on the whole not fear at all. Now and always, the completeness of his victory over Fear will determine how much of a man he is.

It is doubtless very savage that kind of valour of the old Northmen. Snorro tells us they thought it a shame and misery not to die in battle; and if natural death seemed to be coming on, they would cut wounds in their flesh, that Odin might receive them as warriors slain. Old kings, about to die, had their body laid into a ship; the ship sent forth, with sails set and slow fire burning it; that, once out at sea, it might blaze up in flame, and in such manner bury worthily the old hero, at once in the sky and in the ocean! Wild bloody valour; yet valour of its kind; better, I say, than none. In the old Sea-kings too, what an indomitable rugged energy! Silent, with closed lips, as I fancy them, unconscious that they were specially brave; defying the wild ocean with its monsters, and all men and things; — progenitors of our own Blakes and Nelsons. No Homer sang these Norse Sea-kings; but Agamemnon's was a small audacity, and of small fruit in the world, to some of them; — to Hrolf 's of Normandy, for instance! Hrolf, or Rollo Duke of Normandy, the wild Sea-king, has a share in governing England at this hour.

Nor was it altogether nothing, even that wild sea-roving and battling, through so many generations. It needed to be ascertained which was the *strongest* kind of men; who were to be ruler over whom. Among the North-land Sovereigns, too, I find some who got the title *Wood-cutter;* Forest-felling Kings. Much lies in that. I suppose at bottom many of them were forest-fellers as well as fighters, though the Skalds talk mainly of the latter, — misleading certain critics not a little; for no nation of men could ever live by fighting alone; there could not produce enough come out of that! I suppose the right good fighter was oftenest also the right good forest-feller, — the right good improver, discerner, doer and worker in every kind; for true valour, different enough from ferocity, is the basis of all. A more legitimate kind of valour that; shewing itself against the untamed Forests and dark brute Powers of Nature, to conquer Nature for us. In the same direction have not we their descendants since carried it far? May such valour last forever with us!

That the man Odin, speaking with a Hero's voice and heart, as with an impressiveness out of Heaven, told his People the infinite importance of Valour, how man thereby became a god; and that his People, feeling a response to it in their own hearts, believed this message of his, and thought it a message out of Heaven, and him a Divinity for telling it them: this seems to me the primary seed-grain of the Norse Religion, from which all manner of mythologies, symbolic practices, speculations, allegories, songs and sagas would naturally grow. Grow, — how strangely! I called it a small light shining and shaping in the huge vortex of Norse darkness. Yet the darkness itself was *alive;* consider that. It was the eager inarticulate unin-structed Mind of the whole Norse People, longing only to become articu-late, to go on articulating ever farther! The living doctrine grows, grows; — like a Banyan-tree; the first *seed* is the essential thing: any branch strikes itself down into the earth, becomes a new root; and so, in endless complex-ity, we have a whole wood, a whole jungle, one seed the parent of it all. Was not the whole Norse Religion, accordingly, in some sense, what we called 'the enormous shadow of this man's likeness?' Critics trace some affinity in some Norse mythuses, of the Creation and such like, with those of the Hindoos. The Cow Adumbla, 'licking the rime from the rocks,' has a kind of Hindoo look. A Hindoo Cow, transported into frosty countries. Probably enough; indeed we may say undoubtedly, these things will have a kindred with the remotest lands, with the earliest times. Thought does not die, but only is changed. The first man that began to think in this Planet of ours, he was the beginner of all. And then the second man, and the third man; — nay every true Thinker to this hour is a kind of Odin, teaches men *his* way of thought, spreads a shadow of his own likeness over sections of the History of the World.

Of the distinctive poetic character or merit of this Norse Mythology I have not room to speak; nor does it concern us much. Some wild Prophecies we have, as the *Havamal* in the *Elder Edda;* of a rapt, earnest, sibylline sort. But they were comparatively an idle adjunct of the matter, men who as it were but toyed with the matter, these later Skalds; and it is their songs chiefly that survive. In later centuries, I suppose, they would go on singing, poetically symbolizing, as our modern Painters paint, when it was no longer from the innermost heart, or not from the heart at all. This is everywhere to be well kept in mind.

Gray's fragments of Norse Lore, at any rate, will give one no notion of it; — any more than Pope will of Homer. It is no square-built gloomy palace of black ashlar marble, shrouded in awe and horror, as Gray gives it us: no; rough as the North rocks, as the Iceland deserts, it is; with a heartiness, homeliness, even a tint of goodhumour and robust mirth in the middle of these fearful things. The strong old Norse heart did not go upon theatrical sublimities; they had not time to tremble. I like much their robust simplicity; their veracity, directness of conception. Thor 'draws down his brows' in a veritable Norse rage; 'grasps his hammer till the *knuckles grow white.*' Beautiful traits of pity too, an honest pity. Balder 'the white God' dies; the beautiful, benignant; he is the Sungod. They try all Nature for a remedy; but he is dead. Frigga, his mother, sends Hermode to seek or see him: nine days and nine nights he rides, through gloomy deep valleys, a labyrinth of gloom; arrives at the Bridge with its gold roof: the Keeper says, "Yes, Balder did pass here; but the Kingdom of the Dead is down yonder, far towards the North." Hermode rides on; leaps Hell-gate, Hela's gate; does see Balder, and speak with him: Balder cannot be delivered. Inexorable! Hela will not, for Odin or any God, give him up. The beautiful and gentle has to remain there. His Wife had volunteered to go with him, to die with him. They shall forever remain there. He sends his ring to Odin; Nanna his wife sends her *thimble* to Frigga, as a remembrance. — Ah me! —

For indeed Valour is the fountain of Pity too; — of Truth, and all that is great and good in man. The robust homely vigour of the Norse heart attaches one much, in these delineations. Is it not a trait of right honest strength, says Uhland, who has written a fine *Essay* on Thor, that the old Norse heart finds its friend in the Thunder-god? That it is not frightened away by his thunder; but finds that Summer-heat, the beautiful noble summer, must and will have thunder withal! The Norse heart *loves* this Thor and his hammer-bolt; sports with him. Thor is Summer-heat; the god of Peace-able Industry as well as Thunder. He is the Peasant's friend; his true hench-man and attendant is Thialfi, *Manual Labour*. Thor himself engages in all manner of rough manual work, scorns no business for its plebeianism; is ever and anon travelling to the country of the Jötuns, harrying those chaotic Frost-monsters, subduing them, at least straitening and damaging them. There is a great broad humour in some of these things.

Thor, as we saw above, goes to Jötun-land, to seek Hymir's Cauldron, that the Gods may brew beer. Hymir the huge Giant enters, his grey beard all full of hoar-frost; splits pillars with the very glance of his eye; Thor, after much rough tumult, snatches the Pot, claps it on his head; the 'handles of it reach down to his heels.' The Norse Skald has a kind of loving sport with Thor. This is the Hymir whose cattle, the critics have discovered, are Ice-bergs. Huge untutored Brobdignag genius, — needing only to be tamed down; into Shakspeares, Dantes, Goethes! It is all gone now, that old Norse work, — Thor the Thundergod changed into Jack the Giant-killer: but the mind that made it is here yet. How strangely things grow, and die, and do not die! There are twigs of that great world-tree of Norse Belief, still curiously traceable. This poor Jack of the Nursery, with his miraculous shoes of swiftness, coat of darkness, sword of sharpness, he is one. *Childe Etin* in the Scottish Ballads is a Norse Mythus; *Etin* was a *Jötun*. Nay, Shakspeare's *Hamlet* is a twig too of this same world-tree; there seems no doubt of that. Hamlet, *Amleth*, I find, is really a mythic personage; and his Tragedy, of the poisoned Father, poisoned asleep by drops in his ear, and the rest, is a Norse mythus! Old Saxo, as his wont was, made it a Danish history; Shakspeare, out of Saxo, made it what we see. That is a twig of the world-tree that has *grown*, I think; — by nature or accident that one has grown!

In fact, these old Norse songs have a *truth* in them, an inward perennial truth and greatness, — as, indeed, all must have that can very long preserve itself by tradition alone. It is a greatness not of mere body and gigantic bulk, but a rude greatness of soul. There is a sublime uncomplaining melancholy traceable in these old hearts. A great free glance into the very deeps of thought. They seem to have seen, these brave old Northmen, what Medita-tion has taught all men in all ages, That this world is after all but a shew, — a phenomenon or appearance, no real thing. All deep souls see into that, — the Hindoo Mythologist, the German Philosopher, — the Shakspeare, the ear-nest Thinker wherever he may be:

'We are such stuff as Dreams are made of!'

One of Thor's expeditions, to Utgard (the *Outer* Garden, central seat of Jötun-land), is remarkable in this respect. Thialfi was with him, and Loke. After various adventures, they entered upon Giant-land; wandered over plains, wild uncultivated places, among stones and trees. At nightfall they noticed a house; and as the door, which indeed formed one whole side of the house, was open, they entered. It was a simple habitation; one large hall, altogether empty. They staid there. Suddenly in the dead of the night loud noises alarmed them. Thor grasped his hammer; stood in the door, prepared for fight. His companions within ran hither and thither in their terror, seeking some outlet in that rude hall; they found a little closet at last, and took refuge there. Neither had Thor any battle: for, lo, in the morning it turned out that the noise had been only the *snoring* of a certain enormous but peaceable Giant, the Giant Skrymir, who lay peaceably sleeping near by; and this that they took for a house was merely his *Glove*, thrown aside there; the door was the Glove-wrist; the little closet they had fled into was the Thumb! Such a glove; — I remark too that it had not fingers as ours have, but only a thumb, and the rest undivided: a most ancient, rustic glove!

Skrymir now carried their portmanteau all day; Thor, however, had his own suspicions, did not like the ways of Skrymir; determined at night to put an end to him as he slept. Raising his hammer, he struck down into the Giant's face a right thunderbolt blow, of force to rend rocks. The Giant merely awoke; rubbed his cheek, and said, Did a leaf fall? Again Thor struck, so soon as Skrymir again slept; a better blow than before; but the Giant merely murmured, Was that a grain of sand? Thor's third stroke was with both his hands (the 'knuckles white' I suppose), and seemed to dint deep into Skrymir's visage; but he merely checked his snore, and remarked, There must be sparrows roosting in this tree, I think; what is that they have dropt? — At the gate of Utgard, a place so high, that you had to 'strain your neck bending back to see the top of it,' Skrymir went his ways. Thor and his companions were admitted; invited to take share in the games going on. To Thor, for his part, they handed a Drinking-horn; it was a common feat, they told him, to drink this dry at one draught. Long and fiercely, three times over, Thor drank; but made hardly any impression. He was a weak child, they told him: could he lift that Cat he saw there? Small as the feat seemed, Thor with his whole godlike strength could not; he bent up the creature's back, could not raise its feet off the ground, could at the utmost raise one foot. Why, you are no man, said the Utgard people; there is an Old Woman that will wrestle you! Thor, heartily ashamed, seized this haggard Old Woman; but could not throw her.

And now on their quitting Utgard, the chief Jötun, escorting them politely a little way, said to Thor: "You are beaten then: — yet be not so much ashamed; there was deception of appearance in it. That Horn you tried to drink was the *Sea;* you did make it ebb; but who could drink that, the bottomless! The Cat you would have lifted, — why, that is the *Midgard-snake*, the Great World-serpent, which, tail in mouth, girds and keeps up the whole created world; had you torn that up, the world must have rushed to ruin. As for the Old Woman, she was *Time*, Old Age, Duration: with her what can wrestle? No man nor no god with her; gods or men, she prevails over all! And then those three strokes you struck, — look at these *three valleys;* your three strokes made these!" Thor looked at his attendant Jötun: it was Skrymir; — it was, say Norse critics, the old chaotic rocky *Earth* in person, and that glove-*house* was some Earth-cavern! But Skrymir had vanished; Utgard with its skyhigh gates, when Thor grasped his hammer to smite them, had gone to air; only the Giant's voice was heard mocking: "Better come no more to Jötunheim!" —

This is of the allegoric period, as we see, and half play, not of the prophetic and entirely devout: but as a mythus, is there not real antique Norse gold in it? More true metal, rough from the Mimer-stithy, than in many a famed Greek mythus *shaped* far better! A great broad Brobdignag grin of true humour is in this Skrymir; mirth resting on eartnestness [*sic*] and sadness, as the rainbow on black tempest: only a right valiant heart is capable of that. It is the grim humour of our own Ben Jonson, rare old Ben; runs in the blood of us, I fancy; for one catches tones of it, under a still other shape, out of the American Backwoods.

That is also a very striking conception that of the *Ragnarök*, Consummation, or *Twilight of the Gods*. It is in the *Havamal* song; seemingly a very old, prophetic idea. The Gods and Jötuns, the divine Powers and the chaotic brute ones, after long contest and partial victory by the former, meet at last in universal world-embracing wrestle and duel; World-serpent against Thor, strength against strength; mutually extinctive; and ruin, 'twilight' sinking into darkness, swallows the created Universe. The old Universe with its Gods is sunk; but it is not final death: there is to be a new Heaven and a new Earth; a higher supreme God, and Justice to reign among men. Curious: this law of mutation, which also is a law written in man's inmost thought, had been deciphered by these old earnest Thinkers in their rude style; and how, though all dies, and even gods die, yet all death is but a Phœnix fire-death, and new-birth into the Greater and the Better! It is the fundamental Law of Being for a creature made of Time, living in this Place of Hope. All earnest men have seen into it; may still see into it.

And now, connected with this, let us glance at the *last* mythus of the appearance of Thor; and end there. I fancy it to be the latest in date of all these fables: a sorrowing protest against the advance of Christianity, — set forth reproachfully by some Conservative Pagan. King Olaf has been harshly blamed for his over-zeal in introducing Christianity; surely I should have blamed him far more for an underzeal in that! He paid dear enough for it; he died by the revolt of his Pagan people, in battle, in the year 1033, at Stickelstad, near that Drontheim, where the chief Cathedral of the North has now stood for many centuries, dedicated gratefully to his memory as *Saint* Olaf. The mythus about Thor is to this effect. King Olaf, the Christian Reform King, is sailing with fit escort along the shore of Norway, from haven to haven; dispensing justice, or doing other royal work: on leaving a certain haven, it is found that a stranger, of grave eyes and aspect, red beard, of stately robust figure, has stept in. The courtiers address him; his answers surprise by their pertinency and depth: at length he is brought to the King. The stranger's conversation here is not less remarkable, as they sail along the beautiful shore; but after some time, he addresses King Olaf thus: "Yes, King Olaf, it is all beautiful, with the sun shining on it there; green, fruitful, a right fair home for you; and many a sore day had Thor, many a wild fight with the rock Jötuns, before he could make it so. And now you seem minded to put away Thor. King Olaf, have a care!" said the stranger, drawing down his brows; — and when they looked again, he was nowhere to be found. — This is the last appearance of Thor on the stage of this world!

Do we not see well enough how the Fable might arise, without un-veracity on the part of any one: it is the way most Gods have come to appear among men: thus if in Pindar's time 'Neptune was seen once at the Nemean Games,' what was this Neptune too but a 'stranger of noble grave aspect,' —*fit* to be 'seen!' There is something pathetic, tragic for me, in this last voice of Paganism. Thor is vanished, the whole Norse world has vanished; and will not return ever again. In like fashion to that, pass away the highest things. All things that have been in this world, all things that are or will be in it, have to vanish: we have our sad farewell to give them.

That Norse Religion, a rude but earnest, sternly impressive *Consecration of Valour* (so we may define it), sufficed for these old valiant Northmen. Consecration of Valour is not a *bad* thing! We will take it for good, so far as it goes. Neither is there no use in *knowing* something about this old Pagan-ism of our Fathers. Unconsciously, and combined with higher things, it is in *us* yet, that old Faith withal! To know it consciously, brings us into closer and clearer relation with the Past, — with our own possessions in the Past. For the whole Past, as I keep repeating, is the possession of the Present; the Past had always something *true*, and is a precious possession. In a different time, in a different place, it is always some other *side* of our common Human Nature that has been developing itself. The actual True is the *sum* of all these; not any one of them by itself constitutes what of Human Nature is hitherto developed. Better to know them all than misknow them. "To which of these Three Religions do you specially adhere?" inquires Meister of his Teacher. "To all the Three!" answers the other: "To all the Three; for they by their union first constitute the True Religion."

The Hero as Prophet. Mahomet: Islam

FROM the first rude times of Paganism among the Scandinavians in the North, we advance to a very different epoch of religion, among a very different people: Mahometanism among the Arabs. A great change; what a change and progress is indicated here, in the universal condition and thoughts of men!

The Hero is not now regarded as a God among his fellow-men; but as one God-inspired, as a Prophet. It is the second phasis of Hero-worship: the first or oldest, we may say, has passed away without return; in the history of the world there will not again be any man, never so great, whom his fellow-men will take for a god. Nay we might rationally ask, Did any set of human beings ever really think the man they *saw* there standing beside them a god, the maker of this world? Perhaps not: it was usually some man they remembered, or *had* seen. But neither can this, any more, be. The Great Man is not recognised henceforth as a god any more.

It was a rude gross error, that of counting the Great Man a god. Yet let us say that it is at all times difficult to know *what* he is, or how to account of him and receive him! The most significant feature in the history of an epoch is the manner it has of welcoming a Great Man. Ever, to the true instincts of men, there is something godlike in him. Whether they shall take him to be a god, to be a prophet, or what they shall take him to be? that is ever a grand question; by their way of answering that, we shall see, as through a little window, into the very heart of these men's spiritual condition. For at bottom the Great Man, as he comes from the hand of Nature, is ever the same kind of thing: Odin, Luther, Johnson, Burns; I hope to make it appear that these are all originally of one stuff; that only by the world's reception of them, and the shapes they assume, are they so immeasurably diverse. The worship of Odin astonishes us, — to fall prostrate before the Great Man, into *deliquium* of love and wonder over him, and feel in their hearts that he was a denizen of the skies, a god! This was imperfect enough: but to welcome, for example, a Burns as we did, was that what we can call perfect? The most precious gift that Heaven can give to the Earth; a man of 'genius' as we call it; the Soul of a

Man actually sent down from the skies with a God's-message to us, — this we waste away as an idle artificial firework, sent to amuse us a little, and sink it into ashes, wreck and ineffectuality: *such* reception of a Great Man I do not call perfect either! Looking into the heart of the thing, one may perhaps call that of Burns a still uglier phenomenon, betokening still sadder imperfections in mankind's ways, than the Scandinavian method itself! To fall into mere un-reasoning *deliquium* of love and admiration, was not good; but such unreasoning, nay irrational, supercilious no-love at all is perhaps still worse! — It is a thing forever changing, this of Hero-worship; different in each age, difficult to do well in any age. Indeed the heart of the whole business of the age, one may say, is to do it well.

We have chosen Mahomet not as the most eminent Prophet; but as the one we are freest to speak of. He is by no means the truest of Prophets; but I do esteem him a true one. Farther, as there is no danger of our becoming, any of us, Mahometans, I mean to say all the good of him I justly can. It is the way to get at his secret: let us try to understand what *he* meant with the world; what the world meant and means with him, will then be a more answerable question. Our current hypothesis about Mahomet, that he was a scheming Impostor, a Falsehood incarnate, that his religion is a mere mass of quackery and fatuity, begins really to be now untenable to any one. The lies, which well-meaning zeal has heaped round this man, are disgraceful to ourselves only. When Pococke inquired of Grotius, Where the proof was of that story of the pigeon, trained to pick peas from Mahomet's ear, and pass for an angel dictating to him? Grotius answered that there was no proof! It is really time to dismiss all that. The word this man spoke has been the life-guidance now of one hundred and eighty millions of men these twelve hundred years. These hundred and eighty millions were made by God as well as we. A greater number of God's creatures believe in Mahomet's word at this hour than in any other word whatever. Are we to suppose that it was a miserable piece of spiritual legerdemain, this which so many creatures of the Almighty have lived by and died by? I, for my part, cannot form any such supposition. I will believe most things sooner than that. One would be entirely at a loss what to think of this world at all, if quackery so grew and were sanctioned here.

Alas, such theories are very lamentable. If we would attain to knowledge of anything in God's true Creation, let us disbelieve them wholly! They are the product of an Age of Scepticism; indicate the saddest spiritual paralysis, and mere death-life of the souls of men: more godless theory, I think, was never promulgated in this Earth. A false man found a religion? Why, a false man cannot build a brick house! If he do not know and follow *truly* the properties of mortar, burnt clay and what else he works in, it is no house that he makes, but a rubbish-heap. It will not stand for twelve centuries, to lodge a hundred and eighty millions; it will fall straightway. A man must conform himself to Nature's laws, *be* verily in communion with Nature and the truth of things, or Nature will answer him, No, not at all! Speciosities are specious — ah me! — a Cagliostro, many Cagliostros, prominent world-leaders, do prosper by their quackery, for a day. It is like a forged bank-note; they get it passed out of *their* worthless hands: others, not they, have to smart for it. Nature bursts up in fire-flames, French Revolutions and such like, proclaiming with terrible veracity that forged notes are forged.

But of a Great Man especially, of him I will venture to assert that it is incredible he should have been other than true. It seems to me the primary foundation of him, and of all that can lie in him, this. No Mirabeau, Napoleon, Burns, Cromwell, no man adequate to do any thing, but is first of all in right earnest about it; what I call a sincere man. I should say *sincerity*, a deep, great, genuine sincerity, is the first characteristic of all men in any way heroic. Not the sincerity that calls itself sincere; ah no, that is a very poor matter indeed; — a shallow braggart conscious sincerity; oftenest self-conceit mainly. The Great Man's sincerity is of the kind he cannot speak of, is not conscious of: nay, I suppose, he is conscious rather of *in*sincerity; for what man can walk accurately by the law of truth for one day? No, the Great Man does not boast himself sincere, far from that; perhaps does not ask himself if he is so: I would say rather, his sincerity does not depend on himself; he cannot help being sincere! The great Fact of Existence is great to him. Fly as he will, he cannot get out of the awful presence of this Reality. His mind is so made; he is great by that, first of all. Fearful and wonderful, real as Life, real as Death, is this Universe to him. Though all men should forget its truth, and walk in a vain show, he cannot. At all moments the Flame-image glares in upon him; undeniable, there, there! — I wish you to take this as my primary definition of a Great Man. A little man may have this, it is competent to all men that God has made: but a Great Man cannot be without it.

Such a man is what we call an *original* man; he comes to us at first hand. A messenger he, sent from the Infinite Unknown with tidings to us. We may call him Poet, Prophet, God; — in one way or other, we all feel that the words he utters are as no other man's words. Direct from the Inner Fact of things; — he lives, and has to live, in daily communion with that. Hearsays cannot hide it from him; he is blind, homeless, miserable, following hearsays; *it* glares in upon him. Really his utterances, are they not a kind of 'revelation;' — what we must call such for want of some other name? It is from the heart of the world that he comes; he is portion of the primal reality of things. God has made many revelations: but this man too, has not God made him, the latest and newest of all? The 'inspiration of the Almighty giveth *him* understanding:' we must listen before all to him.

This Mahomet, then, we will in no wise consider as an Inanity and Theatricality, a poor conscious ambitious schemer; we cannot conceive him so. The rude message he delivered was a real one withal; an earnest confused voice from the unknown Deep. The man's words were not false, nor his workings here below: no Inanity and Simulacrum; a fiery mass of Life cast up from the great bosom of Nature herself. To *kindle* the world; the world's Maker had ordered it so. Neither can the faults, imperfections, insincerities even, of Mahomet, if such were never so well proved against him, shake this primary fact about him.

On the whole, we make too much of faults; the details of the business hide the real centre of it. Faults? The greatest of faults, I should say, is to be conscious of none. Readers of the Bible above all, one would think, might know better. Who is called there 'the man according to God's own heart?' David, the Hebrew King, had fallen into sins enough; blackest crimes; there was no want of sins. And thereupon the unbelievers sneer and ask, Is this your man according to God's heart? The sneer, I must say, seems to me but a shallow one. What are faults, what are the outward details of a life; if the inner secret of it, the remorse, temptations, true, often-baffled, never-ended struggle of it, be forgotten? 'It is not in man that walketh to direct his steps.' Of all acts is not, for a man, *repentance* the most divine? The deadliest sin, I say, were that same supercilious consciousness of no sin; — that is death; the heart so conscious is divorced from sincerity, humility and fact; is dead: it is 'pure' as dead dry sand is pure. David's life and history, as written for us in those Psalms of his, I consider to be the truest emblem ever given of a man's moral progress and warfare here below. All earnest souls will ever discern in it the faithful struggle of an earnest human soul towards what is good and best. Struggle often baffled, sore baffled, down as into entire wreck; yet a struggle never ended; ever, with tears, repentance, true unconquerable purpose, begun anew. Poor human nature! Is not a man's walking, in truth, always that: 'a succession of falls?' Man can do no other. In this wild element of a Life, he has to struggle onwards; now fallen, deep-abased; and ever, with tears, repentance, with bleeding heart, he has to rise again, struggle again still onwards. That his struggle *be* a faithful unconquerable one: that is the question of questions. We will put up with many sad details, if the soul of it were true. Details by themselves will never teach us what it is. I believe we mis-estimate Mahomet's faults even as faults: but the secret of him will never be got by dwelling there. We will leave all this behind us; and assuring ourselves that he did mean some true thing, ask candidly, what it was or might be.

These Arabs Mahomet was born among are certainly a notable people. Their country itself is notable; the fit habitation for such a race. Savage inaccessible rock-mountains, great grim deserts, alternating with beautiful strips of verdure: wherever water is, there is greenness, beauty; odoriferous balm-shrubs, date-trees, frankincense-trees. Consider that wide waste horizon of sand, empty, silent, like a sand-sea, dividing habitable place from habitable. You are all alone there, left alone with the Universe; by day a fierce sun blazing down on it with intolerable radiance; by night the great deep Heaven with its stars. Such a country is fit for a swift-handed, deep-hearted race of men. There is something most agile, active, and yet most meditative, enthusiastic in the Arab character. The Persians are called the French of the East; we will call the Arabs Oriental Italians. A gifted noble people; a people of wild strong feelings, and of iron restraint over them: the characteristic of noblemindedness, of genius. The wild Bedouin welcomes the stranger to his tent, as one having right to all that is there; were it his worst enemy, he will slay his foal to treat him, will serve him with sacred hospitality for three days, will set him fairly on his way; — and then, by another law as sacred, kill him if he can. In words too, as in action. They are not a loquacious people, taciturn rather; but eloquent, gifted when they do speak. An earnest, truthful kind of men. They are, as we know, of Jewish kindred: but with that deadly terrible earnestness of the Jews they seem to combine something graceful, brilliant, which is not Jewish. They had 'Poetic contests' among them before the time of Mahomet. Sale says, at Ocadh, in the South of Arabia, there were yearly fairs, and there, when the merchandising was done, Poets sang for prizes: — the wild people gathered to hear that.

One Jewish quality these Arabs manifest; the outcome of many or of all high qualities: what we may call religiosity. From of old they had been zealous worshippers, according to their light. They worshipped the stars, as Sabeans; worshipped many natural objects, — recognised them as symbols, immediate manifestations, of the Maker of Nature. It was wrong; and yet not wholly wrong. All God's works are still in a sense symbols of God. Do we not, as I urged, still account it a merit to recognise a certain inexhaustible significance, 'poetic beauty,' as we name it, in all natural objects whatsoever? A man is a poet, and honoured, for doing that, and speaking or singing it, — a kind of diluted worship. They had many Prophets these Arabs; Teachers each to his tribe, each according to the light he had. But indeed, have we not from of old the noblest of proofs, still palpable to every one of us, of what devoutness and noble-mindedness had dwelt in these rustic thoughtful peoples? Biblical critics seem agreed that our own Book of Job was written in that region of the world. I call that, apart from all theories about it, one of the grandest things ever written with pen. One feels, indeed, as if it were not Hebrew; such a noble universality, different from noble patriotism or sectarianism, reigns in it. A noble Book; all men's Book! It is our first, oldest statement of the never-ending Problem, — man's destiny and God's ways with him here in this earth. And all in such free flowing outlines; grand in its sincerity, in its simplicity; in its epic melody, and repose of reconcilement. There is the seeing eye, the mildly under- standing heart. So *true*, every way; true eyesight and vision for all things; material things no less than spiritual: the Horse, — 'hast thou clothed his neck with *thunder?*' — he '*laughs* at the shaking of the spear!' Such living likenesses were never since drawn. Sublime sorrow, sublime reconciliation; oldest choral melody as of the heart of mankind; — so soft, and great; as the summer midnight, as the world with its seas and stars! There is nothing written, I think, in the Bible or out of it, of equal literary merit. —

To the idolatrous Arabs one of the most ancient universal objects of worship was that Black Stone, still kept in the building called Caabah, at Mecca. Diodorus Siculus mentions this Caabah in a way not to be mistaken, as the oldest, most honoured temple in his time; that is, some half-century before our Era. Silvestre de Sacy says there is some likelihood that the Black Stone is an aerolite. In that case, some man might *see* it fall out of Heaven! It stands now beside the Well Zemzem; the Caabah is built over both. A Well is in all places a beautiful affecting object, gushing out like life from the hard earth; — still more so in these hot dry countries, where it is the first condition of being. The Well Zemzem has its name from the bubbling sound of the waters, *zem-zem;* they think it is the Well which Hagar found with her little Ishmael in the wilderness: the aerolite and it have been sacred now, and had a Caabah over them, for thousands of years. A curious object that Caabah! There it stands at this hour, in the black cloth-covering the Sultan sends it yearly; 'twenty-seven cubits high;' with circuit, with double circuit of pillars, with festoon-rows of lamps and quaint ornaments: the lamps will be lighted again *this* night, — to glitter again under the stars. An authentic fragment of the oldest Past. It is the *Keblah* of all Moslem: from Delhi all onwards to Morocco, the eyes of innumerable praying men are turned towards *it*, five times, this day and all days: one of the notablest centres in the Habitation of Men.

It had been from the sacredness attached to this Caabah Stone and Hagar's Well, from the pilgrimings of all tribes of Arabs thither, that Mecca took its rise as a Town. A great town once, though much decayed now. It has no natural advantage for a town; stands in a sandy hollow amid bare barren hills, at a distance from the sea; its provisions, its very bread, have to be imported. But so many pilgrims needed lodgings: and then all places of pilgrimage do, from the first, become places of trade. The first day pilgrims meet, merchants have also met: where men see themselves assembled for one object, they find that they can accomplish other objects which depend on meeting together. Mecca became the Fair of all Arabia. And thereby indeed the chief staple and warehouse of whatever Commerce there was between the Indian and the Western countries, Syria, Egypt, even Italy. It had at one time a population of 100,000; buyers, forwarders of those Eastern and Western products; importers for their own behoof of provisions and corn. The government was a kind of irregular aristocratic republic, not without a touch of theocracy. Ten Men of a chief tribe, chosen in some rough way, were Governors of Mecca, and Keepers of the Caabah. The Koreish were the chief tribe in Mahomet's time; his own family was of that tribe. The rest of the Nation, fractioned and cut asunder by deserts, lived under similar rude patriarchal governments by one or several: herdsmen, carriers, traders, generally robbers too; being oftenest at war, one with another, or with all: held together by no open bond, if it were not this meeting at the Caabah, where all forms of Arab Idolatry assembled in common adoration;—held mainly by the *inward* indissoluble bond of a common blood and language. In this way had the Arabs lived for long ages, unnoticed by the world; a people of great qualities, unconsciously waiting for the day when they should become notable to all the world. Their Idolatries appear to have been in a tottering state; much was getting into confusion and fermentation among them. Obscure tidings of the most important Event ever transacted in this world, the Life and Death of the Divine Man in Judea, at once the symptom and cause of immeasurable change to all people in the world, had in the course of centuries reached into Arabia too; and could not but, of itself, have produced fermentation there.

It was among this Arab people, so circumstanced, in the year 570 of our Era, that the man Mahomet was born. He was of the family of Hashem, of the Koreish tribe as we said; though poor, connected with the chief persons of his country. Almost at his birth he lost his Father; at the age of six years his Mother too, a woman noted for her beauty, her worth and sense: he fell to the charge of his Grandfather, an old man, a hundred years old. A good old man: Mahomet's Father, Abdallah, had been his youngest favourite son. He saw in Mahomet, with his old life-worn eyes, a century old, the lost Abdallah come back again, all that was left of Abdallah. He loved the little orphan Boy greatly; used to say, They must take care of that beautiful little Boy, nothing in their kindred was more precious than he. At his death, while the boy was still but two years old, he left him in charge to Abu Thaleb the eldest of the Uncles, as to him that now was head of the house. By this Uncle, a just and rational man as everything betokens, Mahomet was brought up in the best Arab way.

Mahomet, as he grew up, accompanied his Uncle on trading journeys and such like; in his eighteenth year one finds him a fighter following his Uncle in war. But perhaps the most significant of all his journeys is one we find noted as of some years [*sic*] earlier date: a journey to the Fairs of Syria. The young man here first came in contact with a quite foreign world, — with one foreign element of endless moment to him: the Christian Religion. I know not what to make of that 'Sergius, the Nestorian Monk,' whom Abu Thaleb and he are said to have lodged with; or how much any monk could have taught one still so young. Probably enough it is greatly exaggerated, this of the Nestorian Monk. Mahomet was only fourteen; had no language but his own: much in Syria must have been a strange unintelligible whirl-pool to him. But the eyes of the lad were open; glimpses of many things would doubtless be taken in, and lie very enigmatic as yet, which were to ripen in a strange way into views, into beliefs and insights one day. These journeys to Syria were probably the beginning of much to Mahomet.

One other circumstance we must not forget: that he had no school-learning; of the thing we call school-learning none at all. The art of writing was but just introduced into Arabia; it seems to be the true opinion that Mahomet never could write! Life in the Desert, with its experiences, was all his education. What of this infinite Universe he, from his dim place, with his own eyes and thoughts, could take in, so much and no more of it was he to know. Curious, if we will reflect on it, this of having no books. Except by what he could see for himself, or hear of by uncertain rumour of speech in the obscure Arabian Desert, he could know nothing. The wisdom that had been before him or at a distance from him in the world, was in a manner as good as not there for him. Of the great brother souls, flame-beacons through so many lands and times, no one directly communicates with this great soul. He is alone there, deep down in the bosom of the Wilderness; has to grow up so, — alone with Nature and his own Thoughts.

But, from an early age, he had been remarked as a thoughtful man. His companions named him 'Al Amin, The Faithful.' A man of truth and fidelity; true in what he did, in what he spake and thought. They noted that *he* always meant something. A man rather taciturn in speech; silent when there was nothing to be said; but pertinent, wise, sincere, when he did speak; always throwing light on the matter. This is the only sort of speech *worth* speaking! Through life we find him to have been regarded as an altogether solid, brotherly, genuine man. A serious, sincere character; yet amiable, cordial, companionable, jocose even; — a good laugh in him withal: there are men whose laugh is as untrue as anything about them; who cannot laugh. One hears of Mahomet's beauty: his fine sagacious honest face, brown florid complexion, beaming black eyes; — I somehow like too that vein on the brow, which swelled up black, when he was in anger: like the '*horse-shoe* vein' in Scott's *Redgauntlet*. It was a kind of feature in the Hashem family, this black swelling vein in the brow; Mahomet had it prominent, as would appear. A spontaneous, passionate, yet just, true-meaning man! Full of wild faculty, fire and light; of wild worth, all uncultured; working out his life-task in the depths of the Desert there.

How he was placed with Kadijah, a rich Widow, as her Steward, and travelled in her business to the Fairs of Syria; how he managed all, as one can well understand, with fidelity, adroitness; how her gratitude, her regard for him grew: the story of their marriage is altogether a graceful intelligible one, as told us by the Arab authors. He was twenty-five; she forty, though still beautiful. He seems to have lived in a most affectionate, peaceable, wholesome way with this wedded benefactress; loving her truly, and her alone. It goes greatly against the impostor-theory, the fact that he lived in this entirely unexceptionable, entirely quiet and commonplace way, till the heat of his years was done. He was forty before he talked of any mission from Heaven. All his irregularities, real and supposed, date from after his fiftieth year, when the good Kadijah died. All his 'ambition,' seemingly, had been, hitherto, to live an honest life; his 'fame,' the mere good-opinion of neighbours that knew him, had been sufficient hitherto. Not till he was already getting old, the prurient heat of his life all burnt out, and *peace* growing to be the chief thing this world could give him, did he start on the 'career of ambition;' and, belying all his past character and existence, set up as a wretched empty charlatan to acquire what he could now no longer enjoy! For my share, I have no faith whatever in that.

Ah no: this deep-hearted Son of the Wilderness, with his beaming black eyes, and open social deep soul, had other thoughts in him than ambition. A silent great soul; he was one of those who cannot *but* be in earnest; whom

Nature herself has appointed to be sincere. While others walk in formulas and hearsays, contented enough to dwell there, this man could not screen himself in formulas; he was alone with his own soul and the reality of things. The great Mystery of Existence, as I said, glared in upon him; with its terrors, with its splendours; no hearsays could hide that unspeakable fact, "Here am I!" Such *sincerity*, as we named it, has in very truth something of divine. The word of such a man is a Voice direct from Nature's own Heart. Men do and must listen to that as to nothing else; — all else is wind in comparison. From of old, a thousand thoughts, in his pilgrimings and wanderings, had been in this man: What am I? What *is* this unfathomable Thing I live in, which men name Universe? What is Life; what is Death! What am I to believe? What am I to do? The grim rocks of Mount Hara, of Mount Sinai, the stern sandy solitudes answered not. The great Heaven rolling silent overhead, with its blue-glancing stars, answered not. There was no answer. The man's own soul, and what of God's inspiration dwelt there, had to answer!

It is the thing which all men have to ask themselves; which we too have to ask, and answer. This wild man felt it to be of *infinite* moment; all other things of no moment whatever in comparison. The jargon of argumentative Greek Sects, vague traditions of Jews, the stupid routine of Arab Idolatry: there was no answer in these. A Hero, as I repeat, has this first distinction, which indeed we may call first and last, the Alpha and Omega of his whole Heroism, That he looks through the shews of things into *things*. Use and wont, respectable hearsay, respectable formula: all this is good, or is not good. There is something behind and beyond all these, which all these must correspond with, be the image of, or they are — *Idolatries;* 'bits of black wood pretending to be God:' to the earnest soul a mockery and abomination. Idolatries never so gilded, waited on by heads of the Koreish, will do nothing for this man. Though all men walk by them, what good is it? The great Reality stands glaring there upon *him*. He there has to answer it, or perish miserably. Now, even now, or else through all Eternity never! Answer it; *thou* must find an answer. — Ambition? What could all Arabia do for this man; with the crown of Greek Heraclius, of Persian Chosroes, and all crowns in the Earth; — what could they all do for him? It was not of the Earth he wanted to hear tell; it was of the Heaven above and of the Hell beneath. All crowns and sovereignties whatsoever, where would *they* in a few brief years be? To be Shiek of Mecca or Arabia, and have a bit of gilt wood put into your hand, — will that be one's salvation? I decidedly think, not. We will leave it altogether, this impostor-hypothesis, as not credible; not very tolerable even, worthy chiefly of dismissal by us.

Mahomet had been wont to retire yearly during the month Ramadhan into solitude and silence; as indeed was the Arab custom; a praiseworthy custom, which such a man, above all, would find natural and useful. Communing with his own heart, in the silence of the mountains; himself silent; open to the 'small still voices:' it was a right natural custom! Mahomet was in his fortieth year, when having withdrawn to a cavern in Mount Hara, near Mecca, during this Ramadhan, to pass the month in prayer, and meditation on those great questions, he one day told his wife Kadijah, who with his household was with him or near him this year, That by the unspeakable special favour of Heaven he had now found it all out; was in doubt and darkness no longer, but saw it all. That all these Idols and Formulas were nothing, miserable bits of wood; that there was One God in and over all; and we must leave all Idols, and look to Him. That God is great; and that there is nothing else great! He is the Reality. Wooden Idols are not real; He is real. He made us at first, sustains us yet; we and all things are but the shadow of Him; a transitory garment veiling the Eternal Splendour. '*Allah akbar*, God is great;' — and then also '*Islam*,' That we must *submit* to God. That our whole strength lies in resigned submission to Him, whatsoever He do to us. For this world, and for the other! The thing He sends to us, were it death and worse than death, shall be good, shall be best; we resign ourselves to God. — 'If this be *Islam*,' says Goethe, 'do we not all live in *Islam?*' Yes, all of us that have any moral life; we all live so. It has ever been held the highest wisdom for a man not merely to submit to Necessity, — Necessity will make him submit, — but to know and believe well that the stern thing which Necessity had ordered was the wisest, the best, the thing wanted there. To cease his frantic pretension of scanning this great God's-World in his small fraction of a brain; to know that it *had* verily, though deep beyond his soundings, a Just Law, that the soul of it was Good; — that his part in it was to conform to the Law of the Whole, and in devout silence follow that; not questioning it, obeying it as unquestionable.

I say, this is yet the only true morality known. A man is right and invincible, virtuous and on the road towards sure conquest, precisely while he joins himself to the great deep Law of the World, in spite of all superficial laws, temporary appearances, profit-and-loss calculations; he is victorious while he cooperates with that great central Law, not victorious otherwise; — and surely his first chance of cooperating with it, or getting into the course of it, is to know with his whole soul that it *is;* that it is good, and alone good! This is the soul of Islam; it is properly the soul of Christianity, — for Islam is definable as a confused form of Christianity; had Christianity not been, neither had it been. Christianity also commands us, before all, to be resigned to God. We are to take no counsel with flesh and blood; give ear to no vain cavils, vain sorrows and wishes: to know that we know nothing; that the worst and cruellest to our eyes is not what it seems; that we have to receive whatsoever befals us as sent from God above, and say, It is good and wise, God is great! "Though He slay me, yet will I trust in Him." Islam means in its way Denial of Self, Annihilation of Self. This is yet the highest Wisdom that Heaven has revealed to our Earth.

Such light had come, as it could, to illuminate the darkness of this wild Arab soul. A confused dazzling splendour as of life and Heaven, in the great darkness which threatened to be death: he called it revelation and the angel Gabriel; — who of us yet can know what to call it? It is the 'inspiration of the Almighty' that giveth us understanding. To *know;* to get into the truth of anything, is ever a mystic act, — of which the best Logics can but babble on the surface. 'Is not Belief the true god-announcing Miracle?' says Novalis. — That Mahomet's whole soul, set in flame with this grand Truth vouchsafed him, should feel as if it were important and the only important thing, was very natural. That Providence had unspeakably honoured *him* by revealing it, saving him from death and darkness; that he therefore was bound to make known the same to all creatures: this is what was meant by 'Mahomet is the Prophet of God;' this too is not without its true meaning. —

The good Kadijah, we can fancy, listened to him with wonder, with doubt; at length she answered: Yes, it was *true* this that he said. One can fancy too the boundless gratitude of Mahomet; and how of all the kindnesses she had done him, this of believing the earnest struggling word he now spoke was the greatest. 'It is certain,' says Novalis, 'my Conviction gains infinitely, the moment another soul will believe in it.' It is a boundless favour. — He never forgot this good Kadijah. Long afterwards, Ayesha his young favourite wife, a woman who indeed distinguished herself among the Moslem, by all manner of qualities, through her whole long life; this young brilliant Ayesha was, one day, questioning him: "Now am not I better than Kadijah? She was a widow; old, and had lost her looks: you love me better than you did her?" — "No, by Allah!" answered Mahomet: "No, by Allah! She believed in me when none else would believe. In the whole world I had but one friend, and she was that!" — Seid, his Slave, also believed in him; these with his young Cousin Ali, Abu Thaleb's son, were his first converts.

He spoke of his Doctrine to this man and that; but the most treated it with ridicule, with indifference: in three years, I think, he had gained but thirteen followers. His progress was slow enough. His encouragement to go on, was altogether the usual encouragement that such a man in such a case meets.

After some three years of small success, he invited forty of his chief kindred to an entertainment; and there stood up and told them what his pretension was: that he had this thing to promulgate abroad to all men; that it was the highest thing, the one thing: which of them would second him in that? Amid the doubt and silence of all, young Ali, as yet a lad of sixteen, impatient of the silence, started up, and exclaimed in passionate fierce language, That he would! The assembly, among whom was Abu Thaleb, Ali's Father, could not be unfriendly to Mahomet; yet the sight there, of one unlettered elderly man, with a lad of sixteen, deciding on such an enterprise against all mankind, appeared ridiculous to them; the assembly broke up in laughter. Nevertheless it proved not a laughable thing; it was a very serious thing! As for this young Ali, one cannot but like him. A noble-minded creature, as he shews himself, now and always afterwards; full of affection, of fiery daring. Something chivalrous in him; brave as a lion; yet with a grace, a truth and affection worthy of Christian knighthood. He died by assassination in the Mosque at Bagdad; a death occasioned by his own generous fairness, confidence in the fairness of others: he said, If the wound proved not unto death, they must pardon the Assassin; but if it did, then they must slay him straightway, that so they two in the same hour might appear before God, and see which side of that quarrel was the just one!

Mahomet naturally gave offence to the Koreish, Keepers of the Caabah, superintendents of the Idols. One or two men of influence had joined him: the thing spread slowly, but it was spreading. Naturally he gave offence to everybody: Who is this that pretends to be wiser than we all; that rebukes us all, as mere fools and worshippers of wood! Abu Thaleb the good Uncle spoke with him: Could he not be silent about all that; believe it all for himself, and not trouble others, anger the chief men, endanger himself and them all, talking of it? Mahomet answered: If the Sun stood on his right hand and the Moon on his left, ordering him to hold his peace, he could not obey! No: there was something in this Truth he had got which was of Nature herself; equal in rank to Sun, or Moon, or whatsoever thing Nature had made. It would speak itself there, so long as the Almighty allowed it, in spite of Sun and Moon, and all Koreish and all men and things. It must do that, and could do no other. Mahomet answered so; and, they say, 'burst into tears.' Burst into tears: he felt that Abu Thaleb was good to him; that the task he had got was no soft, but a stern and great one.

He went on speaking to who would listen to him; publishing his Doctrine among the pilgrims as they came to Mecca; gaining adherents in this place and that. Continual contradiction, hatred, open or secret danger attended him. His powerful relations protected Mahomet himself; but by and by, on his own advice, all his adherents had to quit Mecca, and seek refuge in Abyssinia over the sea. The Koreish grew ever angrier; laid plots, and swore oaths among them, to put Mahomet to death with their own hands. Abu Thaleb was dead, the good Kadijah was dead. Mahomet is not solicitous of sympathy from us; but his outlook at this time was one of the dismallest. He had to hide in caverns, escape in disguise; fly hither and thither; homeless, in continual peril of his life. More than once it seemed all over with him; more than once it turned on a straw, some rider's horse taking fright or the like, whether Mahomet and his Doctrine had not ended there, and not been heard of at all. But it was not to end so.

In the thirteenth year of his mission, finding his enemies all banded against him, forty sworn men, one out of every tribe waiting to take his life, and no continuance possible at Mecca for him any longer, Mahomet fled to the place then called Yathreb, where he had gained some adherents; the place they now call Medina, or '*Medinat al Nabi*, the City of the Prophet,' from that circumstance. It lay some 200 miles off, through rocks and deserts; not without great difficulty, in such mood as we may fancy, he escaped thither, and found welcome. The whole East dates its era from this Flight, *Hegira* as they name it: the Year 1 of this Hegira is 622 of our era, the fifty-third of Mahomet's life. He was now becoming an old man; his friends sinking round him one by one; his path desolate, encompassed with danger: unless he could find hope in his own heart, the outward face of things was but hopeless for him. It is so with all men in the like case. Hitherto Mahomet had professed to publish his Religion by the way of preaching and persuasion alone. But now, driven foully out of his native country, since unjust men had not only given no ear to his earnest Heaven's-message, the deep cry of his heart, but would not even let him live if he kept speaking it, — the wild Son of the Desert resolved to defend himself, like a man and Arab. If the Koreish will have it so, they shall have it. Tidings, felt to be of infinite moment to them and all men, they would not listen to these; would trample them down by sheer violence, steel and murder: well, let steel try it then! Ten years more this Mahomet had; all of fighting, of breathless impetuous toil and struggle; with what result we know.

Much has been said of Mahomet's propagating his Religion by the sword. It is no doubt far nobler what we have to boast of the Christian Religion, that it propagated itself peaceably in the way of preaching and conviction. Yet withal, if we take this for an argument of the truth or falsehood of a religion, there is a radical mistake in it. The sword indeed: but where will you get your sword! Every new opinion, at its starting, is precisely in a *minority of one*. In one man's head alone, there it dwells as

yet. One man alone of the whole world believes it; there is one man against
all men. That *he* take a sword, and try to propagate with that, will do little
for him. You must first get your sword! On the whole, a thing will propagate
itself as it can. We do not find, of the Christian Religion either, that it always
disdained the sword, when once it had got one. Charlemagne's conversion
of the Saxons was not by preaching. I care little about the sword: I will
allow a thing to struggle for itself in this world, with any sword or tongue or
implement it has, or can lay hold of. We will let it preach, and pamphleteer,
and fight, and to the uttermost bestir itself, and do, beak and claws, whatsoever is in it; very sure that it will, in the long-run, conquer nothing which
does not deserve to be conquered. What is better than itself, it cannot put
away, but only what is worse. In this great Duel, Nature herself is umpire,
and can do no wrong: the thing which is deepest-rooted in Nature, what we
call *truest*, that thing and not the other will be found growing at last.

Here however, in reference to much that there is in Mahomet and his
success, we are to remember what an umpire Nature is; what a greatness,
composure of depth and tolerance there is in her. You take wheat to cast into
the Earth's bosom: your wheat may be mixed with chaff, chopped straw,
barn-sweepings, dust and all imaginable rubbish; no matter: you cast it into
the kind just Earth; she grows the wheat, — the whole rubbish she silently
absorbs, shrouds *it* in, says nothing of the rubbish. The yellow wheat is
growing there; the good Earth is silent about all the rest, — has silently
turned all the rest to some benefit too, and makes no complaint about it! So
everywhere in Nature. She is true and not a lie; and yet so great, and just,
and motherly, in her truth. She requires of a thing only that it *be* genuine of
heart; she will protect it if so; will not, if not so. There is a soul of truth in all
the things she ever gave harbour to. Alas, is not this the history of all highest
Truth that comes or ever came into the world? The *body* of them all is
imperfection, an element of light *in* darkness: to us they have to come
embodied in mere Logic, in some merely *scientific* Theorem of the Universe; which *cannot* be complete; which cannot but be found, one day,
*in*complete, erroneous, and so die and disappear. The body of all Truth dies;
and yet in all, I say, there is a soul which never dies; which in new and ever-
nobler embodiment lives immortal as man himself! It is the way with
Nature. The genuine essence of Truth never dies. That it be genuine, a voice
from the great Deep of Nature, there is the point at Nature's judgment-seat.
What *we* call pure or impure, is not with her the final question. Not how
much chaff is in you; but whether you have any wheat. Pure? I might say to
many a man: Yes, you are pure; pure enough; but you are chaff, — insincere
hypothesis, hearsay, formality; you never were in contact with the great

heart of the Universe at all; you are properly neither pure nor impure; you *are* nothing, Nature has no business with you.

Mahomet's Creed we called a kind of Christianity; and really, if we look at the wild rapt earnestness with which it was believed and laid to heart, I should say a better kind than that of those miserable Syrian Sects, with their vain janglings about *Homoiousion* and *Homoousion*, the head full of worthless noise, the heart empty and dead! The truth of it is embedded in portentous error and falsehood; but the truth of it makes it be believed, not the falsehood: it succeeded by its truth. A bastard kind of Christianity, but a living kind; with a heart-life in it; not dead, chopping barren logic merely! Out of all that rubbish of Arab idolatries, argumentative theologies, traditions, subtleties, rumours and hypotheses of Greeks and Jews, with their idle wiredrawings, this wild man of the Desert, with his wild sincere heart, earnest as death and life, with his great flashing natural eyesight, had seen into the kernel of the matter. Idolatry is nothing: these Wooden Idols of yours, 'ye rub them with oil and wax, and the flies stick on them,' — these are wood, I tell you! They can do nothing for you; they are an impotent blasphemous pretence; a horror and abomination, if ye knew them. God alone is; God alone has power; He made us, He can kill us and keep us alive: "*Allah akbar*, God is great." Understand that His will is the best for you; that howsoever sore to flesh and blood, you will find it the wisest, best: you are bound to take it so; in this world and in the next, you have no other thing that you can do! — And now if the wild idolatrous men did believe this, and with their fiery hearts lay hold of it to do it, in what form soever it came to them, I say it was well worthy of being believed. In one form or the other, I say it is still the one thing worthy of being believed by all men. Man does hereby become the high-priest of this Temple of a World. He is in harmony with the Decrees of the Author of this World; cooperating with them, not vainly withstanding them: I know, to this day, no better definition of Duty than that same. All that is *right* includes itself in this of cooperating with the real Tendency of the World: you succeed by this (the World's Tendency will succeed), you are good, and in the right course there. *Homoiousion, Homoousion*, vain logical jangle, then or before or at any time, may jangle itself out, and go whither and how it likes: this is the *thing* it all struggles to mean, if it would mean anything. If it do not succeed in meaning this, it means nothing. Not that Abstractions, logical Propositions, be correctly worded or incorrectly; but that living concrete Sons of Adam do lay this to heart: that is the important point. Islam devoured all these vain jangling Sects; and I think had right to do so. It was a Reality, direct from the great Heart of

Nature once more. Arab idolatries. Syrian formulas, whatsoever was not equally real, had to go up in flame, — mere dead *fuel*, in various senses, for this which was *fire*.

It was during these wild warfarings and strugglings, especially after the Flight to Mecca, that Mahomet dictated at intervals his Sacred Book, which they name *Koran*, or *Reading*, 'Thing to be read.' This is the Work he and his disciples made so much of, asking all the world, Is not that a miracle? The Mahometans regard their Koran with a reverence which few Christians pay even to their Bible. It is admitted everywhere as the standard of all law and all practice; the thing to be gone upon in speculation and life: the message sent direct out of Heaven, which this Earth has to conform to, and walk by; the thing to be read. Their Judges decide by it; all Moslem are bound to study it, seek in it for the light of their life. They have mosques where it is all read daily; thirty relays of priests take it up in succession, get through the whole each day. There, for twelve hundred years, has the voice of this Book, at all moments, kept sounding through the ears and the hearts of so many men. We hear of Mahometan Doctors that had read it seventy thousand times!

Very curious: if one sought for 'discrepancies of national taste,' here surely were the most eminent instance of that! We also can read the Koran; our Translation of it, by Sale, is known to be a very fair one. I must say, it is as toilsome reading as I ever undertook. A wearisome confused jumble, crude, incondite; endless iterations, longwindedness, entanglement; most crude, incondite; — insupportable stupidity, in short! Nothing but a sense of duty could carry any European through the Koran. We read in it, as we might in the State-Paper Office, unreadable masses of lumber, that perhaps we may get some glimpses of a remarkable man. It is true we have it under disadvantages: the Arabs see more method in it than we. Mahomet's followers found the Koran lying all in fractions, as it had been written down at first promulgation; much of it, they say, on shoulder-blades of mutton, flung pellmell into a chest: and they published it, without any discoverable order as to time or otherwise; — merely trying, as would seem, and this not very strictly, to put the longest chapters first. The real beginning of it, in that way, lies almost at the end; for the earliest portions were the shortest. Read in its historical sequence it perhaps would not be so bad. Much of it, too, they say, is rhythmic; a kind of wild chaunting song, in the original. Yet with every allowance, one feels it difficult to see how any mortal ever could consider this Koran as a Book written in Heaven, too good for the Earth; as a well-written book, or indeed as a *book* at all; and not a bewildered rhapsody; *written*, so far as writing goes, as badly as almost any book ever was! So much for national discrepancies, and the standard of taste.

Yet I should say, it was not unintelligible how the Arabs might so love it. When once you get this confused coil of a Koran fairly off your hands, and have it behind you at a distance, the essential type of it begins to disclose itself; and in this there is a merit quite other than the literary one. If a book come from the heart, it will contrive to reach other hearts; all art and authorcraft are of small amount to that. One would say the primary character of the Koran is this of its *genuineness*, of its being a *bonâ-fide* book. Prideaux, I know, and others have represented it as a mere bundle of juggleries; chapter after chapter got up to excuse and varnish the author's successive sins, forward his ambitions and quackeries: but really it is time to dismiss all that. I do not assert Mahomet's continual sincerity: who is continually sincere? But I confess I can make nothing of the critic, in these times, who would accuse him of deceit *prepense;* of conscious deceit generally, or perhaps at all; — still more, of living in a mere element of conscious deceit, and writing this Koran as a forger and juggler would have done! Every candid eye, I think, will read the Koran far otherwise than so. It is the confused ferment of a great rude human soul; rude, untutored, that cannot even read; but fervent, earnest, struggling vehemently to utter itself in words. With a kind of breathless intensity he strives to utter himself; the thoughts crowd on him pellmell; for very multitude of things to say he can get nothing said. The meaning that is in him shapes itself into no form of composition, is stated in no sequence, method, or coherence; — they are not *shaped* at all, these thoughts of his; flung out unshaped, as they struggle and tumble there, in their chaotic inarticulate state. We said 'stupid:' yet natural stupidity is by no means the character of Mahomet's Book; it is natural uncultivation rather. The man has not studied speaking; in the haste and pressure of continual fighting, has not time to mature himself into fit speech. The panting breathless haste and vehemence of a man struggling in the thick of battle for life and salvation; this is the mood he is in! A headlong haste; for very magnitude of meaning he cannot get himself articulated into words. The successive utterances of a soul in that mood, coloured by the various vicissitudes of three-and-twenty years; now well uttered, now worse: this is the Koran.

For we are to consider Mahomet, through these three-and-twenty years, as the centre of a world wholly in conflict. Battles with the Koreish and Heathen, quarrels among his own people, backslidings of his own wild heart; all this kept him in a perpetual whirl, his soul knowing rest no more.

In wakeful nights, as one may fancy, the wild soul of the man, tossing amid these vortices, would hail any light of a decision for them as a veritable light from Heaven; *any* making up of his mind, so blessed, indispensable for him there, would seem the inspiration of a Gabriel. Forger and juggler? Ah, no! This great fiery heart, seething, simmering like a great furnace of thoughts, was not a juggler's. His Life was a Fact to him; this God's Universe an awful Fact and Reality. He has faults enough. The man was an uncultured semi-barbarous Son of Nature, much of the Bedouin still clinging to him: we must take him for that. But for a wretched Simulacrum, a hungry Impostor without eyes or heart, practising for a mess of pottage such blasphemous swindlery, forgery of celestial documents, continual high-treason against his Maker and Self, we will not and cannot take him.

Sincerity, in all senses, seems to me the merit of the Koran; what had rendered it precious to the wild Arab men. It is, after all, the first and last merit in a book; gives rise to merits of all kinds, — nay, at bottom, it alone can give rise to merit of any kind. Curiously, through these incondite masses of tradition, vituperation, complaint, ejaculation in the Koran, a vein of true direct insight, of what we might almost call poetry, is found straggling. The body of the Book is made up of mere tradition, and as it were vehement enthusiastic extempore preaching. He returns forever to the old stories of the Prophets as they went current in the Arab memory: how Prophet after Prophet, the Prophet Abraham, the Prophet Hud, the Prophet Moses, Christian and other real and fabulous Prophets, had come to this Tribe and to that, warning men of their sin; and been received by them even as he Mahomet was, — which is a great solace to him. These things he repeats ten, perhaps twenty times; again and ever again, with wearisome iteration; has never done repeating them. A brave Samuel Johnson, in his forlorn garret, might study the Biographies of Authors in that way! This is the great staple of the Koran. But curiously, through all this, comes ever and anon some glance as of the real thinker and seer. He has actually an eye for the world, this Mahomet: with a certain directness and rugged vigour, he brings home still, to our heart, the thing his own heart has been opened to. I make but little of his praises of Allah, which many praise; they are borrowed I suppose mainly from the Hebrew, at least they are far surpassed there. But the eye that flashes direct into the heart of things, and *sees* the truth of them; this is to me a highly interesting object. Great Nature's own gift; which she bestows on all; but which only one in the thousand does not cast sorrowfully away: it is what I call sincerity of vision; the test of a sincere heart. Mahomet can work no miracles; he often answers impatiently: I can work no miracles. I? 'I am a Public Preacher;' appointed to preach this doctrine to all creatures. Yet the world, as we can see, had really from of old been all one great miracle to him. Look over the world, says he; is it not wonderful, the work of Allah; wholly 'a sign to you,' if your eyes were open! This Earth, God made it for you; 'appointed paths in it;' you can live in it, go to and fro on it. — The clouds in the dry country of Arabia, to Mahomet they are very wonderful: Great clouds, he says, born in the deep bosom of the Upper Immensity, where do they come from! They hang there, the great black monsters; pour down their rain-deluges 'to revive a dead earth,' and grass springs, and 'tall leafy palmtrees with their date-clusters hanging round. Is not that a sign?' Your cattle too, — Allah made them: serviceable dumb creatures; they make the grass into milk; you have your clothing from them, very strange creatures; 'and,' adds he, 'and they are a credit to you!' Ships, — he talks often about ships: Huge moving mountains, they spread out their cloth wings, go bounding through the water there, Heaven's wind driving them; anon they lie motionless, God has withdrawn the wind, they lie dead, and cannot stir! Miracles? cries he: What miracle would you have? Are not you yourselves there? God made you, 'shaped you out of a little clay.' Ye were small once; a few years ago ye were not at all. Ye have beauty, strength, thoughts, 'ye have compassion on one another.' Old age comes on you, and grey hairs; your strength fades into feebleness; ye sink down, and again are not. 'Ye have compassion on one another:' this struck me much: Allah might have made you having no compassion on one another, — how had it been then! This is a great direct thought, a glance at first-hand into the very fact of things. Rude vestiges of poetic genius, of whatsoever is best and truest, are visible in this man. A strong untutored intellect; eyesight, heart: a strong wild man, — might have shaped himself into Poet, King, Priest, any kind of Hero.

To his eyes it is forever clear that this world wholly is miraculous. He sees what, as we said once before, all great thinkers, the rude Scandinavians themselves, in one way or other, have contrived to see: That this so solid-looking material world is, at bottom, in very deed, Nothing; is a visual and tactual Manifestation of God's power and presence, — a shadow hung out by Him on the bosom of the void Infinite; nothing more. The mountains, he says, these great rockmountains, they shall dissipate themselves 'like clouds;' melt into the Blue as clouds do, and not be! He figures the Earth, in the Arab fashion, Sale tells us, as an immense Plain or flat Plate of ground, the mountains are set on that to *steady* it. At the Last Day, they shall disappear 'like clouds;' the whole Earth shall go spinning, whirl itself off into wreck, and as dust and vapour vanish in the Inane. Allah withdraws his hand from it, and it ceases to be. The universal empire of Allah, presence everywhere of an unspeakable Power, a Splendour, and a Terror not to be named, as the true force, essence and reality, in all things whatsoever, was continually clear to this man. What a modern talks of by the name, Forces of Nature, Laws of Nature; and does not figure as a divine thing; not even as one thing at all, but as a set of things, undivine enough, — saleable, curious, good for propelling steam-ships! With our Sciences and Cyclopædias, we are apt to forget the *divineness*, in those laboratories of ours. We ought not to forget it! That once well forgotten, I know not what else were worth remembering. Most sciences, I think, were then a very dead thing; withered, contentious, empty; — a thistle in late autumn. The best science, without this, is but as the dead *timber;* it is not the growing tree and forest, — which gives ever-new timber among other things! Man cannot *know* either, unless he can *worship* in some way. His knowledge is a pedantry, and dead thistle, otherwise.

Much has been said and written about the sensuality of Mahomet's Religion; more than was just. The indulgences, criminal to us, which he permitted, were not of his appointment; he found them practised, unquestioned from immemorial time in Arabia; what he did was to curtail them, restrict them, not on one but on many sides. His Religion is not an easy one; with rigorous fasts, lavations, strict complex formulas, prayers five times a day, and abstinence from wine, it did not 'succeed by being an easy religion.' As if indeed any religion, or cause holding of religion, could succeed by that! It is a calumny on men to say that they are roused to heroic action by ease, hope of pleasure, recompense, — sugar-plums of any kind, in this world or the next! In the meanest mortal there lies something nobler. The poor swearing soldier, hired to be shot, has his 'honour of a soldier,' different from drill-regulations and the shilling a day. It is not to taste sweet things, but to do noble and true things, and vindicate himself under God's Heaven as a god-made Man, that the poorest son of Adam dimly longs. Shew him the way of doing that, the dullest daydrudge kindles into a hero. They wrong man greatly who say he is to be seduced by ease. Difficulty, abnegation, martyrdom, death are the *allurements* that act on the heart of man. Kindle the inner genial life of him, you have a flame that burns up all lower considerations. Not happiness, but something higher: one sees this even in the frivolous classes, with their 'point of honour' and the like. Not by flattering our appetites; no, by awakening the Heroic that slumbers in every heart, can any Religion gain followers.

Mahomet himself, after all that can be said about him, was not a sensual man. We shall err widely if we consider this man as a common voluptuary, intent mainly on base enjoyments, — nay on enjoyments of any kind. His household was of the frugalest; his common diet barley-bread and water:

sometimes for months there was not a fire once lighted on his hearth. They record with just pride that he would mend his own shoes, patch his own cloak. A poor, hard-toiling, ill-provided man; careless of what vulgar men toil for. Not a bad man, I should say; something better in him than *hunger* of any sort, — or these wild Arab men, fighting and jostling three and twenty years at his hand, in close contact with him always, would not have reverenced him so! They were wild men, bursting ever and anon into quarrel, into all kinds of fierce sincerity; without right worth and manhood, no man could have commanded them. They called him Prophet, you say? Why, he stood there face to face with them; bare, not enshrined in any mystery; visibly clouting his own cloak, cobbling his own shoes; fighting, counselling, ordering in the midst of them: they must have seen what kind of man he *was*, let him be *called* what you like! No emperor with his tiaras was obeyed as this man in a cloak of his own clouting. During three and twenty years of rough actual trial. I find something of a veritable Hero necessary for that, of itself.

His last words are a prayer; broken ejaculations of a heart struggling up, in trembling hope, towards its Maker. We cannot say that his religion made him *worse;* it made him better; good, not bad. Generous things are recorded of him: when he lost his Daughter, the thing he answers is, in his own dialect, every way sincere, and yet equivalent to that of Christians, 'The Lord giveth, and the Lord taketh away; blessed be the name of the Lord.' He answered in like manner of Seid, his emancipated well-beloved Slave, the second of the believers. Seid had fallen in the War of Tabûc, the first of Mahomet's fightings with the Greeks. Mahomet said, It was well; Seid had done his Master's work, Seid had now gone to his Master: it was all well with Seid. Yet Seid's daughter found him weeping over the body; — the old gray-haired man melting in tears! "What do I see?" said she. — "You see a friend weeping over his friend." — He went out for the last time into the mosque, two days before his death; asked, If he had injured any man? Let his own back bear the stripes. If he owed any man? A voice answered, "Yes, me three drachms," borrowed on such an occasion. Mahomet ordered them to be paid: "Better be in shame now," said he, "than at the Day of Judgment." — You remember Kadijah, and the "No, by Allah!" Traits of that kind shew us the genuine man, the brother of us all, brought visible through twelve centuries, — the veritable Son of our common Mother.

Withal I like Mahomet for his total freedom from cant. He is a rough self-helping son of the wilderness; does not pretend to be what he is not. There is no ostentatious pride in him; but neither does he go much upon humility: he is there as he can be, in cloak and shoes of his own clouting;

speaks plainly to all manner of Persian Kings, Greek Emperors, what it is they are bound to do; knows well enough, about himself, 'the respect due unto thee.' In a life-and-death war with Bedouins, cruel things could not fail; but neither are acts of mercy, of noble natural pity and generosity, wanting. Mahomet makes no apology for the one, no boast of the other. They were each the free dictate of his heart; each called for, there and then. Not a mealy-mouthed man! A candid ferocity, if the case call for it, is in him; he does not mince matters! The War of Tabûc is a thing he often speaks of: his men refused, many of them, to march on that occasion; pleaded the heat of the weather, the harvest, and so forth; he can never forget that. Your harvest? It lasts for a day. What will become of your harvest through all Eternity? Hot weather? Yes, it was hot; but 'Hell will be hotter!' Sometimes a rough sarcasm turns up: He says to the unbelievers, Ye shall have the just measure of your deeds at that Great Day. They will be weighed out to you; ye shall not have short weight! — Everywhere he fixes the matter in his eye; he *sees* it: his heart, now and then, is as if struck dumb by the greatness of it. 'Assuredly,' he says: that word, in the Koran, is written down sometimes as a sentence by itself: 'Assuredly.'

No *Dilettantism* in this Mahomet; it is a business of Reprobation and Salvation with him, of Time and Eternity: he is in deadly earnest about it! Dilettantism, hypothesis, speculation, a kind of amateur-search for Truth, toying and coquetting with Truth: this is the sorest sin. The root of all other imaginable sins. It consists in the heart and soul of the man never having been *open* to Truth; — 'living in a vain show.' Such a man not only utters and produces falsehoods, but *is* himself a falsehood. The rational moral principle, spark of the Divinity, is sunk deep in him, in quiet paralysis of life-death. The very falsehoods of Mahomet are truer than the truths of such a man. He is the insincere man: smooth-polished, respectable in some times and places; inoffensive, says nothing harsh to anybody; most *cleanly*, — just as carbonic acid is, which is death and poison.

We will not praise Mahomet's moral precepts as always of the super-finest sort; yet it can be said that there is always a tendency to good in them; that they are the true dictates of a heart aiming towards what is just and true. The sublime forgiveness of Christianity, turning of the other cheek when the one has been smitten, is not here: you *are* to revenge yourself, but it is to be in measure, not over much, or beyond justice. On the other hand, Islam, like any great Faith, and insight into the essence of man, is a perfect equal-izer of men: the soul of one believer outweighs all earthly kingships; all men, according to Islam too, are equal. Mahomet insists not on the pro-priety of giving alms, but on the necessity of it: he marks down by law how much you are to give, and it is at your peril if you neglect. The tenth part of a man's annual income, whatever that may be, is the *property* of the poor, of those that are afflicted and need help. Good all this: the natural voice of humanity, of pity and equity dwelling in the heart of this wild Son of Nature speaks *so*.

Mahomet's Paradise is sensual, his Hell sensual: true; in the one and the other there is enough that shocks all spiritual feeling in us. But we are to recollect that the Arabs already had it so; that Mahomet, in whatever he changed of it, softened and diminished all this. The worst sensualities, too, are the work of doctors, followers of his, not his work. In the Koran there is really very little said about the joys of Paradise; they are intimated rather than insisted on. Nor is it forgotten that the highest joys even there shall be spiritual; the pure Presence of the Highest, this shall infinitely transcend all other joys. He says, 'Your salutation shall be, Peace.' *Salam*, Have Peace! — the thing that all rational souls long for, and seek, vainly here below, as the one blessing. 'Ye shall sit on seats, facing one another: all grudges shall be taken away out of your hearts.' All grudges! Ye shall love one another freely; for each of you, in the eyes of his brothers, there will be Heaven enough!

In reference to this of the sensual Paradise and Mahomet's sensuality, the sorest chapter of all for us, there were many things to be said; which it is not convenient to enter upon here. Two remarks only I shall make, and therewith leave it to your candour. The first is furnished me by Goethe; it is a casual hint of his which seems well worth taking note of. In one of his Delineations, in *Meister's Travels* it is, the hero comes upon a Society of men with very strange ways, one of which was this: "We require," says the Master, "that each of our people shall restrict himself in one direction," shall go right against his desire in one matter, and *make* himself do the thing he does not wish, "should we allow him the greater latitude on all other sides." There seems to me a great justness in this. Enjoying things which are pleasant; that is not the evil: it is the reducing of our moral self to slavery by them that is. Let a man assert withal that he is king over his habitudes; that he could and would shake them off, on cause shewn: this is an excellent law. The Month Ramadhan for the Moslem, much in Mahomet's Religion, much in his own Life, bears in that direction; if not by forethought, or clear purpose of moral improvement on his part, then by a certain healthy manful instinct, which is as good.

But there is another thing to be said about the Mahometan Heaven and Hell. This namely, that, however gross and material they may be, they are an emblem of an everlasting truth, not always so well remembered elsewhere. That gross sensual Paradise of his: that horrible flaming Hell, the great enormous Day of Judgment he perpetually insists on: what is all this but a rude shadow, in the rude Bedouin imagination, of that grand spiritual Fact, and Beginning of Facts, which it is ill for us too if we do not all know and feel: the Infinite Nature of Duty? That man's actions here are of *infinite* moment to him, and never die or end at all; that man, with his little life, reaches upwards high as Heaven, downwards low as Hell, and in his three-score years of Time holds an Eternity fearfully and wonderfully hidden: all this had burnt itself, as in flame-characters, into the wild Arab soul. As in flame and lightning, it stands written there; awful, unspeakable, ever present to him. With bursting earnestness, with a fierce savage sincerity, half-articulating, not able to articulate, he strives to speak it, bodies it forth in that Heaven and that Hell. Bodied forth in what way you will, it is the first of all truths. It is venerable under all embodiments. What is the chief end of man here below? Mahomet has answered this question, in a way that might put some of *us* to shame! He does not, like a Bentham, a Paley, take Right and Wrong, and calculate the profit and loss, ultimate pleasure of the one and of the other; and summing all up by addition and subtraction into a net result, ask you, Whether on the whole the Right does not preponderate considerably? No: it is not *better* to do the one than the other; the one is to the other as life is to death, — as Heaven is to Hell. The one must in nowise be done, the other in nowise left undone. You shall not measure them; they are incommensurable: the one is death eternal to a man, the other is life eternal. Benthamee Utility, virtue by Profit and Loss; reducing this God's-world to a dead brute Steam-engine, the infinite celestial Soul of Man to a kind of Hay-balance for weighing hay and thistles on, pleasures and pains on: — If you ask me which gives, Mahomet or they, the beggarlier and falser view of Man and his Destinies in this Universe, I will answer, It is not Mahomet! ——

On the whole, we will repeat that this Religion of Mahomet's is a kind of Christianity; has a genuine element of what is spiritually highest looking through it, not to be hidden by all its imperfections. The Scandinavian God *Wish*, the god of all rude men, — this has been enlarged into a Heaven by Mahomet; but a Heaven symbolical of sacred Duty, and to be earned by faith and welldoing, by valiant action, and a divine patience which is still more valiant. It is Scandinavian Paganism, and a truly celestial element superadded to that. Call it not false; look not at the falsehood of it, look at the truth of it. For these twelve centuries, it has been the religion and life-guidance of the fifth part of the whole kindred of Mankind. Above all things, it has been a religion heartily *believed*. These Arabs believe their religion, and try to live by it! No Christians, since the early ages, or only perhaps the English Puritans in modern times, have ever stood by their Faith as the Moslem do by theirs, — believing it wholly, fronting Time with it, and Eternity with it. This night the watchman on the streets of Cairo when he cries, "Who goes?" will hear from the passenger, along with his answer, "There is no God but God." *Allah akbar, Islam*, sounds through the souls, and whole daily existence, of these dusky millions. Zealous missionaries preach it abroad among Malays, black Papuans, brutal Idolators; — displacing what is worse, nothing that is better or good.

To the Arab Nation it was as a birth from darkness into light; Arabia first became alive by means of it. A poor shepherd people, roaming unnoticed in its deserts since the creation of the world: a Hero-Prophet was sent down to them with a word they could believe: see, the unnoticed becomes world-notable, the small has grown world-great; within one century afterwards, Arabia is at Grenada on this hand, at Delhi on that; — glancing in valour and splendour and the light of genius, Arabia shines through long ages over a great section of the world. Belief is great, life-giving. The history of a Nation becomes fruitful, soul-elevating, great, so soon as it believes. These Arabs, the man Mahomet, and that one century, — is it not as if a spark had fallen, one spark, on a world of what seemed black unnoticeable sand; but lo, the sand proves explosive powder, blazes heaven-high from Delhi to Grenada! I said, the Great Man was always as lightning out of Heaven; the rest of men waited for him like fuel, and then they too would flame.

The Hero as Poet. Dante; Shakspeare.

THE Hero as Divinity, the Hero as Prophet are productions of old ages; not to be repeated in the new. They presuppose a certain rudeness of conception, which the progress of mere scientific knowledge puts an end to. There needs to be, as it were, a world vacant, or almost vacant of scientific forms, if men in their loving wonder are to fancy their fellow man either a god or one speaking with the voice of a god. Divinity and Prophet are past. We are now to see our Hero in the less ambitious, but also less questionable, character of Poet; a character which does not pass. The Poet is a heroic figure belonging to all ages; whom all ages possess, when once he is produced, whom the newest age as the oldest may produce; — and will produce, always when Nature pleases. Let Nature send a Hero-soul; in no age is it other than possible that he may be shaped into a Poet.

Hero, Prophet, Poet, — many different names, in different times and places, do we give to Great Men; according to varieties we note in them, according to the sphere in which they have displayed themselves! We might give many more names, on this same principle. I will remark again, however, as a fact not unimportant to be understood, that the different *sphere* constitutes the grand origin of such distinction; that the Hero can be Poet, Prophet, King, Priest or what you will, according to the kind of world he finds himself born into. I confess, I have no notion of a truly great man that could not be *all* sorts of men. The Poet who could merely sit on a chair, and compose stanzas, would never make a stanza worth much. He could not sing the Heroic warrior, unless he himself were at least a Heroic warrior too. I fancy there is in him the Politician, the Thinker, Legislator, Philosopher; — in one or the other degree, he could have been, he is all these. So too I cannot understand how a Mirabeau, with that great glowing heart, with the fire that was in it, with the bursting tears that were in it, could not have written verses, tragedies, poems, and touched all hearts in that way, had his course of life and education led him thitherward. The grand fundamental character is that of Great Man; that the man be great. Napoleon has words in him which are like Austerlitz Battles. Louis Fourteenth's Marshals are a kind of poetical men withal; the things Turenne says are full of sagacity and geniality, like sayings of Samuel Johnson. The great heart, the clear deep-seeing eye: there it lies; no man whatever, in what province soever, can prosper at all without these. Petrarch and Boccaccio did diplomatic messages, it seems, quite well: one can easily believe it; they had done things a little harder than that! Burns, a gifted song-writer, might have made a still better Mirabeau. Shakspeare, — one knows not what *he* could not have made, in the supreme degree.

True, there are aptitudes of Nature too. Nature does not make all great men, more than all other men, in the self-same mould. Varieties of aptitude doubtless; but infinitely more of circumstance; and far oftenest it is the *latter* only that are looked to. But it is as with common men in the learning of trades. You take any man, as yet a vague capability of a man, who could be any kind of craftsman; and make him into a smith, a carpenter, a mason: he is then and thenceforth that and nothing else. And if, as Addison complains, you sometimes see a street-porter staggering under his load on spindle-shanks, and near at hand a tailor with the frame of a Samson, handling a bit of cloth and small Whitechapel needle, — it cannot be considered that aptitude of Nature alone has been consulted here either! The Great Man also, to what shall he be bound apprentice? Given your Hero, is he to become Conqueror, King, Philosopher, Poet? It is an inexplicably complex controversial-calculation between the world and him! He will read the world and its laws; the world with its laws will be there to be read. What the world, on *this* matter, shall permit and bid is, as we said, the most important fact about the world. —

Poet and Prophet differ greatly in our loose modern notions of them. In some old languages, again, the titles are synonymous; *Vates* means both Prophet and Poet: and indeed at all times, Prophet and Poet, well understood, have much kindred of meaning. Fundamentally indeed they are still the same; in this most important respect especially, That they have penetrated both of them into the sacred mystery of the Universe; what Goethe calls 'the open secret!' "Which is the great secret?" asks one. — "The *open* secret," — open to all, seen by almost none! That divine mystery, which lies everywhere in all Beings, 'the Divine Idea of the World, that which lies at the bottom of Appearance,' as Fichte styles it; of which all Appearance, from the starry sky to the grass of the field, but especially the Appearance of Man and his work, is but the *vesture*, the embodiment that renders it visible. This divine mystery *is* in all times and in all places; veritably is. In most times and places it is greatly overlooked; and the Universe, definable always in one or the other dialect, as the realised Thought of God, is considered a trivial, inert, commonplace matter, — as if, says the Satirist, it were a dead thing, which some upholsterer had put together! It could do no good, at present, to *speak* much about this; but it is a pity for every one of us if we do not know it, live ever in the knowledge of it. Really a most mournful pity; — a failure to live at all, if we live otherwise!

But now, I say, whoever may forget this divine mystery, the *Vates*, whether Prophet or Poet, has penetrated into it; is a man sent hither to make it more impressively known to us. That always is his message; he is to reveal that to us, — that sacred mystery which he more than others lives ever present with. While others forget it, he knows it; — I might say, he has been driven to know it; without consent asked of *him*, he finds himself living in it, bound to live in it. Once more, here is no Hearsay, but a direct Insight and Belief; this man too could not help being a sincere man! Whosoever may live in the shows of things, it is for him a necessity of nature to live in the very fact of things. A man, once more, in earnest with the Universe, though all others were but toying with it. He is a *Vates*, first of all, in virtue of being sincere. So far Poet and Prophet, participators in the 'open secret,' are one.

With respect to their distinction again: The *Vates* Prophet, we might say, has seized that sacred mystery rather on the moral side, as Good and Evil, Duty and Prohibition; the *Vates* Poet on what the Germans call the æsthetic side, as Beautiful, and the like. The one we may call a revealer of what we are to do, the other of what we are to love. But indeed these two provinces run into one another, and cannot be disjoined. The Prophet too has his eye on what we are to love: how else shall he know what it is we are to do? The highest Voice ever heard on this Earth said withal, "Consider the lilies of the field; they toil not, neither do they spin: yet Solomon in all his glory was not arrayed like one of these." A glance, that, into the deepest deep of Beauty. 'The lilies of the field,' — dressed finer than earthly princes, springing up there in the humble furrow-field; a beautiful *eye* looking out on you, from the great inner Sea of Beauty! How could the rude Earth make these, if her Essence, rugged as she looks and is, were not inwardly Beauty? — In this point of view, too, a saying of Goethe's, which has staggered several, may have meaning: 'The Beautiful,' he intimates, 'is higher than the Good; the Beautiful includes in it the Good.' The *true* Beautiful; which however, I have said somewhere, 'differs from the *false*, as Heaven does from Vauxhall!' So much for the distinction and identity of Poet and Prophet. —

In ancient and also in modern periods, we find a few Poets who are accounted perfect; whom it were a kind of treason to find fault with. This is noteworthy; this is right: yet in strictness it is only an illusion. At bottom, clearly enough, there is no perfect Poet! A vein of Poetry exists in the hearts of all men; no man is made altogether of Poetry. We are all poets when we *read* a poem well. The 'imagination that shudders at the Hell of Dante,' is not that the same faculty, weaker in degree, as Dante's own? No one but Shakspeare can embody, out of *Saxo Grammaticus*, the story of *Hamlet* as Shakspeare did: but every one models some kind of story out of it; every one embodies it better or worse. We need not spend time in defining. Where there is no specific difference, as between round and square, all definition must be more or less arbitrary. A man that has *so* much more of the poetic element developed in him as to have become noticeable, will be called Poet by his neighbours. World-Poets too, those whom we are to take for perfect Poets, are settled by critics in the same way. One who rises *so* far above the general level of Poets will, to such and such critics, seem a Universal Poet; as he ought to do. And yet it is, and must be, an arbitrary distinction. All Poets, all men, have some touches of the Universal; no man is wholly made of that. Most Poets are very soon forgotten: but not the noblest Shakspeare or Homer of them can be remembered *forever;* — a day comes when he too is not!

Nevertheless, you will say, there must be a difference between true Poetry and true Speech not poetical: what is the difference? On this point many things have been written, especially by late German Critics, some of which are not very intelligible at first. They say, for example, that the Poet has an *infinitude* in him; communicates an *Unendlichkeit*, a certain character of 'infinitude' to whatsoever he delineates. This, though not very precise, yet on so vague a matter is worth remembering: if well meditated, some meaning will gradually be found in it. For my own part, I find considerable meaning in the old vulgar distinction of Poetry being *metrical*, having music in it, being a Song. Truly, if pressed to give a definition, one might say this as soon as anything else: If your delineation be authentically *musical*, musical not in word only, but in heart and substance, in all the thoughts and utterances of it, in the whole conception of it, then it will be poetical; if not, not. — Musical: how much lies in that! A *musical* thought is one spoken by a mind that has penetrated into the inmost heart of the thing; detected the inmost mystery of it, namely the *melody* that lies hidden in it; the inward harmony of coherence which is its soul, whereby it exists, and has a right to be here in this world. All inmost things, we may say, are melodious; naturally utter themselves in Song. The meaning of Song goes deep. Who is there that, in logical words, can express the effect music has on us? A kind of inarticulate unfathomable speech, which leads us to the edge of the Infinite, and lets us for moments gaze into that!

Nay all speech, even the commonest speech, has something of song in it:

not a parish in the world but has its parish-accent; — the rhythm or time to which the people there sing what they have to say! Accent is a kind of chaunting; all men have accent of their own, — though they only *notice* that of others. Observe too how all passionate language does of itself become musical, — with a finer music than the mere accent; the speech of a man even in zealous anger becomes a chaunt, a song. All deep things are Song. It seems somehow the very central essence of us, Song; as if all the rest were but wrappages and hulls! The primal element of us; of us, and of all things. The Greeks fabled of Sphere-Harmonies: it was the feeling they had of the inner structure of Nature; that the soul of all her voices and utterances was perfect music. Poetry, therefore, we will call *musical Thought*. The Poet is he who *thinks* in that manner. At bottom, it turns still on power of intellect; it is a man's sincerity and depth of vision that makes him a Poet. See deep enough, and you see musically; the heart of Nature *being* everywhere music, if you can only reach it.

The *Vates* Poet, with his melodious Apocalypse of Nature, seems to hold a poor rank among us, in comparison with the *Vates* Prophet; his function, and our esteem of him for his function, alike slight. The Hero taken as Divinity; the Hero taken as Prophet; then next the Hero taken only as Poet: does it not look as if our estimate of the Great Man, epoch after epoch, were continually diminishing? We take him first for a god, then for one god-inspired; and now in the next stage of it, his most miraculous word gains from us only the recognition that he is a Poet, beautiful verse-maker, man of genius, or such like! — It looks so; but I persuade myself that intrinsically it is not so. If we consider well, it will perhaps appear that in man still there is the *same* altogether peculiar admiration for the Heroic Gift, by what name soever called, that there at any time was. I should say, if we do not now reckon a Great Man literally divine, it is that our notions of God, of the supreme unattainable Fountain of Splendour, Wisdom and Heroism, are ever rising *higher;* not altogether that our reverence for these qualities, as manifested in our like, is getting lower. This is worth taking thought of. Sceptical Dilettantism, the curse of these ages, a curse which will not last forever, does indeed in this the highest province of human things, as in all provinces, make sad work; and our reverence for great men, all crippled, blinded, paralytic as it is, comes out in poor plight, hardly recognisable. Men worship the shows of great men; the most disbelieve that there is any reality of great men to worship. The dreariest, fatalest faith; believing which, one would literally despair of human things. Nevertheless look, for example, at Napoleon! A Corsican lieutenant of artillery; that is the show of *him:* yet is he not obeyed, *worshipped* after his sort, as all the Tiaraed and

Diademed of the world put together could not be? High duchesses, and ostlers of inns, gather round the Scottish rustic, Burns; — a strange feeling dwelling in each that they never heard a man like this; that on the whole this is the man! In the secret heart of these people it still dimly reveals itself, though there is no accredited way of uttering it at present, that this rustic, with his black brows and flashing sun-eyes, and strange words moving laughter and tears, is of a dignity far beyond all others, incommensurable with all others. Do not we feel it so? But now, were Dilettantism, Scepticism, Triviality, and all that sorrowful brood, cast out of us, — as, by God's blessing, they shall one day be; were faith in the shows of things entirely swept out, replaced by clear faith in the *things*, so that a man acted on the impulse of that only, and counted the other non-extant, what a new livelier feeling towards this Burns were it!

Nay here in these ages, such as they are, have we not two mere Poets, if not deified, yet we may say beatified? Shakspeare and Dante are Saints of Poetry; really, if we will think of it, *canonized*, so that it is impiety to meddle with them. The unguided instinct of the world, working across all these perverse impediments, has arrived at such result. Dante and Shakspeare are a peculiar Two. They dwell apart, in a kind of royal solitude; none equal, none second to them: in the general feeling of the world, a certain transcendentalism, a glory as of complete perfection, invests these two. They *are* canonized, though no Pope or Cardinals took hand in doing it! Such, in spite of every perverting influence, in the most unheroic times, is still our indestructible reverence for heroism. — We will look a little at these Two, the Poet Dante and the Poet Shakspeare: what little it is permitted us to say here of the Hero as Poet, will most fitly arrange itself in that fashion.

Many volumes have been written by way of commentary on Dante and his Book; yet, on the whole, with no great result. His Biography is, as it were, irrecoverably lost for us. An unimportant, wandering, sorrowstricken man, not much note was taken of him while he lived; and the most of that has vanished, in the long space that now intervenes. It is five centuries since he ceased writing and living here. After all commentaries, the Book itself is mainly what we know of him. The Book; — and one might add that Portrait commonly attributed to Giotto, which, looking on it, you cannot help inclining to think genuine, whoever did it. To me it is a most touching face; perhaps of all faces that I know, the most so. Blank there, painted on vacancy, with the simple laurel wound round it; the deathless sorrow and pain, the known victory which is also deathless; — significant of the whole history of Dante! I think it is the mournfulest face that ever was painted from reality; an altogether tragic, heart-affecting face. There is in it, as foundation of it, the softness, tenderness, gentle affection as of a child; but all this is as if congealed into sharp contradiction, into abnegation, isolation, proud hopeless pain. A soft ethereal soul looking out so stern, implacable, grim-trenchant, as from imprisonment of thick-ribbed ice! Withal it is a silent pain too, a silent scornful one: the lip is curled in a kind of godlike disdain of the thing that is eating out his heart, — as if it were withal a mean insignificant thing, as if he whom it had power to torture and strangle were greater than it. The face of one wholly in protest, and life-long unsurrendering battle, against the world. Affection all converted into indignation: an implacable indignation; slow, equable, implacable, silent, like that of a god! The eye too, it looks out as in a kind of *surprise*, a kind of inquiry, Why the world was of such a sort? This is Dante: so he looks, this 'voice of ten silent centuries,' and sings us 'his mystic unfathomable song.'

The little that we know of Dante's Life corresponds well enough with this Portrait and this Book. He was born at Florence, in the upper class of society, in the year 1265. His education was the best then going; much school-divinity, Aristotelean logic, some Latin classics, — no inconsiderable insight into certain provinces of things: and Dante, with his earnest intelligent nature, we need not doubt, learned better than most all that was learnable. He has a clear cultivated understanding, and of great subtlety; this best fruit of education he had contrived to realize from these scholastics. He knows accurately and well what lies close to him; but, in such a time, without printed books or free intercourse, he could not know well what was distant: the small clear light, most luminous for what is near, breaks itself into singular *chiaroscuro* striking on what is far off. This was Dante's learning from the schools. In life, he had gone through the usual destinies; been twice out campaigning as a soldier for the Florentine state, been on embassy; had in his thirty-fifth year, by natural gradation of talent and service, become one of the Chief Magistrates of Florence. He had met in boyhood a certain Beatrice Portinari, a beautiful little girl of his own age and rank, and grown up thenceforth in partial sight of her, in some distant intercourse with her. All readers know his graceful affecting account of this; and then of their being parted; of her being wedded to another, and of her death soon after. She makes a great figure in Dante's Poem; seems to have made a great figure in his life. Of all beings it might seem as if she, held apart from him, far apart at last in the dim Eternity, were the only one he had ever with his whole strength of affection loved. She died: Dante himself was wedded; but it seems not happily, far from happily. I fancy, the rigorous earnest man, with his keen excitabilities, was not altogether easy to make happy.

We will not complain of Dante's miseries: had all gone right with him as he wished it, he might have been Prior, Podestà, or whatsoever they call it, of Florence, well accepted among neighbours, — and the world had wanted one of the most notable words ever spoken or sung. Florence had another prosperous Lord Mayor; and the ten dumb centuries continued voiceless, and the ten other listening centuries (for there will be ten of them and more) had no *Divina Commedia* to hear! We will complain of nothing. A nobler destiny was appointed for this Dante; and he, struggling like a man led towards death and crucifixion, could not help fulfilling it. Give *him* the choice of his happiness! He knew not more than we do what was really happy, what was really miserable.

In Dante's Priorship, the Guelf-Ghibelline, Bianchi-Neri, or some other confused disturbances rose to such a height, that Dante, whose party had seemed the stronger, was with his friends cast unexpectedly forth into banishment; doomed thenceforth to a life of woe and wandering. His property was all confiscated and more; he had the fiercest feeling that it was entirely unjust, nefarious in the sight of God and man. He tried what was in him to get reinstated; tried even by warlike surprisal, with arms in his hand: but it would not do; bad only had become worse. There is a record, I believe, still extant in the Florence Archives, dooming this Dante, wheresoever caught, to be burnt alive. Burnt alive; so it stands, they say: a very curious civic document. Another curious document, some considerable number of years later, is a Letter of Dante's to the Florentine Magistrates, written in answer to a milder proposal of theirs, that he should return on condition of apologizing and paying a fine. He answers, with fixed stern pride, "If I cannot return without calling myself guilty, I will never return, *nunquam revertar.*"

For Dante there was now no home in this world. He wandered from patron to patron, from place to place; proving, in his own bitter words, 'How hard is the path, *Come è duro calle.*' The wretched are not cheerful company. Dante, poor and banished, with his proud earnest nature, with his moody humours, was not a man to conciliate men. Petrarch reports of him that being at Can della Scala's court, and blamed one day for his gloom and taciturnity, he answered in no courtier-like way. Della Scala stood among his courtiers, with mimes and buffoons (*nebulones ac histriones*) making him heartily merry; when turning to Dante, he said: "Is it not strange now that this poor fool should do so much to amuse us; while you, a wise man, sit there day after day, and have nothing to amuse us with at all?" Dante answered bitterly: "No, it is not strange, if you think of the Proverb, *Like to Like;*" — given the amuser, the amusee must also be given! Such a man, with his proud silent ways, with his sarcasms and sorrows, was not made to succeed at court. By degrees, it came to be evident to him that he had no longer any resting place, or hope of benefit, in this earth. The earthly world had cast him forth, to wander, wander; no living heart to love him now; for his sore miseries there was no solace here.

The deeper naturally would the Eternal World impress itself on him; that awful reality over which, after all, this Time-world, with its Florences and banishments, only flutters as an unreal shadow. Florence thou shalt never see: but Hell and Purgatory and Heaven thou shalt surely see! What is Florence, Can della Scala, and the World and Life altogether? ETERNITY: thither, of a truth, not elsewhither, art thou and all things bound! The great soul of Dante, homeless on earth, made its home more and more in that awful other world. Naturally his thoughts brooded on that, as on the one fact important for him. Bodied or bodiless, it is the one fact important for all men: — but to Dante, in that age, it was bodied in fixed certainty of scientific shape; he no more doubted of that *Malebolge* Pool, that it all lay there with its gloomy circles, with its *alti guai*, and that he himself should see it, than we doubt that we should see Constantinople if we went thither. Dante's heart, long filled with this, brooding over it in speechless thought and awe, bursts forth at length into 'mystic unfathomable song;' and this his *Divine Comedy*, the most remarkable of all modern Books, is the result. It must have been a great solacement to Dante, and was, as we can see, a proud thought for him at times, that he, here in exile, could do this work; that no Florence, nor no man or men, could hinder him from doing it, or even much help him in doing it. He knew too, partly, that it was great; the greatest a man could do. 'If thou follow thy star, *Se tu segui la tua stella*' — so could the Hero, in his forsakenness, in his extreme need, still say to himself: "Follow thy star, thou shalt not fail of a glorious haven!" The labour of writing, we find, and indeed could know otherwise, was great and painful for him; he says, This Book 'which has made me lean for many years.' Ah yes, it was won, all of it, with pain and sore toil, — not in sport, but in grim earnest. His Book, as indeed most good Books are, has been written, in many senses, with his heart's blood. It is his whole history this Book. He died after finishing it; not yet very old, at the age of fifty-six; — broken-hearted rather, as is said. He lies buried in his death-city Ravenna: *Hic claudor Dantes patriis extorris ab oris.* The Florentines begged back his body, in a century after; the Ravenna people would not give it. "Here am I Dante laid, shut out from my native shores."

I said, Dante's Poem was a Song: it is Tieck who calls it 'a mystic unfathomable Song;' and such is literally the character of it. Coleridge remarks very pertinently somewhere, that wherever you find a sentence musically worded, of true rhythm and melody in the words, there is something deep and good in the meaning too. For body and soul, word and idea, go strangely together, here as everywhere. Song: we said before, it was the Heroic of Speech! All *old* Poems, Homer's and the rest, are authentically Songs. I would say, in strictness, that all right Poems are; that whatsoever is not *sung* is properly no Poem, but a piece of Prose cramped into jingling lines, — to the great injury of the grammar, to the great grief of the reader, for most part! What we want to get at is the *thought* the man had, if he had any: why should he twist it into jingle, if he *could* speak it out plainly? It is only when the heart of him is rapt into true passion of melody, and the very tones of him, according to Coleridge's remark, become musical by the greatness, depth and music of his thoughts, that we can give him right to rhyme and sing; that we call him a Poet, and listen to him as the Heroic of Speakers, — whose speech *is* Song. Pretenders to this are many; and to an earnest reader, I doubt, it is for most part a very melancholy, not to say an insupportable business, that of reading rhyme! Rhyme that had no inward necessity to be rhymed; — it ought to have told us plainly, without any jingle, what it was aiming at. I would advise all men who *can* speak their thought, not to sing it; to understand that, in a serious time, among serious men, there is no vocation in them for singing it. Precisely as we love the true song, and are charmed by it as by something divine, so shall we hate the false song, and account it a mere wooden noise, a thing hollow, superfluous, altogether an insincere and offensive thing.

I give Dante my highest praise when I say of his *Divine Comedy* that it is, in all senses, genuinely a Song. In the very sound of it there is a *canto fermo;* it proceeds as by a chaunt. The language, his simple *terza rima,* doubtless helped him in this. One reads along naturally with a sort of *lilt.* But I add, that it could not be otherwise; for the essence and material of the work are themselves rhythmic. Its depth, and rapt passion and sincerity, makes it musical; — go *deep* enough, there is music everywhere. A true inward symmetry, what one calls an architectural harmony, reigns in it, proportionates it all: architectural; which also partakes of the character of music. The three kingdoms, *Inferno, Purgatorio, Paradiso,* look out on one another like compartments of a great edifice; a great supernatural world-cathedral, piled up there, stern, solemn, awful; Dante's World of Souls! It is, at bottom, the *sincerest* of all Poems; sincerity, here too, we find to be the measure of worth. It came deep out of the author's heart of hearts; and it goes deep, and through long generations, into ours. The people of Verona, when they saw him on the streets, used to say, *"Eccovi l' uom ch' è stato all' Inferno*, See, there is the man that was in Hell!" Ah, yes, he had been in Hell; — in Hell enough, in long severe sorrow and struggle; as the like of him is pretty sure to have been. Commedias that come out *divine*, are not accomplished otherwise. Thought, true labour of any kind, highest virtue itself, is it not the daughter of Pain? Born as out of the black whirlwind; — true *effort*, in fact, as of a captive struggling to free himself: that is Thought. In all ways we are 'to become perfect through *suffering*.' — But, as I say, no work known to me is so elaborated as this of Dante's. It has all been as if molten, in the hottest furnace of his soul. It had made him 'lean' for many years. Not the general whole only; every compartment of it is worked out, with intense earnestness, into truth, into clear visuality. Each answers to the other; each fits in its place, like a marble stone accurately hewn and po-lished. It is the soul of Dante, and in this the soul of the middle ages, rendered forever rhythmically visible there. No light task; a right intense one: but a task which is *done*.

Perhaps one would say, *intensity*, with the much that depends on it, is the prevailing character of Dante's genius. Dante does not come before us as a large catholic mind; rather as a narrow, and even sectarian mind: it is partly the fruit of his age and position, but partly too of his own nature. His great-ness has, in all senses, concentered itself into fiery emphasis and depth. He is world-great not because he is world-wide, but because he is world-deep. Through all objects he pierces as it were down into the heart of Being. I know nothing so intense as Dante. Consider, for example, to begin with the outermost development of his intensity, consider how he paints. He has a great power of vision; seizes the very type of a thing; presents that and nothing more. You remember that first view he gets of the Hall of Dite: *red* pinnacle, redhot cone of iron glowing through the dim immensity of gloom; — so vivid, so distinct, visible at once and forever! It is as an emblem of the whole genius of Dante. There is a brevity, an abrupt precision in him: Tacitus is not briefer, more condensed; and then in Dante it seems a natural condensation, spontaneous to the man. One smiting word; and then there is silence, nothing more said. His silence is more eloquent than words. It is strange with what a sharp decisive grace he snatches the true likeness of a matter; cuts into the matter as with a pen of fire. Plutus, the blustering giant, collapses at Virgil's rebuke; it is 'as the sails sink, the mast being suddenly broken.' Or that poor Sordello, with the *cotto aspetto*, 'face *baked*,' parched brown and lean; and the 'fiery snow' that falls on them there, a 'fiery snow without wind,' slow, deliberate, never-ending! Or the lids of those Tombs; square sarcophaguses, in that silent dim-burning Hall, each with its Soul in torment; the lids laid open there; they are to be shut at the Day of Judgment, through Eternity. And how Farinata rises; and how Cavalcante falls — at hearing of his Son, and the past tense *'fue!'* The very movements in Dante have something brief; swift, decisive, almost military. It is of the inmost essence of his genius this sort of painting. The fiery, swift Italian nature of the man, so silent, passionate, with its quick abrupt movements, its silent 'pale rages,' speaks itself in these things.

For though this of painting is one of the outermost developments of a man, it comes like all else from the essential faculty of him; it is physiognomical of the whole man. Find a man whose words paint you a likeness, you have found a man worth something; mark his manner of doing it, as very characteristic of him. In the first place, he could not have discerned the object at all, or seen the vital type of it, unless he had, what we may call, *sympathized* with it, — had sympathy in him to bestow on objects. He must have been *sincere* about it too; sincere and sympathetic: a man without worth cannot give you the likeness of any object; he dwells in vague outwardness, fallacy and trivial hearsay, about all objects. And indeed may we not say that intellect altogether expresses itself in this power of discerning what an object is? Whatsoever of faculty a man's mind may have will come out here. Is it even of business, a matter to be done? The gifted man is he who *sees* the essential point, and leaves all the rest aside as surplusage: it is his faculty too, the man of business's faculty, that he discern the true *likeness*, not the false superficial one, of the thing he has got to work in. And how much of *morality* is in the kind of insight we get of anything; 'the eye seeing in all things what it brought with it the faculty of seeing!' To the mean eye all things are trivial, as certainly as to the jaundiced they are yellow. Raphael, the Painters tell us, is the best of all Portrait-painters withal. No most gifted eye can exhaust the significance of any object. In the commonest human face there lies more than Raphael will take away with him.

Dante's painting is not graphic only, brief, true, and of a vividness as of fire in dark night; taken on the wider scale, it is everyway noble, and the outcome of a great soul. Francesca and her Lover, what qualities in that! A thing woven as out of rainbows, on a ground of eternal black. A small flute-voice of infinite wail speaks there, into our very heart of hearts. A touch of womanhood in it too; she speaks of *'questa forma;'* — *so* innocent; and how, even in the Pit of woe, it is a solace that he 'will never part from her.' Saddest tragedy in these alti guai. And the racking winds, in that *aer bruno*, whirl them away again, forever! — Strange to think: Dante was the friend of this poor Francesca's father; Francesca herself may have sat upon the Poet's knee, as a bright innocent little child. Infinite pity, yet also infinite rigour of law: it is so Nature is made; it is so Dante discerned that she was made. What a paltry notion is that of his *Divine Comedy's* being a poor splenetic impotent terrestrial libel; putting those into Hell whom he could not be avenged upon on earth! I suppose if ever pity, tender as a mother's, was in the heart of any man, it was in Dante's. But a man who does not know rigour cannot pity either. His very pity will be cowardly, egoistic, — sentimentality, or little better. I know not in the world an affection equal to that of Dante. It is a tenderness, a trembling, longing, pitying love: like the wail of Æolean harps, soft, soft; like a child's young heart; — and then that stern, sore-saddened heart! These longings of his towards his Beatrice; their meeting together in the *Paradiso;* his gazing in her pure transfigured eyes, her that had been purified by death so long, separated from him so far: ah, one likens it to the song of angels; it is among the purest utterances of affection, perhaps the very purest, that ever came out of a human soul.

For the *intense* Dante is intense in all things; he has got into the essence of all. His intellectual insight, as painter, on occasion too as reasoner, is but the result of all other sorts of intensity. Morally great, above all, we must call him; it is the beginning of all. His scorn, his grief are as transcendent as his love; — as indeed, what are they but the *inverse* or *converse* of his love? '*A Dio spiacenti, ed a' nemici sui*, Hateful to God and to the enemies of God:' lofty scorn, unappeasable silent reprobation and aversion: '*Non ragionam di lor*, We will not speak of *them*, look only and pass.' Or think of this: 'They have not the *hope* to die, *Non han speranza di morte*.' One day, it had risen sternly benign on the scathed heart of Dante, that he, wretched, never-resting, worn as he was, would full surely *die;* 'that Destiny itself could not doom him not to die.' Such words are in this man. For rigour, earnestness and depth, he is not to be paralleled in the modern world; to seek his parallel we must go into the Hebrew Bible, and live with the antique Prophets there.

I do not agree with much modern criticism, in greatly preferring the *Inferno* to the two other parts of the Divine *Commedia*. Such preference belongs, I imagine, to our general Byronism of taste, and is like to be a transient feeling. The *Purgatorio* and *Paradiso*, especially the former, one would almost say, is even more excellent than it. It is a noble thing that *Purgatorio*, 'Mountain of Purification;' an emblem of the noblest conception of that age. If Sin is so fatal, and Hell is and must be so rigorous, awful, yet in Repentance too is man purified; Repentance is the grand Christian act. It is beautiful how Dante works it out. The *tremolar dell' onde*, that 'trembling' of the ocean-waves, under the first pure gleam of morning, dawning afar on the wandering Two, is as the type of an altered mood. Hope has now dawned; never-dying Hope, if in company still with heavy sorrow. The obscure sojourn of dæmons and reprobate is under foot; a soft breathing of penitence mounts higher and higher, to the Throne of Mercy itself. "Pray for me," the denizens of that Mount of Pain all say to him. "Tell my Giovanna to pray for me," my daughter Giovanna; "I think her mother loves me no more!" They toil painfully up by that winding steep, 'bent down like corbels' of a building, some of them, — crushed together so 'for the sin of pride;' yet nevertheless in years, in ages and æons, they shall have reached the top, Heaven's gate, and by Mercy been admitted in. The joy too of all, when one has prevailed; the whole Mountain shakes with joy, and a psalm of praise rises, when one soul has perfected repentance, and got its sin and misery left behind! I call all this a noble embodiment of a true noble thought.

But indeed the Three compartments mutually support one another, are indispensable to one another. The *Paradiso*, a kind of inarticulate music to me, is the redeeming side of the *Inferno;* the *Inferno* without it were untrue. All three make up the true Unseen World, as figured in the Christianity of the Middle Ages; a thing forever memorable, forever true in the essence of it, to all men. It was perhaps delineated in no human soul with such depth of veracity as in this of Dante's; a man *sent* to sing it, to keep it long memorable. Very notable with what brief simplicity he passes out of the every-day reality, into the Invisible one; and in the second or third stanza, we find ourselves in the World of Spirits; and dwell there, as among things palpable, indubitable! To Dante they *were* so; the real world, as it is called, and its facts, was but the threshold to an infinitely higher Fact of a World. At bottom, the one was as *preter*natural as the other. Has not each man a soul? He will not only be a spirit, but is one. To the earnest Dante it is all one visible Fact; he believes it, sees it; is the Poet of it in virtue of that. Sincerity, I say again, is the saving merit, now as always.

Dante's Hell, Purgatory, Paradise, are a symbol withal, an emblematic representation of his Belief about this Universe: — some Critic in a future age, like those Scandinavian ones the other day, who has ceased altogether to think as Dante did, may find this too all an 'Allegory,' perhaps an idle Allegory! It is a sublime embodiment, our sublimest, of the soul of Christianity. It expresses, as in huge worldwide architectural emblems, how the Christian Dante felt Good and Evil to be the two polar elements of this

Creation, on which it all turns; that these two differ not by *preferability* of one to the other, but by incompatibility absolute and infinite; that the one is excellent and high as light and Heaven, the other hideous, black as Gehenna and the Pit of Hell! Everlasting Justice, yet with Penitence, with everlasting Pity, — all Christianity, as Dante and the Middle Ages had it, is emblemed here. Emblemed: and yet, as I urged the other day, with what entire truth of purpose; how unconscious of any embleming! Hell, Purgatory, Paradise: these things were not fashioned as emblems; was there, in our Modern European Mind, any thought at all of their being emblems! Were they not indubitable awful facts; the whole heart of man taking them for practically true, all Nature everywhere confirming them? So is it always in these things. Men do not believe an Allegory. The future Critic, whatever his new thought may be, who considers this of Dante to have been all got up as an Allegory, will commit one sore mistake! — Paganism we recognised as a veracious expression of the earnest awe-struck feeling of man towards the Universe; veracious, true once, and still not without worth for us. But mark here the difference of Paganism and Christianity; one great difference. Paganism emblemed chiefly the Operations of Nature; the destinies, efforts, combinations, vicissitudes of things and men in this world: Christianism emblemed the Law of Human Duty, the Moral Law of Man. One was for the sensuous nature; a rude helpless utterance of the *first* Thought of men, — the chief recognised virtue, Courage, Superiority to Fear. The other was not for the sensuous nature, but for the moral. What a progress is here, if in that one respect only! —

And so in this Dante, as we said, had ten silent centuries, in a very strange way, found a voice. The *Divina Commedia* is of Dante's writing; yet in truth *it* belongs to ten Christian centuries, only the finishing of it is Dante's. So always. The craftsman there, the smith with that metal of his, with these tools, with these cunning methods, — how little of all he does is properly *his* work! All past inventive men work there with him; — as indeed with all of us, in all things. Dante is the spokesman of the Middle Ages; the Thought they lived by stands here, in everlasting music. These sublime ideas of his, terrible and beautiful, are the fruit of the Christian Meditation of all the good men who had gone before him. Precious they; but also is not he precious? Much, had not he spoken, would have been dumb; not dead, yet living voiceless.

On the whole, is it not an utterance, this mystic Song, at once of one of the greatest human souls, and of the highest thing that Europe had hitherto realised for itself? Christianity, as Dante sings it, is another than Paganism in the rude Norse mind; another than 'Bastard Christianism' half-articulately spoken in the Arab Desert, seven hundred years before! — The noblest *idea* made *real* hitherto among men, is sung, and emblemed forth abidingly, by one of the noblest men. In the one sense and in the other, are we not right glad to possess it? As I calculate, it may last yet for long thousands of years. For the thing that is uttered from the inmost parts of a man's soul, differs altogether from what is uttered by the outer part. The outer is of the day, under the empire of mode; the outer passes away, in swift endless changes; the inmost is the same yesterday, today and forever. True souls, in all generations of the world, who look on this Dante, will find a brotherhood in him; the deep sincerity of his thoughts, his woes and hopes, will speak likewise to their sincerity; they will feel that this Dante too was a brother. Napoleon in Saint-Helena is charmed with the genial veracity of old Homer. The oldest Hebrew Prophet, under a vesture the most diverse from ours, does yet, because he speaks from the heart of man, speak to all men's hearts. It is the one sole secret of continuing long memorable. Dante, for depth of sincerity, is like an antique Prophet too; his words, like theirs, come from his very heart. One need not wonder if it were predicted that his Poem might be the most enduring thing our Europe has yet made; for nothing so endures as a truly spoken word. All cathedrals, pontificalities, brass and stone, and outer arrangement, never so lasting, are brief in comparison to an unfathomable heart-song like this: one feels as if it might survive, still of importance to men, when these had all sunk into new irrecognisable combinations, and had ceased individually to be. Europe has made much; great cities, great empires, encyclopædias, creeds, bodies of opinion and practice: but it has made little of the class of Dante's Thought. Homer yet *is*, veritably present face to face with every open soul of us; and Greece, where is *it?* Desolate for thousands of years; away, vanished; a bewildered heap of stones and rubbish, the life and existence of it all gone. Like a dream; like the dust of King Agamemnon! Greece was; Greece, except in the *words* it spoke, is not.

The uses of this Dante? We will not say much about his 'uses.' A human soul who has once got into that primal element of *Song*, and sung forth fitly somewhat therefrom, has worked in the *depths* of our existence; feeding through long times the life-*roots* of all excellent human things whatsoever, — in a way that 'utilities' will not succeed well in calculating! We will not estimate the Sun by the quantity of gas-light it saves us; Dante shall be invaluable, or of no value. One remark I may make: the contrast in this respect between the Hero-Poet and the Hero-Prophet. In a hundred years, Mahomet, as we saw, had his Arabians at Grenada and at Delhi; Dante's Italians seem to be yet very much where they were. Shall we say, then,

Dante's effect on the world was small in comparison? Not so: his arena is far more restricted; but also it is far nobler, clearer; — perhaps not less but more important. Mahomet speaks to great masses of men, in the coarse dialect adapted to such; a dialect filled with inconsistencies, crudities, follies: on the great masses alone can he act, and there with good and with evil strangely blended. Dante speaks to the noble, the pure and great, in all times and places. Neither does he grow obsolete, as the other does. Dante burns as a pure star, fixed there in the firmament, at which the great and the high of all ages kindle themselves: he is the possession of all the chosen of the world for uncounted time. Dante, one calculates, may long survive Mahomet. In this way the balance may be made straight again.

But, at any rate, it is not by what is called their effect on the world, by what *we* can judge of their effect there, that a man and his work are measured. Effect? Influence? Utility? Let a man *do* his work; the fruit of it is the care of Another than he. It will grow its own fruit; and whether embodied in Caliph Thrones and Arabian Conquests, so that it 'fills all Morning and Evening Newspapers,' and all Histories, which are a kind of distilled Newspapers; or not embodied so at all; — what matters that? That is not the real fruit of it! The Arabian Caliph, in so far only as he did something, was something. If the great Cause of Man, and Man's work in God's Earth, got no furtherance from the Arabian Caliph, then no matter how many scimetars he drew, how many gold piastres pocketed, and what uproar and blaring he made in this world, — *he* was but a loud-sounding inanity and futility; at bottom, he *was* not at all. Let us honour the great empire of *Silence*, once more! Ah yes, the boundless treasury which we do *not* jingle in our pockets, or count up and present before men. It is perhaps, of all things, the usefulest for each of us to do, in these loud times. ——

As Dante, the Italian man, was sent into our world to embody musically the Religion of the Middle Ages, the Religion of our Modern Europe, its Inner Life; so Shakspeare, we may say, embodies for us the Outer Life of our Europe as developed then, its chivalries, courtesies, humours, ambitions, what practical way of thinking, acting, looking at the world, men then had. As in Homer we may still construe Old Greece; so in Shakspeare and Dante, after thousands of years, what our Modern Europe was, in Faith and in Practice, will still be legible. Dante has given us the Faith or soul; Shakspeare, in a not less noble way, has given us the Practice or body. This latter also we were to have; a man was sent for it, the man Shakspeare. Just when that chivalry-way of life had reached its last finish, and was on the point of breaking down into slow or swift dissolution, as we now see it

everywhere, this other sovereign Poet, with his seeing eye, with his perennial singing voice, was sent to take note of it, to give long-enduring record
of it. Two fit men: Dante, deep, fierce as the central fire of the world;
Shakspeare, wide, placid, far-seeing, as the Sun, the upper light of the
world. Italy produced the one world-voice; we English had the honour of
producing the other.

Curious enough how, as it were by mere accident, this man came to us. I
think always, so great, quiet, complete and self-sufficing is this Shakspeare,
had the Warwickshire Squire not prosecuted him for deer-stealing, we had
perhaps never heard of him as a Poet! The woods and skies, the rustic Life
of Man in Stratford there, had been enough for this man! But indeed that
strange outbudding of our whole English Existence, which we call the
Elizabethan Era, did not it too come as of its own accord? The 'Tree
Igdrasil' buds and withers by its own laws, — too deep for our scanning. Yet
it does bud and wither, and every bough and leaf of it is there, by fixed
eternal laws; not a Sir Thomas Lucy but comes at the hour fit for him.
Curious, I say, and not sufficiently considered: how every thing does coop-
erate with all; not a leaf rotting on the highway but is indissoluble portion of
solar and stellar systems; no thought, word or act of man but has sprung
withal out of all men, and works sooner or later, recognisably or irrecog-
nisably, on all men! It is all a Tree: circulation of sap and influences, mutual
communication of every minutest leaf with the lowest talon of a root, with
every other greatest and minutest portion of the whole. The Tree Igdrasil,
that has its roots down in the Kingdoms of Hela and Death, and whose
boughs overspread the highest Heaven! —

In some sense it may be said that this glorious Elizabethan Era with its
Shakspeare, as the outcome and flowerage of all which had preceded it, is
itself attributable to the Catholicism of the Middle Ages. The Christian
Faith, which was the theme of Dante's Song, had produced this Practical
Life which Shakspeare was to sing. For Religion then, as it now and always
is, was the soul of Practice; the primary vital fact in men's life. And remark
here, as rather curious, that Middle-Age Catholicism was abolished, so far
as Acts of Parliament could abolish it, before Shakspeare, the noblest product of it, made his appearance. He did make his appearance nevertheless.
Nature at her own time, with Catholicism or what else might be necessary,
sent him forth; taking small thought of Acts of Parliament. King Henrys,
Queen-Elizabeths go their way; and Nature too goes hers. Acts of Parliament, on the whole, are small, notwithstanding the noise they make. What
Act of Parliament, debate at St. Stephen's, on the hustings or elsewhere,

was it that brought this Shakspeare into being? No dining at Freemasons' Tavern, opening subscription-lists, selling of shares, and infinite other jangling and true or false endeavouring! This Elizabethan Era, and all its nobleness and blessedness, came without proclamation, preparation of ours. Priceless Shakspeare was the free gift of Nature; given altogether silently; — received altogether silently, as if it had been a thing of little account. And yet, very literally, it is a priceless thing. One should look at that side of matters too.

Of this Shakspeare of ours, perhaps the opinion one sometimes hears a little idolatrously expressed is, in fact, the right one; I think the best judgment not of this country only, but of Europe at large, is slowly pointing to the conclusion, That Shakspeare is the chief of all Poets hitherto; the greatest intellect who, in our recorded world, has left record of himself in the way of Literature. On the whole, I know not such a power of vision, faculty of thought, if we take all the characters of it, in any other man. Such a calmness of depth, placid joyous strength; all things imaged in that great soul of his so true and clear, as in a tranquil unfathomable sea! It has been said, that in the constructing of Shakspeare's Dramas there is, apart from all other 'faculties' as they are called, an understanding manifested, equal to that in Bacon's *Novum Organum*. That is true; and it is not a truth that strikes every one. It would become more apparent if we tried, any of us for himself, how, out of Shakspeare's dramatic materials, *we* could fashion such a result! The built house seems all so fit, every way as it should be, as if it came there by its own law and the nature of things; we forget the rude disorderly quarry it was shaped from. The very perfection of the house, as if Nature herself had made it, hides the builder's merit. Perfect, more perfect than any other man, we may call Shakspeare in this: he discerns, knows as by instinct, what condition he works under, what his materials are, what his own force and its relation to them is. It is not a transitory glance of insight that will suffice; it is deliberate illumination of the whole matter; it is a calmly *seeing* eye; a great intellect, in short. How a man, of some wide thing that he has witnessed, will construct a narrative, what kind of picture and delineation he will give of it, — is the best measure you could get of what intellect is in the man. Which circumstance is vital and shall stand prominent; which unessential, fit to be suppressed; where is the true *beginning*, the true sequence and ending? To find out this, you task the whole force of insight that is in the man. He must *understand* the thing; according to the depth of his understanding, will the fitness of his answer be. You will try him so. Does like join itself to like; the spirit of method stir in that confusion, so that its embroilment becomes order? Can the man say, *Fiat lux*, and out of chaos make a world? Precisely as there is *light* in himself, will he accomplish this.

Or indeed we may say again, it is in what I called Portrait-painting, delineating of men and things, especially of men, that Shakspeare is great. All the greatness of the man comes out decisively here. It is unexampled, I think, that calm creative perspicacity of Shakspeare. The thing he looks at reveals not this or that face of it, but its inmost heart and generic secret: it dissolves itself as in light before him, so that he discerns the perfect structure of it. Creative, we said: poetic creation, what is this too but *seeing* the thing sufficiently? The *word* that will describe the thing follows, of itself, from such clear intense sight of the thing. And is not Shakspeare's *morality*, his valour, candour, tolerance, truthfulness; his whole victorious strength and greatness, which can triumph over such obstructions, visible there too? Great as the world! No *twisted*, poor convex-concave mirror, reflecting all objects with its own convexities and concavities; a perfectly *level* mirror; — that is to say withal, if we will understand it, a man justly related to all things and men, a good man. It is truly a lordly spectacle how this great soul takes in all kinds of men and objects, a Falstaff, an Othello, a Juliet, a Coriolanus; sets them all forth to us in their round completeness; loving, just, the equal brother of all. *Novum Organum*, and all the intellect you will find in Bacon, is of a quite secondary order; earthy, material, poor in comparison with this. Among modern men, one finds, in strictness, almost nothing of the same rank. Goethe alone, since the days of Shakspeare, reminds me of it. Of him too you say that he *saw* the object; you may say what he himself says of Shakspeare: 'His characters are like watches with dial-plates of transparent crystal; they shew you the hour like others, and the inward mechanism also is all visible.'

The seeing eye! It is this that discloses the inner harmony of things; what Nature meant, what musical idea Nature has wrapped up in these often rough embodiments. Something she did mean. To the seeing eye that something were discernible. Are they base, miserable things? You can laugh over them, you can weep over them; you can in some way or other genially relate yourself to them; — you can, at lowest, hold your peace about them, turn away your own and others' face from them, till the hour come for practically exterminating and extinguishing them! At bottom, it is the Poet's first gift, as it is all men's, that he have intellect enough. He will be a Poet if he have: a Poet in word; or failing that, perhaps still better, a Poet in act. Whether he write at all; and if so, whether in prose or in verse, will depend on accidents: who knows on what extremely trivial accidents, — perhaps on his having had a singing-master, on his being taught to sing in his boyhood! But the faculty which enables him to discern the inner heart of things, and the harmony that dwells there (for whatsoever exists has a harmony in the heart of it, or it would not hold together and exist), is not the result of habits or accidents, but the gift of Nature herself; the primary outfit for a Heroic Man in what sort soever. To the Poet, as to every other, we say first of all, *See.* If you cannot do that, it is of no use to keep stringing rhymes together, jingling sensibilities against each other, and *name* yourself a Poet; there is no hope for you. If you can, there is, in prose or verse, in action or speculation, all manner of hope. The crabbed old Schoolmaster used to ask, when they brought him a new pupil, "But are ye sure he's *not a dunce?*" Why, really one might ask the same thing, in regard to every man proposed for whatsoever function; and consider it as the one inquiry needful: Are ye sure he's not a dunce? There is, in this world, no other entirely fatal person.

For, in fact, I say the degree of vision that dwells in a man is a correct measure of the man. If called to define Shakspeare's faculty, I should say superiority of Intellect, and think I had included all under that. What indeed are faculties? We talk of faculties as if they were distinct, things separable; as if a man had intellect, imagination, fancy, &c., as he has hands, feet and arms. That is a capital error. Then again, we hear of a man's 'intellectual nature,' and of his 'moral nature,' as if these again were divisible, and existed apart. Necessities of language do indeed require us so to speak; we must speak, I am aware, in that way, if we are to speak at all. But words ought not to harden into things for us. It seems to me, our apprehension of this matter is, for most part, radically falsified thereby. We ought to know withal, and to keep forever in mind, that these divisions are at bottom but *names;* that man's spiritual nature, the vital Force which dwells in him, is essentially one and indivisible; that what we call imagination, fancy, understanding, and so forth, are but different figures of the same Power of Insight, all indissolubly connected with each other, physiognomically related; that if we knew one of them, we might know all of them. Morality itself, what we call the moral quality of a man, what is this but another *side* of the one vital Force whereby he is and works? All that a man does is physiognomical of him. You may see how a man would fight, by the way in which he sings; his courage, or want of courage, is visible in the word he utters, in the opinion he has formed, no less than in the stroke he strikes. He is *one;* and preaches the same Self abroad in all these ways.

Without hands a man might have feet, and could still walk: but, consider it, without morality, intellect were impossible for him, he could not know anything at all! To know a thing, what we can call knowing, a man must first *love* the thing, sympathize with it: that is, be *virtuously* related to it. If he have not the justice to put down his own selfishness at every turn, the courage to stand by the dangerous-true at every turn, how shall he know? His virtues, all of them, will lie recorded in his knowledge. Nature with her truth remains to the bad, the selfish and the pusillanimous, forever a sealed book: what such can know of Nature is mean, superficial, small; for the uses of the day merely. — But does not the very Fox know something of Nature? Exactly so: it knows where the geese lodge! The human Reynard, very frequent everywhere in the world, what more does he know but this and the like of this? Nay, it should be considered too, that if the Fox had not a certain vulpine *morality*, he could not even know where the geese were, or get at the geese! If he spent his time in splenetic atrabiliar reflexions on his own misery, his ill usage by Nature, Fortune and other Foxes, and so forth; and had not courage, promptitude, practicality, and other suitable vulpine gifts and graces, he would catch no geese. We may say of the Fox too, that his morality and insight are of the same dimensions; different faces of the same internal unity of vulpine life! — These things are worth stating, for the contrary of them acts with manifold very baleful perversion, in this time: what limitations, modifications they require, your own candour will supply.

If I say, therefore, that Shakspeare is the greatest of Intellects, I have said all about him. But there is more in Shakspeare's intellect than we have yet seen. It is what I call an unconscious intellect; there is more virtue in it than he himself is aware of. Novalis beautifully remarks of him, that those Dramas of his are Products of Nature too, deep as Nature herself. I find a great truth in this saying. Shakspeare's Art is not Artifice; the noblest worth of it is not there by plan or precontrivance. It grows up from the deeps of Nature, through this noble sincere soul, who is a voice of Nature. The latest generations of men will find new meanings in Shakspeare, new elucidations of their own human being; 'new harmonies with the infinite structure of the Universe; concurrences with later ideas, affinities with the higher powers and senses of man.' This well deserves meditating. It is Nature's highest reward to a true simple great soul, that he get thus to be *a part of herself.* Such a man's works, whatsoever he with utmost conscious exertion and forethought shall accomplish, grow up withal *un*consciously, from the unknown deeps in him; — as the oak-tree grows from the Earth's bosom, as the mountains and waters shape themselves; with a symmetry grounded on Nature's own laws, conformable to all Truth whatsoever. How much in Shakspeare lies hid; his sorrows, his silent struggles known to himself; much that was not known at all, not speakable at all: like *roots*, like sap and forces working under ground! Speech is great; but Silence is greater.

Withal the joyful tranquillity of this man is notable. I will not blame Dante for his misery: it is as battle without victory; but true battle, — the first, indispensable thing. Yet I call Shakspeare greater than Dante, in that he fought truly, and did conquer. Doubt it not, he had his own sorrows: those *Sonnets* of his will even testify expressly in what deep waters he had waded, and swum struggling for his life; — as what man like him ever had not to do? It seems to me a heedless notion, our common one, that he sat like a bird on the bough; and sang forth, free and offhand, never knowing the troubles of other men. Not so; with no man is it so. How could a man travel forward from rustic deer-poaching to such tragedy-writing, and not fall in with sorrows by the way? Or, still better, how could a man delineate a Hamlet, a Coriolanus, a Macbeth, so many suffering heroic hearts, if his own heroic heart had never suffered? — And now, in contrast with all this, observe his mirthfulness, his genuine overflowing love of laughter! You would say, in no point does he *exaggerate* but only in laughter. Fiery objurgations, words that pierce and burn, are to be found in Shakspeare: yet he is always in measure here; never what Johnson would remark as a specially 'good hater.' But his laughter seems to pour from him in floods; he heaps all manner of ridiculous nicknames on the butt, tumbles and tosses him in all sorts of horse-play; you would say, roars and laughs. And then, if not always the finest, it is always a genial laughter. Not at mere weakness, at misery or poverty; never. No man who *can* laugh, what we call laughing, will laugh at these things. It is some poor character only *desiring* to laugh, and have the credit of wit, that does so. Laughter means sympathy; good laughter is not 'the crackling of thorns under the pot.' Even at stupidity and pretension this Shakspeare does not laugh otherwise than genially. Dog-berry and Verges tickle our very hearts; and we dismiss them covered with explosions of laughter: but we like the poor fellows only the better for our laughing; and hope that they will get on well there, and continue Presidents of the City-watch. — Such laughter, like sunshine on the deep sea, is very beautiful to me.

We have no room to speak of Shakspeare's individual works; though perhaps there is much still waiting to be said on that head. Had we, for instance, all his Plays reviewed as *Hamlet*, in *Wilhelm Meister*, is! A thing which might, one day, be done. August Wilhelm Schlegel has a remark on his Historical Plays, *Henry Fifth* and the others, which is worth remembering. He calls them a kind of National Epic. Marlborough, you recollect, said, he knew no English History but what he had learned from Shakspeare. There are really, if we look to it, few as memorable Histories. The great salient points are admirably seized; all rounds itself off, into a kind of rhythmic coherence: it is, as Schlegel says, *epic;* — as indeed all delineation by a great thinker will be. There are right beautiful things in those Pieces, which indeed together form one beautiful thing. That battle of Agincourt strikes me as one of the most perfect things, in its sort, we anywhere have of Shakspeare's. The description of the two hosts: the worn-out, jaded English; the dread hour, big with destiny, when the battle shall begin; and then that deathless valour: "Ye good yeomen, whose limbs were made in England!" There is a noble Patriotism in it, — far other than the 'indifference' you sometimes hear ascribed to Shakspeare. A true English heart breathes, calm and strong, through the whole business; not boisterous, protrusive; all the better for that. There is a sound in it like the ring of steel. This man too had a right stroke in him, had it come to that!

But I will say, of Shakspeare's works generally, that we have no full impress of him there; even as full as we have of many men. His works are so many windows, through which we see a glimpse of the world that was in him. All his works seem, comparatively speaking, cursory, imperfect, written under cramping circumstances; giving only here and there a note of the full utterance of the man. Passages there are that come upon you like splendour out of Heaven; bursts of radiance, illuminating the very heart of the thing: you say, "That is *true,* spoken once and forever; wheresoever and whensoever there is an open human soul, that will be recognised as true!" Such bursts, however, make us feel that the surrounding matter is not radiant; that it is, in part, temporary, conventional. Alas, Shakspeare had to write for the Globe Playhouse: his great soul had to crush itself, as it could, into that and no other mould. It was with him, then, as it is with us all. No man works save under conditions. The sculptor cannot set his own free Thought before us; but his Thought as he could translate it into the stone that was given, with the tools that were given. *Disjecta membra* are all that we find of any Poet, or of any man.

Whoever looks intelligently at this Shakspeare may recognise that he too was a *Prophet,* in his way; of an insight analogous to the Prophetic, though he took it up in another strain. Nature seemed to this man also divine; *un*speakable, deep as Tophet, high as Heaven: 'We are such stuff as Dreams are made of!' That scroll in Westminster Abbey, which few read with understanding, is of the depth of any Seer. But the man sang; did not preach, except musically. We called Dante the melodious Priest of Middle-Age Catholicism. May we not call Shakspeare the still more melodious Priest of a *true* Catholicism, the 'Universal Church' of the Future and of all times? No narrow superstition, harsh asceticism, intolerance, fanatical

fierceness or perversion: a Revelation, so far as it goes, that such a thousandfold hidden beauty and divineness dwells in all Nature; which let all
men worship as they can! We may say without offence, that there rises a
kind of universal Psalm out of this Shakspeare too; not unfit to make itself
heard among the still more sacred Psalms. Not in disharmony with these, if
we understood them, but in unison! — I cannot call this Shakspeare a 'Sceptic,' as some do; his indifference to the creeds and theological quarrels of
his time misleading them. No: neither unpatriotic, though he says little
about his Patriotism; nor sceptic, though he says little about his Faith. Such
'indifference' was the fruit of his greatness withal: his whole heart was in
his own grand sphere of worship (we may call it such); these other controversies, vitally important to other men, were not vital to him.

But call it worship, call it what you will, is it not a right glorious thing,
and set of things, this that Shakspeare has brought us? For myself, I feel that
there is actually a kind of sacredness in the fact of such a man being sent
into this Earth. Is he not an eye to us all; a blessed heaven-sent Bringer of
Light? — And, at bottom, was it not perhaps far better that this Shakspeare,
every way an unconscious man, was *conscious* of no Heavenly message?
He did not feel, like Mahomet, because he saw into those internal Splendours, that he specially was the 'Prophet of God:' I ask, was he not greater
than Mahomet in that? Greater; and also, if we compute strictly, as we did in
Dante's case, more successful. It was intrinsically an error that notion of
Mahomet's, of his supreme Prophethood; and has come down to us inextricably involved in error to this day; dragging along with it such a coil of
fables, impurities, intolerances, as makes it a questionable step for me here
and now to say, as I have done, that Mahomet was a true Speaker at all, and
not rather an ambitious charlatan, perversity and simulacrum, no Speaker,
but a Babbler! Even in Arabia, as I compute, Mahomet will have exhausted
himself and become obsolete, while this Shakspeare, this Dante may be still
young; — while this Shakspeare may still pretend to be a Priest of Mankind,
of Arabia as of other places, for unlimited periods to come! Compared with
any speaker or singer one knows, even with Æschylus or Homer, why
should he not, for veracity and universality, last like them? He is *sincere* as
they; reaches deep down like them, to the universal and perennial. But as
for Mahomet, I think it had been better for him *not* to be so conscious! Alas,
poor Mahomet; all that he was *conscious* of was a mere error; a futility and
triviality, — as indeed such ever is. The truly great in him too was the
unconscious: that he was a wild Arab lion of the desert, and did speak out
with that great thunder-voice of his, not by words which he *thought* to be
great, but by actions, by feelings, by a history which *were* great! His Koran

has become a stupid piece of prolix absurdity; we do not believe, like him, that God wrote that! The Great Man here too, as always, is a Force of Nature; whatsoever is truly great in him springs up from the *in*articulate deeps.

Well: this is our poor Warwickshire Peasant, who rose to be Manager of a Playhouse, so that he could live without begging; whom the Earl of South-ampton cast some kind glances on; whom Sir Thomas Lucy, many thanks to him, was for sending to the Treadmill! We did not account him a god, like Odin, while he dwelt with us; — on which point there were much to be said. But I will say rather, or repeat, [*sic*] In spite of the sad state Hero-worship now lies in, consider what this Shakspeare has actually become among us. Which Englishman we ever made, in this land of ours, which million of Englishmen, would we not give up rather than the Stratford Peasant? There is no regiment of highest Dignitaries that we would sell him for. He is the grandest thing we have yet done. For our honour among foreign nations, as an ornament to our English Household, what item is there that we would not surrender rather than him? Consider now, if they asked us, Will you give up your Indian Empire or your Shakspeare, you English; never have had any Indian Empire, or never have had any Shakspeare? Really it were a grave question. Official persons would answer doubtless in official language; but we, for our part too, should not we be forced to answer: Indian Empire, no Indian Empire; we cannot do without Shakspeare! Indian Empire will go, at any rate, some day; but this Shakspeare does not go, he lasts forever with us; we cannot give up our Shakspeare!

Nay, apart from spiritualities; and considering him merely as a real, mar-ketable, tangibly useful possession. England, before long, this Island of ours, will hold but a small fraction of the English: in America, in New Holland, east and west to the very Antipodes, there will be a Saxondom covering great spaces of the Globe. And now, what is it that can keep all these together into virtually one Nation, so that they do not fall out and fight, but live at peace, in brotherlike intercourse, helping one another? This is justly regarded as the greatest practical problem, the thing all manner of sovereignties and govern-ments are here to accomplish: what is it that will accomplish this? Acts of Parliament, administrative prime-ministers cannot. America is parted from us, so far as Parliament could part it. Call it not fantastic, for there is much reality in it: Here, I say, is an English King, whom no time or chance, Parlia-ment or combination of Parliaments, can dethrone! This King Shakspeare, does not he shine, in crowned sovereignty, over us all, as the noblest, gen-tlest, yet strongest of rallying-signs; *in*destructible; really more valuable in that point of view, than any other means or appliance whatsoever? We can fancy him as radiant aloft over all the Nations of Englishmen, a thousand years hence. From Paramatta, from New York, wheresoever, under what sort of Parish-Constable soever, English men and women are, they will say to one another: "Yes, this Shakspeare is ours; we produced him, we speak and think by him; we are of one blood and kind with him." The most common-sense politician too, if he pleases, may think of that.

Yes, truly, it is a great thing for a Nation that it get an articulate voice; that it produce a man who will speak forth melodiously what the heart of it means! Italy, for example, poor Italy lies dismembered, scattered asunder, not appearing in any protocol or treaty as a unity at all; yet the noble Italy is actually *one:* Italy produced its Dante; Italy can speak! The Czar of all the Russias, he is strong, with so many bayonets, Cossacks and cannons; and does a great feat in keeping such a tract of Earth politically together; but he cannot yet speak. Something great in him, but it is a dumb greatness. He has had no voice of genius, to be heard of all men and times. He must learn to speak. He is a great dumb monster hitherto. His cannons and Cossacks will all have rusted into nonentity, while that Dante's voice is still audible. The Nation that has a Dante is bound together as no dumb Russia can be. — We must here end what we had to say of the *Hero-Poet.*

LECTURE IV.

The Hero as Priest. Luther; Reformation: Knox; Puritanism.

Our present discourse is to be of the Great Man as Priest. We have repeatedly endeavoured to explain that all sorts of Heroes are intrinsically of the same material; that given a great soul, open to the Divine Significance of Life, then there is given a man fit to speak of this, to sing of this, to fight and work for this, in a great, victorious, enduring manner; there is given a Hero, — the outward shape of whom will depend on the time and the environment he finds himself in. The Priest too, as I understand it, is a kind of Prophet; in him too there is required to be a light of inspiration, as we must name it. He presides over the worship of the people; is the Uniter of them with the Unseen Holy. He is the spiritual Captain of the people; as the Prophet is their spiritual King with many captains: he guides them heavenward, by wise guidance through this Earth and its work. The ideal of him is, that he too be what we can call a voice from the unseen Heaven; interpreting, even as the Prophet did, and in a more familiar manner unfolding the same to men. The unseen Heaven, — the 'open secret of the Universe,' which so few have an eye for! He is the Prophet shorn of his more awful splendour; burning with mild equable radiance, as the enlightener of daily life. This, I say, is the ideal of a Priest. So in old times; so in these, and in all times. One knows very well that, in reducing ideals to practice, great latitude of tolerance is needful; very great. But a Priest who is not this at all, who does not any longer aim or try to be this, is a character — of whom we had rather not speak in this place.

Luther and Knox were by express vocation Priests, and did faithfully perform that function in its common sense. Yet it will suit us better here to consider them chiefly in their historical character, rather as Reformers than Priests. There have been other Priests perhaps equally notable, in calmer times, for doing faithfully the office of a Leader of Worship; bringing down, by faithful heroism in that kind, a light from Heaven into the daily life of their people; leading them forward, as under God's guidance, in the way wherein they were to go. But when this same *way* was a rough one, of battle, confusion and danger, the spiritual Captain who led through that, becomes, especially to us who live under the fruit of his leading, more notable than any other. He is the warfaring and battling Priest; who led his people, not to quiet faithful labour as in smooth times, but to faithful valorous conflict, in times all violent, dismembered: a more perilous service, a more memorable one, be it higher or not. These two men we will account our best Priests, inasmuch as they were our best Reformers. Nay I may ask, Is not every true Reformer, by the nature of him, a *Priest* first of all? He appeals to Heaven's invisible justice against Earth's visible force; knows that it, the invisible, is strong and alone strong. He is a believer in the divine truth of things, a *seer*, seeing through the shows of things; a worshipper, in one way or the other, of the divine truth of things: a Priest, that is. If he be not first a Priest, he will never be good for much as a Reformer.

Thus then, as we have seen Great Men, in various situations, building up Religions, heroic Forms of human Existence in this world, Theories of Life worthy to be sung by a Dante, Practices of Life by a Shakspeare, — we are now to see the reverse process; which also is necessary, which also may be carried on in the Heroic manner. Curious how this should be necessary: yet necessary it is. The mild shining of the Poet's light has to give place to the fierce lightning of the Reformer: unfortunately the Reformer too is a personage that cannot fail in History! The Poet indeed, with his mildness, what is he but the product and ultimate adjustment of Reform, or Prophecy, with its fierceness? No wild Saint Dominics and Thebaid Eremites, there had been no melodious Dante; rough Practical Endeavour, Scandinavian and other, from Odin to Walter Raleigh, from Ulfila to Cranmer, enabled Shakspeare to speak. Nay the finished Poet, I remark sometimes, is a symptom that his epoch itself has reached perfection and is finished; that before long there will be a new epoch, new Reformers needed.

Doubtless it were finer, could we go along always in the way of *music;* be tamed and taught by our Poets, as the rude creatures were by their Orpheus of old. Or failing this rhythmic *musical* way, how good were it could we get so much as into the *equable* way; I mean, if *peaceable* Priests, reforming from day to day, would always suffice us! But it is not so; even this latter has not yet been realised. Alas, the battling Reformer too is, from time to time, a needful and inevitable phenomenon. Obstructions are never wanting: the very things that were once indispensable furtherances become obstructions; and need to be shaken off, and left behind us, — a business often of enormous difficulty. It is notable enough, surely, how a Theorem or spiritual Representation, so we may call it, which once took-in the whole Universe, and was completely satisfactory in all parts of it to the highly discursive acute intellect of Dante, one of the greatest in the world, — had in the course of another century become dubitable to common intellects; become deniable; and is now, to every one of us, flatly incredible, obsolete as Odin's Theorem! To Dante, human Existence, and God's ways with men, were all well represented by those *Malebolges, Purgatorios;* to Luther not well. How was this? Why could not Dante's Catholicism continue; but Luther's Protestantism must needs follow? Alas, nothing will *continue.*

I do not make much of 'Progress of the Species,' as handled in these times of ours; nor do I think you would care to hear much about it. The talk on that subject is too often of the most extravagant, confused sort. Yet I may say, the fact itself seems certain enough; nay we can trace out the inevitable necessity of it in the nature of things. Every man, as I have stated somewhere, is not only a learner but a doer: he learns with the mind given him what has been; but with the same mind he discovers farther, he invents and desires somewhat of his own. Absolutely without originality there is no man. No man whatever believes, or can believe, exactly what his grandfather believed: he enlarges somewhat, by fresh discovery, his view of the Universe, and consequently his Theorem of the Universe, — which is an *infinite* Universe, and can never be embraced wholly or finally by any view or Theorem, in any conceivable enlargement: he enlarges somewhat, I say; finds somewhat that was credible to his grandfather incredible to him, false to him, inconsistent with some new thing he has discovered or observed. It is the history of every man; and in the history of Mankind we see it summed up into great historical amounts, — revolutions, new epochs. Dante's Mountain of Purgatory does *not* stand 'in the ocean of the other Hemisphere,' when Columbus has once sailed thither! Men find no such thing extant in the other Hemisphere. It is not there. It must cease to be believed to be there. So with all beliefs whatsoever in this world, — all Systems of Belief, and Systems of Practice that spring from these.

If we add now the melancholy fact that when Belief waxes uncertain, Practice too becomes unsound, and errors, injustices and miseries everywhere more and more prevail, we shall see material enough for revolution. At all turns, a man who will *do* faithfully, needs to believe firmly. If he have to ask at every turn the world's suffrage; if he cannot dispense with the world's suffrage, and make his own suffrage serve, he is a poor eye-servant; the work committed to him will be *mis*done. Every such man is a daily contributor to the inevitable downfal. Whatsoever work he does, dishonestly, with an eye to the outward look of it, is a new offence, parent of new misery to somebody or other. Offences accumulate till they become insupportable; and are then violently burst through, cleared off as by explosion. Dante's sublime Catholicism, incredible now in theory, and defaced still worse by faithless, doubting and dishonest practice, has to be torn asunder by a Luther, Shakspeare's noble Feudalism, as beautiful as it once looked and was, has to end in a French Revolution. The accumulation of offences is, as we say, too literally *exploded*, blasted asunder volcanically; and there are long troublous periods, before matters come to a settlement again.

Surely it were mournful enough to look only at this face of the matter, and find in all human opinions and arrangements only the fact that they were uncertain, temporary, subject to the law of death! At bottom, it is not so: all death, here too, we find, is but of the body, not of the essence or soul; all destruction, by violent revolution or howsoever it be, is but new creation on a wider scale. Odinism was *Valour;* Christianity was *Humility*, a nobler kind of Valour. No thought that ever dwelt honestly as true in the heart of man but *was* an honest insight into God's truth on man's part, and *has* an essential truth in it which endures through all changes, an everlasting possession for us all. And, on the other hand, what a melancholy notion is that, which has to represent all men, in all countries and times except our own, as having spent their life in blind condemnable error, mere lost Pagans, Scandinavians, Mahometans, only that we might have the true ultimate knowledge! All generations of men were lost and wrong, only that this present little section of a generation might be saved and right. They all marched forward there, all generations since the beginning of the world, like the Russian soldiers into the ditch of Schweidnitz Fort, only to fill up the ditch with their dead bodies, that we might march over and take the place! It is an incredible hypothesis.

Such incredible hypothesis we have seen maintained with fierce emphasis; and this or the other poor individual man, with his sect of individual men, marching as over the dead bodies of all men, towards sure victory: but when he too, with his hypothesis and ultimate infallible credo, sank into the ditch, and became a dead body, what was to be said? — Withal, it is an important fact in the nature of man, that he tends to reckon his own insight as final, and goes upon it as such. He will always do it, I suppose, in one or the other way; but it must be in some wider, wiser way than this. Are not all true men that live, or that ever lived, soldiers of the same army; enlisted, under Heaven's captaincy, to do battle against the same enemy, the empire of Darkness and Wrong? Why should we misknow one another, fight not against the enemy but against ourselves, from mere difference of uniform? All uniforms shall be good, so they hold in them true valiant men. All fashions of arms, the Arab turban and swift scimetar, Thor's strong hammer smiting down *Jötuns*, shall be welcome. Luther's battle-voice, Dante's march-melody, all genuine things are with us, not against us. We are all under one Captain, soldiers of the same host. — Let us now look a little at this Luther's fighting; what kind of battle it was, and how he comported himself in it. Luther too was of our spiritual Heroes; a Prophet to his country and time.

As introductory to the whole, a remark about Idolatry will perhaps be in place here. One of Mahomet's characteristics, which indeed belongs to all Prophets, is unlimited implacable zeal against Idolatry. It is the grand theme of Prophets: Idolatry, the worshipping of dead Idols as the Divinity, is a thing they cannot away with, but must denounce continually, and brand with inexpiable reprobation; it is the chief of all the sins they see done under the sun. This is worth noting. We will not enter here into the theological question about Idolatry. Idol is *Eidolon*, a thing seen, a symbol. It is not God, but a Symbol of God; and perhaps one may question whether any the most benighted mortal ever took it for more than a Symbol. I fancy, he did not think that the poor image his own hands had made *was* God; but that God was emblemed by it, that God was in it some way or other. And now in this sense, one may ask, Is not all worship whatsoever a worship by Symbols, by *eidola*, or things seen? Whether *seen*, rendered visible as an image or picture to the bodily eye; or visible only to the inward eye, to the imagination, to the intellect: this makes a superficial, but no substantial difference. It is still a Thing Seen, significant of Godhood; an Idol. The most rigorous Puritan has his Confession of Faith, and intellectual Representation of Divine things, and worships thereby; thereby is worship first made possible for him. All creeds, liturgies, religious forms, conceptions that fitly invest religious feelings, are in this sense *eidola*, things seen. All worship whatsoever must proceed by Symbols, by Idols: — we may say, all Idolatry is comparative, and the worst Idolatry is only *more* idolatrous.

Where then lies the evil of it? Some fatal evil must lie in it, or earnest prophetic men would not on all hands so reprobate it. Why is Idolatry so hateful to Prophets? It seems to me as if, in the worship of those poor wooden symbols, the thing that had chiefly provoked the Prophet, and filled his inmost soul with indignation and aversion, was not exactly what suggested itself to his own thought, and came out of him in words to others, as the thing. The rudest heathen that worshipped Canopus, or the Caabah Black-stone, he, as we saw, was superior to the horse that worshipped nothing at all! Nay there was a kind of lasting merit in that poor act of his; analogous to what is still meritorious in Poets: recognition of a certain endless *divine* beauty and significance in stars and all natural objects whatsoever. Why should the Prophet so mercilessly condemn him? The poorest mortal worshipping his

Fetish, while his heart is full of it, may be an object of pity, of contempt and avoidance, if you will; but cannot surely be an object of hatred. Let his heart *be* honestly full of it, the whole space of his dark narrow mind illuminated thereby; in one word, let him entirely *believe* in his Fetish, — it will then be, I should say, if not well with him, yet as well as it can readily be made to be, and you will leave him alone, unmolested there.

But here enters the fatal circumstance of Idolatry, that, in the era of the Prophets, no man's mind *is* any longer honestly filled with his Idol, or Symbol. Before the Prophet can arise who, seeing through it, knows it to be mere wood, many men must have begun dimly to doubt that it was little more. Condemnable Idolatry is *insincere* Idolatry. Doubt has eaten out the heart of it: a human soul is seen clinging spasmodically to an Ark of the Covenant, which it half-feels now to have become a Phantasm. This is one of the balefulest sights. Souls are no longer *filled* with their Fetish; but only pretend to be filled, and would fain make themselves feel that they are filled. "You do not believe," said Coleridge; "you only believe that you believe." It is the final scene in all kinds of Worship and Symbolism; the sure symptom that death is now nigh. It is equivalent to what we call Formulism, and Worship of Formulas, in these days of ours. No more immoral act can be done by a human creature; for it is the beginning of all immorality, or rather it is the impossibility henceforth of any morality whatsoever: the innermost moral soul is paralyzed thereby, cast into fatal magnetic sleep! Men are no longer *sincere* men. I do not wonder that the earnest man denounces this, brands it, prosecutes it with inextinguishable aversion. He and it, all good and it, are at death-feud. Blameable Idolatry is *Cant*, and even what one may call Sincere-Cant. Sincere-Cant: that is worth thinking of! Every sort of Worship ends with this phasis. — I find Luther to have been a Breaker of Idols, no less than any other Prophet. The wooden gods of the Koreish, made of timber and bees'-wax, were not more hateful to Mahomet than Tetzel's Pardons of Sin, made of sheepskin and ink, were to Luther. It is the property of every Hero, in every time, in every place and situation, that he come back to reality; that he stand upon things, and not shows of things. According as he loves, and venerates, articulately or with deep speechless thought, the awful realities of things, so will the hollow shows of things, however regular, decorous, accredited by Koreishes or Conclaves, be intolerable and detestable to him. Protestantism too is the work of a Prophet: the prophet-work of that sixteenth century. The first stroke of honest demolition to an ancient thing grown false and idolatrous; preparatory afar off to a new thing, which shall be true, and authentically divine! —

At first view it might seem as if Protestantism were entirely destructive to this that we call Hero-worship, and represent as the basis of all possible good, religious or social, for mankind. One often hears it said that Protestantism introduced a new era, radically different from any the world had ever seen before: the era of 'private judgment,' as they call it. By this revolt against the Pope, every man became his own Pope; and learnt, among other things, that he must never trust any Pope, or spiritual Hero-captain, any more! Whereby, is not spiritual union, all hierarchy and subordination among men, henceforth an impossibility? So we hear it said. — Now I need not deny that Protestantism was a revolt against spiritual sovereignties, Popes and much else. Nay I will grant that English Puritanism, revolt against earthly sovereignties, was the second act of it; that the enormous French Revolution itself was the third act, whereby all sovereignties earthly and spiritual were, as might seem, abolished or made sure of abolition. Protestantism is the grand root from which our whole subsequent European History branches out. For the spiritual will always body itself forth in the temporal history of men; the spiritual is the beginning of the temporal. And now, sure enough, the cry is everywhere for Liberty and Equality, Independence and so forth; instead of Kings, Ballot-boxes and Electoral suffrages: it seems made out that any Hero-sovereign, or loyal obedience of men to a man, in things temporal or things spiritual, has passed away forever from the world. I should despair of the world altogether, if so. One of my deepest convictions is, that it is not so. Without sovereigns, true sovereigns, temporal and spiritual, I see nothing possible but an anarchy; the hatefulest of things. But I find Protestantism, whatever anarchic democracy it have produced, to be the beginning of new genuine sovereignty and order. I find it to be a revolt against *false* sovereigns; the painful but indispensable first preparative for *true* sovereigns getting place among us! This is worth explaining a little.

Let us remark, therefore, in the first place, that this of 'private judgment' is, at bottom, not a new thing in the world, but only new at that epoch of the world. There is nothing generically new or peculiar in the Reformation; it was a return to Truth and Reality in opposition to Falsehood and Semblance, as all kinds of Improvement and genuine Teaching are and have been. Liberty of private judgment, if we will consider it, must at all times have existed in the world. Dante had not put out his eyes, or tied shackles on himself; he was at home in that Catholicism of his, a free-seeing soul in it, — if many a poor Hogstraten, Tetzel and Dr. Eck had now become slaves in it. Liberty of judgment? No iron chain, or outward force of any kind, could ever compel the soul of a man to believe or to disbelieve: it is his own indefeasible light, that judgment of his; he will reign, and believe there, by the grace of God alone! The sorriest sophistical Bellarmine preaching sightless faith and passive obedience, must first, by some kind of *conviction*, have abdicated his right to be convinced. His 'private judgment' indicated that, as the adviseablest step *he* could take. The right of private judgment will subsist, in full force, wherever true men subsist. A true man *believes* with his whole judgment, with all the illumination and discernment that is in him, and has always so believed. A false man, only struggling to 'believe that he believes,' will naturally manage it in some other way. Protestantism said to this latter, Woe! and to the former, Well done! At bottom, it was no new saying; it was a return to all old sayings that ever had been said. Be genuine, be sincere: that was, once more, the meaning of it. Mahomet believed with his whole mind; Odin with his whole mind, — he, and all *true* Followers of Odinism. They, by their private judgment, had 'judged' — *so*.

And now I venture to assert, that the exercise of private judgment, faithfully gone about, does by no means necessarily end in selfish independence, isolation, but rather ends necessarily in the opposite of that. It is not honest inquiry that makes anarchy; but it is error, insincerity, half-belief, and untruth that makes it. A man protesting against error is on the way towards uniting himself with all men that believe in truth. There is no communion possible among men who believe only in hearsays. The heart of each is lying dead; has no power of sympathy even with *things*, — or he would believe *them* and not hearsays. No sympathy even with things; how much less with his fellow-men! He cannot unite with men; he is an anarchic man. Only in a world of sincere men is unity possible; — and there, in the long-run, it is as good as *certain*.

For observe one thing, a thing too often left out of view, or rather altogether lost sight of in this controversy: That it is not necessary a man should himself have *discovered* the truth he is to believe in never so sincerely. A Great Man, we said, was always sincere, as the first condition of him. But a man need not be great in order to be sincere; that is not the necessity of Nature and all Time, but only of certain corrupt unfortunate epochs of Time. A man can believe, and make his own, in the most genuine way, what he has received from another; — and with boundless gratitude to that other! The merit of *originality* is not novelty; it is sincerity. The believing man is the original man; whatsoever he believes he believes it for himself, not for another. Every son of Adam can become a sincere man, an original man, in this sense; no mortal is doomed to be an insincere man. Whole ages, what we call ages of Faith, are original, — all men in them, or the most of men in them, sincere. These are the great and fruitful ages: every worker, in all spheres, is a worker not on semblance but on substance; every work issues in a result: the general sum of such work is great; for all of it, as genuine, tends towards one goal; all of it is *additive*, none of it subtractive. There is true union, true kingship, loyalty, all true and blessed things, so far as the poor Earth can produce blessedness for men. Hero-worship? Ah me, that a man be self-subsistent, original, true, or what we call it, is surely the farthest in the world from indisposing him to reverence and believe other men's truth! It only disposes, necessitates and invincibly compels him to *dis*believe other men's dead formulas, hearsays and untruths. A man embraces truth with his eyes open, and because his eyes are open: does he need to shut them before he can love his Teacher of truth? He alone can love, with a right gratitude and genuine loyalty of soul, the Hero-Teacher who has delivered him out of darkness into light. Is not such a one a true Hero, and Serpent-queller; worthy of all reverence! The black monster, Falsehood, our one enemy in this world, lies prostrate by his valour; it was he that conquered the world for us! — See, accordingly, was not Luther himself reverenced as a true Pope, or Spiritual Father, *being* verily such? Napoleon, from amid boundless revolt of Sansculottism, became a King. Hero-worship never dies, nor can die. Loyalty and Sovereignty are everlasting in the world: — and there is this in them, that they are grounded not on garnitures and semblances, but on realities and sincerities. Not by shutting your eyes, your 'private judgment;' no, but by opening them, and by having something to see! Luther's message was deposition and abolition to all false Popes and Potentates, but life and strength, though afar off, to new genuine ones.

All this of Liberty and Equality, Electoral Suffrages, Independence and so forth, we will take, therefore, to be a temporary phenomenon, by no means a final one. Though likely to last a long time, with sad enough embroilments for us all, we must welcome it, as the penalty of sins that are past, the pledge of inestimable benefits that are coming. In all ways, it behoved men to quit simulacra and return to fact; cost what it might, that did behove to be done. With spurious Popes, and believers having no private judgment, — quacks pretending to command over dupes, — what can you do? Misery and mischief only. You cannot make an association out of insincere men; you cannot build an edifice except by plummet and level, — at *right*-angles to one another! In all this wild revolutionary work, from Protestantism downwards, I see the blessedest result preparing itself: not abolition of Hero-worship, but rather what I would call a whole World of Heroes. If Hero mean *sincere man*, why may not every one of us be a Hero? A world all sincere, a believing world: the like has been; the like will again be, — cannot help being. That were the right sort of Worshippers for Heroes:

never could the truly Better be so reverenced as where all ~~~~ True and Good! — But we must hasten to Luther and his Life.

Luther's birthplace was Eisleben in Saxony; he came into the world there on the 10th of November, 1483. It was an accident that gave this honour to Eisleben. His parents, poor mine-labourers in a village of that region, named Mohra, had gone to the Eisleben Winter-Fair: in the tumult of this scene the Frau Luther was taken with travail, found refuge in some poor house there, and the boy she bore was named MARTIN LUTHER. Strange enough to reflect upon it. This poor Frau Luther, she had gone with her husband to make her small merchandisings; perhaps to sell the lock of yarn she had been spinning, to buy the small winter-necessaries for her narrow hut or household: in the whole world, that day, there was not a more entirely unimportant-looking pair of people than this Miner and his Wife. And yet what were all Emperors, Popes and Potentates, in comparison? There was born here, once more, a Mighty Man; whose light was to flame as the beacon over long centuries and epochs of the world; the whole world and its history was waiting for this man. It is strange, it is great. It leads us back to another Birth-hour, in a still meaner environment, Eighteen Hundred years ago, — of which it is fit that we *say* nothing, that we think only in silence; for what words are there! The Age of Miracles past? The Age of Miracles is forever here! —

I find it altogether suitable to Luther's function in this Earth, and doubtless wisely ordered to that end by the Providence presiding over him and us and all things, that he was born poor, and brought up poor, one of the poorest of men. He had to beg, as the schoolchildren in those times did; singing for alms and bread, from door to door. Hardship, rigorous Necessity was the poor boy's companion; no man nor no thing would put-on a false face to flatter Martin Luther. Among things, not among the shows of things, had he to grow. A boy of rude figure, yet with weak health, with his large greedy soul, full of all faculty and sensibility, he suffered greatly. But it was his task to get acquainted with *realities*, and keep acquainted with them, at whatever cost: his task was to bring the whole world back to reality, for it had dwelt too long with semblance! A youth nursed up in wintry whirlwinds, in desolate darkness and difficulty, that he may step forth at last from his stormy Scandinavia, strong as a true man, as a god: a Christian Odin, — a right Thor once more, with his thunder-hammer, to smite asunder ugly enough *Jötuns* and Giant-monsters!

Perhaps the turning incident of his life, we may fancy, was that death of his friend Alexis, by lightning, at the gate of Erfurt. Luther had struggled up through boyhood, better and worse; displaying in spite of all hindrances the largest intellect, eager to learn: his father judging doubtless that he might promote himself in the world, set him upon the study of Law. This was the path to rise; Luther, with little will in it either way, had consented: he was now nineteen years of age. Alexis and he had been to see the old Luther people at Mansfeldt; were got back again near Erfurt, when a thunderstorm came on; the bolt struck Alexis, he fell dead at Luther's hand. What is this Life of ours; — gone in a moment, burnt up like a scroll, into the blank Eternity! What are all earthly preferments, Chancellorships, Kingships? They lie shrunk together — there! The Earth has opened on them; in a moment they are not, and Eternity is. Luther, struck to the heart, determined to devote himself to God, and God's service alone. In spite of all dissuasions from his father and others, he became a Monk in the Augustine Convent at Erfurt.

This was probably the first light-point in the history of Luther, his purer will now first decisively uttering itself; but, for the present, it was still as one light-point in an element all of darkness. He says he was a pious monk, *ich bin ein frommer Mönch gewesen;* faithfully, painfully struggling to work out the truth of this high act of his; but it was to little purpose. His misery had not lessened; had rather, as it were, increased into infinitude. The drudgeries he had to do, as novice in his Convent, all sorts of slave-work, were not his grievance: the deep earnest soul of the man had fallen into all manner of black scruples, dubitations; he believed himself likely to die soon, and far worse than die. One hears with a new interest for poor Luther that, at this time, he lived in terror of the unspeakable misery; fancied that he was doomed to eternal reprobation. Was it not the humble sincere nature of the man? What was he, that he should be raised to Heaven! He that had known only misery, and mean slavery: the news was too blessed to be credible. It could not become clear to him how, by fasts, vigils, formalities and mass-work, a man's soul could be saved. He fell into the blackest wretchedness; had to wander staggering as on the verge of bottomless Despair.

It must have been a most blessed discovery, that of an old Latin Bible which he found in the Erfurt Library about this time. He had never seen the Book before. It taught him another lesson than that of fasts and vigils. A brother monk too, of pious experience, was helpful. Luther learned now that a man was saved not by singing masses, but by the infinite grace of God: a more credible hypothesis. He gradually got himself founded, as on the rock. No wonder he should venerate the Bible, which had brought this blessed help to him. He prized it as the Word of the Highest must be prized by such a man. He determined to hold by that; as through life and to death he firmly did.

This then is his deliverance from darkness, his final triumph over darkness, what we call his conversion; for himself the most important of all epochs. That he should now grow daily in peace and clearness; that, unfolding now the great talents and virtues implanted in him, he should rise to importance in his Convent, in his country, and be found more and more useful in all honest business of life, is a natural result. He was sent on missions by his Augustine Order, as a man of talent and fidelity fit to do their business well: the Elector of Saxony, Friedrich, named the Wise, a truly wise and just prince, had cast his eye on him as a valuable person; made him Professor in his new University of Wittenberg, Preacher too at Wittenberg; in both which capacities, as in all duties he did, this Luther, in the peaceable sphere of common life, was gaining more and more esteem with all good men.

It was in his twenty-seventh year that he first saw Rome; being sent thither, as I said, on mission from his Convent. Pope Julius the Second, and what was going on at Rome, must have filled the mind of Luther with amazement. He had come as to the Sacred City, throne of God's Highpriest on Earth; and he found it—what we know! Many thoughts it must have given the man; many which we have no record of, which perhaps he did not himself know how to utter. This Rome, this scene of false priests, clothed not in the beauty of holiness, but in far other vesture, is *false:* but what is it to Luther? A mean man he, how shall he reform a world? That was far from his thoughts. A humble, solitary man, why should he at all meddle with the world? It was the task of quite higher men than he. His business was to guide his own footsteps wisely through the world. Let him do his own obscure duty in it well; the rest, horrible and dismal as it looks, is in God's hand, not in his.

It is curious to reflect what might have been the issue, had Roman Popery happened to pass this Luther by; to go on in its great wasteful orbit, and not come athwart his little path, and force him to assault it! Conceivable enough that, in this case, he might have held his peace about the abuses of Rome; left Providence, and God on high, to deal with them! A modest quiet man; not prompt he to attack irreverently persons in authority. His clear task, as I say, was to do his own duty; to walk wisely in this world of confused wickedness, and save his own soul alive. But the Roman Highpriesthood did come athwart him: afar off at Wittenberg he, Luther, could not get lived in honesty for it; he remonstrated, resisted, came to extremity; was struck at, struck again, and so it came to wager of battle between them! This is worth attending to, in Luther's history. Perhaps no man of so humble, peaceable a disposition ever filled the world with contention. We cannot but see that he would have loved privacy, quiet diligence in the shade; that it was against his will he ever became a notoriety. Notoriety: what would that do for him? The goal of his march through this world was the Infinite Heaven; an indubitable goal for him: in a few years, he should either have attained that, or lost it forever! We will say nothing at all, I think, of that sorrowfulest of theories, of its being some mean shopkeeper grudge, of the Augustine Monk against the Dominican, that first kindled the wrath of Luther, and produced the Protestant Reformation. We will say to the people who maintain it, if indeed any such exist now, Get first into the sphere of thought by which it is so much as possible to judge of Luther, or of any man like Luther, otherwise than distractedly; we may then begin arguing with you.

The Monk Tetzel, sent out carelessly in the way of trade, by Leo Tenth, — who merely wanted to raise a little money, and for the rest seems to have been a Pagan rather than a Christian, so far as he was anything, — arrived at Wittenberg, and drove his scandalous trade there. Luther's flock bought Indulgences; in the confessional of his Church, people pleaded to him that they had already got their sins pardoned. Luther, if he would not be found wanting at his own post, a false sluggard and coward at the very centre of the little space of ground that was his own and no other man's, had to step forth against Indulgences, and declare aloud that *they* were a futility and sorrowful mockery, that no man's sins could be pardoned by *them*. It was the beginning of the whole Reformation. We know how it went; forward from this first public challenge of Tetzel, on the last day of October 1517, through remonstrance and argument; — spreading ever wider, rising ever higher; till it became unquenchable, and enveloped all the world. Luther's heart's desire was to have this grief and other griefs amended; his thought was still far from introducing separation in the Church, or revolting against the Pope, Father of Christendom. The elegant Pagan Pope cared little about this Monk and his doctrines; wished, however, to have done with the noise of him: in a space of some three years, having tried various softer methods, he thought good to end it by *fire*. He dooms the Monk's writings to be burnt by the hangman, and his body to be sent bound to Rome — probably for a similar purpose. It was the way they had ended with Huss, with Jerome, the century before. A short argument, fire. Poor Huss: he came to that Constance Council, with all imaginable promises and safe-conducts; an earnest, not rebellious kind of man: they laid him instantly in a stone dungeon 'three feet wide, six feet high, seven feet long;' *burnt* the true voice out of this world; choked it in smoke and fire. That was *not* well done!

I, for one, pardon Luther for now altogether revolting against the Pope. The elegant Pagan, by this fire-decree of his, had kindled into noble just wrath the bravest heart then living in this world. The bravest, if also one of the humblest, peaceablest; it was now kindled. These words of mine, words of truth and soberness, aiming faithfully, as human inability would allow, to promote God's truth on Earth, and save men's souls, you, God's vicegerent on earth, answer them by the hangman and fire? You will burn me and them, for answer to the God's-message they strove to bring you? *You* are not God's vicegerent; you are *another's*, I think! I take your Bull, as an emparchmented Lie, and burn *it*. You will do what you see good next; this is what I do. — It was on the tenth of December 1520, three years after the beginning of the business, that Luther 'with a great concourse of people,' took this indignant step of burning the Pope's fire-decree in the market-place of Wittenberg. Wittenberg looked on 'with shoutings;' the whole world was looking on. The Pope should not have provoked that 'shout!' It was the shout of the awakening of nations. The quiet German heart, modest, patient of much, had at length got more than it could bear. Formulism, Pagan Popism, and other Falsehood and corrupt Semblance had ruled long enough: and here once more was a man found who durst tell all men that God's-world stood not on semblances but on realities; that Life was a truth, and not a lie!

At bottom, as was said above, we are to consider Luther as a Prophet Idol-breaker; a bringer back of men to reality. It is the function of great men and teachers. Mahomet said, These idols of yours are wood; you put wax and oil on them, the flies stick on them: they are not God, I tell you, they are black wood! Luther said to the Pope, This thing of yours that you call a Pardon of Sins, it is a bit of rag-paper with ink. It *is* nothing else; it, and so much like it, is nothing else. God alone can pardon sins. Popeship, spiritual Fatherhood of God's Church, is that a vain semblance, of cloth and parchment? It is an awful fact. God's Church is not a semblance, Heaven and Hell are not semblances. I stand on this, since you drive me to it. Standing on this, I a poor German Monk am stronger than you all. I stand solitary, friendless, one man, on God's Truth; you with your tiaras, triple-hats, with your treasuries and armories, thunders spiritual and temporal, stand on the Devil's Lie, and are not so strong! —

The Diet of Worms, Luther's appearance there on the 17th of April 1521, may be considered as the greatest scene in Modern European History; the point, indeed, from which the whole subsequent history of civilization takes its rise. After multiplied negotiations, disputations, it had come to this. The young Emperor Charles Fifth, with all the Princes of Germany, Papal nuncios, dignitaries spiritual and temporal, are assembled there: Luther is to appear and answer for himself, whether he will recant or not. The world's pomp and power sits there on this hand: on that, stands up for God's Truth, one man, Hans Luther the poor miner's Son. Friends had reminded him of Huss, advised him not to go; he would not be advised. A large company of friends rode out to meet him, with still more earnest warnings; he answered, "Were there as many Devils in Worms as there are roof-tiles, I would on." The people, on the morrow, as he went to the Hall of the Diet, crowded the windows and housetops, some of them calling out to him, in solemn words, not to recant: "Whosoever denieth me before men!" they cried to him, — as in a kind of solemn petition and adjuration. Was it not in reality our petition too, the petition of the whole world, lying in dark bondage of soul, para- lysed under a black spectral Nightmare and triple-hatted Chimera, calling itself Father in God, and what not: "Free us; it rests with thee; desert us not!" Luther did not desert us. His speech, of two hours, distinguished itself by its respectful, wise and honest tone; submissive to whatsoever could lawfully claim submission, not submissive to any more than that. His writ- ings, he said, were partly his own, partly derived from the Word of God. As to what was his own, human infirmity entered into it; unguarded anger, blindness, many things doubtless which it were a blessing for him could he abolish altogether. But as to what stood on sound truth and the Word of God, he could not recant it. How could he? "Confute me," he concluded, "by proofs of Scripture, or else by plain just arguments: I cannot recant otherwise. For it is neither safe nor prudent to do aught against conscience. Here stand I; I can do no other: God assist me!" — It is, as we say, the greatest moment in the Modern History of Men. English Puritanism, En- gland and its Parliaments, Americas, and vast work these two centuries; French Revolution, Europe and its work everywhere at present: the germ of it all lay there: had Luther in that moment done other, it had all been otherwise! The European World was asking him: Am I to sink ever lower into falsehood, stagnant putrescence, loathsome accursed death; or, with whatever paroxysm, to cast the falsehoods out of me, and be cured and live? —

Great wars, contentions, and disunion followed out of this Reformation; which last down to our day, and are yet far from ended. Great talk and crimination has been made about these. They are lamentable, undeniable; but after all, what has Luther or his cause to do with them? It seems strange reasoning to charge the Reformation with all this. When Hercules turned the purifying river into King Augeas's stables, I have no doubt the confusion that resulted was considerable all around; but I think it was not Hercules's blame; it was some other's blame! The Reformation might bring what results it liked when it came, but the Reformation simply could not help coming. To all Popes and Popes' advocates, expostulating, lamenting and accusing, the answer of the world is: Once for all, your Popehood has become untrue. No matter how good it was, how good you say it is, we cannot believe it; the light of our whole mind, given us to walk by from Heaven above, finds it henceforth a thing unbelievable. We will not believe it, we will not try to believe it, — we dare not! The thing is *untrue;* we were traitors against the Giver of all Truth, if we durst pretend to think it true. Away with it; let whatsoever likes come in the place of it: with *it* we can have no farther trade! — Luther and his Protestantism is not responsible for wars; the false Simulacra that forced him to protest, they are responsible. Luther did what every man that God has made has not only the right, but lies under the sacred duty, to do: answered a Falsehood when it questioned him, Dost thou believe me? — No! — At what cost soever, without counting of costs, this thing behoved to be done. Union, organisation spiritual and material, a far nobler than any Popedom or Feudalism in their truest days, I never doubt, is coming for the world; sure to come. But on Fact alone, not on Semblance and Simulacrum, will it be able either to come, or to stand when come. With union grounded on falsehood, and ordering us to speak and act lies, we will not have anything to do. Peace? A brutal lethargy is peaceable, the noisome grave is peaceable. We hope for a living peace, not a dead one!

And yet, in prizing justly the indispensable blessings of the New, let us not be unjust to the Old. The Old *was* true, if it no longer is. In Dante's days it needed no sophistry, self-blinding or other dishonesty, to get itself reckoned true. It was good then; nay there is in the soul of it a deathless good. The cry of 'No Popery,' is foolish enough in these days. The speculation that Popery is on the increase, building new chapels, and so forth, may pass for one of the idlest ever started. Very curious: to count up a few Popish chapels, listen to a few Protestant logic-choppings, — to much dull-droning drowsy inanity that still calls itself Protestant, and say: See, Protestantism is *dead;* Popism is more alive than it, will be alive after it! — Drowsy inanities, not a few, that call themselves Protestant are dead; but *Protestantism* has not died yet, that I hear of! Protestantism, if we will look, has in these days produced its Goethe, its Napoleon; German Literature and the French Revolution; rather considerable signs of life! Nay, at bottom, what else is alive *but* Protestantism? The life of most else that one meets is a galvanic one merely, — not a pleasant, not a lasting sort of life!

Popery can build new chapels; welcome to do so, to all lengths. Popery cannot come back, any more than Paganism can, — *which* also still lingers in some countries. But, indeed, it is with these things, as with the ebbing of the sea: you look at the waves oscillating hither, thither on the beach; for *minutes* you cannot tell how it is going: look in half an hour where it is, — look in half a century where your Popehood is! Alas, would there were no greater danger to our Europe than the poor old Pope's revival! Thor may as soon try to revive. — And withal this oscillation has a meaning. The poor old Popehood will not die away entirely, as Thor has done, for some time yet; nor ought it. We may say, the Old never dies till this happen, Till all the soul of good that was in it have got itself transfused into the practical New. While a good work remains capable of being done by the Romish form; or, what is inclusive of all, while a *pious life* remains capable of being led by it, just so long, if we consider, will this or the other human soul adopt it, go about as a living witness of it. So long it will obtrude itself on the eye of us who reject it, till we in our practice too have appropriated whatsoever of truth was in it. Then, but also not till then, it will have no charm more for any man. It lasts here for a purpose. Let it last as long as it can. —

Of Luther I will add now, in reference to all these wars and bloodshed, the noticeable fact that none of them began so long as he continued living. The controversy did not get to fighting so long as he was there. To me it is proof of his greatness in all senses, this fact. How seldom do we find a man that has stirred up some vast commotion, who does not himself perish, swept away in it. Such is the usual course of revolutionists. Luther continued, in a good degree, sovereign of this greatest revolution; all Protestants, of what rank or function soever, looking much to him for guidance: and he held it peaceable, continued firm at the centre of it. A man to do this must have a kingly faculty: he must have the gift to discern at all turns where the true heart of the matter lies, and to plant himself courageously on that, as a strong true man, that other true men may rally round him there. He will not continue leader of men otherwise. Luther's clear deep force of judgment, his force of all sorts, of *silence*, of tolerance and moderation, among others, are very notable in these circumstances.

Tolerance, I say; a very genuine kind of tolerance: he distinguishes what is essential, and what is not; the unessential may go as it will. A complaint comes that such and such a Reformed Preacher 'will not preach without a cassock.' Well, answers Luther, what harm will a cassock do the man? 'Let him have a cassock to preach in; let him have three cassocks if he find benefit in them!' His conduct in the matter of Karlstadt's wild image breaking, or the Anabaptists; of the Peasants' War, shews a noble strength, very different from spasmodic violence. With sure prompt insight he discriminates what is what: a strong just man speaks forth what is the wise course, and all men follow him in that. Luther's written works give similar testimony of him. The dialect of these speculations is now grown obsolete for us; but one still reads them with a singular attraction. And indeed the mere grammatical diction is still legible enough; Luther's merit in literary history is of the greatest: his dialect became the language of all writing. They are not well written, these four-and-twenty quartos of his; written hastily, with quite other than literary objects. But in no Books have I found a more robust, genuine, I will say noble faculty of a man than in these. A rugged honesty, homeliness, simplicity; a rugged sterling sense and strength. He flashes out illumination from him; his smiting idiomatic phrases seem to cleave into the very secret of the matter. Good humour too, nay tender affection, nobleness, and depth: this man could have been a Poet too! He had to *work* an Epic Poem, not write one. I call him a great Thinker; as indeed his greatness of heart already betokens that.

Richter says of Luther's words, 'his words are half-battles.' They may be called so. The essential quality of him was that he could fight and conquer; that he was a right piece of human Valour. No more valiant man, no mortal heart to be called *braver*, that one has record of, ever lived in that Teutonic Kindred, whose character is valour. His defiance of the 'Devils' in Worms was not a mere boast, as the like might be if now spoken. It was a faith of Luther's that there were Devils, spiritual denizens of the Pit, continually besetting men. Many times, in his writings, this turns up; and a most small sneer has been grounded on it by some. In the room of the Wartburg where he sat translating the Bible, they still shew you a black spot on the wall; the strange memorial of one of these conflicts. Luther sat translating one of the Psalms; he was worn down with long labour, with sickness, abstinence from food: there rose before him some hideous indefinable Image, which he took for the Evil One, to forbid his work: Luther started up, with fiend-defiance; flung his inkstand at the spectre, and it disappeared! The spot still remains there; a curious monument of several things. Any apothecary's apprentice can now tell us what we are to think of this apparition, in a scientific sense: but the man's heart that dare rise defiant, face to face, against Hell itself, can give no higher proof of fearlessness. The thing he will quail before, exists not on this Earth or under it. — Fearless enough! They spoke once about his not being at Leipzig, as if 'Duke George had hindered him,' a great enemy of his. It was not for Duke George, answered he: No; "if I had business at Leipzig, I would go, though it rained Duke Georges for nine days running."

At the same time, they err greatly who imagine that this man's courage was ferocity, mere coarse disobedient obstinacy and savagery, as many do. Far from that. There may be an absence of fear which arises from the absence of thought or affection, from the presence of hatred and stupid fury. We do not value the courage of the tiger highly! With Luther it was far otherwise; no accusation could be more unjust than this of mere ferocious violence brought against him. A most gentle heart withal, full of pity and love, as indeed the truly valiant heart ever is. The tiger before a *stronger* foe — flies: the tiger is not what we call valiant, only fierce and cruel. I know few things more touching than those soft breathings of affection, soft as a child's or a mother's, in this great wild heart of Luther. So honest, unadulterated with any cant; homely, rude in their utterance; pure as water welling from the rock. What, in fact, was all that downpressed mood of despair and reprobation, which we saw in his youth, but the outcome of preeminent thoughtful gentleness, affections too keen and fine? It is the course such men as the poor Poet Cowper fall into. Luther, to a slight observer, might have seemed a timid, weak man; modesty, affectionate shrinking tenderness the chief distinction of him. It is a noble valour which is roused in a heart like this, once stirred up into defiance; all kindled into a heavenly blaze.

In Luther's *Table-talk*, a posthumous Book of anecdotes and sayings collected by his friends, the most interesting now of all the Books proceeding from him, we have many beautiful unconscious displays of the man, and what sort of nature he had. His behaviour at the deathbed of his little Daughter, so still, so great and loving, is among the most affecting things. He is resigned that his little Margaret should die, yet longs inexpressibly that she might live; — follows, in awestruck thought, the flight of her little soul through those unknown realms. Awestruck; most heartfelt, we can see; and sincere, — for after all dogmatic creeds and articles, he feels what nothing it is that we know, or can know: His little Margaret shall be with God, as God wills; for Luther too that is all; *Islam* is all.

Once, he looks out from his solitary 'Patmos,' the Wartburg, in the middle of the night: The great vault of Immensity, long flights of clouds sailing through it, — dumb, gaunt, huge, — who supports all that? "None ever saw the pillars of it; yet it is supported." God supports it. We must know that God is great, that God is good; and trust, where we cannot see. — Returning home from Leipzig once, he is struck by the beauty of the harvest-fields: How it stands, that golden yellow corn, on its fair taper stem, its golden head bent, all rich and waving there. — the meek Earth, at God's kind bidding, has produced it once again; the bread of man! — In the garden at Wittenberg one evening at sunset, a little bird has perched for the night: That little bird, says Luther, above it are the stars and deep Heaven of worlds; yet it has folded its little wings; gone trustfully to rest there as in its home: the Maker of it has given it too a home! —— Neither are mirthful turns wanting: there is a great free human heart in this man. The common speech of him has a rugged nobleness, idiomatic, expressive, genuine; gleams here and there with beautiful poetic tints. One feels him to be a great brother man. His love of Music, indeed, is not this, as it were, the summary of all these affections in him? Many a wild unutterability he spoke forth from him in the tones of his flute. The Devils fled from his flute, he says. Death-defiance on the one hand, and such love of music on the other: I could call these the two opposite poles of a great soul; between these two all great things had room.

Luther's face is to me expressive of him; in Kranach's best portraits I find the true Luther. A rude, plebeian face; with its huge craglike brows and bones, the emblem of rugged energy; at first, almost a repulsive face. Yet in the eyes especially there is a wild silent sorrow; an unnameable melancholy, the element of all gentle and fine affections; giving to the rest the true stamp of nobleness. Laughter was in this Luther, as we said; but tears also were there. Tears also were appointed him; tears and hard toil. The basis of his life was Sadness, Earnestness. In his latter days, after all triumphs and victories, he expresses himself heartily weary of living; he considers that God alone can and will regulate the course things are taking, and that perhaps the Day of Judgment is not far. As for him, he longs for one thing: that God would release him from his labour, and let him depart and be at rest. They understand little of the man who cite this in *dis*credit of him! — I will call this Luther a true Great Man; great in intellect, in courage, affection and integrity; one of our most loveable and precious men. Great, not as a hewn obelisk; but as an Alpine mountain, — so simple, honest, spontaneous, not setting up to be great at all; there for quite another purpose than being great! Ah yes, unsubduable granite, piercing far and wide into the Heavens; — yet in the clefts of it fountains, green beautiful valleys with flowers! A right Spiritual Hero and Prophet; once more, a true Son of Nature and Fact, for whom these centuries, and many that are to come yet, will be thankful to Heaven.

The most interesting phasis which the Reformation anywhere assumes, especially for us English, is that of Puritanism. In Luther's own country, Protestantism soon dwindled into a rather barren affair: not a religion or faith, but rather now a theological jangling of argument, the proper seat of it not the heart; the essence of it sceptical contention: which indeed has jangled more and more, down to Voltairism itself, — through Gustavus-Adolphus contentions onward to French-Revolution ones! But in our Island there arose a Puritanism, which even got itself established as a Presbyterianism and National Church among the Scotch; which came forth as a real business of the heart; and has produced in the world very notable fruit. In some senses, one may say it is the only phasis of Protestantism that ever got to the rank of being a Faith, a true heart-communication with Heaven, and of exhibiting itself in History as such. We must spare a few words for Knox; himself a brave and remarkable man; but still more important as Chief Priest and Founder, which one may consider him to be, of the Faith that became Scotland's, New England's, Oliver Cromwell's. History will have something to say about this, for some time to come!

We may censure Puritanism as we please; and no one of us, I suppose, but would find it a very rough defective thing. But we, and all men, may understand that it was a genuine thing; for Nature has adopted it, and it has grown, and grows. I say sometimes, that all goes by wager of battle in this world; that *strength*, well understood, is the measure of all worth. Give a thing time; if it can succeed, it is a right thing. Look now at American Saxondom; and at that little Fact of the sailing of the Mayflower, two hundred years ago, from Delft Haven in Holland! Were we of open sense as the Greeks were, we had found a Poem here; one of Nature's own Poems, such as she writes in broad facts over great continents. For it was properly the beginning of America: there were straggling settlers in America before, some material as of a body was there; but the soul of it was first this. These poor men, driven out of their own country, not able well to live in Holland, determine on settling in the New World. Black untamed forests are there, and wild savage creatures; but not so cruel as Star-chamber hangmen. They thought the Earth would yield them food, if they tilled honestly; the everlasting Heaven would stretch, there too, overhead; they should be left in peace, to prepare for Eternity by living well in this world of Time; worshipping in what they thought the true, not the idolatrous way. They clubbed their small means together; hired a ship, the little ship Mayflower, and made ready to set sail. In *Neale's History of the Puritans* is an account of the ceremony of their departure: solemnity, we might call it rather, for it was a real act of worship. Their minister went down with them to the beach, and their brethren whom they were to leave behind; all joined in solemn prayer (the Prayer to is given), That God would have pity on His poor children, and *go* with them into that waste wilderness, for He also had made that, He was

there also as well as here. — Hah! These men, I think, had a work! The weak
thing, weaker than a child, becomes strong one day, if it be a true thing.
Puritanism was only despicable, laughable then; but nobody can manage to
laugh at it now. Puritanism has got weapons and sinews; it has fire-arms,
war-navies; it has cunning in its ten fingers, strength in its right arm: it can
steer ships, fell forests, remove mountains; — it is one of the strongest
things under this sun at present!

In the history of Scotland too, I can find properly but one epoch: we may
say, it contains nothing of world-interest at all but this Reformation by
Knox. A poor barren country, full of continual broils, dissensions, mas-
sacrings; a people in the last state of rudeness and destitution, little better
perhaps than Ireland at this day. Hungry fierce barons, not so much as able
to form any arrangement with each other *how to divide* what they fleeced
from these poor drudges; but obliged, as the Columbian Republics are at
this day, to make of every alteration a revolution; no way of changing a
ministry but by hanging the old ministers on gibbets: this is a historical
spectacle of no very singular significance! 'Bravery' enough, I doubt not;
fierce fighting in abundance: but not braver or fiercer than that of their old
Scandinavian Sea-king ancestors; *whose* exploits we have not found worth
dwelling on! It is a country as yet without a soul; nothing developed in it but
what is rude, external, semi-animal. And now at the Reformation, the internal life is kindled, as it were, under the ribs of this outward material death.
A cause, the noblest of causes kindles itself, like a beacon set on high; high
as Heaven, yet attainable from Earth; — whereby the meanest man becomes
not a Citizen only, but a Member of Christ's visible Church; a veritable
Hero, if he prove a true man!

Well; this is what I mean by a whole 'nation of heroes;' a *believing*
nation. There needs not a great soul to make a hero; there needs a god-
created soul which will be true to its origin; that will be a great soul! The
like has been seen, we find. The like will be again seen, under wider forms
than the Presbyterian: there can be no lasting good done till then. — Impossible! say some. Possible? Has it not *been*, in this world, as a practised fact?
Did Hero-worship fail in Knox's case? Or are we made of other clay now?
Did the Westminster Confession of Faith add some new property to the soul
of man? God made the soul of man. He did not doom any soul of man to live
as a Hypothesis and Hearsay, in a world filled with such, and with the fatal
work and fruit of such! ——

But to return: This that Knox did for his Nation, I say, we may really call
a resurrection as from death. It was not a smooth business; but it was
welcome surely, and cheap at that price, had it been far rougher. On the

whole, cheap at any price; — as life is. The people began to *live:* they needed first of all to do that, at what cost and costs soever. Scotch Literature and Thought, Scotch Industry; James Watt, David Hume, Walter Scott, Robert Burns: I find Knox and the Reformation acting in the heart's core of every one of these persons and phenomena; I find that without the Reformation they would not have been. Or what of Scotland? The Puritanism of Scotland became that of England, of New England. A tumult in the High Church of Edinburgh spread into a universal battle and struggle over all these realms; — there came out, after fifty years struggling, what we all call the *'Glorious* Revolution,' a *Habeas-Corpus* Act, Free Parliaments, and much else! — Alas, is it not too true what we said, That many men in the van do always, like Russian soldiers, march into the ditch of Schwiednitz [*sic*], and fill it up with their dead bodies, that the rear may pass over them dry-shod, and gain the honour? How many earnest rugged Cromwells, Knoxes, poor Peasant Covenanters, wrestling, battling for very life, in rough miry places, have to struggle, and suffer, and fall, greatly censured, *bemired,* — before a beautiful Revolution of Eighty-eight can step over them in official pumps and silkstockings, with universal three-times-three!

. It seems to me hard measure that this Scottish man, now after three hundred years, should have to plead like a culprit before the world; intrinsically for having been, in such way as it was then possible to be, the bravest of all Scotchmen! Had he been a poor Half-and-half, he could have crouched into the corner, like so many others; Scotland had not been delivered; and Knox had been without blame. He is the one Scotchman to whom, of all others, his country and the world owe a debt. He has to plead that Scotland would forgive him for having been worth to it any million 'unblameable' Scotchmen that need no forgiveness! He bared his breast to the battle; had to row in French galleys, wander forlorn in exile, in clouds and storms; was censured, shot at through his windows; had a right sore fighting life: if this world were his place of recompense, he had made but a bad venture of it. I cannot apologize for Knox. To him it is very indifferent, these two hundred and fifty years or more, what men say of him. But we, having got above all those details of his battle, and living now in clearness on the fruits of his victory, we for our own sake ought to look through the rumours and controversies enveloping the man, into the man himself.

For one thing, I will remark that this post of Prophet to his Nation was not of his seeking; Knox had lived forty years quietly obscure, before he became conspicuous. He was the son of poor parents; had got a college-education; become a Priest; adopted the Reformation, and seemed well content to guide his own steps by the light of it, nowise unduly intruding it on others. He had lived as Tutor in gentlemen's families: preaching when any body of persons wished to hear his doctrine: resolute he to walk by the truth, and speak the truth when called to do it; not ambitious of more; not fancying himself capable of more. In this entirely obscure way he had reached the age of forty; was with the small body of Reformers who were standing siege in St. Andrew's Castle, — when one day in their chapel, the Preacher after finishing his exhortation to these fighters in the forlorn hope, said suddenly, That there ought to be other speakers, that all men who had a priest's heart and gift in them ought now to speak; — which gifts and heart one of their own number, John Knox the name of him, had: Had he not? said the Preacher, appealing to all the audience: What then is *his* duty? The people answered affirmatively; it was a criminal forsaking of his post, if such a man held the word that was in him silent. Poor Knox was obliged to stand up; he attempted to reply; he could say no word; — burst into a flood of tears, and ran out. It is worth remembering, that scene. He was in grievous trouble for some days. He felt what a small faculty was his for this great work. He felt what a baptism he was called to be baptized withal. He 'burst into tears.'

Our primary characteristic of a Hero, that he is sincere, applies emphatically to Knox. It is not denied anywhere that this, whatever might be his other qualities or faults, is among the truest of men. With a singular instinct he holds to the truth and fact; the truth alone is there for him, the rest a mere shadow and deceptive nonentity. However feeble, forlorn the reality may seem, on that and that only *can* he take his stand. In the Galleys of the River Loire, whither Knox and the others, after their Castle of St. Andrew's was taken, had been sent as Galley-slaves, — some officer or priest, one day, presented them an Image of the Virgin Mother, requiring that they, the blasphemous heretics, should do it reverence. Mother? Mother of God? said Knox, when the turn came to him: This is no Mother of God: this is "a *pented bredd*," — a piece of wood, I tell you, with paint on it! She is fitter for swimming, I think, than for being worshipped, added Knox: and flung the thing into the river. It was not very cheap jesting there: but come of it what might, this thing to Knox was and must continue nothing other than the real truth; it was a *pented bredd:* worship it he would not. He told his fellow-prisoners, in this darkest time, to be of courage; the Cause they had was the true one, and must and would prosper; the whole world could not put it down. Reality is of God's making; it is alone strong. How many *pented bredds*, pretending to be real, are fitter to swim than to be worshipped! — This Knox cannot live but by fact: he clings to reality as the shipwrecked sailor to the cliff. He is an instance to us how a man, by sincerity itself, becomes heroic: it is the grand gift he has. We find in Knox a good honest intellectual talent, no transcendent one; — a narrow, inconsiderable man, as compared with Luther: but in heartfelt instinctive adherence to truth, in *sincerity*, as we say, he has no superior; nay, one might ask, What equal he has? The heart of him is of the true Prophet cast. "He lies there," said the Earl of Morton at his grave, "who never feared the face of man." He resembles, more than any of the moderns, an Old-Hebrew Prophet. The same inflexibility, intolerance, rigid narrow-looking adherence to God's truth, stern rebuke in the name of God to all that forsake truth: an Old-Hebrew Prophet in the guise of an Edinburgh Minister of the Sixteenth Century. We are to take him for that; not require him to be other.

Knox's conduct to Queen Mary, the harsh visits he used to make in her own palace, to reprove her there, have been much commented upon. Such cruelty, such coarseness fills us with indignation. On reading the actual narrative of the business, what Knox said, and what Knox meant, I must say one's tragic feeling is rather disappointed. They are not so coarse, these speeches; they seem to me about as fine as the circumstances would permit! Knox was not there to do the courtier; he came on another errand. Whoever, reading these colloquies of his with the Queen, thinks they are vulgar insolences of a plebeian priest to a delicate high lady, mistakes the purport and essence of them altogether. It was unfortunately not possible to be polite with the Queen of Scotland, unless one proved untrue to the Nation and Cause of Scotland. A man who did not wish to see the land of his birth made a hunting-field for intriguing ambitious Guises, and the Cause of God trampled under foot of Falsehoods, Formulas and the Devil's Cause, had no method of making himself agreeable! "Better that women weep," said Morton, "than that bearded men be forced to weep." Knox was the constitutional opposition-party in Scotland: the Nobles of the country, called by their station to take that post, were not found in it; Knox had to go, or no one. The hapless Queen; — but the still more hapless Country, if *she* were made happy! Mary herself was not without sharpness enough, among her other qualities: "Who are you," said she once, "that presume to school the nobles and sovereign of this realm?" — "Madam, a subject born within the same," answered he. Reasonably answered! If the 'subject' have truth to speak, it is not the 'subject's' footing that will fail him here. —

We blame Knox for his intolerance. Well, surely it is good that each of us be as tolerant as possible. Yet, at bottom, after all the talk there is and has been about it, what is tolerance? Tolerance has to tolerate the *un*essential; and to see well what that is. Tolerance has to be noble, measured, just in its very wrath, when it can tolerate no longer. But, on the whole, we are not

altogether here to tolerate! We do not tolerate Falsehoods, Thieveries, Iniq-
uities, when they fasten on us; we say to them, Thou art false and unjust! We
are here to *extinguish* Falsehoods in some wise way! I will not quarrel so
much with the way; the doing of the thing is our great concern. In this sense,
Knox was, full surely, intolerant.

A man sent to row in French Galleys, and such like, for teaching the
Truth in his own land, cannot always be in the mildest humour! I am not
prepared to say that Knox had a soft temper; nor do I know that he had what
we call an ill temper. An ill nature he decidedly had not. Kind honest
affections dwelt in the much-enduring, hard-worn, ever-battling man. That
he *could* rebuke Queens, and had such weight among those proud turbulent
Nobles, proud enough whatever else they were; and could maintain to the
end a kind of virtual Presidency and Sovereignty in that wild realm, he who
was only 'a subject born within the same:' this of itself will prove to us that
he was found, close at hand, to be no mean acrid man; but at heart, a
healthful, strong, sagacious man. Such alone can bear rule in that kind.
They blame him for pulling down cathedrals, and so forth, as if he were a
seditious rioting demagogue: precisely the reverse is seen to be the fact, in
regard to cathedrals and the rest of it, if we examine! Knox wanted no pulling down of stone edifices; he wanted leprosy and darkness to be thrown out
of the lives of men. Tumult was not his element; it was the tragic feature of
his life that he was forced to dwell so much in that. Every such man is the
born enemy of Disorder; hates to be in it: but what then? Smooth Falsehood
is not Order; it is the general sumtotal of *Dis*order. Order is *Truth*, — each
thing standing on the basis that belongs to it: Order and Falsehood cannot
subsist together.

Withal, unexpectedly enough, this Knox has a vein of drollery in him;
which I like much, in combination with his other qualities. He has a true eye
for the ridiculous. His *History*, with its rough earnestness, is curiously
enlivened with this. When the two Prelates, entering Glasgow Cathedral,
quarrel about precedence; march rapidly up, take to hustling one another,
twitching one another's rochets, and at last flourishing their croziers like
quarter-staves, it is a great sight for him every way! Not mockery, scorn,
bitterness alone; though there is enough of that too. But a true, loving,
illuminating laugh mounts up over the earnest visage; not a loud laugh; you
would say, a laugh in the *eyes* most of all. An honesthearted, brotherly man;
brother to the high, brother also to the low; sincere in his sympathy with
both. He had his pipe of Bourdeaux too, we find, in that old Edinburgh
house of his; a cheery social man, with faces that loved him! They go far
wrong who think this Knox was a gloomy, spasmodic, shrieking fanatic.

Not at all: he is one of the solidest of men. Practical, cautious-hopeful, patient; a most shrewd, observing, quietly discerning man. In fact, he has very much the type of character we assign to the Scotch at present: a certain sardonic taciturnity is in him; insight enough; and a stouter heart than he himself knows of. He has the power of holding his peace over many things which do not vitally concern him, — "They? what are they?" But the thing which does vitally concern him, that thing he will speak of; and in a tone the whole world shall be made to hear: all the more emphatic for his long silence. This Prophet of the Scotch is to me no hateful man! — He had a sore fight of an existence; wrestling with Popes and Principalities; in defeat, contention, life-long struggle; rowing as a galley-slave, wandering as an exile. A sore fight: but he won it. "Have you hope?" they asked him in his last moment, when he could no longer speak. He lifted his finger, 'pointed upwards with his finger,' and so died. Honour to him. His works have not died. The letter of his work dies, as of all men's; but the spirit of it never.

One word more as to the letter of Knox's work. The unforgiveable offence in him is, that he wished to set up Priests over the head of Kings. In other words, he strove to make the Government of Scotland a *Theocracy*. This indeed is properly the sum of his offences; the essential sin, for which what pardon can there be? It is most true, he did, at bottom, consciously or unconsciously, mean a Theocracy, or Government of God. He did mean that Kings and Prime Ministers, and all manner of persons, in public or private, diplomatising or whatever else they might be doing, should walk according to the Gospel of Christ, and understand that this was their Law, supreme over all laws. He hoped once to see such a thing realised; and the Petition, *Thy Kingdom come*, no longer an empty word. He was sore grieved when he saw greedy worldly Barons clutch hold of the Church's property; when he expostulated that it was not secular property, that it was spiritual property, and should be turned to *true* churchly uses, education, schools, worship; — and the Regent Murray had to answer, with a shrug of the shoulders, "It is a devout imagination!" This was Knox's scheme of right and truth; this he zealously endeavoured after, to realise it. If we think his scheme of truth was too narrow, was not true; we may rejoice that he could not realise it; that it remained, after two centuries of effort, unrealisable, and is a 'devout imagination' still. But how shall we blame *him* for struggling to realise it? Theocracy, Government of God, is precisely the thing to be struggled for! All Prophets, zealous Priests, are there for that purpose. Hildebrand wished a Theocracy; Cromwell wished it, fought for it; Mahomet attained it. Nay, is it not what all zealous men, whether called Priests, Prophets, or whatsoever else called, do essentially wish, and must wish? That right and truth, or

God's Law, reign supreme among men, this is the Heavenly Ideal (well-named in Knox's time, and nameable in all times, a revealed 'Will of God'), towards which the Reformer will insist that all be more and more approximated. All true Reformers, as I said, are by the nature of them Priests, and strive for a Theocracy.

How far such Ideals can ever be introduced into Practice, and at what point our impatience with their non-introduction ought to begin, is always a question. I think we may say safely, Let them introduce themselves as far as they can contrive to do it! If they are the true faith of men, all men ought to be more or less impatient always where they are not found introduced. There will never be wanting Regent-Murrays enough to shrug their shoulders, and say, "A devout imagination!" We will praise the Hero-Priest rather, who does what is in *him* to bring them in; and wears out, in toil, calumny, contradiction, a noble life, to make a God's Kingdom of this Earth. The Earth will not become too godlike!

LECTURE V.

[TUESDAY, 19TH MAY, 1840.]

The Hero as Man of Letters.
Johnson, Rousseau, Burns.

HERO-GODS, Prophets, Poets, Priests are forms of Heroism that belong to the old ages, make their appearance in the remotest times; some of them have ceased to be possible long since, and cannot any more shew themselves in this world. The Hero as *Man of Letters*, again, of which class we are to speak today, is altogether a product of these new ages; and so long as the wondrous art of *Writing*, or of Ready-writing which we call *Printing*, subsists, he may be expected to continue, as one of the main forms of Heroism for all future ages. He is, in various respects, a very singular phenomenon.

He is new, I say; he has hardly lasted above a century in the world yet. Never, till about a hundred years ago, was there seen any figure of a Great Soul living apart in that anomalous manner; endeavouring to speak forth the inspiration that was in him by Printed Books, and find place and subsistence by what the world would please to give him for doing that. Much had been sold and bought, and left to make its own bargain in the marketplace; but the inspired wisdom of a Heroic Soul never till then, in that naked manner. He, with his copy-rights and copy-wrongs, in his squalid garret, in his rusty coat; ruling (for this is what he does), from his grave, after death, whole nations and generations who would, or would not, give him bread while living, — is a rather curious spectacle! Few shapes of Heroism can be more unexpected.

Alas, the Hero from of old has had to cramp himself into strange shapes: the world knows not well at any time what to do with him, so foreign is his aspect in the world! It seemed absurd to us that men, in their rude admiration, should take some wise great Odin for a god, and worship him as such; some wise great Mahomet for one god-inspired, and religiously follow his Law for twelve centuries: but that a wise great Johnson, a Burns, a Rousseau, should be taken for some idle nondescript, extant in the world to amuse idleness, and have a few coins and applauses thrown him, that he might live thereby; *this* perhaps, as before hinted, will one day seem a still absurder phasis of things! — Meanwhile, since it is the spiritual always that determines the material, this same Man-of-Letters Hero must be regarded as our most important modern person. He, such as he may be, is the soul of all. What he teaches, the whole world will do and make. The world's manner of dealing with him is the most significant feature of the world's general position. Looking well at his life, we may get a glance as deep as is readily possible for us into the life of those singular centuries which have produced him, in which we ourselves live and work.

There are genuine Men of Letters, and not genuine; as in every kind there is a genuine and a spurious. If *Hero* be taken to mean genuine, then I say the Hero as Man of Letters will be found discharging a function for us which is ever honourable, ever the highest; and was once well known to be the highest. He is uttering forth, in such way as he has, the inspired soul of him; all that a man, in any case, can do. I say *inspired;* for what we call 'originality,' 'sincerity,' 'genius,' the heroic quality we have no good name for, signifies that. The Hero is he who lives in the inward sphere of things, in the True, Divine and Eternal, which exists always, unseen to most, under the Temporary, Trivial: his being is in that; he declares that abroad, by act or speech as it may be, in declaring himself abroad. His life, as we said before, is a piece of the everlasting heart of Nature herself: all men's life is, — but the weak many know it not, in most times; the strong few are strong, heroic, perennial, because it cannot be hidden from them. The Man of Letters, like every Hero, is there to proclaim this in such sort as he can. Intrinsically it is the same function which the old generations named a man Prophet, Priest, Divinity for doing; which all manner of Heroes, by speech or by act, are sent into the world to do.

Fichte the German Philosopher delivered, some forty years ago at Jena, a highly remarkable Course of Lectures on this subject: '*Ueber das Wesen des Gelehrten*, On the Nature of the Literary Man.' Fichte, in conformity with the Transcendental Philosophy, of which he was a distinguished teacher, declares first, That all things which we see or work with in this Earth, especially we ourselves and all persons, are as a kind of vesture or sensuous Appearance; that under all there lies, as the essence of them, what he calls the 'Divine Idea of the World;' this is the Reality which 'lies at the bottom of all Appearance.' To the mass of men no such Divine Idea is recognisable in the world; they live merely, says Fichte, among the superficialities, practicalities and shews of the world, not dreaming that there is anything divine under them. But the Man of Letters is sent hither specially that he may discern for himself, and make manifest to us, this same Divine Idea: in every new generation it will manifest itself in a new dialect; and he is there for the purpose of doing that. Such is Fichte's phraseology; with which we need not quarrel. It is his way of naming what I here, by other words, am striving imperfectly to name; what there is at present no name for: The unspeakable Divine Significance, full of splendour, of wonder and terror, that lies in the being of every man, of every thing, — the Presence of the God who made every man and thing. Mahomet taught this in his dialect; Odin in his: it is the thing which all thinking hearts, in one dialect or another, are here to teach. Fichte calls the Man of Letters, therefore, a Prophet, or as he prefers to phrase it, a Priest, continually unfolding the Godlike to men: Men of Letters are a perpetual Priesthood, from age to age, teaching all men that a God is still present in their life; that all 'Appearance,' whatsoever we see in the world, is but as a vesture for the 'Divine Idea of the World,' for 'that which lies at the bottom of Appearance.' In the true Literary Man there is thus ever, acknowledged or not by the world, a sacredness: he is the light of the world; the world's Priest; — guiding it, like a sacred Pillar of Fire, in its dark pilgrimage through the waste of Time. Fichte discriminates with sharp zeal the *true* Literary Man, what we here call the *Hero* as Man of Letters, from multitudes of false unheroic. Whoever lives not wholly in this Divine Idea, or living partially in it, struggles not, as for the one good, to live wholly in it, — he is, let him live where else he like, in what pomps and prosperities he like, no Literary Man; he is, says Fichte, a 'Bungler, *Stümper*.' Or at best, if he belong to the prosaic provinces, he may be a 'Hodman;' Fichte even calls him elsewhere a 'Nonentity,' and has in short no mercy for him, no wish that *he* should continue happy among us! This is Fichte's notion of the Man of Letters. It means, in its own form, precisely what we here mean.

In this point of view, I consider that, for the last hundred years, by far the notablest of all Literary Men is Fichte's countryman, Goethe. To that man too, in a strange way, there was given what we may call a life in the Divine Idea of the World; vision of the inward divine mystery: and strangely, out of his Books, the world rises imaged once more as godlike, the workmanship and temple of a God. Illuminated all, not in fierce impure fire-splendour as of Mahomet, but in mild celestial radiance; — really a Prophecy in these most unprophetic times; to my mind, by far the greatest, though one of the quietest, among all the great things that have come to pass in them! Our chosen specimen of the Hero as Literary Man would be this Goethe. And it were a very pleasant plan for me here, to discourse of his heroism: for I consider him to be a true Hero; heroic in what he said and did, and perhaps still more in what he did not say and did not do; to me a noble spectacle: a great heroic ancient man, speaking and keeping silence as an ancient Hero, in the guise of a most modern, high-bred, high-cultivated Man of Letters! We have had no such spectacle; no man capable of affording such, for the last hundred and fifty years. But at present, such is the general state of knowledge about Goethe, it were worse than useless to attempt speaking of him in this case. Speak as I might, Goethe, to the great majority of you, would remain problematic, vague; no impression but a false one could be realised. Him we must leave to future times. Johnson, Burns, Rousseau, three great figures from a prior time, from a far inferior state of circumstances, will suit us better here. Three men of the Eighteenth Century; the conditions of their life far more resemble what those of ours still are in England, than what Goethe's in Germany were. Alas, these men did not conquer like him; they fought bravely, and fell. They were not heroic bringers of the light, but heroic seekers of it. They lived under galling conditions; struggling as under mountains of impediment, and could not unfold themselves into clearness, victorious interpretation of that 'Divine Idea.' It is rather the *Tombs* of three Literary Heroes that I have to shew you. These are the monumental heaps, under which three spiritual giants lie buried. Very mournful, but also great and full of interest for us. We will linger by them for a while.

Complaint is often made, in these times, of what we call the disorganised condition of society: how ill many arranged forces of society fulfil their work; how many powerful forces are seen working in a wasteful, chaotic, altogether unarranged manner. It is too just a complaint, as we all know. But perhaps if we look at this of Books and the Writers of Books, we shall find here, as it were, the summary of all other disorganization; — a sort of *heart*, from which and to which all other confusion circulates in the world! Considering what Book-writers do in the world, and what the world does with Book-writers, I should say, It is the most anomalous thing the world at present has to shew. — We should get into a sea far beyond sounding, did we attempt to give account of this: but we must glance at it for the sake of our subject. The worst element in the life of these three Literary Heroes was, that they found their business and position such a chaos. On the beaten road there is tolerable travelling; but it is sore work, and many have to perish, fashioning a path through the impassable! Our pious Fathers, feeling well what importance lay in the speaking of man to men, founded churches, made endowments, regulations; everywhere in the civilised world there is a Pulpit, environed with all manner of complex dignified appurtenances and furtherances, that therefrom a man with the tongue may, to best advantage, address his fellow-men. They felt that this was the most important thing; that without this there was no good thing. It is a right pious work, that of theirs; beautiful to behold! But now with the art of Writing, with the art of

Printing, a total change has come over that business. The Writer of a Book, is not he a Preacher preaching, not to this parish or that, on this day or that, but to all men in all times and places? Surely it is of the last importance that *he* do his work right, whoever do it wrong; — that the *eye* report not falsely, for then all the other members are astray! Well; how he may do his work, whether he do it right or wrong, or do it at all, is a point which no man in the world has taken the pains to think of. To a certain shopkeeper, trying to get some money for his books, if lucky, he is of some importance; to no other man of any. Whence he came, whither he is bound, by what ways he arrived, by what he might be furthered on his course, no one asks. He is an accident in society. He wanders like a wild Ishmaelite, in a world of which he is as the spiritual light, either the guidance or the misguidance!

Certainly the Art of Writing is the most miraculous of all things man has devised. Odin's *Runes* were the first form of the work of a Hero; *Books*, written words, are still miraculous *Runes*, the latest form! In Books lies the *soul* of the whole Past Time; the articulate audible voice of the Past, when the body and material substance of it has altogether vanished like a dream. Mighty fleets and armies, harbours and arsenals, vast cities, high-domed, many-engined, — they are precious, great: but what do they become? Agamemnon, the many Agamemnons, Pericleses, and their Greece; all is gone now to some ruined fragments, dumb mournful wrecks and blocks: but the Books of Greece! There Greece, to every thinker, still very literally lives; can be called up again into life. No magic *Rune* is stranger than a Book. All that Mankind has done, thought, gained or been: it is lying as in magic preservation in the pages of Books. They are the chosen possession of men.

Do not Books still accomplish *miracles*, as *Runes* were fabled to do? They persuade men. Not the wretchedest circulating-library novel, which foolish girls thumb and con in remote villages, but will help to regulate the actual practical weddings and households of those foolish girls. So 'Celia' felt, so 'Clifford' acted: the foolish Theorem of Life, stamped into those young brains, comes out as a solid Practice one day. Consider whether any *Rune* in the wildest imagination of Mythologist ever did such wonders as, on the actual firm Earth, some Books have done! What built St. Paul's Cathedral? Look at the heart of the matter, it was that divine HEBREW Book, — the word partly of the man Moses, an outlaw tending his Midianitish herds, four thousand years ago, in the wildernesses of Sinai! It is the strangest of things, yet nothing is truer. With the art of Writing, of which Printing is a simple, an inevitable and comparatively insignificant corollary, the true reign of miracles for mankind commenced. It related, with a wondrous new contiguity and perpetual closeness, the Past and Distant with the

Present in time and place; all times and all places with this our actual Here and Now. All things were altered for men; all modes of important work of men: teaching, preaching, governing, and all else.

To look at Teaching, for instance. Universities are a notable, respectable product of the modern ages. Their existence too is modified, to the very basis of it, by the existence of Books. Universities arose while there were yet no Books procurable; while a man, for a single Book, had to give an estate of land. That, in those circumstances, when a man had some knowledge to communicate, he should do it by gathering the learners round him, face to face, was a necessity for him. If you wanted to know what Abelard knew, you must go and listen to Abelard. Thousands, as many as thirty thousand, went to hear Abelard and that metaphysical theology of his. And now for any other teacher who had also something of his own to teach, there was a great convenience opened: so many thousands eager to learn were already assembled yonder; of all places the best place for him was that. For any third teacher it was better still; and grew ever the better, the more teachers there came. It only needed now that the King took notice of this new phenomenon; combined or agglomerated the various schools into one school; gave it edifices, privileges, encouragements, and named it *Universitas*, or School of all Sciences: the University of Paris, in its essential characters, was there. The model of all subsequent Universities; which down even to these days, for six centuries now, have gone on to found themselves. Such, I conceive, was the origin of Universities.

It is clear, however, that with this simple circumstance, facility of getting Books, the whole conditions of the business from top to bottom were changed. Once invent Printing, you metamorphosed all Universities, or superseded them! The teacher needed not now to gather men personally round him, that he might *speak* to them what he knew: print it in a Book, and all learners far and wide, for a trifle, had it each at his own fireside, much more effectually to learn it! — Doubtless there is still peculiar virtue in Speech; even writers of Books may still, in some circumstances, find it convenient to speak also, — witness our present meeting here! There is, one would say, and must ever remain while man has a tongue, a distinct province for Speech as well as for Writing and Printing. In regard to all things this must remain; to Universities among others. But the limits of the two have nowhere yet been pointed out, ascertained; much less put in practice: the University which would completely take in that great new fact, of the existence of Printed Books, and stand on a clear footing for the Nineteenth Century as the Paris one did for the Thirteenth, has not yet come into existence. If we think of it, all that a University, or final highest School can do for us, is still but what the first School began doing, — teach us to *read*. We learn to *read*, in various languages, in various sciences; we learn the alphabet and letters of all manner of Books. But the place where we are to get knowledge, even theoretic knowledge, is the Books themselves! It depends on what we read, after all manner of Professors have done their best for us. The true University of these days is a Collection of Books.

But to the Church itself, as I hinted already, all is changed, in its preaching, in its working, by the introduction of Books. The Church is the working recognised Union of our Priests or Prophets, of those who by wise teaching guide the souls of men. While there was no Writing, even while there was no Easy-writing, or *Printing*, the preaching of the voice was the natural sole method of performing this. But now with Books! — He that can write a true Book, to persuade England, is not he the Bishop and Archbishop, the Primate of England and of all England? I many a time say, the writers of Newspapers, Pamphlets, Poems, Books, these *are* the real working effective Church of a modern country. Nay, not only our preaching, but even our worship, is not it too accomplished by means of Printed Books? The noble sentiment which a gifted soul has clothed for us in melodious words, which brings melody into our hearts, — is not this essentially, if we will understand it, of the nature of worship? There are many, in all countries, who, in this confused time, have no other method of worship. He who, in any way, shews us better than we knew before that a lily of the fields is beautiful, does he not shew it us as an effluence of the Fountain of all Beauty; as the *handwriting*, made visible there, of the great Maker of the Universe? He has sung for us, made us sing with him, a little verse of a sacred Psalm. Essentially so. How much more he who sings, who says, or in any way brings home to our heart the noble doings, feelings, darings and endurances of a brother man! He has verily touched our hearts as with a live coal *from the altar*. Perhaps there is no worship more authentic. Literature, so far as it is Literature, is an 'apocalypse of Nature,' a revealing of the 'open secret.' It may well enough be named, in Fichte's style, a 'continuous revelation' of the Godlike in the Terrestrial and Common. The Godlike does ever, in very truth, endure there; is brought out, now in this dialect, now in that, with various degrees of clearness: all true gifted Singers and Speakers are, consciously or unconsciously, doing so. The dark stormful indignation of a Byron, so wayward and perverse, may have touches of it; nay, the withered mockery of a French sceptic, — his mockery of the False, a love and worship of the True. How much more the sphere-harmony of a Shakspeare, of a Goethe; the cathedral-music of a Milton; the humble genuine lark-notes of a Burns, — skylark, starting from the humble furrow, far overhead into the blue depths, and singing to us so genuinely there! Fragments of a real 'Church Liturgy' and 'body of Homilies,' strangely disguised from the common eye, are to be found weltering in that huge froth-ocean of Printed Speech we loosely call Literature! Books are our Church too.

Or turning now to the Government of men. Witenagemote, old Parliament, was a great thing. The affairs of the nation were there deliberated and decided; what we were to *do* as a nation. But does not, though the name Parliament subsists, the parliamentary debate go on now, everywhere and at all times, in a far more comprehensive way, *out* of Parliament altogether? Burke said there were Three Estates in Parliament; but, in the Reporters' Gallery yonder, there sat a *Fourth Estate* more important far than they all. It is not a figure of a speech, or a witty saying; it is a literal fact, — very momentous to us in these times. Literature is our Parliament too. Printing, which comes necessarily out of Writing, I say often, is equivalent to Democracy: invent Writing, Democracy is inevitable. Writing brings Printing; brings universal every-day extempore Printing, as we see at present. Whoever can speak, speaking now to the whole nation, becomes a power, a branch of government, with inalienable weight in law-making, in all acts of authority. It matters not what rank he has, what revenues or garnitures: the requisite thing is, that he have a tongue which others will listen to; this and nothing more is requisite. The nation is governed by all that has tongue in the nation: Democracy is virtually *there*. Add only that whatsoever power exists will have itself by and by organised; working secretly under bandages, obscurations, obstructions, it will never rest till it get to work free, unincumbered, visible to all. Democracy virtually extant will insist on becoming palpably extant. —

On all sides, are we not driven to the conclusion that, of the things which man can do or make here below, by far the most momentous, wonderful and worthy are the things we call Books! Those poor bits of rag-paper with black ink on them; — from the Daily Newspaper to the sacred Hebrew Book, what have they not done, what are they not doing! — For indeed, whatever be the outward form of the thing (bits of paper, as we say, and black ink), is it not verily, at bottom, the highest act of man's faculty that produces a Book? It is the *Thought* of man; the true thaumaturgic virtue; by which man works all things whatsoever. All that he does, and brings to pass, is the vesture of a Thought. This London City, with all its houses, palaces, steamengines, cathedrals, and huge immeasurable traffic and tumult, what is it but a Thought, but millions of Thoughts made into One; — a huge immeasurable Spirit of a Thought, embodied in brick, in iron, smoke, dust, Palaces, Parliaments, Hackney Coaches, Katherine Docks, and the rest of it! Not a brick was made but some man had to *think* of the making of that brick. — The thing we called 'bits of paper with traces of black ink,' is the *purest* embodiment a Thought of man can have. No wonder it is, in all ways, the activest and noblest.

All this, of the importance and supreme importance of the Man of Letters in modern Society, and how the Press is to such a degree superseding the Pulpit, the Senate, the *Senatus Academicus* and much else, has been admitted for a good while; and recognised often enough, in late times, with a sort of sentimental triumph and wonderment. It seems to me, the Sentimental by and by will have to give place to the Practical. If Men of Letters *are* so incalculably influential, actually performing such work for us from age to age, and even from day to day, then I think we may conclude that Men of Letters will not always wander like unrecognised unregulated Ishmaelites among us! Whatsoever thing, as I said above, has virtual unnoticed power will cast off its wrappages, bandages, and step forth one day with palpably articulated, universally visible power. That one man wear the clothes, and take the wages, of a function which is done by quite another: there can be no profit in this; this is not right, it is wrong. And yet, alas, the *making* of it right, — what a business, for long times to come! Sure enough, this that we call Organisation of the Literary Guild is still a great way off, incumbered with all manner of complexities. If you asked me what were the best possible organisation for the Men of Letters in modern society; the arrangement, of furtherance and regulation, grounded the most accurately on the actual facts of their position and of the world's position, — I should beg to say that the problem far exceeded my faculty! It is not one man's faculty; it is that of many successive men turned earnestly upon it, that will bring out even an approximate solution. What the best arrangement were, none of us could say. But if you ask, Which is the worst? I answer: This which we now have, that Chaos should sit umpire in it; this is the worst. To the best, or any good one, there is yet a long way.

One remark I must not omit, That royal or parliamentary grants of money are by no means the chief thing wanted! To give our Men of Letters stipends, endowments, and all furtherance of cash, will do little towards the business. On the whole, one is weary of hearing about the omnipotence of money. I will say rather that, for a genuine man, it is no evil to be poor; that there ought to be Literary Men poor, — to shew whether they are genuine or not! Mendicant Orders, bodies of good men doomed to *beg*, were instituted in the Christian Church; a most natural and even necessary development of the spirit of Christianity. It was itself founded on Poverty, on Sorrow, Contradiction, Crucifixion, every species of worldly Distress and Degradation.

We may say that he who has not known those things, and learned from them the priceless lessons they have to teach, has missed a good opportunity of schooling. To beg, and go barefoot, in coarse woollen cloak with a rope round your loins, and be despised of all the world, was no beautiful business; — nor an honourable one in any eye, till the nobleness of those who did so had made it honoured of some! Begging is not in our course at the present time: but for the rest of it, who will say that a Johnson is not perhaps the better for being poor? It is needful for him, at all rates, to know that outward profit, that success of any kind is *not* the goal he has to aim at. Pride, vanity, ill-conditioned egoism of all sorts, are bred in his heart, as in every heart; need, above all, to be cast out of his heart, — to be, with whatever pangs, torn out of it, cast forth from it, as a thing worthless. Byron, born rich and noble, made out even less than Burns, poor and plebeian. Who knows but, in that same 'best possible organisation' as yet far off, Poverty may still enter as an important element? What if our Men of Letters, men setting up to be Spiritual Heroes, were still *then*, as they now are, a kind of 'involuntary monastic order;['] bound still to this same ugly Poverty, — till they had tried what was in it too, till they had learned to make it too do for them! Money, in truth, can do much, but it cannot do all. We must know the province of it, and confine it there; and even spurn it back, when it wishes to get farther.

Besides, were the money-furtherances, the proper season for them, the fit assigner of them, all settled, — how is the Burns to be recognised that merits these? He must pass through the ordeal, and prove himself. *This* ordeal; this wild welter of a chaos which is called Literary Life: this too is a kind of ordeal! There is clear truth in the idea that a struggle from the lower classes of society, towards the upper regions and rewards of society, must ever continue. Strong men are born there, who ought to stand elsewhere than there. The manifold, inextricably complex, universal struggle of these constitutes, and must constitute, what is called the progress of society. For Men of Letters, as for all other sorts of men. How to regulate that struggle? There is the whole question. To leave it as it is, at the mercy of blind Chance; a whirl of distracted atoms, one cancelling the other; one of the thousand arriving saved, nine hundred and ninety-nine lost by the way; your royal Johnson languishing inactive in garrets, or harnessed to the yoke of Printer Cave, your Burns dying brokenhearted as a Gauger, your Rousseau driven into mad exasperation, kindling French Revolutions by his paradoxes: this, as we said, is clearly enough the *worst* regulation. The *best*, alas, is far from us!

And yet there can be no doubt but it is coming; advancing on us, as yet hidden in the bosom of centuries: this is a prophecy one can risk. For so soon as men get to discern the importance of a thing, they do infallibly set about arranging it, facilitating, forwarding it; and rest not till, in some approximate degree, they have accomplished that. I say, of all Priesthoods, Aristocracies, Governing Classes at present extant in the world, there is no class comparable for importance to that Priesthood of the Writers of Books. This is a fact which he who runs may read, — and draw inferences from. "Literature will take care of itself," answered Mr. Pitt, when applied to for some help for Burns. "Yes," answers Mr. Southey, "it will take care of itself; *and of you too*, if you do not look to it!"

The result to individual Men of Letters is not the momentous one; they are but individuals, an infinitesimal fraction of the great body; they can struggle on, and live or else die, as they have been wont. But it deeply concerns the whole society, whether it will set its *light* on high places, to walk thereby; or trample it under foot, and scatter it in all ways of wild waste (not without conflagration), as heretofore! Light is the one thing wanted for the world. Put wisdom in the head of the world, it will fight its battle victoriously, and be the best world man can make it. I called this anomaly of a disorganic Literary Class the heart of all other anomalies, at once product and parent; some good arrangement for that would be as the *punctum saliens* of a new vitality and just arrangement for all. Already, in some European countries, in France, in Prussia, one traces some beginnings of an arrangement for the Literary Class; indicating the gradual possibility of such. I believe that it is possible; that it will have to be possible.

By far the most interesting fact I hear about the Chinese is one on which we cannot arrive at clearness, but which excites endless curiosity even in the dim state: this namely, that they do attempt to make their Men of Letters their Governors! It would be rash to say, one understood how this was done, or with what degree of success it was done. All such things must be very *un*successful; yet a small degree of success is precious; the very attempt how precious! There does seem to be, all over China, a more or less active search everywhere to discover the men of talent that grow up in the young generation. Schools there are for every one: a foolish sort of training, yet still a sort. The youths who distinguish themselves in the lower school are promoted into favourable stations in the higher, that they may still more distinguish themselves, — forward and forward: it appears to be out of these that the Official Persons, and incipient Governors, are taken. These are they whom they *try* first, whether they can govern or not. And surely with the best hope; for they are the men that have already shewn intellect. Try them, they have not governed or administered as yet; perhaps they cannot; but there is no doubt they *have* some understanding, — without which no man can! Neither is Understanding a *tool*, as we are too apt to figure; 'it is a *hand* which can handle any tool.' Try these men: they are of all others the best worth trying. — Surely there is no kind of government, constitution, revolution, social apparatus or arrangement, that I know of in this world, so promising to one's scientific curiosity as this. The man of intellect at the top of affairs: this is the aim of all constitutions and revolutions, if they have any aim. For the man of true intellect, as I assert and believe always, is the noblehearted man withal, the true, just, humane and valiant man. Get *him* for governor, all is got; fail to get him, though you had Constitutions plentiful as blackberries, and a Parliament in every village, there is nothing yet got! —

These things look strange, truly; and are not such as we commonly speculate upon. But we are fallen into strange times; these things will require to be speculated upon; to be rendered practicable, to be in some way put in practice. These, and many others. On all hands of us, there is the announcement, audible enough, that the old Empire of Routine has ended; that to say a thing has long been, is no reason for its continuing to be. The things which have been are fallen into decay, are fallen into incompetence; large masses of mankind, in every society of our Europe, are no longer capable of living at all by the things which have been. When millions of men can no longer by their utmost exertion gain food for themselves, and 'the third man for thirty-six weeks each year is short of third-rate potatoes,' the things which have been must decidedly prepare to alter themselves! — I will now quit this of the organisation of Men of Letters.

Alas, the evil that pressed heaviest on those Literary Heroes of ours was not the want of organisation for Men of Letters, but a far deeper one; out of which, indeed, this and so many other evils for the Literary Man, and for all men, had, as from their fountain, taken rise. That our Hero as Man of Letters had to travel without highway, companionless, through an inorganic chaos, — and to leave his own life and faculty lying there, as a partial contribution towards *pushing* some highway through it: this, had not his faculty itself been so perverted and paralysed, he might have put up with, might have considered to be but the common lot of Heroes. His fatal misery was the *spiritual paralysis*, so we may name it, of the age in which his life lay; whereby his life too, do what he might, was half-paralysed! The Eighteenth was a *Sceptical* Century; in which little word there is a whole Pandora's Box of miseries. Scepticism means not intellectual Doubt alone, but moral Doubt; all sorts of *in*fidelity, insincerity, spiritual paralysis. Perhaps, in few centuries that one could specify since the world began, was a life of Heroism more difficult for a man. That was not an age of Faith, — an age of Heroes! The very possibility of Heroism had been, as it were, formally abnegated in the minds of all. Heroism was gone forever; Triviality, Formalism and Commonplace were come forever. The 'age of miracles' had been, or perhaps had not been; but it was not any longer. An effete world; wherein Wonder, Greatness, Godhood could not now dwell; — in one word, a godless world!

How mean, dwarfish are their ways of thinking, in this time, — compared not with the Christian Shakspeares and Miltons, but with the old Pagan Skalds, with any species of believing men. The living TREE Igdrasil, with the melodious prophetic waving of its world-wide boughs, deep-rooted as Hela, has died out into the clanking of a World-MACHINE. 'Tree' and 'machine:' contrast these two things. I, for my share, declare the world to be no Machine; it does not go by wheels and pinions at all! The old Norse Heathen had a truer notion of God's-world than these poor Machine-Sceptics: the old Heathen Norse were *sincere* men. But for these poor Sceptics there was no sincerity, no truth. Half-truth and hearsay was called truth. Truth, for most men, meant plausibility; to be measured by the number of votes you could get. They had lost any notion that sincerity was possible, or of what sincerity was. How many Plausibilities asking, with unaffected surprise and the air of offended virtue, What! am not I sincere? Spiritual Paralysis, I say, nothing left but a Mechanical life, was the characteristic of that century. For the common man, unless happily he stood *below* his century and belonged to another prior one, it was impossible to be a Believer, a Hero; he lay buried, unconscious, under these baleful influences. To the strongest man, only with infinite struggle and confusion was it possible to work himself half-loose; and lead as it were, in an enchanted, most tragical way, a spiritual death-in-life, and be a Half-Hero!

Scepticism is the name we give to all this; as the chief symptom, as the chief origin of all this. Concerning which so much were to be said! It would take many Discourses, not a small fraction of one Discourse, to state what one feels about that Eighteenth Century and its ways. As indeed this, and the like of this, which we now call Scepticism, is precisely the black malady and life-foe, against which all teaching and discoursing since man's life began has directed itself: the battle of Belief against Unbelief is the never-ending battle! Neither is it in the way of crimination that one would wish to speak. Scepticism, for that century, we must consider as the decay of old ways of believing, the preparation afar off for new better and wider ways, — an inevitable thing. We will not blame men for it; we will lament their hard fate. We will understand that destruction of old *forms* is not destruction of everlasting *substances;* that Scepticism, as sorrowful and hateful as we see it, is not an end but a beginning.

The other day speaking, without prior purpose that way, of Bentham's theory of man and man's life, I chanced to call it a more beggarly one than Mahomet's. I am bound to say, now when it is once uttered, that such is my deliberate opinion. Not that one would mean offence against the man Jeremy Bentham, or those who respect and believe him. Bentham himself, and even the creed of Bentham, seems to me comparatively worthy of praise. It is a determinate *being* what all the world, in a cowardly half-and-half manner, was tending to be. Let us have the crisis; we shall either have death or the cure. I call this gross, steamengine Utilitarianism an approach towards new Faith. It was a laying down of cant; a saying to oneself: "Well then, this world is a dead iron machine, the god of it Gravitation and selfish Hunger; let us see what, by checking and balancing, and good adjustment of tooth and pinion, can be made of it!" Benthamism has something complete, manful, in such fearless committal of itself to what it finds true; you may call it Heroic, though a Heroism with its *eyes* put out! It is the culminating point, and fearless ultimatum, of what lay in the half-and-half state, pervading man's whole existence in that Eighteenth Century. It seems to me, all deniers of Godhood, and all lip-believers of it, are bound to be Benthamites, if they have courage and honesty. Benthamism is an *eyeless* Heroism: the Human Species, like a hapless blinded Samson grinding in the Philistine Mill, clasps convulsively the pillars of its Mill; brings huge ruin down, but ultimately deliverance withal. Of Bentham I meant to say no harm.

But this I do say, and would wish all men to know and lay to heart, that he who discerns nothing but Mechanism in the Universe, has in the fatalest way missed the secret of the Universe altogether. That all Godhood should vanish out of men's conception of this Universe seems to me precisely the most brutal error, — I will not disparage Heathenism by calling it a Heathen error, — that men could fall into. It is not true; it is false at the very heart of it. A man who thinks so will think *wrong* about all things in the world; this original sin will vitiate all other conclusions he can form. One might call it the most lamentable of Delusions, — not forgetting Witchcraft itself! Witchcraft worshipped at least a living Devil; but this worships a dead iron Devil; no God, not even a Devil! — Whatsoever is noble, divine, inspired, drops thereby out of life. There remains everywhere in life a despicable *caputmortuum;* the mechanical hull, all soul fled out of it. How can a man act heroically? The 'Doctrine of Motives' will teach him that it is, under more or less disguise, nothing but a wretched love of Pleasure, fear of Pain; that

Hunger, of applause, of cash, of whatsoever victual it may be, is the ultimate fact of man's life. Atheism, in brief; — which does indeed frightfully punish itself. The man, I say, is become spiritually a paralytic man; this godlike Universe a dead mechanical Steamengine, all working by motives, checks, balances, and I know not what; wherein, as in the detestable belly of some Phalaris'-Bull of his own contriving, he the poor Phalaris sits miserably dying! —

Belief I define to be the healthy act of a man's mind. It is a mysterious indescribable process that of getting to believe; — indescribable, as all vital acts are. We have our mind given us, not that it may cavil and argue, but that it may see into something, give us clear belief and understanding about something, whereon we are then to proceed to act. Doubt, truly, is not itself a crime. Certainly we do not rush out, clutch up the first thing we find, and straightway believe that! All manner of doubt, inquiry, σκέψις as it is named, about all manner of objects, dwells in every reasonable mind. It is the mystic working of the mind, on the object it is *getting* to know and believe. Belief comes out of all this, above ground, like the tree from its hidden *roots*. But now if, even on common things, we require that a man keep his doubts *silent*, and not babble of them till they in some measure become affirmations or denials; how much more in regard to the highest things, impossible to speak of in words at all! That a man parade his doubt, and get to imagine that debating and logic (which means at best only the manner of *telling* us your thought, belief or disbelief, about a thing) is the triumph and true work of what intellect he has: alas, this is as if you should *overturn* the tree, and instead of green boughs, leaves and fruits, shew us ugly taloned roots turned up into the air, — and no growth, only death and misery going on!

For the Scepticism, as I said, is not intellectual only; it is moral also; a chronic atrophy and disease of the whole soul. A man lives by believing something; not by debating and arguing about many things. A sad case for him when all that he can manage to believe is something he can button in his pocket, and with one or the other organ eat and digest! Lower than that he will not get. We call those ages in which he gets so low the mournfulest, sickest and meanest of all ages. The world's heart is palsied, sick: how can any limb of it be whole? Genuine Acting ceases in all departments of the world's work; dexterous Similitude of Acting begins. The world's wages are pocketed, the world's work is not done. Heroes have gone out; Quacks have come in. Accordingly, what Century, since the end of the Roman world, which also was a time of scepticism, simulacra and universal decadence, so abounds with Quacks as that Eighteenth? Consider them, with their tumid sentimental vapouring about virtue, benevolence — the wretched Quack squadron, Cagliostro at the head of them! Few men were without quackery; they had got to consider it a necessary ingredient and amalgam for truth. Chatham, our brave Chatham himself, comes down to the House, all wrapt and bandaged; he "has crawled out in great bodily suffering," and so on; — *forgets*, says Walpole, that he is acting the sick man; in the fire of debate, snatches his arm from the sling, and oratorically swings and brandishes it! Chatham himself lives the strangest mimetic life, half-hero, half-quack, all along. For indeed the world is full of dupes; and you have to gain the *world's* suffrage! How the duties of the world will be done in that case, what quantities of error, which means failure, which means sorrow and misery, to some and to many, will gradually accumulate in all provinces of the world's business, we need not compute.

It seems to me, you lay your finger here on the heart of the world's maladies, when you call it a Sceptical World. An insincere world; a godless untruth of a world! It is out of this, as I consider, that the whole tribe of social pestilences, French Revolutions, Chartisms, and what not, have derived their being, — their chief necessity to be. This must alter. Till this alter, nothing can beneficially alter. My one hope of the world, my inexpugnable consolation in looking at the miseries of the world, is that this is altering. Here and there one does now find a man who knows, as of old, that this world is a Truth, and no Plausibility and Falsity; that he himself is alive, not dead or paralytic; and the world is alive, instinct with Godhood, beautiful and awful, even as in the beginning of days! One man once knowing this, many men, all men, must by and by come to know it. It lies there clear, for whosoever will take the *spectacles* off his eyes and honestly look, to know! For such a man the Unbelieving Century, with its unblessed Products, is already past; a new century is already come. The old unblessed Products and Performances, as solid as they look, are Phantasms, preparing speedily to vanish. To this and the other noisy, very great-looking Simulacrum with the whole world huzzahing at its heels, he can say, composedly stepping aside: Thou art not *true;* thou art not extant, only semblant; go thy way! — Yes, hollow Formulism, gross Benthamism, and other unheroic atheistic Insincerity is visibly and even rapidly declining. An unbelieving Eighteenth Century is but an exception, — such as now and then occurs. I prophesy that the world will once more become *sincere;* a believing world; with *many* Heroes in it, a Heroic World! It will then be a victorious world; never till then.

Or indeed what of the world and its victories? Men speak too much about the world. Each one of us here, let the world go how it will, and be victorious or not victorious, has he not a Life of his own to lead? One Life; a little gleam of Time between two Eternities; no second chance to us forevermore! It were well for *us* to live not as fools and simulacra, but as wise and realities. The world's being saved will not save us; nor the world's being lost destroy us. We should look to ourselves: there is great merit here in the 'duty of staying at home!' And, on the whole, to say truth, I never heard of 'worlds' being 'saved' in any other way. That mania of saving worlds is itself a piece of the Eighteenth Century with its windy sentimentalism. Let us not follow it too far. For the saving of the *world* I will trust confidently to the Maker of the world; and look a little to my own saving, which I am more competent to! — In brief, for the world's sake, and for our own, we will rejoice greatly that Scepticism, Insincerity, Mechanical Atheism, with all their poison-dews, are going, and as good as gone.

Now it was under such conditions, in those times of Johnson, that our Men of Letters had to live. Times in which there was properly no truth in life. Old Truths had fallen nigh dumb; the new lay yet hidden, not trying to speak. That Man's Life here below was a Sincerity and Fact, and would forever continue such, no new intimation in that dusk of the world, had yet dawned. No intimation; not even any French Revolution, — which we define to be a Truth once more, though a Truth clad in hellfire! How different was the Luther's pilgrimage, with its assured goal, from the Johnson's girt with mere traditions, suppositions, grown now incredible, unintelligible! Mahomet's Formulas were of 'wood waxed and oiled,' and could be *burnt* out of one's way: poor Johnson's were far more difficult to burn. — The strong man will ever find *work*, which means difficulty, pain, to the full measure of his strength. But to make out a victory, in those circumstances of our poor Hero as Man of Letters, was perhaps more difficult than in any. Not obstruction, disorganisation, Bookseller Osborne and Fourpence-halfpenny a day; not this alone; but the light of his own soul was taken from him. No landmark on the Earth; and, alas, what is that to having no loadstar in the Heaven! We need not wonder that none of those Three men rose to victory. That they fought truly, is the highest praise. With a mournful sympathy we will contemplate, if not three living victorious Heroes, as I said, the Tombs of three fallen Heroes! They fell for us too; making a way for us. There are the mountains which they hurled abroad in their confused War of the Giants; under which, their strength and life spent, they now lie buried.

I have already written of these three Literary Heroes, expressly or incidentally; what I suppose is known to most of you; what need not be spoken or written a second time. They concern us here as the singular *Prophets* of that singular age; for such they virtually were; and the aspect they and their world exhibit, under this point of view, might lead us into reflexions enough! I call them, all three, Genuine Men more or less; faithfully, for most part unconsciously, struggling to be genuine, and plant themselves on the everlasting truth of things. This to a degree that eminently distinguishes them from the poor artificial mass of their contemporaries; and renders them worthy to be considered as Speakers, in some measure, of the everlasting truth, as Prophets in that age of theirs. By Nature herself a noble necessity was laid on them to be so. They were men of such magnitude that they could not live on unrealities, — clouds, froth and all inanity gave way under them: there was no footing for them but on firm earth; no rest or regular motion for them, if they got not footing there. To a certain extent, they were Sons of Nature once more in an age of Artifice; once more, Original Men.

As for Johnson, I have always considered him to be, by nature, one of our great English souls. A strong and noble man; so much left undeveloped in him to the last: in a kindlier element what might he not have been, — Poet, Priest, sovereign Ruler! On the whole, a man must not complain of his 'element,' of his 'time,' or the like; it is thriftless work doing so. His time is bad: well then, he is there to make it better! — Johnson's youth was poor, isolated, hopeless, very miserable. Indeed, it does not seem possible that, in any the favourablest outward circumstances, Johnson's life could have been other than a painful one. The world might have had more of profitable *work* out of him, or less; but his *effort* against the world's work could never have been a light one. Nature, in return for his nobleness, had said to him, Live in an element of diseased sorrow. Nay, perhaps the sorrow and the nobleness were intimately and even inseparably connected with each other. At all events, poor Johnson had to go about girt with continual hypochondria, physical and spiritual pain. Like a Hercules with the burning Nessus'-shirt on him, which shoots in on him dull incurable misery: the Nessus'-shirt not to be stript off, which is his own natural skin! In this manner, *he* had to live. Figure him there, with his scrofulous diseases, with his great greedy heart, and unspeakable chaos of thoughts; stalking mournful as a stranger in this Earth; eagerly devouring what spiritual thing he could come at: school-languages and other merely grammatical stuff, if there were nothing better! The largest soul that was in all England; and provision made for it of 'fourpence halfpenny a day.' Yet a giant invincible soul; a true man's. One remembers always that story of the shoes at Oxford: the rough, seamy-faced, rawboned College Servitor stalking about, in winter-season, with his shoes worn out; how the charitable Gentleman Commoner secretly places a new pair at his door; and the rawboned Servitor, lifting them, looking at them near, with his dim eyes, with what thoughts, — pitches them out of window! Wet feet, mud, frost, hunger or what you will; but not beggary: we cannot stand beggary! Rude stubborn self-help here; a whole world of squalor, rudeness, confused misery and want, yet of nobleness and manfulness withal. It is a type of the man's life, this pitching away of the shoes. An original man; — not a secondhand, borrowing or begging man. Let us stand on our own basis, at any rate! On such shoes as we ourselves can get. On frost and mud, if you will, but honestly on that; — on the reality and substance which Nature gives *us*, not on the semblance, on the thing she has given another than us! —

And yet with all this rugged pride of manhood and self-help, was there ever soul more tenderly affectionate, loyally submissive to what was really higher than he? Great souls are always loyally submissive, reverent to what is over them; only small mean souls are otherwise. I could not find a better proof of what I said the other day, That the sincere man was by nature the obedient man; that only in a World of Heroes was there loyal Obedience to the Heroic. The essence of *originality* is not that it be *new*: Johnson believed altogether in the old; he found the old opinions credible for him, fit for him; and in a right heroic manner, lived under them. He is well worth study in regard to that. For we are to say that Johnson was far other than a mere man of words and formulas; he was a man of truths and facts. He stood by the old formulas; the happier was it for him that he could so stand: but in all formulas that *he* could stand by, there needed to be a most genuine substance. Very curious how, in that poor Paper-age, so barren, artificial, thick-quilted with Pedantries, Hearsays, the great Fact of this Universe glared-in forever, wonderful, indubitable, unspeakable, divine-infernal, upon this man too! How he harmonised his Formulas with it, how he managed at all under such circumstances: that is a thing worth seeing. A thing 'to be looked at with reverence, with pity, with awe.' That Church of St. Clement Danes, where Johnson still *worshipped* in the era of Voltaire, is to me a venerable place.

It was in virtue of his *sincerity*, of his speaking still in some sort from the heart of Nature, though in the current artificial dialect, that Johnson was a Prophet. Are not all dialects 'artificial?' Artificial things are not all false; — nay every true Product of Nature will infallibly *shape* itself; we may say all artificial things are, at the starting of them, *true*. What we call 'Formulas' are not in their origin bad; they are indispensably good. Formula is *method*, habitude; found wherever man is found. Formulas fashion themselves as Paths do, as beaten Highways, leading towards some sacred or high object, whither many men are bent. Consider it. One man, full of heartfelt earnest impulse, finds out a way of doing somewhat. — were it of uttering his soul's reverence for the Highest, were it but of fitly saluting his fellow-man. An inventor was needed to do that, a *poet;* he has articulated the dim-struggling thought that dwelt in his own and many hearts. This is his way of doing that; these are his footsteps, the beginning of a 'Path.' And now see: the second man travels naturally in the footsteps of his foregoer, it is the *easiest* method. In the footsteps of his foregoer; yet with improvements, changes where such seem good; at all events with enlargements, the Path ever *widening* itself as more travel it; — till at last there is a broad Highway whereon the whole world may travel and drive. While there remains a City or Shrine, or any Reality to drive to, at the farther end, the Highway shall be right welcome! When the City is gone, we will forsake the Highway. In this manner all Institutions, Practices, Regulated Things in the world have come into existence, and gone out of existence. Formulas all begin by being *full* of substance; you may call them the *skin*, the articulation into shape, into limbs and skin, of a substance that is already there: *they* had not been there otherwise. Idols, as we said, are not idolatrous till they become doubtful, empty for the worshipper's heart. Much as we talk against Formulas, I hope no one of us is ignorant withal of the high significance of *true* Formulas; that they were, and will ever be, the indispensablest furniture of our habitation in this world. —

Mark, too, how little Johnson boasts of his 'sincerity.' He has no suspicion of his being particularly sincere, — of his being particularly anything! A hard-struggling, weary-hearted man, or 'scholar' as he calls himself, trying hard to get some honest livelihood in the world, not to starve, but to live — without stealing! A noble unconsciousness is in him. He does not 'engrave *Truth* on his watch-seal;' no, but he stands by truth, speaks by it, works and lives by it. Thus it ever is. Think of it once more. The man whom Nature has appointed to do great things is, first of all, furnished with that openness to Nature which renders him incapable of being *in*sincere! To his large, open, deep-feeling heart Nature is a Fact: all hearsay is hearsay; the unspeakable greatness of this Mystery of Life, let him acknowledge it or not, nay even though he seem to forget it or deny it, is ever present to *him*, — fearful and wonderful, on this hand and on that. He has a basis of sincerity; unrecognised, because never questioned or capable of question. Mirabeau, Mahomet, Cromwell, Napoleon: all the Great Men I ever heard of have this as the primary material of them. Innumerable commonplace men are debating, are talking everywhere their commonplace doctrines, which they have learned by logic, by rote, at second-hand: to that kind of man all this is still nothing. He must have truth; truth which *he* feels to be true. How shall he stand otherwise? His whole soul, at all moments, in all ways, tells him that there is no standing. He is under the noble necessity of being true. Johnson's way of thinking about this world is not mine, any more than Mahomet's was: but I recognise the everlasting element of heart-*sincerity* in both; and see with pleasure how neither of them remains ineffectual. Neither of them is as *chaff* sown; in both of them is something which the seed-field will *grow*.

Johnson was a Prophet to his people; preached a Gospel to them, — as all like him always do. The highest Gospel he preached we may describe as a kind of Moral Prudence: 'in a world where much is to be done and little is to be known,' see how you will *do* it! A thing well worth preaching. 'A world where much is to be done and little is to be known:' do not sink yourselves in boundless bottomless abysses of Doubt, of wretched godforgetting Unbelief; — you were miserable then, powerless, mad: how could you *do* or work at all? Such Gospel Johnson preached and taught; — coupled, theoretically and practically, with this other great Gospel, 'Clear your mind of Cant!' Have no trade with Cant: stand on the cold mud in the frosty weather, but let it be in your own *real* torn shoes: 'that will be better for you,' as Mahomet says! I call this, call these two things *joined together*, a great Gospel, the greatest perhaps that was possible at that time.

Johnson's Writings, which once had such currency and celebrity, are now as it were disowned by the young generation. It is not wonderful; Johnson's opinions are fast becoming obsolete: but his style of thinking and of living, we may hope, will never become obsolete. I find in Johnson's Books the indisputablest traces of a great intellect and great heart; — ever welcome, under what obstructions and perversions soever. They are *sincere* words, those of his; he means things by them. A wondrous buckram style, — the best he could get to then; a measured grandiloquence, stepping or rather stalking along in a very solemn way, grown obsolete now; sometimes a tumid *size* of phraseology not in proportion to the contents of it: all this you will put up with. For the phraseology, tumid or not, has always *something within it*. So many beautiful styles, and books, with *nothing* in them; — a man is a *male*factor to the world who writes such! *They* are the avoidable kind! — Had Johnson left nothing but his *Dictionary*, one might have traced there a great intellect, a genuine man. Looking to its clearness of definition, its general solidity, honesty, insight and successful method, it may be called the best of all Dictionaries. There is in it a kind of architectural nobleness; it stands there like a great solid square-built edifice, finished, symmetrically complete: you judge that a true Builder did it.

One word, in spite of our haste, must be granted to poor Bozzy. He passes for a mean, inflated, gluttonous creature; and was so in many senses.

Yet the fact of his reverence for Johnson will ever remain noteworthy. The foolish conceited Scotch Laird, the most conceited man of his time, approaching in such awestruck attitude the great dusty irascible Pedagogue in his mean garret there: it is a genuine reverence for Excellence; a *worship* for Heroes, at a time when neither Heroes nor worship were surmised to exist. Heroes, it would seem, exist always, and a certain worship of them! We will also take the liberty to deny altogether that of the witty Frenchman, That no man is a Hero to his valet-de-chambre. Or if so, it is not the Hero's blame, but the Valet's: that his soul, namely, is a mean *valet*-soul! He expects his Hero to advance in royal stage-trappings, with measured step, trains borne behind him, trumpets sounding before him. It should stand rather, No man can be a *Grand-Monarque* to his valet-de-chambre. Strip your Louis Quatorze of his king-gear, and there *is* left nothing but a poor forked radish with a head fantastically carved; — admirable to no valet. The Valet does not know a Hero when he sees him! Alas, no: it requires a kind of *Hero* to do that; — and one of the world's wants, in *this* as in other senses, is for most part want of such.

On the whole, shall we not say, that Boswell's admiration was well bestowed; that he could have found no soul in all England so worthy of bending down before? Shall we not say, of this great mournful Johnson too, that he guided his difficult confused existence wisely; led it *well*, like a right valiant man? That waste chaos of Authorship by Trade; that waste chaos of Scepticism in religion and politics, in life-theory and life-practice; in his poverty, in his dust and dimness, with the sick body and the rusty coat: he made it do for him, like a brave man. Not wholly without a loadstar in the Eternal; he had still a loadstar, as the brave all need to have: with his eye set on that, he would change his course for nothing in these confused vortices of the lower sea of Time. 'To the Spirit of Lies, bearing death and hunger, he would in no wise strike his flag.' Brave old Samuel: *ultimus Romanorum!*

Of Rousseau and his Heroism I cannot say so much. He is not what I call a strong man. A morbid, excitable, spasmodic man; at best, intense rather than strong. He had not 'the talent of Silence,' an invaluable talent; which few Frenchmen, or indeed men of any sort in these times, excel in! The suffering man ought really 'to consume his own smoke;' there is no good in emitting *smoke* till you have made it into *fire*, — which, in the metaphorical sense too, all smoke is capable of becoming! Rousseau has not depth or width, not calm force for difficulty; the first characteristic of true greatness. A fundamental mistake to call vehemence and rigidity strength! A man is not strong who takes convulsion-fits; though six men cannot hold him then.

He that can walk under the heaviest weight without staggering, he is the strong man. We need forever, especially in these loud-shrieking days, to remind ourselves of that. A man who cannot *hold his peace*, till the time come for speaking and acting, is no right man.

Poor Rousseau's face is to me expressive of him. A high, but narrow contracted intensity in it: bony brows; deep, strait-set eyes, in which there is something bewildered-looking, — bewildered, peering with lynx-eagerness. A face full of misery, even ignoble misery, and also of the antagonism against that; something mean, plebeian there, redeemed only by *intensity:* the face of what is called a Fanatic, — a sadly *contracted* Hero! We name him here because, with all his drawbacks, and they are many, he has the first and chief characteristic of a Hero: he is heartily *in earnest.* In earnest, if ever man was; as none of these French Philosophes were. Nay, one would say, of an earnestness too great for his otherwise sensitive, rather feeble nature; and which indeed in the end drove him into the strangest incoherences, almost delirations. There had come, at last, to be a kind of madness in him: his Ideas *possessed* him like demons; hurried him so about, drove him over steep places! —

The fault and misery of Rousseau was what we easily name by a single word, *Egoism;* which is indeed the source and summary of all faults and miseries whatsoever. He had not perfected himself into victory over mere Desire; a mean Hunger, in many sorts, was still the motive principle of him. I am afraid he was a very vain man; hungry for the praises of men. You remember Genlis's experience of him. She took Jean Jacques to the Theatre; he bargaining for a strict incognito, — "*He* would not be seen there for the world!" The curtain did happen nevertheless to be drawn aside: the Pit recognised Jean Jacques, but took no great notice of him! He expressed the bitterest indignation; gloomed all evening, spake no other than surly words. The glib Countess remained entirely convinced that his anger was not at being seen, but at not being applauded when seen. How the whole nature of the man is poisoned; nothing but suspicion, self-isolation, fierce moody ways! He could not live with anybody. A man of some rank from the country, who visited him often, and used to sit with him, expressing all reverence and affection for him, comes one day; finds Jean Jacques full of the sourest unintelligible humour. "Monsieur," said Jean Jacques, with flaming eyes, "I know why you come here. You come to see what a poor life I lead; how little is in my poor pot that is boiling there. Well, look into the pot! There is half a pound of meat, one carrot and three onions; that is all: go and tell the whole world that, if you like, Monsieur!" — A man of this sort was far gone. The whole world got itself supplied with anecdotes, for light laughter, for a certain theatrical interest, from these perversions and contorsions of poor Jean Jacques. Alas, to him they were not laughing or theatrical; too real to him! The contorsions of a dying gladiator: the crowded amphitheatre looks on with entertainment; but the gladiator is in agonies and dying.

And yet this Rousseau, as we say, with his passionate appeals to Mothers, with his *Contrat-social*, with his celebrations of Nature, even of savage life in Nature, did once more touch upon Reality, struggle towards Reality; was doing the function of a Prophet to his Time. As *he* could, and as the Time could! Strangely through all that defacement, degradation and almost madness, there is in the inmost heart of poor Rousseau a spark of real heavenly fire. Once more, out of the element of that withered mocking Philosophism, Scepticism, and Persiflage, there has arisen in this man the ineradicable feeling and knowledge that this Life of ours is *true;* not a Scepticism, Theorem, or Persiflage, but a Fact, an awful Reality. Nature had made that revelation to him; had ordered him to speak it out. He got it spoken out; if not well and clearly, then ill and dimly, — as clearly as he could. Nay what are all errors and perversities of his, even those stealings of ribbons, aimless confused miseries and vagabondisms, if we will interpret them kindly, but the blinkard dazzlement and staggerings to and fro of a man sent on an errand he is too weak for, by a path he cannot yet find? Men are led by strange ways. One should have tolerance for a man, hope of him; leave him to try yet what he will do. While life lasts, hope lasts for every man.

Of Rousseau's literary talents, greatly celebrated still among his countrymen, I do not say much. His Books, like himself, are what I call unhealthy; not the good sort of Books. There is a sensuality in Rousseau. Combined with such an intellectual gift as his, it makes pictures of a certain gorgeous attractiveness: but they are not genuinely poetical. Not white sunlight: something *operatic;* a kind of rosepink, artificial bedizenment. It is frequent, or rather it is universal, among the French since his time. Madame de Staël has something of it; St. Pierre; and down onwards to the present astonishing convulsionary 'Literature of Desperation,' it is everywhere abundant. That same *rosepink* is not the right hue. Look at a Shakspeare, at a Goethe, even at a Walter Scott! He who has once seen into this, has seen the difference of the True from the Sham-True, and will discriminate them ever afterwards.

We had to observe in Johnson how much good a Prophet, under all disadvantages and disorganisations, can accomplish for the world. In Rousseau we are called to look rather at the fearful amount of evil which, under such disorganisation, may accompany the good. Historically it is a most pregnant spectacle, that of Rousseau. Banished into Paris garrets, in the gloomy company of his own Thoughts and Necessities there; driven from post to pillar; fretted, exasperated till the heart of him went mad, he had grown to feel deeply that the world was not his friend nor the world's law. It was expedient, if any way possible, that such a man should *not* have been set in flat hostility with the world. He could be cooped into garrets, laughed at as a maniac, left to starve like a wild beast in his cage; — but he could not be hindered from setting the world on fire. The French Revolution found its Evangelist in Rousseau. His semi-delirious speculations on the miseries of civilised life, the preferability of the savage to the civilised, and such like, helped well to produce a whole delirium in France generally. True, you may well ask, What could the world, the governors of the world, do with such a man? Difficult to say what the governors of the world could do with him! What he could do with them is unhappily clear enough, — *guillotine* a great many of them! Enough now of Rousseau.

It was a curious phenomenon, in the withered, unbelieving, secondhand Eighteenth Century, that of a Hero starting up, among the artificial pasteboard figures and productions, in the guise of a Robert Burns. Like a little well in the rocky desert places, — like a sudden splendour of Heaven in the artificial Vauxhall! People knew not what to make of it. They took it for a piece of the Vauxhall fire-work; alas, it *let* itself be so taken, though struggling half-blindly, as in bitterness of death, against that! Perhaps no man had such a false reception from his fellow-men. Once more a very wasteful life-drama was enacted under the sun.

The tragedy of Burns's life is known to all of you. Surely we may say, if discrepancy between place held and place merited constitute perverseness of lot for a man, no lot could be more perverse than Burns's. Among those secondhand acting-figures, *mimes* for most part, of the Eighteenth Century, once more a giant Original Man; one of those men who reach down to the perennial Deeps, who take rank with the Heroic among men: and he was born in a poor Ayrshire hut. The largest soul of all the British lands came among us in the shape of a hard-handed Scottish Peasant. — His Father, a poor toiling man, tried various things; did not succeed in any; was involved in continual difficulties. The Steward, Factor as the Scotch call him, used to send letters and threatenings, Burns says, 'which threw us all into tears.' The brave hard-toiling, hard-suffering Father, his brave heroine of a wife; and those children, of whom Robert was one! In this Earth, so wide otherwise, no shelter for *them*. The letters 'threw us all into tears:' figure it. The brave Father, I say always; — a *silent* Hero and Poet; without whom the son had never been a speaking one! Burns's Schoolmaster came afterwards to London, learnt what good society was; but declares that in no meeting of men did he ever enjoy better discourse than at the hearth of this peasant. And his poor 'seven acres of nursery-ground,' nor the miserable patch of clay-farm, nor anything he tried to get a living by, would prosper with him; he had a sore unequal battle all his days. But he stood to it valiantly; a wise, faithful, unconquerable man; — swallowing down how many sore sufferings daily into silence; fighting like an unseen Hero, — nobody publishing newspaper-paragraphs about his nobleness; voting pieces of plate to him! However, he was not lost; nothing is lost. Robert is there; the outcome of him, — and indeed of many generations of such as him.

This Burns appeared under every disadvantage: uninstructed, poor, born only to hard manual toil; and writing, when it came to that, in a rustic special dialect, known only to a small province of the country he lived in. Had he written, even what he did write, in the general language of England, I doubt not he had already become universally recognised as being, or capable to be, one of our greatest men. That he should have tempted so many to penetrate through the rough husk of that dialect of his, is proof that there lay something far from common within it. He has gained a certain recognition, and is continuing to do so over all quarters of our wide Saxon world: wheresoever a Saxon dialect is spoken, it begins to be understood, by personal inspection of this and the other, that one of the most considerable Saxon men of the Eighteenth century was an Ayrshire Peasant named Robert Burns. Yes, I will say, here too was a piece of the right Saxon stuff: strong as the Harz-rock, rooted in the depths of the world; — rock, yet with wells of living softness in it! A wild impetuous whirlwind in passion and faculty slumbered quiet there; such heavenly *melody* dwelling in the heart of it. A noble rough genuineness; homely, rustic, honest; true simplicity of strength; with its lightning-fire, with its soft dewy pity; — like the old Norse Thor, the Peasant-god! —

Burns's Brother Gilbert, a man of much sense and worth, has told me that Robert, in his young days, in spite of their hardship, was usually the gayest of speech; a fellow of infinite frolic, laughter, sense, and heart; far pleasanter to hear there, stript cutting peats in the bog, or such like, than he ever afterwards knew him. I can well believe it. This basis of mirth (*'fond gaillard,'* as old Marquis Mirabeau calls it), a primal-element of sunshine and joyfulness, coupled with his other deep and earnest qualities, is one of the most attractive characteristics of Burns. A large fund of Hope dwells in him; spite of his tragical history, he is not a mourning man. He shakes his sorrows gallantly aside; bounds forth victorious over them. It is as the lion shaking 'dew-drops from his mane;' as the swift-bounding horse, that *laughs* at the shaking of the spear. — But indeed, Hope, Mirth, of the sort like Burns's, are they not the outcome properly of warm generous affection, — such as is the beginning of all to every man?

You would think it strange if I called Burns the most gifted British soul we had in all that century of his: and yet I believe the day is coming when there will be little danger in saying so. His writings, all that he *did* under such obstructions, are only a poor fragment of him. Professor Stewart remarked very justly, what indeed is true of all Poets good for much, that his poetry was not any particular faculty; but the general result of a naturally vigorous original mind expressing itself in that way. Burns's gifts, expressed in conversation, are the theme of all that ever heard him. All kinds of gifts: from the gracefulest utterances of courtesy, to the highest fire of passionate speech; loud floods of mirth, soft wailings of affection, laconic emphasis, clear piercing insight: all was in him. Witty duchesses celebrate him as a man whose speech 'led them off their feet.' This is beautiful: but still more beautiful that which Mr. Lockhart has recorded, which I have more than once alluded to, How the waiters and ostlers at inns would get out of bed, and come crowding to hear this man speak! Waiters and ostlers: — they too were men, and here was a man! I have heard much about his speech; but one of the best things I ever heard of it was, last year, from a venerable gentleman long familiar with him, That it was speech distinguished by always *having something in it*. "He spoke rather little than much," this old man told me; "sat rather silent in those early days, as in the company of persons above him; and always when he did speak, it was to throw new light on the matter." I know not why any one should ever speak otherwise! — But if we look at his general force of soul, his healthy *robustness* every way, the rugged downrightness, penetration, generous valour and manfulness that was in him, — where shall we readily find a better gifted man?

Among the great men of the Eighteenth Century, I sometimes feel as if Burns might be found to resemble Mirabeau more than any other. They differ widely in vesture; yet look at them intrinsically. There is the same burly thicknecked strength of body as of soul; — built, in both cases, on what the old Marquis calls a *fond gaillard*. By nature, by course of breeding, indeed by nation, Mirabeau has much more of bluster; a noisy, forward, unresting man. But the characteristic of Mirabeau too is veracity and sense, power of true *insight*, superiority of vision. The thing that he says is worth remembering. It is a flash of insight into some object or other: so do both these men speak. The same raging passions; capable too in both of manifesting themselves as the tenderest noble affections. Wit, wild laughter, energy, directness, sincerity: these were in both. The types of the two men were not dissimilar. Burns too could have governed, debated in National Assemblies; politicised, as few could. Alas, the courage which had to exhibit itself in capture of smuggling schooners in the Solway Frith; in keeping *silence* over so much, where no good speech, but only inarticulate rage was possible: this might have bellowed forth Ushers de Brézé and the like; and made itself visible to all men, in managing of kingdoms, in ruling of great ever-memorable epochs! But they said to him reprovingly, his Official Superiors said, and wrote: 'You are to work, not think.' Of your *thinking-*faculty, the greatest in this land, we have no need; you are to gauge beer there; for that only are *you* wanted. Very notable; — and worth mentioning, though we know what is to be said and answered! As if Thought, Power of Thinking, were not, at all times, in all places and situations of the world, precisely the thing that *was* wanted. The fatal man, is he not always the *un*thinking man, the man who cannot think and *see;* but only grope, and hallucinate, and *mis*see the nature of the thing he works with? He missees it, mis*takes* it, as we say; takes it for one thing, and it *is* another thing, — and leaves him standing like a Futility there! He is the fatal man; unutterably fatal, put in the high places of men. — Why complain of this? say some. Strength is mournfully denied its arena; that was true from of old. Doubtless; and the worse for the *arena*, say I! *Complaining* profits little; stating of the truth may profit. That a Europe, with its French Revolution just breaking out, finds no need of a Burns except for gauging beer, — is a thing I, for one, cannot *rejoice* at! —

Once more we have to say here that the chief quality of Burns is the *sincerity* of him. So in his Poetry, in his Life. The Song he sings is not of fantasticalities; it is of a thing felt, really there; the prime merit of this, as of all in him, and of his Life generally, is truth. The Life of Burns is what we may call a great tragic sincerity. A sort of savage sincerity, — not cruel, far from that; but wild, wrestling naked with the truth of things. In that sense, there is something of the savage in all great men.

Hero-worship, — Odin, Burns? Well; these Men of Letters too were not without a kind of Hero-worship: but what a strange condition has that got into now! The waiters and ostlers of Scotch inns, prying about the door, eager to catch any word that fell from Burns, were doing unconscious reverence to the Heroic. Johnson had his Boswell for worshipper. Rousseau had worshippers enough; princes calling on him in his mean garret; the great, the beautiful doing reverence to the poor moonstruck man. For himself a most portentous contradiction; the two ends of his life not to be brought into harmony. He sits at the tables of grandees; and has to copy music for his own living. He cannot even get his music copied: "By dint of dining out," says he, "I run the risk of dying by starvation at home." For his worshippers too a most questionable thing! If doing Hero-worship well or badly be the test of vital wellbeing or illbeing to a generation, can we say that *these* generations are very first-rate? — And yet our heroic Men of Letters do teach, govern, are kings, priests, or what you like to call them; intrinsically there is no preventing it by any means whatever. The world *has* to obey him who thinks and sees in the world. The world can alter the manner of that; can either have it as blessed continuous summer-sunshine, or as unblessed black thunder and tornado, — with unspeakable difference of profit for the world! The manner of it is very alterable; the matter and fact of it not, by any power under the sky. Light; or, failing that, lightning: the world can take its choice. Not whether we call an Odin god, prophet, priest or what we call him; but whether we believe the word he tells us: there it all lies. If it be a true word, we shall have to believe it; believing it, we shall have to do it. What *name* or welcome we give him or it, is a point that concerns ourselves mainly. *It*, the new Truth, new deeper revealing of the Secret of this Universe, is verily of the nature of a message from on high; and must and will have itself obeyed. ——

My last remark is on that notablest phasis of Burns's history his visit to Edinburgh. Often it seems to me as if his demeanour there were the highest proof he gave of what a fund of worth and genuine manhood was in him. If we think of it, few heavier burdens could be laid on the strength of a man. So sudden; all common *Lionism*, which ruins innumerable men, was as nothing to this. It is as if Napoleon had been made a King of, not gradually, but at once from the Artillery Lieutenancy in the Regiment La Fère. Burns, still only in his twenty-seventh year, is no longer even a ploughman; he is flying to the West Indies to escape disgrace and a jail. This month he is a ruined peasant, his wages seven pounds a year, and these gone from him: next month he is in the blaze of rank and beauty, handing down jewelled Duchesses to dinner; the cynosure of all eyes! Adversity is sometimes hard upon a man; but for one man who can stand prosperity, there are a hundred that will stand adversity. I admire much the way in which Burns met all this. Perhaps no man one could point out, was ever so sorely tried, and so little forgot himself. Tranquil, unastonished; not abashed, not inflated, neither awkwardness nor affectation: he feels that *he* there is the man Robert Burns; that the 'rank is but the guinea-stamp;' that the celebrity is but the candle-light, which will shew *what* man, not in the least make him a better or other man! Alas, it may readily, unless he look to it, make him a *worse* man; a wretched inflated windbag, — inflated till he *burst* and become a dead lion; for whom, as some one has said, 'there is no resurrection of the body:' worse than a living dog! — Burns is admirable here.

And yet, alas, as I have observed elsewhere, these Lion-hunters were the ruin and death of Burns. It was they that rendered it impossible for him to live! They gathered round him in his Farm; hindered his industry; no place was remote enough from them. He could not get his Lionism forgotten, honestly as he was disposed to do so. He falls into discontents, into miseries, faults; the world getting ever more desolate for him; health, character, peace of mind, all gone; — solitary enough now. It is tragical to think of! These men came but to *see* him; it was out of no sympathy with him, nor no hatred to him. They came to get a little amusement: they got their amusement; — and the Hero's life went for it!

Richter says, in the Island of Sumatra there is a kind of 'Light-chafers,' large Fire-flies, which people stick upon spits, and illuminate the ways with at night. Persons of condition can thus travel with a pleasant radiance, which they much admire. Great honour to the Fire-flies! But — ! —

The Hero as King. Cromwell, Napoleon: Modern Revolutionism.

WE come now to the last form of Heroism; that which we call Kingship. The Commander over Men; he to whose will our wills are to be subordinated, and loyally surrender themselves, and find their welfare in doing so, may be reckoned the most important of Great Men. He is practically the *summary* for us of *all* the various figures of Heroism; Priest, Teacher, whatsoever of earthly or of spiritual dignity we can fancy to reside in a man, embodies itself here, to *command* over us, furnish us with constant practical teaching, tell us for the day and hour what we are to *do*. He is called *Rex*, Regulator, *Roi:* our own name is still better; King, *Könning*, which means *Can*-ning, Able-man.

Numerous considerations, pointing towards deep, questionable, and indeed unfathomable regions, present themselves here: on the most of which we must resolutely for the present forbear to speak at all. As Burke said that perhaps fair *Trial by Jury* was the soul of Government, and that all legislation, administration, parliamentary debating, and the rest of it, went on, in order 'to bring twelve impartial men into a jury-box;' — so, by much stronger reason, may I say here, that the finding of your *Able-man*, and getting him invested with the *symbols of ability*, with dignity, worship (*worth*-ship), royalty, kinghood, or whatever we call it, so that *he* may actually have room to guide according to his faculty of doing it, — is the business, well or ill accomplished, of all social procedure whatsoever in this world! Hustings-speeches, Parliamentary motions, Reform Bills, French Revolutions, all mean at heart this; or else nothing. Find in any country the Ablest Man that exists there; raise *him* to the supreme place, and loyally reverence him: you have a perfect government for that country; no ballot-box, parliamentary eloquence, voting, constitution-building, or other machinery whatsoever can improve it a whit. It is in the perfect state; an ideal country. The Ablest Man; he means also the truest-hearted, justest, the Noblest Man: what he *tells us to do* must be precisely the wisest, fittest, that we could anywhere or anyhow learn; — the thing which it will in all ways behove us, with right loyal thankfulness, and nothing doubting, to do! Our *doing* and life were then, so far as government could regulate it, well regulated; that were the ideal of constitutions.

Alas, we know very well that Ideals can never be completely embodied in practice. Ideals must ever lie a very great way off; and we will right thankfully content ourselves with any not intolerable approximation thereto! Let no man, as Schiller says, too querulously 'measure by a scale of perfection the meagre product of reality' in this poor world of ours. We will esteem him no wise man; we will esteem him a sickly, discontented, foolish man. And yet, on the other hand, it is never to be forgotten that Ideals do exist; that if they be not approximated to at all, the whole matter goes to wreck! Infallibly. No bricklayer builds a wall *perfectly* perpendicular, mathematically this is not possible; a certain degree of perpendicularity suffices him; and he, like a good bricklayer, who must have done with his job, leaves it so. And yet if he sway *too much* from the perpendicular; above all, if he throw plummet and level quite away from him, and pile brick on brick heedless, just as it comes to hand — ! Such bricklayer, I think, is in a bad way. *He* has forgotten himself: but the Law of Gravitation does not forget to act on him; he and his wall rush down into confused welter of ruin! —

This is the history of all rebellions, French Revolutions, social explosions in ancient or modern times. You have put the too *Un*able Man at the head of affairs! The too ignoble, unvaliant, fatuous man. You have forgotten that there is any rule, or natural necessity whatever, of putting the Able Man there. Brick must lie on brick as it may and can. Unable Simulacrum of Ability, *quack*, in a word, must adjust himself with quack, in all manner of administration of human things; — which accordingly lie unadministered, fermenting into unmeasured masses of failure, of indigent misery: in the outward, and in the inward or spiritual, miserable millions stretch out the hand for their due supply, and *it* is not there. The 'law of gravitation' acts; Nature's laws do none of them forget to act. The miserable millions burst forth into Sansculottism, or some other sort of madness: bricks and bricklayer lie as a fatal chaos! —

Much sorry stuff, written some hundred years ago or more, about the 'Divine right of Kings,' moulders unread now in the Public Libraries of this country. Far be it from us to disturb the calm process by which it is disappearing harmlessly from the earth, in those repositories! At the same time, not to let the immense rubbish go without leaving us, as it ought, some soul of it behind, — I will say that it did mean something; something true, which it is important for us and all men to keep in mind. To assert that in whatever man you chose to lay hold of (by this or the other plan of clutching at him); and clapt a round piece of metal on the head of, and called King, — there straightway came to reside a divine virtue, so that *he* became a kind of god, and a Divinity inspired him with faculty and right to rule over you to all lengths: this, — what can we do with this but leave it to rot silently in the Public Libraries? But I will say withal, and that is what these Divine-right men meant, That in Kings, and in all human Authorities, and relations that men god-created can form among each other, there is verily either a Divine Right or else a Diabolic Wrong; one or the other of these two! For it is false altogether, what the last Sceptical Century taught us, that this world is a steamengine. There is a God in this world; and a God's-sanction, or else the violation of such, does look out from all ruling and obedience, from all moral acts of men. There is no act more moral between men than that of rule and obedience. Wo to him that claims obedience when it is not due; wo to him that refuses it when it is! God's law is in that, I say, however the Parchment-laws may run: there is a Divine Right or else a Diabolic Wrong at the heart of every claim that one man makes upon another.

It can do none of us harm to reflect on this: in all the relations of life it will concern us; in Loyalty and Royalty, the highest of these. I esteem the modern error, That all goes by self-interest and the checking and balancing of greedy knaveries, and that in short there is nothing divine whatever in the association of men, a still more despicable error, natural as it is to an unbelieving century, than that of a 'divine right' in people *called* Kings. I say, Find me the true *Könning*, King, or Able-man, and he *has* a divine right over me. That we knew in some tolerable measure how to find him, and that all men were ready to acknowledge his divine right when found: this is precisely the healing which a sick world is everywhere, in these ages, seeking after! The true King, as guide of the practical, has ever something of the Pontiff in him, — guide of the spiritual, from which all practice has its rise. This too is a true saying, That the *King* is head of the *Church*. — But we will leave the Polemic stuff of a dead century to lie quiet on its book-shelves.

Certainly it is a fearful business, that of having your Able-man to *seek*, and not knowing in what manner to proceed about it! That is the world's sad predicament in these times of ours. They are times of revolution, and have long been. The bricklayer with his bricks, no longer heedful of plummet or the law of gravitation, have toppled, tumbled, and it all welters as we see! But the beginning of it was not the French Revolution; that is rather the *end*, we can hope. It were truer to say, the *beginning* was three centuries farther back: in the Reformation of Luther. That the thing which still called itself Christian Church had become a Falsehood, and brazenly went about pretending to pardon men's sins for metallic coined money, and to do much else which in the everlasting truth of Nature it did *not* now do: here lay the vital malady. The inward being wrong, all outward went ever more and more wrong. Belief died away; all was Doubt, Disbelief. The builder *cast away* his plummet; said to himself, "What is gravitation? Brick lies on brick there!" Alas, does it not still sound strange to many of us, the assertion that there *is* a God's-truth in the business of god-created men; that all is not a kind of grimace, an 'expediency,' diplomacy, one knows not what! —

From that first necessary assertion of Luther's, "You, self-styled *Papa*, you are no Father in God at all; you are a Chimera, whom I know not how to name in polite language!" — from that onwards to the shout which rose round Camille Desmoulins in the Palais Royal, "*Aux armes!*" when the people had burst up against *all* manner of Chimeras, — I find a natural historical sequence. That shout too, so frightful, half-infernal, was a great matter. Once more the voice of awakened nations; — starting confusedly, as out of nightmare, as out of death-sleep, into some dim feeling that Life was real; that God's-world was not an expediency and diplomacy! Infernal; — yes, since they would not have it otherwise. Infernal, since not celestial or terrestrial! Hollowness, insincerity *has* to cease; sincerity of some sort has to begin. Cost what it may, reigns of terror, horrors of French Revolution or what else, we have to return to truth. Here is a Truth, as I said: a Truth clad in hellfire, since they would not but have it so! —

A common theory among considerable parties of men in England and elsewhere used to be, that the French Nation had, in those days, as it were gone *mad;* that the French Revolution was a general act of insanity, a temporary conversion of France and large sections of the world into a kind of Bedlam. The Event had risen and raged; but was a madness and nonentity, — gone now happily into the region of Dreams and the Picturesque! — To such comfortable philosophers, the Three Days of July, 1830, must have been a surprising phenomenon. Here is the French Nation risen again, in musketry and death-struggle, out shooting and being shot, to make that same mad French Revolution good! The sons and grandsons of those men, it would seem, persist in the enterprise: they do not disown it; they will have it made good; will have themselves shot, if it be not made good! To philosophers who had made up their life-system on that madness-quietus, no phenomenon could be more alarming. Poor Niebuhr, they say, the Prussian Professor and Historian, fell broken-hearted in consequence; sickened, if we can believe it, and died of the Three Days! It was surely not a very heroic death; — little better than Racine's, dying because Louis Fourteenth looked sternly on him once. The world had stood some considerable shocks in its time; might have been expected to survive the Three Days too, and be found turning on its axis after even them! The Three Days told all mortals that the old French Revolution, mad as it might look, was not a transitory ebullition of Bedlam, but a genuine product of this Earth where we all live; that it was verily a Fact, and the world in general would do well everywhere to regard it as such.

Truly, without the French Revolution, one would not know what to make of an age like this at all. We will hail the French Revolution, as shipwrecked mariners might the sternest rock, in a world otherwise all of baseless sea and waves. A true Apocalypse, though a terrible one, to this false withered artificial time; testifying once more that Nature is *preter*natural, if not divine, then diabolic; that Semblance is not Reality; that it has to become Reality, or the world will take fire under it, — burn *it* into what it is, namely Nothing! Plausibility has ended; empty Routine has ended; much has ended. This, as with a Trump of Doom, has been proclaimed to all men. They are the wisest who will learn it soonest. Long confused generations before it be learned; peace impossible till it be! The earnest man, surrounded, as ever, with a world of inconsistencies, can await patiently, patiently strive to do *his* work, in the midst of that. Sentence of Death is written down in Heaven against all that; sentence of Death is now proclaimed on the Earth against it: this he with his eyes may see. And surely, I should say, considering the other side of the matter, what enormous difficulties lie there, and how fast, fearfully fast, in all countries, the inexorable demand for solution of them is pressing on, — he may easily find other work to do than labouring in the Sansculottic province at this time of day!

To me, in these circumstances, that of 'Hero-worship' becomes a fact inexpressibly precious; the most solacing fact one sees in the world at present. There is an everlasting hope in it for the management of the world. Had all traditions, arrangements, creeds, societies that men ever instituted, sunk away, this would remain. The certainty of Heroes being sent us; our faculty, our necessity, to reverence Heroes when sent: it shines like a polestar through smoke-clouds, dustclouds, and all manner of down-rushing and conflagration.

Hero-worship would have sounded very strange to those workers and fighters in the French Revolution. Not reverence for Great Men; not any hope, or belief, or even wish, that Great Men could again appear in the world! Nature, turned into a 'Machine,' was as if effete now; could not any longer produce Great Men: — I can tell her, she may give up the trade altogether, then; we cannot do without Great Men! — But neither have I any quarrel with that of 'Liberty and Equality;' with the faith that, wise great men being impossible, a level immensity of foolish small men would suffice. It was a natural faith then and there. "Liberty and Equality; no Authority needed any longer. Hero-worship, reverence for *such* Authorities, has proved false, is itself a falsehood; no more of it! We have had such *forgeries*, we will now trust nothing. So many base plated coins passing in the market, the belief has now become common that no gold any longer exists, —and even that we can do very well without gold!"—I find this, among other things, in that universal cry of Liberty and Equality; and find it very natural, as matters then stood.

And yet surely it is but the *transition* from false to true. Considered as the whole truth, it is false altogether;—the product of entire sceptical blindness, as yet only *struggling* to see. Hero-worship exists forever, and everywhere: not Loyalty alone; it extends from divine adoration down to the lowest practical regions of life. 'Bending before men,' if it is not to be a mere empty grimace, better dispensed with than practised, is Hero-worship; a recognition that there does dwell in that presence of our brother something divine; that every created man, as Novalis said, is a 'revelation in the Flesh.' They were Poets too, that devised all those graceful courtesies which make life noble! Courtesy is not a falsehood or grimace; it need not be such. And Loyalty, religious Worship itself, are still possible; nay still inevitable.

May we not say, moreover, while so many of our late Heroes have worked rather as revolutionary men, that nevertheless every Great Man, every genuine man, is by the nature of him a son of Order, not of Disorder? It is a tragical position for a true man to work in revolutions. He seems an anarchist; and indeed a painful element of anarchy does encumber him at every step,—him to whose whole soul anarchy is hostile, hateful. His mission is Order; every man's is. He is here to make what was disorderly, chaotic, into a thing ruled, regular. He is the missionary of Order. Is not all work of man in this world a *making of Order?* The carpenter finds rough trees; shapes them, constrains them into square fitness, into purpose and use. We are all born enemies of Disorder: it is tragical for us all to be concerned in image-breaking and down-pulling; for the Great Man, *more* a man than we, it is doubly tragical.

Thus too all human things, maddest French Sansculottisms, do and must work towards Order. I say, there is not a *man* in them, raging in the thickest of the madness, but is impelled withal, at all moments, towards Order. His very life means that; Disorder is dissolution, death. No chaos but it seeks a *centre* to revolve round. While man is man, some Cromwell or Napoleon is the necessary finish of a Sansculottism.—Curious: in those days when Hero-worship was the most incredible thing to every one, how it does come out nevertheless, and assert itself practically, in a way which all have to credit. Divine *right*, take it on the great scale, is found to mean divine *might* withal! While old false Formulas are getting trampled everywhere into destruction, new genuine Substances unexpectedly unfold themselves indestructible. In rebellious ages, when Kingship itself seems dead and abolished, Cromwell, Napoleon step forth again as Kings. The history of these men is what we have now to look at, as our last phasis of Heroism. The old ages are brought back to us; the manner in which Kings were made, and Kingship itself first took rise, is again exhibited in the history of these Two.

We have had many civil-wars in England; wars of Red and White Roses, wars of Simon de Montfort; wars enough, which are not very memorable. But that war of the Puritans has a significance which belongs to no one of the others. Trusting to your candour, which will suggest on the other side what I have not room to say, I will call it a section once more of that great universal war which alone makes up the true History of the World, — the war of Belief against Unbelief! The struggle of men intent on the real essence of things, against men intent on the semblances and forms of things. The Puritans, to many, seem mere savage Iconoclasts, fierce destroyers of Forms; but it were more just to call them haters of *untrue* Forms. I hope we know how to respect Laud and his King as well as them. Poor Laud seems to me to have been weak and ill-starred, not dishonest; an unfortunate Pedant rather than anything worse. His 'Dreams' and superstitions, at which they laugh so, have an affectionate, loveable kind of character. He is like a College-Tutor, whose whole world is forms, College-rules; whose notion is that these are the life and safety of the world. He is placed suddenly, with that unalterable luckless notion of his, at the head not of a College but of a Nation, to regulate the most complex deep-reaching interests of men. He thinks they ought to go by the old decent regulations; nay that their salvation will lie in extending and improving these. Like a weak man, he drives with spasmodic vehemence towards his purpose; cramps himself to it, heeding no voice of prudence, no cry of pity: He will have his College-rules obeyed by his Collegians; that first; and till that, nothing. He is an ill-starred Pedant, as I said. He would have it the world was a College of that kind, and the world *was not* that. Alas, was not his doom stern enough? Whatever wrongs he did, were they not all frightfully avenged on him?

It is meritorious to insist on forms; Religion and all else naturally clothes itself in forms. Everywhere the *formed* world is the only habitable one. The naked formlessness of Puritanism is not the thing I praise in the Puritans; it is the thing I pity, — praising only the spirit which had rendered that inevitable! All substances clothe themselves in forms: but there are suitable true forms, and then there are untrue unsuitable. As the briefest definition, one might say, Forms which *grow* round a substance, if we rightly understand that, will correspond to the real nature and purport of it, will be true, good; forms which are consciously *put* round a substance, bad. I invite you to reflect on this. It distinguishes true from false in Ceremonial Form, earnest solemnity from empty pageant, in all human things.

There must be a veracity, a natural spontaneity in forms. In the commonest meeting of men, a person making, what we call, 'set speeches,' is not he an offence? In the mere drawing-room, whatsoever courtesies you see to be grimaces, prompted by no spontaneous reality within, are a thing you wish to get away from. But suppose now it were some matter of vital concernment, some transcendent matter (as Divine Worship is), about which your whole soul, struck dumb with its excess of feeling, knew not how to *form* itself into utterance at all, and preferred formless silence to any utterance there possible, — what should we say of a man coming forward to represent or utter it for you in the way of upholsterer-mummery? Such a man, — let him depart swiftly, if he love himself! You have lost your only son; are mute, struck down, without even tears: an importunate man importunately offers to celebrate Funeral Games for him in the manner of the Greeks! Such mummery is not only not to be accepted; it is hateful, unendurable. It is what the old Prophets called 'Idolatry,' worshipping of hollow *shows;* what all earnest men do and will reject. We can partly understand what those poor Puritans meant. Laud dedicating that St. Catherine Creed's Church, in the manner we have it described; with his multiplied ceremonial bowings, gesticulations, exclamations: surely it is rather the rigorous formal *Pedant,* intent on his 'College-rules,' than the earnest Prophet, intent on the essence of the matter!

Puritanism found *such* forms insupportable; trampled on such forms; — we have to excuse it for saying, No form at all rather than such! It stood preaching in its bare pulpit, with nothing but the Bible in its hand. Nay, a man preaching from his earnest *soul* into the earnest *souls* of men: is not this virtually the essence of all Churches whatsoever? The nakedest, savagest reality, I say, is preferable to any semblance, however dignified. Besides, it will clothe itself with *due* semblance by and by, if it be real. No fear of that; actually no fear at all. Given the living *man,* there will be found *clothes* for him; he will find himself clothes. But the suit-of-clothes pretending that *it* is both clothes and man — ! We cannot 'fight the French' by three hundred thousand red uniforms; there must be *men* in the inside of them! Semblance, I assert, must actually *not* divorce itself from Reality. If Semblance do, — why then there must be men found to rebel against Semblance, for it has become a lie! These two Antagonisms at war here, in the case of Laud and the Puritans, are as old nearly as the world. They went to fierce battle over England in that age; and fought out their confused controversy to a certain length, with many results for all of us.

In the age which directly followed that of the Puritans, their cause or themselves were little likely to have justice done them. Charles Second and his Rochesters were not the kind of men you would set to judge what the worth or meaning of such men might have been. That there could be any faith or truth in the life of a man, was what these poor Rochesters, and the age they ushered in, had forgotten. Puritanism was hung on gibbets, — like the bones of the leading Puritans. Its work nevertheless went on accomplishing itself. All true work of a man, hang the author of it on what gibbet you like, must and will accomplish itself. We have our *Habeas-Corpus*, our free Representation of the People; acknowledgment, wide as the world, that all men are, or else must, shall, and will become, what we call *free* men; — men with their life grounded on reality and justice, not on tradition, which has become unjust and a chimera! This in part, and much besides this, was the work of the Puritans.

And indeed, as these things became gradually manifest, the character of the Puritans began to clear itself. Their memories were, one after another, taken *down* from the gibbet; nay a certain portion of them are now, in these days, as good as canonized. Eliot, Hampden, Pym, nay Ludlow, Hutcheson, Vane himself, are admitted to be a kind of Heroes; political Conscript Fathers, to whom in no small degree we owe what makes us a free England: it would not be safe for anybody to designate these men as wicked. Few Puritans of note but find their apologists somewhere, and have a certain reverence paid them by earnest men. One Puritan, I think, and almost he alone, our poor Cromwell, seems to hang yet on the gibbet, and find no hearty apologist anywhere. Him neither saint nor sinner will acquit of great wickedness. A man of ability, infinite talent, courage, and so forth: but he betrayed the Cause! Selfish ambition, dishonesty, duplicity; a fierce, coarse, hypocritical *Tartuffe;* turning all that noble Struggle for constitutional Liberty into a sorry farce played for his own benefit: this and worse is the character they give of Cromwell. And then there come contrasts with Washington and others; above all, with these noble Pyms and Hampdens, whose noble work he stole for himself, and ruined into a futility and deformity.

This view of Cromwell seems to me the not unnatural product of a century like the Eighteenth. As we said of the Valet, so of the Sceptic: He does not know a Hero when he sees him! The Valet expected purple mantles, gilt sceptres, bodyguards and flourishes of trumpets: the Sceptic of the Eighteenth century looks for regulated respectable Formulas, 'Principles,' or what else he may call them; a style of speech and conduct which has got to seem 'respectable,' which can plead for itself in a handsome articulate manner, and gain the suffrages of an enlightened sceptical Eighteenth century! It is, at bottom, the same thing that both the Valet and he expect: the garnitures of some *acknowledged* royalty, which *then* they will acknowledge! The King coming to them in the rugged *un*formulistic state shall be no King.

For my own share, far be it from me to say or insinuate a word of disparagement against such characters as Hampden, Eliot, Pym; whom I believe to have been right worthy and useful men. I have read diligently what books and documents about them I could come at; — with the honestest wish to admire, to love, and worship them like Heroes; but I am sorry to say, if the real truth must be told, with very indifferent success! At bottom, I found that it would not do. They are very noble men these; step along in their stately way, with their measured euphuisms, philosophies, parliamentary eloquences, Ship-monies, *Monarchies of Man;* a most constitutional, unblameable, dignified set of men. But the heart remains cold before them; the fancy alone endeavours to get up some worship of them. What man's heart does, in reality, break forth into any fire of brotherly love for these men? They are become dreadfully dull men! One breaks down often enough in the constitutional eloquence of the admirable Pym, with his 'seventhly and lastly.' You find that it may be the admirablest thing in the world, but that it is heavy, — heavy as lead, barren as brick clay; that, in a word, for you there is little or nothing now surviving there! One leaves all these Nobilities standing in their niches of honour: the rugged outcast Cromwell, he is the man of them all, in whom one still finds human stuff. The great savage *Baresark:* he could write no euphuistic *Monarchy of Man;* did not speak, did not work with glib regularity; had no straight story to tell for himself anywhere. But he stood bare, not cased in euphuistic coat-of-mail; he grappled like a giant, face to face, heart to heart, with the naked truth of things! That, after all, is the sort of man for one. I plead guilty to valuing such a man beyond all other sorts of men. Smooth-shaven Respectabilities not a few one finds, that are not good for much. Small thanks to a man for keeping his hands clean, who would not touch the work but with gloves on!

Neither, on the whole, does this constitutional tolerance of the Eighteenth century for the other happier Puritans seem to be a very great matter. One might say, it is but a piece of Formulism and Scepticism like the rest. They tell us, It was a sorrowful thing to consider that the foundation of our English Liberties should have been laid by 'Superstition.' These Puritans came forward with Calvinistic incredible Creeds, Anti-Laudisms, West-minster Confessions; demanding, chiefly of all, that they should have liberty to *worship* in their own way. Liberty to *tax* themselves: that was the thing they should have demanded! It was Superstition, Fanaticism, disgraceful ignorance of Constitutional Philosophy to insist on the other thing! — Liberty to *tax* oneself? Not to pay out money from your pocket except on reason shewn? No century, I think, but a rather barren one would have fixed on that as the first right of man! I should say, on the contrary, A just man will generally have better cause than *money* in what shape soever, before deciding to revolt against his Government. Ours is a most confused world; in which a good man will be thankful to see any kind of Government maintain itself in a not insupportable manner: and here in England, to this hour, if he is not ready to pay a great many taxes which *he* can see very small reason in, it will not go well with him, I think! He must try some other climate than this. Taxgatherer? Money? He will say: "Take my money, since you *can*, and it is so desirable to you; take it, — and take yourself away with it; and leave me alone to my work here. *I* am still here; can still work, after all the money you have taken from me!" But if they come to him, and say, "Acknowledge a Lie; pretend to say you are worshipping God, when you are not doing it: believe not the thing that *you* find true, but the thing that I find, or pretend to find true!" He will answer: "No; by God's help, No! You may take my purse; but I cannot have my moral Self annihilated. The cash is any Highwayman's who might meet me with a loaded pistol: but the Self is mine and God my Maker's; it is not yours; and I will resist you to the death, and revolt against you, and on the whole front all manner of extremities, accusations and confusions, in defence of that!" —

Really, it seems to me the one reason which could justify revolting, this of the Puritans. It has been the soul of all just revolts among men. Not *Hunger* alone produced even the French Revolution; no, but the feeling of the insupportable all-pervading *Falsehood* which had now embodied itself in Hunger, in universal material Scarcity and Nonentity, and thereby become *indisputably* false in the eyes of all! We will leave the Eighteenth century with its 'liberty to tax itself.' We will not astonish ourselves that the meaning of such men as the Puritans remained dim to it. To men who believe in no reality at all, how shall a *real* human soul, the intensest of all realities, as it were the Voice of this world's Maker still speaking to *us*, — be intelligible? What it cannot reduce into constitutional doctrines relative to 'taxing,' or other the like material interest, gross, palpable to the sense, such a century will needs reject as an amorphous heap of rubbish. Hampdens, Pyms and Ship-money will be the theme of much constitutional eloquence, striving to be fervid; — which will glitter, if not as fire does, then as ice does. and the irreducible Cromwell will remain a chaotic mass of 'Madness,' 'Hypocrisy,' and much else.

From of old, I will confess, this theory of Cromwell's falsity has been incredible to me. Nay, I cannot believe the like, of any Great Man whatever. Multitudes of Great Men figure in History as false selfish men; but if we will consider it, they are but *figures* for us, unintelligible shadows: we do not see into them as men that could have existed at all. A superficial unbelieving generation only, with no eye but for the surfaces and semblances of things, could form such notions of Great Men. Can a great soul be possible without a *conscience* in it, the essence of all *real* souls, great or small? — No, we cannot figure Cromwell as a Falsity and Fatuity; the longer I study him and his career, I believe this the less. Why should we? There is no evidence of it. Is it not strange that, after all the mountains of calumny this man has been subject to, after being represented as the very prince of liars, who never, or hardly ever, spoke truth, but always some cunning counterfeit of truth, there should not yet have been one falsehood brought clearly home to him? A prince of liars, and no lie spoken by him. Not one that I could yet get sight of. It is like Pococke asking Grotius, Where is your *proof* of Mahomet's Pigeon? No proof! — Let us leave all these calumnious chimeras, as chimeras ought to be left. They are not portraits of the man; they are distracted phantasms of him, the joint product of hatred and darkness.

Looking at the man's life with our own eyes, it seems to me, a very different hypothesis suggests itself. What little we know of his earlier obscure years, distorted as it has come down to us, does it not all betoken an earnest, hearty, sincere kind of man? His nervous melancholic temperament indicates rather a seriousness *too* deep for him. You remember that story of his having a vision of the Evil Spirit, predicting that he should be Sovereign of England, and so forth. In broad daylight, some huge white Spectre, which he took to be the Devil, with preternatural monitions of some sort, shews itself to him: the Royalists made immense babble about it; but apart from their speculations, we can suppose this story of the Spectre to be true. Then there are afterwards those hypochondriacal visions: the Doctor sent for; Oliver imagining that 'the steeple of Huntingdon was about to tumble on him.' Such an excitable deep-feeling nature, in that rugged stubborn bulk of his; in other words, a soul of such *intensity*, such sensibility, with all its strength!

The young Oliver is sent to study Law; falls, for a little period, into some of the dissipations of youth; but speedily repents, abandons all this: not much above twenty, he is married, settled as an altogether grave and quiet man. He pays back what money he had won at gambling; — he does not think any gain of that kind could be really *his*. It is very interesting, very natural, this 'conversion,' as they well name it; this awakening of a great true soul from the worldly slough, to see into the awful *truth* of things; — to see that Time and its shows all rested on Eternity, and this poor Earth of ours was the threshold either of Heaven or of Hell! Oliver's life at Ely as a sober industrious Farmer, is it not altogether as that of a true devout man? He has renounced the world and its ways; *its* prizes are not the thing that can enrich him. He tills the earth; he reads his Bible; daily assembles his servants round him to worship God. He comforts persecuted ministers, is fond of preachers; nay, can himself preach, — exhorts his neighbours to be wise, to redeem the time. In all this, what 'hypocrisy,' 'ambition,' 'cant,' or other falsity? The man's hopes, I do believe, were fixed on the other Higher World; his aim to get well *thither* by walking well through his humble course in *this* world. He courts no notice: what could notice here do for him? 'Ever in his great Taskmaster's eye.' — It is striking, too, how he comes out once into public view; he, since no other is willing to come: in resistance to a public grievance. I mean, in that matter of the Bedford Fens. No one else will go to law with Authority; therefore he will. That matter once settled, he returns back into obscurity, to his Bible and his Plough. 'Gain influence?' His influence is the most legitimate; derived from personal knowledge of him, as a just, religious, reasonable and determined man. In this way he has lived till past forty; old age is now in view of him, and the earnest portal of Death and Eternity; — it was at this point that he suddenly became 'ambitious!' I do not interpret his Parliamentary mission in that way!

His successes in Parliament, his successes through the war, are honest successes of a brave man; who has more resolution in the heart of him, more light in the head of him than other men. His prayers to God; his spoken thanks to the God of Victory, who had preserved him safe, and carried him forward so far, through the furious clash of a world all set in conflict, through desperate-looking envelopments at Dunbar; through the death-hail of so many battles; mercy after mercy; to the 'crowning mercy' of Worcester Fight: all this is good and genuine for a deephearted Calvinistic Cromwell. Only to vain unbelieving Cavaliers, worshipping not God but their own 'love-locks,' frivolities and formalities, living quite apart from contemplations of God, living *without* God in the world, need it seem hypocritical.

Nor will his participation in the King's death involve him in condemnation with us. It is a stern business killing of a King! But if you once go to

war with him, it lies *there;* this and all else lies there. Once at war, you have
made wager of battle with him: it is he to die, or else you. Reconciliation is
problematic; may be possible, or, far more likely, is impossible. It is now
pretty generally admitted that the Parliament, having vanquished Charles
First, had no way of making any tenable arrangement with him. The large
Presbyterian party, apprehensive now of the Independents, were most anxious to do so; anxious indeed as for their own existence; but it could not be.
The unhappy Charles, in those final Hampton-Court negotiations, shews
himself as a man fatally incapable of being dealt with. A man who, once for
all, could not and would not *understand:* — whose thought did not in any
measure represent to him the real fact of the matter; nay, worse, whose *word*
did not at all represent his thought. We may say this of him without cruelty,
with deep pity rather: but it is true and undeniable. Forsaken there of all but
the *name* of Kingship, he still, finding himself treated with outward respect
as a King, fancied that he might play off party against party, and smuggle
himself into his old power by deceiving both. Alas, they both *discovered*
that he was deceiving them. A man whose *word* will not inform you at all
what he means or will do, is not a man you can bargain with. You must get
out of that man's way, or put him out of yours! The Presbyterians, in their
despair, were still for believing Charles, though found false, unbelievable
again and again. Not so Cromwell: "For all our fighting," says he, "we are
to have a little bit of paper?" No! —

In fact, everywhere we have to note the decisive practical *eye* of this
man; how he drives towards the practical and practicable; has a genuine
insight into what *is* fact. Such an intellect, I maintain, does not belong to a
false man: the false man sees false shows, plausibilities, expediencies: the
true man is needed to discern even practical truth. Cromwell's advice about
the Parliament's Army, early in the contest, How they were to dismiss their
city-tapsters, flimsy riotous persons, and choose substantial yeomen, whose
heart was in the work, to be soldiers for them: this is advice by a man who
saw. Fact answers, if you see into Fact! Cromwell's *Ironsides* were the
embodiment of this insight of his; men fearing God; and without any other
fear. No more conclusively genuine set of fighters ever trod the soil of
England, or of any other land.

Neither will we blame greatly that word of Cromwell's to them; which
was so blamed: "If the King should meet me in battle, I would kill the
King." Why not? These words were spoken to men who stood as before a
Higher than Kings. They had set more than their own lives on the cast. The
Parliament may call it, in official language, a fighting '*for* the King:' but we,
for our share, cannot understand that. To us it is no dilettante work, no sleek

officiality; it is sheer rough death and earnest. They have brought it to the calling forth of *War;* horrid internecine fight, man grappling with man in fire-eyed rage, — the *infernal* element in man called forth, to try it by that! *Do* that therefore; since that is the thing to be done. — The successes of Cromwell seem to me a very natural thing! Since he was not shot in battle, they were an inevitable thing. That such a man, with the eye to see, with the heart to dare, should advance, from post to post, from victory to victory, till the Huntingdon Farmer became, by whatever name you might call him, the acknowledged Strongest Man in England, virtually the King of England, requires no magic to explain it! —

Truly it is a sad thing for a people, as for a man, to fall into Scepticism, into dilettantism, insincerity; not to know a Sincerity when they see it. For this world, and for all worlds, what curse is so fatal? The heart lying dead, the eye cannot see. What intellect remains is merely the *vulpine* intellect. That a true *King* be sent them is of small use; they do not know him when sent. They say scornfully, Is this your King? The Hero wastes his heroic faculty in bootless contradiction from the unworthy; and can accomplish little. For himself he does accomplish a heroic life, which is much, which is all; but for the world he accomplishes comparatively nothing. The wild rude Sincerity, direct from Nature, is not glib in answering from the witness-box: in your small-debt *pie-powder* court, he is scouted as a counterfeit. The vulpine intellect 'detects' him. For being a man worth any thousand men, the response your Knox, your Cromwell gets, is an argument for two centuries whether he was a man at all. God's greatest gift to this Earth is sneeringly flung away. The miraculous talisman is a paltry plated coin, not fit to pass in the shops as a common guinea.

Lamentable this! I say, this must be remedied. Till this be remedied in some measure, there is nothing remedied. 'Detect quacks?' Yes do, for Heaven's sake; but know withal the men that are to be trusted! Till we know that, what is all our knowledge; how shall we so much as 'detect?' The vulpine sharpness, which considers itself to be knowledge, and 'detects' in that fashion, is far mistaken. Dupes indeed are many: but, of all *dupes*, there is none so fatally situated as he who lives in undue terror of being duped. The world does exist; the world has truth in it, or it would not exist! First recognise what is true, we shall *then* discern what is false; and properly never till then.

'Know the men that are to be trusted:' alas, this is yet, in these days, very far from us. The sincere alone can recognise sincerity. Not a Hero only is needed, but a world fit for him; a world not of *Valets;* — the Hero comes almost in vain to it otherwise! Yes, it is far from us: but it must come, thank God, it is visibly coming. Till it do come, what have we? Ballot-boxes, suffrages, French Revolutions: — if we are as Valets, and do not know the Hero when we see him, what good are all these? A heroic Cromwell comes; and for a hundred and fifty years he cannot have a vote from us. Why, the insincere, unbelieving world is the *natural property* of the Quack, and of the Father of Quacks and Quackeries! Misery, confusion, unveracity are alone possible there. By ballot-boxes we alter the *figure* of our Quack; but the substance of him continues. The Valet-World *has* to be governed by the Sham-Hero, by the King merely *dressed* in King-gear. It is his; he is its! One of two things: We shall either learn to know a Hero, a true Governor and Captain, somewhat better, when we see him; or else go on to be forever governed by the Unheroic; — had we ballot-boxes clattering at every street-corner, there were no remedy in these.

Poor Cromwell, — great Cromwell! The inarticulate Prophet; Prophet who could not *speak*. Rude, confused, struggling to utter himself, with his savage depth, with his wild sincerity; and he looked so strange, among the elegant Euphuisms; dainty little Falklands, didactic Chillingworths, diplomatic Clarendons! Consider him. An outer hull of chaotic confusion, visions of the Devil, nervous dreams, almost semi-madness; and yet such a clear determinate man's-energy working in the heart of that. A kind of chaotic man. The ray as of pure starlight and fire, working in such an element of boundless hypochondria, *un*formed black of darkness! And yet withal this hypochondria, what was it but the very greatness of the man? The depth and tenderness of his wild affections; the quantity of *sympathy* he had with things, — the quantity of insight he would yet get into the heart of things, the mastery he would yet get over things: this was his hypochondria. The man's misery, as man's misery always does, came of his greatness. Samuel Johnson too is that kind of man. Sorrow-stricken, half-distracted; the wide element of mournful *black* enveloping him, — wide as the world. It is the character of a prophetic man; a man with his whole soul *seeing* and struggling to see.

On this ground, too, I explain to myself Cromwell's reputed confusion of speech. To himself the internal meaning was sun-clear; but the material with which he was to clothe it in utterance was not there. He had *lived* silent; a great unnamed sea of Thought round him all his days; and in his way of life little call to attempt *naming* or uttering that. With his sharp power of vision, resolute power of action, I doubt not he could have learned to write Books withal, and speak fluently enough; — he did harder things than writing of Books. This kind of man is precisely he who is fit for doing manfully all things you will set him on doing. Intellect is not speaking and logicizing; it is seeing and ascertaining. Virtue, *Vir-tus*, manhood, *hero-hood*, is not fairspoken immaculate regularity; it is first of all, what the Germans well name it, *Tugend* (*Taugend, dow*-ing or *Dough*tiness), Courage and the Faculty to *do*. This basis of the matter Cromwell had in him.

One understands moreover how, though he could not speak in Parliament, he might *preach*, rhapsodic preaching; above all, how he might be great in extempore prayer. These are the free outpouring utterances of what is in the heart: method is not required in them; warmth, depth, sincerity are all that is required. Cromwell's habit of prayer is a notable feature of him. All his great enterprises were commenced with prayer. In dark inextricable-looking difficulties, his Officers and he used to assemble, and pray alternately, for hours, for days, till some definite resolution rose among them, some 'door of hope,' as they would name it, disclosed itself. Consider that. In tears, in fervent prayers, and cries to the great God, to have pity on them, to make His light shine before them. They, armed Soldiers of Christ, as they felt themselves to be; a little band of Christian Brothers, who had drawn the sword against a great black devouring world not Christian, but Mammonish, Devilish, — they cried to God in their straits, in their extreme need, not to forsake the Cause that was His. The light which now rose upon them, — how could a human soul, by any means at all, get better light? Was not the purpose so formed like to be precisely the best, wisest, the one to be followed without hesitation any more? To them it was as the shining of Heaven's own Splendour in the waste-howling darkness; the Pillar of Fire by night, that was to guide them on their desolate perilous way. *Was* it not such? Can a man's soul, to this hour, get guidance by any other method than intrinsically by that same, — devout prostration of the earnest struggling soul before the Highest, the Giver of all Light; be such *prayer* a spoken, articulate, or be it a voiceless, inarticulate one? There is no other method. 'Hypocrisy?' One begins to be weary of all that. They who call it so, have no right to speak on such matters. They never formed a purpose, what one can call a purpose. They went about balancing expediencies, plausibilities; gathering votes, advices; they never were alone with the *truth* of a thing at all. — Cromwell's prayers were likely to be 'eloquent,' and much more than that. His was the heart of a man who *could* pray.

But indeed his actual Speeches, I apprehend, were not nearly so ineloquent, incondite, as they look. We find he was, what all speakers aim to be, an impressive speaker, even in Parliament; one who, from the first, had weight. With that rude passionate voice of his, he was always understood to *mean* something, and men wished to know what. He disregarded eloquence, nay despised and disliked it; spoke always without premeditation of the words he was to use. The Reporters, too, in those days, seem to have been singularly candid; and to have given the Printer precisely what they found on their own note-paper. And withal, what a strange proof is it of Cromwell's being the premeditative ever-calculating hypocrite, acting a play before the world, That to the last he took no more charge of his Speeches! How came he not to study his words a little, before flinging them out to the public? If the words were true words, they could be left to shift for themselves.

But with regard to Cromwell's 'lying,' we will make one remark. This, I suppose, or something like this, to have been the nature of it. All parties found themselves deceived in him; each party understood him to be meaning *this*, heard him even say so, and behold he turns out to have been meaning *that!* He was, cry they, the chief of liars. But now, intrinsically, is not all this the inevitable fortune, not of a false man in such times, but simply of a superior man? Such a man must have *reticences* in him. If he walk wearing his heart upon his sleeve for daws to peck at, his journey will not extend far! There is no use for any man's taking up his abode in a house built of glass. A man always is to be himself the judge how much of his mind he will shew to other men; even to those he would have work along with him. There are impertinent inquiries made: your rule is, to leave the inquirer *un*informed on that matter; not, if you can help it, *mis*informed, but precisely as dark as he was! This, could one hit the right phrase of response, is what the wise and faithful man would aim to answer in such a case.

Cromwell, no doubt of it, spoke often in the dialect of small subaltern parties; uttered to them a *part* of his mind. Each little party thought him all its own. Hence their rage, one and all, to find him not of their party, but of his own party! Was it his blame? At all seasons of his history, he must have felt, among such people, how, if he explained to them the deeper insight he had, they must either have shuddered aghast at it, or believing it, their own little compact hypothesis must have gone wholly to wreck. They could not have worked in his province any more; nay perhaps they could not now have worked in their own province. It is the inevitable position of a great man among small men. Small men, most active, useful, are to be seen everywhere, whose whole activity depends on some conviction which to you is palpably a limited one; imperfect, what we call an *error*. But would it be a kindness always, is it a duty always or often, to disturb them in that? Many a man, doing loud work in the world, stands only on some thin traditionality, conventionality; to him indubitable, to you incredible: break that beneath him, he sinks to endless depths! "I might have my hand full of truth," said Fontenelle, "and open only my little finger."

And if this be the fact even in matters of doctrine, how much more in all departments of practice. He that cannot withal *keep his mind to himself* cannot practise any considerable thing whatever. And we call it 'dissimulation,' all this? What would you think of calling the general of an army a dissembler because he did not tell every corporal and private soldier, who pleased to put the question, what his thoughts were about everything? — Cromwell, I should rather say, managed all this in a manner we must admire for its perfection. An endless vortex of such questioning 'corporals' rolled confusedly round him through his whole course; whom he did answer. It must have been as a great true-seeing man that he managed this too. Not one proved falsehood, as I said; not one! Of what man that ever wound himself through such a coil of things will you say so much? —

But, in fact, there are two errors, widely prevalent, which pervert to the very basis our judgments formed about such men as Cromwell; about their 'ambition,' 'falsity,' and such like. The first is what I might call substituting the *goal* of their career for the course and starting-point of it. The vulgar Historian of a Cromwell fancies that he had determined on being Protector of England, at the time when he was ploughing the marsh lands of Cambridgeshire. His career lay all mapped out; a program of the whole drama; which he then step by step dramatically unfolded, with all manner of cunning, deceptive dramaturgy, as he went on, — the hollow, scheming Ὑποκριτής or Play-actor that he was! This is a radical perversion; all but universal in such cases. And think for an instant how different the fact is! How much does one of *us* foresee of his own life? Short way ahead of us it is all dim; an *un*wound skein of possibilities, of apprehensions, attemptabilities, vague-looming hopes. This Cromwell had *not* his life lying all in that fashion of Program, which he needed then, with that unfathomable cunning of his, only to enact dramatically, scene after scene! Not so. We see it so; but to him it was in no measure so. What absurdities would fall away of themselves, were this one undeniable fact kept honestly in view by History! Historians indeed will tell you that they do keep it in view; — but look whether such is practically the fact! Vulgar History, as in this Cromwell's case, omits it altogether; even the best kinds of History only remember it now and then. To remember it duly, with rigorous perfection, as in the fact it *stood*, requires indeed a rare faculty; rare, nay impossible. A very Shakspeare for faculty; or more than Shakspeare; who could *enact* a brother man's biography, see with the brother man's eyes at all points of his course what things *he* saw; in short, *know* his course and him, as few 'Historians' are like to do. Half or more of all the thick-plied perversions which distort our image of Cromwell, will disappear, if we honestly so much as try to represent them so; in sequence, as they *were;* not in the lump, as they are thrown down before us.

But a second error, which I think the generality commit, refers to this same 'ambition' itself. We exaggerate the ambition of Great Men; we mistake what the nature of it is. Great Men are not ambitious in that sense; he is a small poor man that is ambitious so. Examine the man who lives in misery because he does not shine above other men; who goes about producing himself, pruriently anxious about his gifts and claims; struggling to force everybody, as it were begging everybody for God's sake, to acknowledge him a great man, and set him over the heads of men! Such a creature is among the wretchedest sights seen under this sun. A *great* man? A poor morbid prurient empty man; fitter for the ward of a hospital, than for a throne among men. I advise you to keep out of his way. He cannot walk on quiet paths; unless you will look at him, wonder at him, write paragraphs about him, he cannot live. It is the *emptiness* of the man, not his greatness. Because there is nothing in himself, he hungers and thirsts that you would find something in him. In good truth, I believe no great man, not so much as a genuine man who had health and real substance in him of whatever magnitude, was ever much tormented in this way.

Your Cromwell, what good could it do him to be 'noticed' by noisy crowds of people? God his Maker already noticed him. He, Cromwell, was already there; no notice would make *him* other than he already was. Till his hair was grown grey; and Life from the downhill slope was all seen to be limited, not infinite but finite, and all a measurable matter *how* it went, — he had been content to plough the ground, and read his Bible. He in his old days could not support it any longer, without selling himself to Falsehood, that he might ride in gilt carriages to Whitehall, and have clerks with bundles of papers haunting him, "Decide this, decide that," which in utmost sorrow of heart no man can perfectly decide! What could gilt carriages do for this man? From of old, was there not in his life a weight of meaning, a terror and a splendour as of Heaven itself? His existence there as man, set him beyond the need of gilding. Death, Judgment and Eternity: these already lay as the background of whatsoever he thought or did. All his life lay begirt as in a sea of nameless Thoughts, which no speech of a mortal could name. God's Word, as the Puritan prophets of that time had read it: this was great, and all else was little to him. To call such a man 'ambitious,' to figure him as the prurient windbag described above, seems to me the poorest solecism. Such a man will say: "Keep your gilt carriages and huzzaing mobs, keep your red-tape clerks, your influentialities, your important businesses. Leave me alone, leave me alone; there is *too much life* in me already!" Old Samuel Johnson, the greatest soul in England in his day, was not ambitious. 'Corsica Boswell' flaunted at public shows with printed ribbons round his hat; but the great old Samuel staid at home. The world-wide soul wrapt up in its thoughts, in its sorrows; — what could paradings and ribbons in the hat do for it?

Ah yes, I will say again: The great *silent* men! Looking round on the noisy inanity of the world, words with little meaning, actions with little worth, one loves to reflect on the great Empire of *Silence*. The noble silent men, scattered here and there, each in his department; silently thinking, silently working; whom no Morning Newspaper makes mention of! They are the salt of the Earth. A country that has none or few of these is in a bad way. Like a forest which had no *roots;* which had all turned into leaves and boughs; — which must soon wither and be no forest. Wo for us if we had nothing but what we can *shew*, or speak. Silence, the great Empire of Silence: higher than the stars; deeper than the Kingdoms of Death! It alone is great; all else is small. — I hope we English will long maintain our *grand talent pour le silence*. Let others that cannot do without standing on barrel-heads, to spout, and be seen of all the market-place, cultivate speech exclusively, — become a most green forest without roots! Solomon says, There is a time to speak; but also a time to keep silence. Of some great silent Samuel, not urged to writing, as old Samuel Johnson says he was, by *want of money*, and nothing other, one might ask, "Why do not you too get up and speak; promulgate your system, found your sect?" — "Truly," he will answer, "I am *continent* of my thought hitherto; I happily have yet had the ability to keep it in me, no compulsion strong enough to speak it. My 'system' is not for promulgation first of all; it is for serving myself to live by. That is the great purpose of it to me. And then the 'honour?' Alas, yes; — but as Cato said of the statue: So many statues in that Forum of yours, may it not be better if they ask, Where is Cato's statue? than say, There it is!" ——

But now, by way of counterpoise to this of Silence, let me say that there are two kinds of ambition; one wholly blameable, the other laudable and inevitable. Nature has provided that the great silent Samuel shall not be silent too long. The selfish wish to shine over others, let it be accounted altogether poor and miserable. 'Seekest thou great things, seek them not:' this is most true. And yet, I say, there is an irrepressible tendency in every man to develope himself according to the magnitude which Nature has made him of; to speak out, to act out, what Nature has laid in him. This is proper, fit, inevitable; nay it is a duty, and even the summary of duties for a man. The meaning of life here on earth might be defined as consisting in this: To unfold your *self*, to work what thing you have the faculty for. It is a necessity for the human being, the first law of our existence. Coleridge beautifully remarks that the infant learns to *speak* by this necessity it feels. — We will say therefore, To decide about ambition, whether it is bad or not, you have two things to take into view. Not the coveting of the place alone, but the fitness of the man for the place withal: that is the question. Perhaps the place was *his;* perhaps he had a natural right, and even obligation, to seek the place! Mirabeau's ambition to be Prime Minister, how shall we blame it, if he were 'the only man in France that could have done any good there?' Hopefuler perhaps had he not so clearly *felt* how much good he could do! But a poor Necker, who could do no good, and had even felt that he could do none, yet sitting broken-hearted because they had flung him out, and he was now quit of it, well might Gibbon mourn over him. — Nature, I say, has provided amply that the silent great man shall strive to speak withal; *too* amply, rather!

Fancy, for example, you had revealed to the brave old Samuel Johnson, in his shrouded-up existence, that it was possible for him to do a priceless divine work for his country and the whole world. That the perfect Heavenly Law might be made Law on this Earth, that the prayer he prayed daily, 'Thy kingdom come,' was at length to be fulfilled! If you had convinced his judgment of this; that it was possible, practicable; that he the mournful silent Samuel was called to take a part in it! Would not the whole soul of the man have flamed up into a divine clearness, into noble utterance and determination to act; casting all sorrows and misgivings under his feet, counting all affliction and contradiction small, — the whole dark element of his existence blazing into articulate radiance of light and lightning? It were a true ambition this! And think now how it actually was with Cromwell. From of old, the sufferings of God's Church, true zealous Preachers of the truth flung into dungeons, whipt, set on pillories, their ears cropt off, God's Gospel-cause trodden under foot of the unworthy: all this had lain heavy on his soul. Long years he had looked upon it, in silence, in prayer; seeing no remedy on Earth; trusting well that a remedy in Heaven's goodness would come, — that such a course was false, unjust, and could not last forever. And now behold the dawn of it; after twelve years silent waiting, all England stirs itself; there is to be once more a Parliament, the Right will get a voice for itself: inexpressible well-grounded hope has come again into the Earth. Was not such a Parliament worth being a member of? Cromwell threw down his ploughs, and hastened thither. He spoke there, — rugged bursts of earnestness, of a self-seen truth, where we get a glimpse of them. He worked there; he fought and strove, like a strong true giant of a man, through cannon-tumult and all else, — on and on, till the Cause *triumphed,* its once so formidable enemies all swept from before it, and the dawn of hope had become clear light of victory and certainty. That *he* stood there as the strongest soul of England, the undisputed Hero of all England, — what of this? It was possible that the Law of Christ's Gospel could now establish itself in the world! The Theocracy which John Knox in his pulpit might dream of as a 'devout imagination,' this practical man, experienced in the whole chaos of most rough practice, dared to consider as capable of being *realised*. Those that were highest in Christ's Church, the devoutest wisest men, were to rule the land: in some considerable degree, it might be so and should be so. Was it not *true*, God's truth? And if *true*, was it not then the very thing to do? The strongest practical intellect in England dared to answer, Yes! This I call a noble true purpose: is it not, in its own dialect, the noblest that could enter into the heart of Statesman or man? For a Knox to take it up was something; but for a Cromwell, with his great sound sense and experience of what our world *was*, — History, I think, shews it only this once in such a degree. I account it the culminating point of Protestantism; the most heroic phasis that 'Faith in the Bible' was appointed to exhibit here below. Fancy it: that it were made manifest to one of us, how we could make the Right supremely victorious over Wrong, and all that we had longed and prayed for, as the highest good to England and all lands, an attainable fact!

Well, I must say, the *vulpine* intellect, with its knowingness, its alertness and expertness in 'detecting hypocrites,' seems to me a rather sorry business. We have had but one such Statesman in England; one man, that I can get sight of, who ever had in the heart of him any such purpose at all. One man, in the course of fifteen hundred years; and this was his welcome. He had adherents by the hundred or the ten; opponents by the million. Had England rallied all round him, — England might have been a *Christian* land! As it is, vulpine knowingness sits yet at its hopeless problem, 'Given a world of Knaves, to educe an Honesty from their joint action;' — how cumbrous a problem you may see in Chancery Law-Courts, and some other places! Till at length, by Heaven's just anger, but also by Heaven's great grace, the matter begins to stagnate; and this problem is becoming to all men a *palpably* hopeless one. —

But with regard to Cromwell and his purposes: Hume, and a multitude following him, come upon me here with an admission that Cromwell *was* sincere at first; a sincere 'Fanatic' at first, but gradually became a 'Hypocrite' as things opened round him. This of the Fanatic-Hypocrite is Hume's theory of it; extensively applied since, — to Mahomet and many others. Think of it seriously, you will find something in it; not much, not all, very far from all. Sincere hero-hearts do not sink in this miserable manner. The Sun flings forth impurities, gets balefully incrusted with spots; but it does not quench itself, and become no Sun at all, but a mass of Darkness! I will venture to say that such never befel a great deep Cromwell; I think, never. Nature's own lion-hearted Son; Antæus-like, his strength is got by *touching the Earth*, his Mother; lift him up from the Earth, lift him up into Hypocrisy, Inanity, his strength is gone. We will not assert that Cromwell was an immaculate man; that he fell into no faults, no insincerities among the rest. He was no dilettante professor of 'perfections,' 'immaculate conducts.' He was a rugged Orson, rending his rough way through actual true *work*, — doubtless with many a *fall* therein. Insincerities, faults, very many faults daily and hourly: it was too well known to him; known to God and him! The Sun was dimmed many a time; but the Sun had not himself grown a Dimness. Cromwell's last words, as he lay waiting for death, are those of a Christian heroic man. Broken prayers to God, that He would judge him, He since man could not, in justice yet in pity. They are most touching words. He breathed out his wild great soul, its toils and sins all ended now, into the presence of his Maker, in this manner.

I, for one, will not call the man a Hypocrite! Hypocrite, mummer, the life of him a mere theatricality; empty barren quack, hungry for the shouts of mobs? The man had made obscurity do very well for him till his head was grey; and now he *was*, there as he stood recognised unblamed, the virtual King of England. Cannot a man do without King's Coaches and Cloaks? Is it such a blessedness to have clerks forever pestering you with bundles of papers in red tape? A simple Diocletian prefers planting of cabbages; a George Washington, no very immeasurable man, does the like. One would say, it is what any genuine man could do; and would do. The instant his real work were out in the matter of Kingship, — away with it!

Let us remark, meanwhile, how indispensable everywhere a *King* is, in all movements of men. It is strikingly shewn, in this very war, what becomes of men when they cannot find a Chief Man, and their enemies can. The Scotch Nation was all but unanimous in Puritanism; zealous and of one mind about it, as in this English end of the Island was always far from being the case. But there was no great Cromwell among them; poor tremulous, hesitating, diplomatic Argyles and such like: none of them had a heart true enough for the truth, or durst commit himself to the truth. They had no leader; and the scattered Cavalier party in that country had one: Montrose, the noblest of all the Cavaliers; an accomplished, gallant-hearted, splendid man; what one may call the Hero-Cavalier. Well, look at it: on the one hand subjects without a King; on the other a King without subjects! The subjects without King can do nothing; the subjectless King can do something. This Montrose, with a handful of Irish or Highland savages, few of them so much as guns in their hand, dashes at the drilled Puritan armies like a wild whirlwind; sweeps them, time after time, some five times over, from the field before him. He was at one period, for a short while, master of all Scotland. One man; but he was a man: a million zealous men, but *without* the one; they against him were powerless! Perhaps of all the persons in that Puritan struggle, from first to last, the single indispensable one was verily Cromwell. To see and dare, and decide; to be a fixed pillar in the welter of uncertainty; — a King among them, whether they called him so or not.

Precisely here, however, lies the rub for Cromwell. His other proceedings have all found advocates, and stand generally justified; but this dismissal of the Rump Parliament and assumption of the Protectorship, is what no one can pardon him. He had fairly grown to be King in England, Chief Man of the victorious party in England: but it seems he could not do without the King's Cloak, and sold himself to perdition in order to get it. Let us see a little how this was.

England, Scotland, Ireland, all lying now subdued at the feet of the Puritan Parliament, the practical question arose, What was to be done with it? How will you govern these Nations, which Providence in a wondrous way has given up to your disposal? Clearly those hundred surviving members of the Long Parliament, who sit there as supreme authority, cannot continue forever to sit. What *is* to be done? — It was a question which theoretical constitution-builders may find easy to answer; but to Cromwell, looking there into the real practical facts of it, there could be none more complicated. He asked of the Parliament, What it was they would decide upon? It was for the Parliament to say. Yet the Soldiers too, however contrary to Formula, they who had purchased this victory with their blood, it seemed to them that they also should have something to say in it! We will not "for all our fighting have nothing but a little piece of paper." We understand that the Law of God's Gospel, to which He through us has given the victory, shall establish itself, or try to establish itself, in this land!

For three years, Cromwell says, this question had been sounded in the ears of the Parliament. They could make no answer; nothing but talk, talk. Perhaps it lies in the nature of parliamentary bodies; perhaps no Parliament could in such case make any answer but even that of talk, talk! Nevertheless the question must and shall be answered. You sixty men there, becoming fast odious, even despicable, to the whole nation, whom the nation already call Rump Parliament, *you* cannot continue to sit there: who or what then is to follow? 'Free Parliament,' right of Election, Constitutional Formulas of one sort or the other, — the thing is a hungry Fact coming on us, which we must answer or be devoured by it! And who are you that prate of Constitutional Formulas, rights of Parliament? You have had to kill your King, to make Pride's Purges, to expel and banish by the law of the stronger whosoever would not let your Cause prosper: there are but fifty or three-score of you left there, debating in these days. Tell us what we shall do; not in the way of Formula, but of practicable Fact!

How they did finally answer, remains obscure to this day. The diligent Godwin himself admits that he cannot make it out. The likeliest is, that this poor Parliament still would not, and indeed could not dissolve and disperse; that when it came to the point of actually dispersing, they again, for the tenth or twentieth time, adjourned it, — and Cromwell's patience failed him. But we will take the favourablest hypothesis ever started for the Parliament; the favourablest, though I believe it is not the true one, but too favourable. According to this version: At the uttermost crisis, when Cromwell and his Officers were met on the one hand, and the fifty or sixty Rump Members on the other, it was suddenly told Cromwell that the Rump in its despair *was* answering in a very singular way; that in their splenetic envious despair, to keep out the Army at least, these men were hurrying through the House a kind of Reform Bill, — Parliament to be chosen by the whole of England; equable electoral division into districts; free suffrage, and the rest of it! A very questionable, or indeed for *them* an unquestionable thing. Reform Bill, free suffrage of Englishmen? Why, the Royalists themselves, silenced indeed but not exterminated, perhaps out*number* us; the great numerical majority of England was always indifferent to our Cause, merely looked at it and submitted to it. It is in weight and force, not by counting of heads, that we are the majority! And now with your Formulas and Reform Bills, the whole matter, sorely won by our swords, shall again launch itself to sea; become a mere hope, and likelihood, *small* even as a likelihood? And it is not a likelihood; it is a certainty, which we have won, by God's strength and our own right hands, and do now hold *here*. Cromwell walked down to these refractory Members; interrupted them in that rapid speed of their Reform Bill; — ordered them to begone, and talk there no more. — Can we not forgive him? Can we not understand him? John Milton, who looked on it all near at hand, could applaud him. The Reality had swept the Formulas away before it. I fancy, most men who were Realities in England might see into the necessity of that.

The strong daring man, therefore, has set all manner of Formulas and logical superficialities against him; has dared appeal to the genuine Fact of this England, Whether it will support him or not? It is curious to see how he struggles to govern in some constitutional way; find some Parliament to support him; but cannot. His first Parliament, the one they call Barebones's Parliament, is, so to speak, a *Convocation of the Notables*. From all quarters of England the leading Ministers and chief Puritan Officials nominate the men most distinguished by religious reputation, influence and attachment to the true Cause: these are assembled to shape out a plan. They sanctioned what was past; shaped as they could what was to come. They were scornfully called *Barebones's Parliament*: the man's name, it seems, was not *Barebones*, but Barbone, — a good enough man. Nor was it a jest, their work; it was a most serious reality, — a trial on the part of these Puritan Notables how far the Law of Christ could become the Law of this England. There were men of sense among them, men of some quality; men of deep piety I suppose the most of them were. They failed, it seems, and broke down, endeavouring to reform the Court of Chancery! They appointed Cromwell Protector, and went their ways.

The second Parliament, chosen by the rule these notables had fixed upon, did assemble, and worked; — but got, before long, into bottomless questions as to the Protector's *right*, as to 'usurpation,' and so forth; and had at the earliest legal day to be dismissed. Cromwell's concluding Speech to these men is a remarkable one. Most rude, chaotic, as all his Speeches are; but most earnest-looking. You would say, it was a sincere helpless man; not used to *speak* the great inorganic thought of him, but to act it rather! A helplessness of utterance, in such bursting fulness of meaning. He talks much about 'births of Providence:' All these changes, so many victories and events, were not forethoughts, and theatrical contrivances of men, of *me* or of men; it is blind blasphemers that will persist in calling them so! He insists with a heavy sulphurous wrathful emphasis on this. As he well might! As if a Cromwell in that dark huge game he had been playing, the world wholly thrown into chaos round him, had *foreseen* it all, played it all off like a precontrived puppetshow by wood and wire! These things were foreseen by no man, he says; no man could tell what a day would bring forth: they were 'births of Providence,' God's finger guided us on, and we came at last to clear height of victory, God's Cause triumphant in these Nations; and you as a Parliament could assemble together, and say in what manner all this could be *organised*, reduced into rational feasibility among the affairs of men. You were to help with your wise counsel in doing that. "You have had such an opportunity as no Parliament in England ever had." Christ's Law, the Right and True, was to be in some measure made the Law of this land. In place of that, you have got into your idle pedantries, constitutionalities, bottomless cavillings and questionings about written laws for my coming here;— and would send the whole matter into Chaos again, because I have no Notary's parchment, but only God's voice from the battle-whirlwind, for being President among you! That opportunity is gone; and we know not when it will return. You have had your constitutional Logic; and Mammon's Law, not Christ's Law rules yet in this land. "God be judge between you and me!" These are his final words to them: Take you your constitution-formulas in your hand; and I my *in*formal struggles, purposes, realities and acts; and "God be judge between you and me!" —

We said above what shapeless, involved chaotic things these printed Speeches of Cromwell's are. *Wilfully* ambiguous, unintelligible, say the most: a hypocrite shrouding himself in confused Jesuistic jargon! To me they do not seem so. I will say rather, they afforded the first glimpses I could ever get into the reality of this Cromwell, nay into the possibility of him. Try to believe that he means something, search lovingly what that may be: you will find a real *speech* lying imprisoned in these broken rude tortuous utterances; a meaning in the great heart of this inarticulate man! You will, for the first time, begin to see that he was a man; not an enigmatic chimera, unintelligible to you, incredible to you. The Histories and Biographies written of this Cromwell, written in shallow sceptical generations that could not know or conceive of a deep believing man, are far more *obscure* than Cromwell's Speeches. You look through them only into the infinite vague of Black and the Inane. 'Heats and jealousies,' says Lord Clarendon himself: 'heats and jealousies,' mere crabbed whims, theories, and crotchets; these induced slow sober quiet Englishmen to lay down their ploughs and work; and fly into red fury of confused war against the best-conditioned of Kings! *Try* if you can find that true. Scepticism writing about Belief may have great gifts; but it is really *ultra vires* there. It is Blindness laying down the Laws of Optics. —

Cromwell's third Parliament split on the same rock as his second. Ever the constitutional Formula: How came *you* there? Shew us some Notary parchment! Blind pedants: — "Why, surely the same power which makes you a Parliament, that, and something more, made me a Protector!" If my Protectorship is nothing, what in the name of wonder is your Parliamenteership, a reflex and creation of that? —

Parliaments having failed, there remained nothing but the way of Despotism. Military Dictators, each with his district, to *coerce* the Royalist and other gainsayers, to govern them, if not by act of Parliament, then by the sword. Formula shall *not* carry it, while the Reality is here! I will go on, protecting oppressed Protestants abroad, appointing just judges, wise managers, at home, cherishing true Gospel ministers; doing the best I can to make England a Christian England, greater than old Rome, the Queen of Protestant Christianity; I, since you will not help me; I while God leaves me life! — Why did he not give it up; retire into obscurity again, since the Law would not acknowledge him? cry several. That is where they mistake. For him there was no giving of it up! Prime Ministers have governed countries, Pitt, Pombal, Choiseul; and their word was a law while it held: but this Prime Minister was one that *could not get resigned*. Let him once resign, Charles Stuart and the Cavaliers wanted to kill him; to kill the Cause *and* him. Once embarked, there is no retreat, no return. This Prime Minister could *retire* no-whither except into his tomb.

One is sorry for Cromwell in his old days. His complaint is incessant of the heavy burden Providence has laid on him. Heavy; which he must bear till death. Old Colonel Hutcheson, as his wife relates it, Hutcheson his old battle-mate, coming to see him on some indispensable business, much against his will, — Cromwell 'follows him to the door,' in a most fraternal, domestic, conciliatory style; begs that he would be reconciled to him, his old brother in arms; says how much it grieves him to be misunderstood, deserted by true fellow soldiers, dear to him from of old: the rigorous Hutcheson, cased in his Presbyterian formula, sullenly goes his way. — And the man's head now white; his strong arm growing weary with its long work! I think always too of his poor Mother, now very old, living in that Palace of his; a right brave woman; as indeed they lived all an honest God-fearing Household there: if she heard a shot go off, she thought it was her son killed. He had to come to her twice a day that she might see with her own eyes that he was yet living. The poor old Mother! —— What had this man gained; what had he gained? He had a life of sore strife and toil, to his last day. Fame, ambition, place in History? His dead body was hung in chains; his 'place in History' — place in History forsooth — has been a place of ignominy, accusation, blackness and disgrace; and here, this day, who knows if it is not rash in me to be among the first that ever ventured to pronounce him not a knave and liar, but a genuinely honest man! Peace to him. Did he not, in spite of all, accomplish much for us? *We* walk smoothly over his great rough heroic life; step over his body sunk in the ditch there. We need not *spurn* it, as we step on it! — Let the Hero rest. It was not to *men's* judgment that he appealed; nor have men judged him very well.

Precisely a century and a year after this of Puritanism had got itself hushed up into decent composure, and its results made smooth, in 1688, there broke out a far deeper explosion, much more difficult to hush up, known to all mortals, and like to be long known, by the name of French Revolution. It is properly the third and final act of Protestantism; the explosive confused return of mankind to Reality and Fact, now that they were perishing of Semblance and Sham. We call our English Puritanism the second act: "Well then the Bible is true; let us go by the Bible!" "In Church," said Luther; "In Church and State," said Cromwell, "let us go by what actually *is* God's Truth." Men have to return to reality; they cannot live on semblance. The French Revolution, or third act, we may well call the final one; for lower than that savage *Sansculottism* men cannot go. They stand there on the nakedest haggard Fact, undeniable in all seasons and circumstances; and may and must begin again confidently to build up from that. The French explosion, like the English one, got its King, — who had no Notary parchment to shew for himself. We have still to glance for a moment at Napoleon, our second modern King.

Napoleon does by no means seem to me so great a man as Cromwell. His enormous victories which reached over all Europe, while Cromwell abode mainly in our little England, are but as the high *stilts* on which the man is seen standing; the stature of the man is not altered thereby. I find in him no such *sincerity* as in Cromwell; only a far inferior sort. No silent walking, through long years, with the Awful, Unnameable of this Universe; 'walking with God,' as he called it; and faith and strength in that alone: *latent* thought and valour, content to lie latent, then burst out as in blaze of Heaven's lightning! Napoleon lived in an age when God was no longer believed; the meaning of all Silence, Latency, was thought to be Nonentity: he had to begin not out of the Puritan Bible, but out of poor Sceptical *Encyclopédies*. This was the length the man carried it. Meritorious to get so far. His compact, prompt, every-way articulate character is in itself perhaps small, compared with our great chaotic *in*articulate Cromwell's. Instead of '*dumb* Prophet struggling to speak,' we have a portentous mixture of the Quack withal! Hume's notion of the Fanatic-Hypocrite, with such truth as it has, will apply much better to Napoleon, than it did to Cromwell, to Mahomet or the like, — where indeed taken strictly it has hardly any truth at all. An element of blameable ambition shews itself, from the first, in this man; gets the victory over him at last, and involves him and his work in ruin.

'False as a bulletin' became a proverb in Napoleon's time. He makes what excuse he could for it: that it was necessary to mislead the enemy, to keep up his own men's courage, and so forth. On the whole, these are no excuses. A man in no case has any liberty to tell lies. It had been in the long-run *better* for Napoleon too if he had not told any. In fact, if a man have any purpose reaching beyond the hour and day, meant to be found extant *next* day, what good can it ever be to promulgate lies? The lies are found out; ruinous penalty is exacted for them. No man will believe the liar next time even when he speaks truth, when it is of the last importance that he be believed. The old cry of wolf! — A Lie is *no*-thing; you cannot of nothing make something; you make *nothing* at last, and lose your labour into the bargain.

Yet Napoleon *had* a sincerity: we are to distinguish between what is superficial and what is fundamental in insincerity. Across these outer manoeuvrings and quackeries of his, which were many and most blameable, let us discern withal that the man had a certain instinctive ineradicable feeling for reality; and did base himself upon fact, so long as he had any basis. He has an instinct of Nature better than his culture was. His *savans*, Bourrienne tells us, in that voyage to Egypt were one evening busily occupied arguing that there could be no God. They had proved it, to their satisfaction, by all manner of logic. Napoleon looking up into the stars, answers, "Very ingenious, Messieurs: but *who made* all that?" The Atheistic logic runs off from him like water; the great Fact stares him in the face: "Who made all that?" So too in Practice: he, as every man that can be great, or have victory in this world, sees, through all entanglements, the practical heart of the matter; drives straight towards that. When the steward of his Tuileries Palace was exhibiting the new upholstery, with praises, and demonstration how glorious it was, and how cheap withal, Napoleon, making little answer, asked for a pair of scissors, clipt one of the gold tassels from a window-curtain, put it in his pocket, and walked on. Some days afterwards, he produced it at the right moment, to the horror of his upholstery functionary: it was not gold but tinsel! In Saint Helena, it is notable how he still, to his last days, insists on the practical, the real. "Why talk and complain; above all, why quarrel with one another? There is no *resultat* in it; it comes to nothing that one can *do*. Say nothing, if one can do nothing!" He speaks often so, to his poor discontented followers; he is like a piece of silent strength in the middle of their morbid querulousness there.

And accordingly was there not what we can call a *faith* in him, genuine so far as it went? That this new enormous Democracy asserting itself here in the French Revolution is an insuppressible Fact, which the whole world, with its old forces and institutions, cannot put down: this was a true insight of his, and took his conscience and enthusiasm along with it, — a *faith*. And did he not interpret the dim purport of it well? '*La carrière ouverte aux talens*, The implements to him who can handle them:' this actually is the truth, and even the whole truth; it includes whatever the French Revolution or any Revolution could mean. Napoleon, in his first period, was a true Democrat. And yet by the nature of him, fostered too by his military trade, he knew that Democracy, if it were a true thing at all, could not be an anarchy: the man had a heart-hatred for anarchy. On that Twentieth of June (1792), Bourrienne and he sat in a coffee-house, as the mob rolled by: Napoleon expresses the deepest contempt for persons in authority that they do not restrain this rabble. On the Tenth of August he wonders why there is no man to command these poor Swiss; they would conquer if there were. Such a faith in Democracy, yet hatred of anarchy, it is that carries Napoleon through all his great work. Through his brilliant Italian Campaigns, onwards to the Peace of Lœben, one would say, his inspiration is: 'Triumph to the French Revolution; assertion of it against these Austrian Simulacra that pretend to call it a Simulacrum!' Withal, however, he feels, and has a right to feel, how necessary a strong Authority is; how the Revolution cannot prosper or last without such. To bridle in that great devouring, self-devouring French Revolution; to *tame* it, so that its intrinsic purpose can be made good, that it may become *organic*, and be able to live among other organisms and *formed* things, not as a wasting destruction alone: is not this still what he partly aimed at, as the true purport of his life; nay what he actually managed to do? Through Wagrams, Austerlitzes; triumph after triumph, — he triumphed so far. There was an eye to see in this man, a soul to dare and do. He rose naturally to be the King. All men saw that he *was* such. The common soldiers used to say on the march: "These babbling *Avocats*, up at Paris; all talk and no work! What wonder it runs all wrong? We shall have to go and put our *Petit Caporal* there!" They went, and put him there; they and France at large. Chief-consulship, Emperorship, victory over Europe; — till the poor Lieutenant of *La Fère*, not unnaturally, might seem to himself the greatest of all men that had been in the world for some ages.

But at this point, I think, the fatal charlatan-element got the upper hand. He apostatised from his old faith in Facts, took to believing in Semblances; strove to connect himself with Austrian Dynasties, Popedoms, with the old false Feudalities which he once saw clearly to be false; — considered that *he* would found "his Dynasty" and so forth; that the enormous French Revolution meant only that! The man was 'given up to strong delusion, that he should believe a lie;' a fearful but most sure thing. He did not know true from false now when he looked at them, — the fearfulest penalty a man pays for yielding to untruth of heart. *Self* and false ambition had now become his god: *self*-deception once yielded to, *all* other deceptions follow naturally more and more. What a paltry patchwork of theatrical paper-mantles, tinsel and mummery, had this man wrapt his own great reality in, thinking to make it more real thereby! His hollow Pope's-*Concordat*, pretending to be a re-

establishment of Catholicism, felt by himself to be the method of extirpat-
ing it, "*la vaccine de la religion:*" his ceremonial Coronations, consecra-
tions by the old Italian Chimera in Notre-Dame there, — "wanting nothing
to complete the pomp of it," as Augereau said, "nothing but the half-
million of men who had died to put an end to all that!" Cromwell's Inauguration was by the Sword and Bible; what we must call a genuinely *true* one.
Sword and Bible were borne before him, without any chimera: were not
these the *real* emblems of Puritanism; its true decoration and insignia? It
had used them both in a very real manner, and pretended to stand by them
now! But this poor Napoleon mistook: he believed too much in the *Dupeability* of men; saw no fact deeper in man than Hunger and this! He was
mistaken. Like a man that should build upon cloud: his house and he fall
down in confused wreck, and depart out of the world. Alas, in all of us this
charlatan-element exists; and *might* be developed, were the temptation
strong enough. 'Lead us not into temptation!' But it is fatal, I say, that it *be*
developed. The thing into which it enters as a cognisable ingredient is
doomed to be altogether transitory; and, however huge it may *look*, is in
itself small. Napoleon's working, accordingly, what was it with all the noise
it made? A flash as of gunpowder wide-spread; a blazing-up as of dry heath.
For an hour the whole Universe seems wrapt in smoke and flame; but only
for an hour. It goes out: the Universe with its old mountains and streams, its
stars above and kind soil beneath, is still there. The Duke of Weimar told his
friends always, To be of courage; this Napoleonism was *unjust*, a falsehood,
and could not last. It is true doctrine. The heavier this Napoleon trampled on
the world, holding it tyrannously down, the fiercer would the world's recoil
against him be, one day. Injustice pays itself with frightful compound-
interest. I am not sure but he had better have lost his best park of artillery, or
had his best regiment drowned in the sea, than shot that poor German Bookseller, Palm! It was a palpable tyrannous murderous injustice, which no
man, let him paint an inch thick, could make out to be other. It burnt deep
into the hearts of men, it and the like of it; suppressed fire flashed in the eyes
of men, as they thought of it, — waiting their day! Which day *came:* Germany rose round him. — What Napoleon *did* will in the long-run amount to
what he did *justly;* what Nature with her laws will sanction. To what of
reality was in him; to that and nothing more. The rest was all smoke and
waste. *La carrière ouverte aux talens:* that great true Message, which has
yet to articulate and fulfil itself everywhere, he left in a most inarticulate
state. He was a great *ébauche*, a rude-draught; as indeed what great man is
not? Left in *too* rude a state, alas! His notions of the world, as he expresses
them there at St. Helena, are almost tragical to consider. He seems to feel

the most unaffected surprise that it has all gone so: that he is flung out on the rock here, and the World is still moving on its axis. France is great, and all-great; and at bottom, he is France. England itself, he says, is by Nature only an appendage of France; 'another Isle of Oleron to France.' So it was *by Nature*, by Napoleon-Nature; and yet look how in fact — HERE AM I! He cannot understand it: inconceivable that the reality has not corresponded to his program of it; that France was not all-great, that he was not France. 'Strong delusion,' that he should believe the thing to be which *is* not! The compact, clear-seeing, decisive Italian nature of him, strong, genuine, which he once had, has enveloped itself, half dissolved itself, in a turbid atmosphere of French Fanfaronade. The world was not disposed to be trodden down underfoot; to be bound into masses, and built together, as *he* liked, for a pedestal to France and him: the world had quite other purposes in view! Napoleon's astonishment is extreme. But alas, what help now? He had gone that way of his; and Nature also had gone her way. Having once parted with Reality, he tumbles helpless in Vacuity; no rescue for him. He had to sink there, mournfully as man seldom did; and break his great heart, and die, — this poor Napoleon: a great implement too soon wasted, till it was useless: our last Great Man!

Our last, in a double sense. For here finally these wide roamings of ours through so many times and places, in search and study of Heroes, are to terminate. I am sorry for it: there was pleasure for me in this business, if also much pain. It is a great subject, and a most grave and wide one, this which, not to be too grave about it, I have named *Hero-worship*. It enters deeply, as I think, into the secret of Mankind's ways and vitalest interests in this world, and is well worth explaining at present. With six months, instead of six days, we might have done better. I promised to break ground on it; I know not whether I have even managed to do that. I have had to tear it up in the rudest manner in order to get into it at all. Often enough, with these abrupt utterances thrown out isolated, unexplained, has your tolerance been put to the trial. Tolerance, patient candour, all-hoping favour and kindness, which I will not speak of at present. The accomplished and distinguished, the beautiful, the wise, something of what is best in England, have listened patiently to my rude words. With many feelings, I heartily thank you all; and say, Good be with you all!

THE END.

Essays

"The Tone of the Preacher"

Carlyle as Public Lecturer in *On Heroes, Hero-Worship, and the Heroic in History*

OWEN DUDLEY EDWARDS

His Lectures on Heroes and Hero-Worship . . . are just his recorded talk — the eloquent droppings of his mind. To them we could refer all who have never met him.
— George Gilfillan, *A First Gallery of Literary Portraits* (1851) 92

The tone is even more consistently earnest than *Sartor;* it is the tone of the preacher, who feels that he stands between the living and the dead.
— Archibald MacMechan, Introduction to Carlyle's *Heroes* (1901)

Thomas Carlyle's *On Heroes, Hero-Worship, and the Heroic in History* (1841) holds a unique place among his works, and perhaps in modern literature. The book consolidated his conquest of London, evangelized listeners and readers effectively enough to distance competitors, and thundered literary and historical judgments that won its foremost intellectual responses from the social sciences. *Heroes and Hero-Worship* preached a doctrine enshrining schoolboy adulation and elevated it to a British creed. One Carlylean "Fact" needs to be kept in the ascendant here: the book originated in a series of public lectures, delivered from 5 to 22 May 1840, and its decisive shape seems to have been achieved a few days before the lectures began, a shape that would transform Carlyle's literary and philosophical career. It was also the culmination of a four-year period in which he had previously delivered talks on German literature (1 to 26 May 1837), the history of literature (30 April to 11 June 1837), and revolutions of modern Europe (1 to 18 May 1839). To a considerable degree the format of *Heroes and Hero-Worship* committed its creator to a reactionary logic, but ironically, its two leading male midwives were probably the leading British and American radicals of their generation. It was repudiated by subsequent intellectual generations whose best efforts failed to escape its enchantments. *Heroes and Hero-Worship* proclaimed its Englishness by ostentatious Scots speech and subjects, and its cosmopolitanism was without peer for its times.

In his biography of Carlyle, James Anthony Froude notes, "In the summer of 1834 [he] left Craigenputtock and its solitary moors and removed to London, there to make a last experiment whether it would be possible for him to abide by literature as a profession, or whether he must seek another employment and perhaps another country" (*Life in London* 1:8). Froude here struck the economic note that Carlyle preferred to reserve for high denunciation of the literary establishment's neglect of figures such as Samuel Johnson and Robert Burns, but it was the right note. Carlyle knew that the Johnson and Burns with whom he would identify himself had had long to wait before London and Edinburgh respectively would surrender to provincials, however heroic. Notwithstanding the topicality of the French Revolution, he suspected that writing might not be enough. He was familiar enough with the appeal of public lecturing. He himself had studied speaking from his boyhood Sundays listening to preachers, regurgitating and perhaps even parodying their discourses. As a student, this verbal awareness began to bring power to his expositions written as he and his colleagues flowered in a university where the lecture was king and paymaster. As a teacher, he kept classes quiet with his powerful voice, privately entrancing his listeners, one of whom — Jane Welsh Carlyle — later married him.

A visit from Ralph Waldo Emerson to Craigenputtoch in 1833 had whetted Carlyle's appetite for public speaking. The sublime transcendentalist was a New Englander, with business shrewdness in his bones, who recognized Carlyle's potential. The lecture, tolerated in London and deified in Edinburgh, was in America a means of shrinking the Atlantic as well as consolidating the country. Emerson persisted in his efforts to lure Carlyle across the Atlantic. Writing to him on 30 April 1835, he seconded the "opinion of many friends whose judgment I value" that Carlyle as biographer of Schiller, friend of Goethe, essayist on Burns, and author of *Sartor Resartus* "would ... batter down opposition, and command all ears on whatever topic pleased him, and that, quite independently of the merit of his lectures, merely for so many names' sake" (Slater 123). Emerson baited his hook with his own success as a speaker: "I found much indulgence, in reading, last winter, some Biographical Lectures, which were meant for theories or portraits of Luther, Michelangelo, Milton, George Fox, Burke" (122). Emerson had anticipated the excitement essential to encouraging Carlyle to emigrate, ridiculing the apathetic English but treating their "apathy or antipathy" (122) as an opportunity for Carlyle to try his luck as a lecturer in the United States. A year later Emerson was still pressing his case. In a letter of 8 April 1836, he reminded his friend that the "orator is only responsible for what his lips articulate.... You may handle every member & relation of humanity....

Why may you not give the reins to your wit, your pathos, your philosophy, — and become that good despot which the virtuous orator is?" (143). The deft allusion likening Carlyle to St. Paul would not have been missed, but the "Macedonia" (Acts 16:9–10) to which Emerson hoped to attract the Scotsman would at this stage only renew the latter's thirst for London conquest.

Emerson's example might be attractive, but Carlyle would not follow him in "reading . . . Biographical Lectures" (Slater 122). As he stressed to his sister Jean on 29 December 1836, "I mean to speak the Lectures (having grown ill-haired [ill-tempered], and impudent enough for that)" (*CL* 9:109). He told John Stuart Mill that his plan was to deliver a series of talks on German literature, "a project [that] does not seem to promise much" (*CL* 9:130; 28 Jan. 1837). Carlyle underestimated the enthusiasm of his friends and admirers. One of them, James Spedding, wrote to Richard Monckton Milnes on 4 April 1837, and urged him to attend: "Of course you will be here to attend the said lectures, but I want you to come up a little before they begin, that you may assist in procuring the attendance of others. The list of subscribers is at present not large, and you are just the man to make it grow. As it is Carlyle's first essay of this kind, it is important that there should be a respectable muster of hearers" (Reid 1:192). Carlyle himself informed his literary agent Jane Wilson that "if she or other friends could find me forty or fifty human beings really desirous to know something about German Literature, I would with perfect promptitude actually open my mouth to them and tell them what I knew" (*CL* 9:146; to John A. Carlyle, 17 Feb. 1837). He need not have worried about the reception he would receive. His sponsors opened up larger sheepfolds, knowing that to make the lectures succeed, they would need to secure bellwethers whose promised presence would summon the cultural multitude.

Though he feared that his Scots accent and Scotticisms would alienate his listeners, his accent and his demeanor proved no barrier to auditors. Following the first lecture the *Spectator* reported on 6 May that "Mr. Carlyle may be deficient in the mere mechanism of oratory; but this minor defect is far more than counterbalanced by his perfect mastery of his subject, the originality of his manner, the perspicuity of his language, his simple but genuine eloquence, and his vigorous grasp of a large and difficult question" (qtd. in Wilson, *Cromwell* 5). Carlyle was more dubious of his acceptability than was his audience, informing his mother on 19 May, after his fifth lecture, that it "is very curious to hear the wild Annandale voice speaking down upon these high-cultivated dignitaries and marchionesses; and how patient and silent they sit under it" (*CL* 9:206). His parents had once thought him a candidate for the Presbyterian ministry, and however unorthodox his current brand of theism, he clearly still thought of a lecture in such terms, with his audience rapt "under" his "deliverances." His doctrine was heretical, but his vision was clerical, gleaned from a culture that situated "deliverance" at the heart of priesthood. The significance of this lineage was clear enough three years later, when Carlyle included Knox and Luther in "The Hero as Priest." The seven lectures in 1837 were followed by twelve in 1838, this time on European literature from Homer to Goethe. Eleven of these survive in attempted full transcriptions by Thomas Chisholm Anstey (1816–73), published in 1892. Press summaries of several other lectures were published, and some private versions have been found. Two texts of the Chisholm Anstey reports (edited respectively by R. P. Karkaria and J. Reay Greene), largely in agreement, show the contrast in the lecturer's maturity between 1838 and 1840, allowing for what Carlyle said in 1840 to what he wrote and passed for printing. For the third series, six lectures in 1839 on "The Revolutions of Modern Europe," we have less text, whether reported, reduced, or revised. What we lose in print is what contemporaries saw and heard, or picked up by word of mouth, which is the young Carlyle in full artistic bloom radiating unquenchable energy and creativity.

After attending a lecture by Carlyle, the future Massachusetts senator Charles Sumner (1811–74) wrote home to George Hillard on 14 June 1838: "He seemed like an inspired boy; truths and thoughts that made one move on the benches came from his apparently unconscious mind, couched in the most grotesque style, and yet condensed to a degree of intensity . . . childlike in manner and feeling, and yet reaching by intuition points and extremes of ratiocination which others could not so well accomplish after days of labor, if indeed they ever could" (Pierce 1:318–19). Monckton Milnes shared Sumner's vision of Carlyle in 1838: "There he stands, simple as a child, and his happy thought dances on his lips and in his eyes, and takes word and goes away, as he bids it God speed, whatever it be" (Reid 1:220). G. K. Chesterton (1874–1936) observed in *The Victorian Age in Literature* (1913), "It was one of [Carlyle's] innumerable crotchets . . . to encourage prose as against poetry. But as a matter of fact, he himself was much greater considered as a kind of poet than considered as anything else; and the central idea of poetry is the idea of guessing right, like a child" (443). The element of play, of game, of son performing for mother, and childlike husband maneuvered by amused wife, kept his language youthful, his eye bright, and his intellect rapier sharp.

What was new about the third set of lectures, this time on the revolutions of modern Europe, was the way in which Carlyle shaped them around

Oliver Cromwell and the prophetic part that he played in the English Revolution. Perhaps inevitably, the content of his lectures was beginning to fuse itself with his preacher-like manner of delivering them. Carlyle announced to his mother on 13 January 1839, "I have my face turned partly towards Oliver Cromwell and the *Covenant* time in England and Scotland, and am reading books and meaning to read more on the matter (for it is large and full of meaning); but what I shall make of it, or whether I shall make anything at all; it would be premature to say as yet" (*CL* 11:4). The language was appropriately biblical, yet faintly reminiscent of God speaking of the Old Testament kings, a tone Carlyle never quite lost in all his admiration for Cromwell. The lectures, he announced to his brother John on February 4, 1839, would allow him to "*get acquainted with England* (a great secret to me always hitherto), and I may as well begin here as elsewhere" (*CL* 11:15).

The lectures on revolutions caused an immediate stir. Following the second, entitled "Protestantism, Faith in the Bible, Luther, Knox, and Gustavus Adolphus," Jane Welsh Carlyle described the impact of her husband's words on the assemblage: "Our second lecture '*transpired*' yesterday, and with surprising success — literally surprising — for he was imputing the profound attention with which they . . . listened, to an awful sympathizing expectation on their part of his momentary, complete break-down, when all at once they broke into loud plaudits, and he thought they must all have gone clear out of their wits!" (*CL* 11:93; 5 May 1839). Characteristically, she put her finger on the pivotal moment in this series and in the next: "Even John Knox, tho' they must have been very angry at him for demolishing so much beautiful architecture, which is quite a passion with the English, they were quite willing to let good be said of, so that it was indisputably true — nay it was in reference to Knox that they first applauded yesterday — Perhaps his being a Countryman of their favorite Lecturer's might have something to do with it! — but we will hope better things tho we thus speak" (*CL* 11:93–94). To the expression "better things," Carlyle noted on the letter after his wife's death, "Common preacher's phrase in Scotl*d*" (*CL* 11:94), thereby acknowledging her familiarity with the clerical code that he shared with his mother. In this instance the "better things" were what Knox was to open up, to wit Cromwell and English Puritanism in the third lecture.

Carlyle must have been disappointed when he learnt from a review written by Leigh Hunt in the *Examiner* on 12 May 1839, that his attempted redemption of Cromwell had failed. In Hunt's estimate, "Cromwell himself [Carlyle] certainly over-reached; for after all, in what did *he* succeed, except in making himself for a short time an unhappy prince? And why did our philosophical lecturer, who sees nothing enduring in a Napoleon compared with a book, say not a syllable of such intellectual master-spirits as Vane and Milton?" (qtd. in Shepherd 1:205–6). Unwittingly, Hunt had set out the agenda for another lecture series. The absence in the lectures of any reference to Sir Henry Vane the Younger (1613–62) would be dealt with by Carlyle in 1840 when he worked up his case for Cromwell as a hero. The absence of John Milton was a very different matter, the poet having loomed fairly large in the 1838 lecture series on European literature. Then Carlyle had regarded him as a "summing up, as it were, of . . . Shakespeare and Knox," but neatly diminishing Milton by making him an heir rather than a progenitor of Puritanism: "He got his knowledge out of Knox, for Knox's influence was not confined to Scotland. It was planted there at first, and continued growing in his own country till it filled it, and then it spread itself into England, working great events, and . . . it ended in the Revolution of 1688" (*Lectures* 165). Hence Knox became integral to English history, not only superior to Milton but the "Chief Priest and Founder . . . of the Faith that became Scotland's, New England's, Oliver Cromwell's" (*Heroes* 124). Here was the vital Scottish context for Carlyle's next set of lectures on heroes and hero-worship. A better and more convincing receptacle than Milton had been found to fill the vacancy in Scotland's theological legacy. Cromwell not only provided continuity, he also secured Carlyle's entry to the realm of Englishness.

Still committed to speaking to an audience rather than reading from a text, Carlyle began sketching ideas for a new set of six lectures. On 2 March 1840, he wrote to his brother John, "I am to talk about gods, prophets, priests, kings, poets, teachers . . . and may probably call it 'On the Heroic' " (*CL* 12:67). The subject material, he explained, "is not so much historic as didactic; a partly new arrangement; which I must try to get thro' as I best may" (12:94). The lectures were highly successful if controversial, and the second on Mohammed Carlyle considered to be "the *best* I ever delivered" (*CL* 12:142). By the end of the lecture series Carlyle had clearly had enough of lecturing, which he equated with being "spitted on the spear's point like a Surinam *fire-fly* to give light to the fashionable classes" (*CL* 12:141). The change in approach from historian to social commentator for the series had opened up new possibilities for Carlyle, who was familiar with the lucrative marketplace for printed versions of sermons. He was now prepared to contemplate the possibility of publishing his talks. He toyed with the idea of selling transcripts of them, but as he explained, the transcripts themselves were inadequate — "it is like soda-water with the gas out of it" (*CL* 12:144;

[to Henry Cole,] 14 May 1840). He finally resolved to rewrite the lectures from his preparatory notes once the series was concluded. The process was no easier later than it was when he prepared. On February 5, 1841, he told John, "We are now far into the second Lecture: the First needed very heavy correction; paragraphs to be added &c.: twice I sat a whole day; sometimes like the *cooking of a cucumber,* after getting something all ready with great labour, I flung it out of the window, as the best course!" (*CL* 13:29). To John Sterling on 2 March 1841, he announced: "The Hero-Lectures are . . . printed, and away from me. With great pleasure I bequeath them . . . to the Prince of the Power of the Air to work *his* good pleasure with them: it is not probable that he dislikes them much worse than I do, — under many points of view" (*CL* 13:48).

Carlyle had succeeded in keeping the printed texts far more suggestive of verbal performances than published lectures normally achieve, clearly striving to effect a full partnership between tongue and pen. For some reviewers, the oratorical quality of the book brought back sour memories of the lectures themselves. The newspaper editor James Grant (1802–79), perhaps resentful of Carlyle's successful effort to reinvent himself in *Heroes* as an Englishman, complained bitterly in his anonymous *Portraits of Public Characters* (1841) about the lecturer's incomprehensible Scottish accent: "At times . . . he so unnaturally distorts his features, as to give to his countenance a very unpleasant expression. . . . And his manner of speaking, and the ungracefulness of his gesticulation, are greatly aggravated by his strong Scotch accent. Even to the generality of Scotchmen his pronunciation is harsh in no ordinary degree. Need I say, then, what it must be to an English ear?" (154–55). But English ears were more receptive to "the Chelsea Sage" than those that belonged to Scotsmen self-consciously striving to be English. Reviewers were exceptionally keen to quote as much of the spoken text from *Heroes* as their editors would permit. For instance, in his review of the book in April 1841, John Abraham Heraud (1799–1887), editor of the *Monthly Magazine,* devoted twenty-two pages to it, of which eighteen were in fact excerpts from *Heroes.* Carlyle had earlier condemned Heraud in a letter to Emerson, 26 September 1840, as a "cockney windbag" (Slater 281), but on this occasion Heraud had left it to Carlyle to provide four-fifths of the wind.

Reviewers, however well disposed, were generally anxious about the religious dimension of *Heroes.* An anonymous contributor to *Tait's Edinburgh Magazine* admitted that "there is fervour in its tone, which feels as if it came direct from the heart; and there is moral courage, though it requires more courage in our society to attack one social abuse than fifty doctrinal systems" (383). A writer in the *Monthly Review* in May 1841 wondered about the "Last Judgment" on Carlyle's judgments: "What might not such a writer have made Mahomet or Cromwell, had he taken up another theory? — What, if he had managed to look at first upon his hero in a different light? — What, above all, is or will be the Eternal's judgment? — So that however gratifying, purifying, and ennobling, are the spirit and matter of these Lectures, something not short of distrust has accompanied our reading of them" (21). In the *Monthly Magazine* Heraud concluded in mock-apocalyptic fashion, "Look to thyself, O man! and to the God in thee! See (not to make thyself, but) to be made by him the ablest and the worthiest! Let each man do this — and we shall have a world of heroes, not worshipping one another, but worshipping God. All is idolatry, except this. This alone is the True Faith, in which whoso believeth not, is damned!" (412). Across the Atlantic, Margaret Fuller, transcendentalist editor of the Boston *Dial* and protégée of Emerson, demurely ended her review in 1842 by echoing the view of an "acute observer" that "the best criticism on [Carlyle's] works would be his own remark, that a man in convulsions is not proved strong because six healthy men cannot hold him." She was less harsh in her appraisal: "We are not consoled by his brilliancy and the room he has obtained for an infinity of quips and cranks and witty turns for the corruption of his style. . . . Yet let thanks, manifold thanks, close this and all chapters that begin with his name" (133).

In perhaps the most astute twentieth-century commentary on *Heroes*, David DeLaura saw an "autobiographical pressure" imposed by Carlyle "upon his most congenial heroes — Mahomet, Dante, Luther, Knox, Johnson, Cromwell" (718). According to DeLaura, Carlyle shared and experienced their destiny as prophets because they seemed above "the beautiful people [who] applauded and bought his books, and [the] young men [who] wrote letters in playful mock-Carlylese" (725). Carlyle never lost sight of his own conviction that "the Great Man was always as lightning out of Heaven; the rest of men waited for him like fuel, and then they too would flame" (*Heroes* 76). The exceptions to DeLaura's list were as intriguing as the inclusions. Both Emerson and Carlyle thought they knew Shakespeare, but their love for him was a love for the works, not the man. Rousseau and Napoleon were by now lost loves and served as foils to others, either explicitly or implicitly. Odin was a brilliant contrivance but, once contrived, more or less impossible to maintain as a human. Burns was a different matter. He had brought Carlyle real success as an essay topic, and that love had not died. Ironically, Carlyle did not see how fully Burns had realized heroic specifications, but his miscalculation has stimulated modern scholarship into correcting him. Nigel Leask's *Robert Burns and Pastoral* (2010) expands Carlyle's vision of Burns as the heaven-taught ploughman and explores his poetry in the context of his own age, from agricultural improvement to learning for its own sake. Burns was a figure of the Scottish Enlightenment, all the more in its Christian contrast from the secularist European version. Carlyle's conviction that "his writings, all that he *did* under such obstructions, are only a poor fragment of him" (*Heroes* 158) has been amply vindicated by Leask, who has revealed the extent to which science and art have penetrated Burns's poetry.

In the conclusion of his magisterial essay, DeLaura claimed that "Carlyle had discovered a series of formulas which led him to the precise point where his fundamental doctrine and his personal quest for self-definition met, enabling him to write what is perhaps the most openly 'prophetic' book of the nineteenth century in England and a masterpiece of Romantic art" (732). The danger of the superlatives here is that they half concede that the great art of *Heroes* might not be compatible with good history, or that it might diminish the historical sensitivity of Carlyle, whose essays "On History" (1830) and "On History Again" (1833) had been exemplary and influential. Carlyle's success in conquering London had come at the cost of admiration rather than of acceptance, and the result of this tradeoff was considerable bitterness on his part. Gradually he hardened into a self-regarding icon. The shift from historian to social commentator that had inspired him to publish the lectures on heroes as a book also contained the seeds for future perceptions of his legacy. In a characteristically generous piece of understatement, Leslie Stephen (1832–1904) commented in his entry on Carlyle in the *Encyclopædia Britannica* (1902), "As he won greater recognition as a prophet, he indulged too freely in didactic monologue" (26:596).

Yet *Heroes* had opened up historical truths perhaps more remarkably than Carlyle grasped. He knew or could guess at most of the heroic outcomes, his most recent exertion having rescued Cromwell to an extent from the dustbin of history. But Odin and Mahomet were new to him. He mentioned to Emerson on 6 January 1840, that he had "read rubbish of Books: Eichhorn, Grimm &c.; very considerable rubbish, one grain in the cartload worth pocketing" (Slater 259). Johann G. Eichhorn's three volumes on the Old Testament, with their preoccupation with "higher criticism," probably succeeded in driving Carlyle away from the use of biblical heroes. But the brothers Grimm, or at least Jacob Grimm, would have steered him in the direction of Teutonic mythology, where he found "grains" enough to define Odin as a human hero. From the standpoint of historical research, the novelty of Carlyle's first lecture defined a great truth, thereafter largely ignored by historians for more than a century: folklore and oral tradition as clues to prehistory, on which his own knowledge of the Scottish borders would have educated him. Carlyle's passionate insistence that paganism's self-belief had to be taken seriously was also a long-avoided reality. Christians had told themselves pagans had not believed their official dogmas; agnostics had told themselves that nobody had believed these either. Only in the aftermath of James George Frazer's *Golden Bough* (1906–15) did many thinkers come to recognize what Carlyle implicitly had demonstrated in *Heroes:* the all-important connections among folklore, myth, and comparative religion.

Carlyle roared about sincerity as though nobody else had understood its importance, but he was perfectly right to make it a test on which the probabilities lay strongly with its reality. He extended the thesis in "The Hero as Prophet" with greater success, because here he had an obviously real hero in Mahomet and an obviously real falsifier in Voltaire, whose contemptible play *La Fanatisme ou Mahomet le prophète* (1741) represented its subject as a fraud, lecher, and murderer. Voltaire tried to justify the drama by simultaneously using it to ingratiate himself with the pope and implying that it was really a satire on Catholicism. The defamation of Islam was not even carried out for its own sake but made a contrivance to further Western neuroses. "The Hero as Prophet" was one of the most ferocious yet fair-minded demolitions that Voltaire ever received, even if Carlyle went a little far in seeking to demolish the entire eighteenth century while he was at it. The great Orientalist Owen Lattimore valued *Heroes* above all for forcing its European audience to look beyond its own Continental frontiers and to take Asian civilization among the hunting grounds for its heroes. *Heroes* has been reviled as racist and proto-Fascist, but its second lecture pioneered rejection of racism against Islam, an achievement far beyond that of most of Carlyle's critics. In a letter to his mother on 9 May 1840, Carlyle referred to the lecture on Mahomet, which "I vomited it forth on them like wild Annandale grapeshot; they laughed, applauded, &c., &c.: in short, it was all right, and I suppose it is by much the best Lecture I shall have the luck to give this time" (*CL* 12:139). Heroic in his humility, Carlyle had underestimated his most enduring strengths as a historian — his profound insight, intelligence, and imagination.

In Defense of "Religiosity"

Carlyle, Mahomet, and the Force of Faith in History

DAVID R. SORENSEN

Were he alive today it is safe to assume that Carlyle would have regarded the emergence of radical Islamism as a threat to civilization, both Eastern and Western. But he would also have insisted that the motives of its leaders, however violent and destructive, had to be gauged in relation to larger "affinities with the higher powers and senses of man" (*Heroes* 98). There is a Carlylean familiarity to the pattern of events in the late twentieth century. In the sanguine aftermath of the Cold War, latter-day "Progress of the Species" (106) philosophers such as Francis Fukuyama too confidently assumed that "there is a fundamental process at work that dictates a common evolutionary pattern for all human societies — in short, something like a Universal History of mankind in the direction of liberal democracy" (48). With startling suddenness, religious extremists brutally disrupted this apparently irresistible march of progress. Carlyle would not have been shocked. He knew better than to weave such neat "endings" from the "immeasurable mass of threads and thrums" that composed the raw material of "Universal History" ("On History Again" [1833], *Historical Essays* 22). In his lectures on heroes, he chided those in his audience who smugly reckoned that "all generations of men were lost and wrong, only that this present little section of a generation might be saved and right." From his perspective, such an "incredible hypothesis" treated the past as a thinly disguised homage to the present and revealed to Carlyle an astonishing parochialism peculiar to nineteenth-century liberalism: "What a melancholy notion . . . to represent all men, in all countries and times except our own, as having spent their life in blind condemnable error, mere lost Pagans, Scandinavians, Mahometans, only that we might have the true ultimate knowledge!" (*Heroes* 107).

The self-satisfied cultural myopia of such dismissals of the past lay at the heart of Carlyle's rejection of the logically honed "scientific" verdicts of the Utilitarians about the correlation between happiness and material gratification. Carlyle's lecture on Mahomet reflected his lifelong effort to repudiate this Benthamite orthodoxy, and to identify dynamic "religiosity"

(*Heroes* 55), rather than rational self-interest, as the surest measure of social stability and harmony in history. His attempt to redeem the "rude message" (54) of Islam inevitably overlapped with his desire to expose the coruscated condition of spirituality, as he perceived it, in Victorian society. Bentham and his disciples had rendered history a science of progress, philosophy a justification of self-interest, and faith a matter of social convenience. The "infinite celestial Soul of Man" (75) was reduced to a mechanical balance between pleasure and pain. The questions that Mahomet posed while wandering among the "grim rocks of Mount Hara" — "What is life; what is Death! What am I to believe? What am I to do?" (60) — no longer mattered. Religion had become irrelevant in English society. More significantly, in Carlyle's view, "Belief," the "life-giving" core of any true faith, had retreated into sentimentally bland expressions of philanthropy and good-will.

Carlyle's attempt to redeem religion and religiosity by acknowledging the legitimacy of Islam was controversial to say the least. In a letter to Ralph Waldo Emerson, 2 July 1840, Carlyle reported that the "Lecture on Mahomet . . . astonished my worthy friends beyond measure. It seems that this Mahomet was not a quack? Not a bit of him! That he is a better Christian, with his 'bastard Christianity,' than most of us shovel-hatted? . . . On the whole, I fear I did little but confuse my esteemed audience: I was amazed after all their reading of me, to be understood so ill" (*CL* 12:183–84). It is clear that Carlyle intended to provoke his audience to question the claims of Christianity as the sole possessor of divine truth. In the first lecture, he had drawn from paganism the apparently nonthreatening core element of his argument, that "a man's religion is the chief fact with regard to him" (*Heroes* 22). But at the outset of his second lecture, he conceded that "we have chosen Mahomet not as the most eminent Prophet: but as the one we are freest to speak of" (52). Carlyle, of course, recognizes that he cannot discuss Christ in the historical and intellectual register that he required. For both personal and professional reasons, Carlyle knew that he could not transgress the orthodox limits imposed by his "esteemed audience" (*CL* 12:184) in Portman Square. He had rejected the miraculous aspects of Christianity because he could never reconcile the natural Jesus with his supernatural incarnation. If he wrote the life of Jesus, he knew he would have to expose the "rude gross error" (*Heroes* 51) of the Son of God's divinity, and lift the veil of theological "quackery" behind which the doctrinal Savior lived, moved, and breathed. Mahomet offered him a much safer subject, he drolly conceded, since "there is no danger of our becoming, any of us, Mahometans" (52). Under his breath he may have been tempted to add, "or Christians, for that matter."

Although the lecture confused and no doubt angered many of his listeners, Carlyle's essay on Mahomet permanently reshaped Victorian attitudes to the Prophet. Twenty years after he delivered the lecture, a commentary in the radical journal the *Leader* concluded, "For a long period it had been the custom for Jewish and Christian writers to regard Mohammed as an imposter; — but the philosophical minds of this century have formed a more favourable opinion of his character. For the most part, they seem disposed to recognise his mission; at any rate, they are not prepared to dispute that it was accomplished. This, undoubtedly, is a great fact in his favour, and to Mr. Thos. Carlyle in particular conclusive of his claims" ("Islamism" 165). Carlyle's positive influence on the reception of Islam in the West carried on well into the twentieth century. In an address to the Carlyle Society on 24 October 1953, W. Montgomery Watt, future professor of Arabic at Edinburgh University, asserted that Carlyle's essay on Mahomet marked "an important step forward in the process of reversing the medieval world-picture of Islam as the great enemy, and rehabilitating its founder, Muhammad" (254).

In the early twenty-first century, Carlyle's reputation as a champion of Islam has survived, though it coexists awkwardly with the equally resilient caricature of him as a racist, imperialist, and forerunner of Fascism and National Socialism. Still, it is a testimony to Carlyle's enigmatic appeal that the author of the biographical sketch in *Heroes* could at once be credited by Ruth apRoberts and Geoffrey Tillotson for having "laid the groundwork for James Frazer, Emile Durkheim, and Mircea Eliade" (apRoberts, *Ancient Dialect* 101) as well as for the founding of comparative religion, and cited by John Casey and David Westerlund for justifying the violence of the Lebanese Hizbollah movement and the anti-Christian polemics of the African Muslim populist and preacher Ahmed Deedat (1918–2005). Postcolonialist critics such as Albert Pionke who defer to Edward Said have been eager to point out that Carlyle's "thinking remains limited by and vulnerable to the prejudices of his period" (509).[1] Others are less certain that Carlyle's "prejudices" matter very much. For example, Minou Reeves, until 1979 an Iranian career diplomat, singled out Carlyle as a persuasive advocate who "condemned the hostile attitudes of Europeans towards Muhammed . . . by celebrating the Prophet of Islam as an upright, sincere and great man of history" (5). And Muhammed A. Al-Da'mi, professor of English and linguistics at Baghdad University, lauded Carlyle's essay on Mahomet as "a rare document of great literary merit which attempts a revaluation of established attitudes" (84).

If there seems to be a favorable consensus for Carlyle's attitude toward Mahomet, it is that his intention in the lecture had never been hagiography. The preliminary sketch of his portrait of the Prophet in *Heroes* can be found in *Lectures on the History of Literature,* which had been delivered between April and July 1838. In his earlier discussion he qualifies his praise for Mahomet, "an enthusiastic man, who had by the powers of his own mind gained a flash of the truth," by implicitly contrasting him with Shakespeare, with whom "there are always the noblest sympathies, no sectarianism, no cruelty, no narrowness, no vain egotism" (*Lectures* 106–7, 158). Carlyle would elaborate this distinction between the Prophet and the Bard with considerable vehemence in his lecture on heroes. Less a sign of cultural chauvinism than an indication of spiritual restlessness, it was Carlyle's energetic "religiosity" that enabled him to re-create the circumstances of Mahomet's conversion with open-eyed verisimilitude. Watt rightly stressed that Carlyle "was the first writer in either east or west to attempt to fathom the inner experience of the founder of Islam. . . . [He] alone was interested in the man, the human person, grappling with the problems of human life and destiny that are common to all men" (253). That Carlyle places Shakespeare above Mahomet in his pantheon of heroes is a mark of the dramatist's superior intellectual freedom, not of his superior cultural worth.

Carlyle's biographical approach to Mahomet was heavily influenced by his sources, which in turn influenced his use of these sources. He was wary of relying heavily on the two supposedly authoritative versions of the Prophet's life that were available to him — George Sale's translation of the Koran published in 1734, to which he added an introductory essay, and Edward Gibbon's *History of the Decline and Fall of the Roman Empire* (1776–88). Sale (1696–1736) was a London solicitor who had worked at one point for the Society for the Promotion of Christian Knowledge and, according to Robert Irwin, "regarded the Arabs as the scourge of God visited on the Christians for their errors and schisms" (121). Sale admitted in his "Preliminary Discourse" that the "protestants alone are able to attack the Koran with success; and for them, I trust, Providence has reserved the glory of its overthrow" (iv). Gibbon, who relied heavily on Sale's work, was more familiar to Carlyle as the withering prosecutor of Christianity, but his attitude to Islam was only slightly less critical. He cautioned that the "talents of Mahomet are entitled to our applause, but his success has perhaps too strongly attracted our admiration. Are we surprised that a multitude of proselytes should embrace the doctrine and the passions of an eloquent fanatic?" (5:394). Notwithstanding his accomplishments, the founder of Islam was, for Gibbon, a "victorious impostor" driven by the "ruling passion" of "ambition" (5:377). From their respective vantage points, Sale and Gibbon each provided Carlyle with a clear if stringently Western view of the social and political context of Islam, yet neither threw much light on Mahomet's inner world. Sale's synopsis of Mahomet's "personal qualifications" is grudgingly narrow: "He was a man of at least tolerable morals, and not such a monster of wickedness as he is usually represented. And indeed it is scarce possible to conceive, that a wretch of so profligate a character should ever have succeeded in an enterprize of this nature; a little hypocrisy and saving of appearances, at least, must have been absolutely necessary; and the sincerity of his intentions is what I pretend not to inquire into" (41).

Gibbon's tendency to treat spiritual matters as political conflicts in disguise was appealing to Carlyle on one level. He valued the contrast that the author of *The Decline and Fall* established between seventh-century Christianity, fractured by increasingly arcane and mystical theological disputes, and Islam, strengthened by a resolutely nonmiraculous faith in one God and His apostle Mahomet. Gibbon reinforced Carlyle's conviction that theology had little to do with true religion, a conviction that had been buttressed by the latter's distaste for the controversies of the Oxford Movement. For Gibbon, Mahomet embodies the worldly practicality and the independent bent of the Arab nature. He resists the tendency to deify himself, and instead forges a creed that is austere in both form and substance:

> The creed of Mohammed is free from suspicion or ambiguity; and the Koran is a glorious testimony to the unity of God. The prophet of Mecca rejected the worship of idols and men, of stars and planets, on the rational principle that whatever rises must set, that whatever is born must die, that whatever is corruptible must decay and perish. In the author of the universe his rational enthusiasm confessed and adored an infinite and eternal being, without form or place, without issue or similitude, present to our most secret thoughts, existing by the necessity of his own nature, and deriving from himself all moral and intellectual perfection. (5:339)

But Carlyle objected to the manner in which Gibbon diminished the integrity of Mahomet's spiritual affirmation by distinguishing too rigidly between its Mecca and Medina phases. According to Gibbon, Mahomet became obsessed with the expulsion of idolaters and unbelievers following his flight from Mecca to Medina. In his view, the Prophet's injunctions to convert or destroy the infidels transformed the creed into a militant doctrine of punishment and submission, informed by a fatalistic resignation to the will of Allah. Gibbon perceived a dangerous confusion of political and religious authority: "From his establishment at Medina, Mahomet assumed the exercise of the regal and sacerdotal office; and it was impious to appeal from a judge whose decrees were inspired by the divine wisdom" (5:358). In consequence, Gibbon's Mahomet was corrupted by his own power: "Of his last years, ambition was the ruling passion; and a politician will suspect that he secretly smiled . . . at the enthusiasm of his youth and the credulity of his proselytes." Gibbon concludes that both the Prophet and his religion became "gradually stained" (5:377) by their association with war, violence, and imperialism.

Despite his disagreements with Sale and Gibbon, Carlyle appreciated the historical specificity of their respective accounts. But neither author provided him with the most salient feature of his own portrait — the intimate narrative of Mahomet's personal and spiritual development. Carlyle's most important source, unknown to his twentieth-century defenders and detractors, had been written by Antoine Isaac Silvestre de Sacy (1758–1838), whom Irwin refers to as "the most distinguished scholar of classical Arabic in the early nineteenth century" (7).[2] The essay provided Carlyle with a powerful refutation of the arguments advanced by Sale and Gibbon that Mahomet was an ambitious charlatan consumed by a lust for worldly power. Sacy showed that the personal life of the Prophet demonstrated a quite contrary reality, namely that Islam had flourished — and continued to flourish — because of the moral and spiritual vitality of its founder's creed. Throughout the essay, Sacy underscores Mahomet's role as an inspired leader, governor, and administrator. He abstracts the Prophet of his miraculous aspects, while highlighting the humanity and the basic decency of his religious vision. From the outset, Sacy is determined to separate Mahomet from the accretions of legend and myth: "We have tried to resist using the accounts of the Prophet's life that have been transmitted in the writings of his most fervent disciples, accounts in which the Muslims have embellished both his public and private life" (187). Instead, he concentrates on the steady expansion of Mahomet's spiritual receptivity. In his handling of Mahomet's conversion in his fortieth year, Sacy gives prominence to the Prophet's social and political objectives, yet he never underestimates the autonomy and the integrity of the founder's faith. Unlike Sale and Gibbon, Sacy refuses to treat the doctrines of Islam primarily as political maneuvers. Sacy agrees with Gibbon that Mahomet's world was torn apart by religious and tribal factionalism: "The Arabs, divided by many tribal rivalries, were plunged into the most grotesque idolatries. . . . The eastern Christians were broken up into an infinite number of sects, who persecuted one another with fanatical fervor. . . . Persia itself had for a long period been wracked by civil war and by conquest" (188). But there was nothing cynical or self-serving about Mahomet's aim to unify the Arabs under one coherent faith, which he hoped would form the basis of a new civil society. Sacy observes, "It was in these circumstances that Mahomet sought the inspiration of God to serve as a prophet and apostle, and to establish a religion that would unify heathens, jews, and even lapsed Christians" (188). Drawing from this thesis, Carlyle sets the Prophet's spiritual education in the context of the "Arab idolatries, argumentative theologies, traditions, subtleties, rumours and hypotheses of Greeks and Jews." Mahomet's heroism lies in his capacity to look "through the shews of things into *things*" (*Heroes* 66, 60). Sacy offers vivid testimony of the Prophet's intellectual abilities. He possesses "a penetrating spirit, a capacious memory, an alert and lively eloquence, a rare presence of person, a tenacious strength and courage, a robust and strong temperament, a grave and imposing demeanor, a deep knowledge of men, an art of dissimulation that was necessary to harness the passions and conscience of men, and that was crucial to the success of his mission" (188–89). Sacy effectively refutes Gibbon's "impostor" theory by showing that the Prophet's use of artifice was self-defensive and necessary. Without well-practiced cunning, Mahomet could not have survived, let alone prevailed, in the dangerously fractious and violent atmosphere of his times.

Sacy also pays close attention to Mahomet's domestic domain because it intimately discloses the personal qualities that will later distinguish him as a ruler: "The private sphere was where he revealed the leading traits of his character. He would demonstrate his quickness of perception, his prudence, his steady devotion to the one true God, the sweetness of his character, the reliability of his finances; his noble and exquisite manners in the company of strangers, his vivacity and jocularity with his friends, his kindness and patience with servants" (206). Sacy uses anecdotes throughout the essay to highlight the formidable challenges that the Prophet confronts in attempting to realize his goals. When Mahomet appointed Ali his lieutenant in front of family members, "a universal laughter erupted, and everyone said that Abu-Thaleb, from now on, had better obey the injunctions of his nephew" (190). Carlyle includes the story but counsels his readers that "it proved not a laughable thing; it was a very serious thing!" (*Heroes* 63). Mahomet's growing fame eventually frightens his enemies, and they warn his uncle to curb the young man's preaching. Sacy's report of the conversation between Abu-Thaleb and Mahomet stresses the Prophet's tender emotions: "Abu-

Thaleb thought he would warn his nephew about the dangers to which he was exposing his friends. The Prophet, who was fearless, told his Uncle that even if he placed the sun on his right shoulder and the moon on his left, he could not renounce his enterprise; at the same time, his eyes filled with tears" (190). Sacy's version contrasts pointedly with that of Gibbon, who regarded Mahomet's reply as the utterance of "an intrepid fanatic" (5:353). For Carlyle, the episode yields insight into the inner struggle of Mahomet, who "felt that Abu Thaleb was good to him; that the task he had got was no soft, but a stern and great one" (*Heroes* 63). Sacy complements this sketch of Mahomet's character with a vivid physical description of him: "He was of medium height with a ruddy temperament; he had a large head, a tanned complexion, which was animated by bright colors, and physical traits that were regular yet strongly pronounced; wide eyes, black and fiery, with a forehead slightly projected, an aquiline nose, full cheeks, and the shape of his jaw exquisitely curved; his large mouth, white teeth, slightly crooked; he had a little black mole below his bottom lip, and between his eyebrows, a vein that tended to color when he became angry. His physiognomy was graceful and majestic, and his gait was relaxed despite his stoutness" (205–6). For Carlyle, Mahomet's features betray the depth and intensity of his character: "One hears of [his] beauty: his fine sagacious honest face, brown florid complexion, beaming black eyes; — I somehow like too that vein on the brow, which swelled up black, when he was in anger" (59).

Sacy's essay prompted Carlyle to reconsider Sale and Gibbon's argument that might and right were synonymous in Mahomet's religion. Sale believed that it "is certainly one of the most convincing proofs that Mohammedism was no other than a human invention, that it owed its progress and establishment almost entirely to the sword" (49–50). Gibbon's analysis was more subtle, but he arrived at a similar conclusion. Islam survived because it shaped itself in response to human needs while maintaining strict limits to its supernatural claims: "The Mohammedans have uniformly withstood the temptation of reducing the object of their faith and devotion to a level with the senses and imagination of man. 'I believe in one God, and Mohammed the apostle of God,' is the simple and invariable profession of Islam. The intellectual image of the Deity has never been degraded by any visible idol; the honours of the prophet have never transgressed the measure of human virtue" (5:394). Gibbon contends that such a creed was conducive to fanaticism because it checked independence and inquiry among the faithful and promoted "a spirit of charity and friendship," while at the same time it encouraged enmity toward unbelievers: "The hostile tribes were united in faith and obedience, and the valour which had been idly spent in domestic quarrels was vigorously directed against a foreign enemy" (5:396). Conversely, Sacy sets the issue of the Prophet's penchant for conflict in another context. More emphatically than Gibbon, Sacy insists on the humane aspect of Mahomet's desire for a religion stripped of miracles, one intended to "substitute idolatrous cults with a more dignified Divinity that conformed to the interests of human nature and society" (207). In defending Mahomet against the accusation that he transformed himself into a cult, Sacy insists that "he abolished a large number of brutal and inhuman rituals that were revolting to reason, that had been sanctioned by the traditions of the Arabs" (207).

Carlyle follows Sacy in denying that Mahomet was exclusively dedicated to "propagating his Religion by the sword" (*Heroes* 64). Like all great religions, in Carlyle's view, Islam succeeded because of the truthfulness of its teachings, rather than because of the strength of its battalions. As Carlyle expresses it in his lecture, the Prophet's message could not have endured for long if it were rooted in violence. It triumphed and prospered because it fulfilled an eternal human desire for peace, order, beauty, conduct, and purpose. Gibbon mentions Mahomet's mild character but adds that "the clemency of the prophet was decided by his interest" (5:360). Sacy points out that in comparison with most rulers of the time, Mahomet was a mild and tolerant governor, who rarely resorted to bloodlust: "His leniency was denied very rarely, and he seldom demanded the sort of horrible and bloody punishments that have polluted the annals of history" (206). Islam progressed in compliance with the genius of its founder and the aspirations of his followers: "The impartial judgment of history will assign a distinguished place to this extraordinary man, who through the force of his genius began one of the most shocking and astonishing revolutions of all times. Despite the errors and imperfections of his doctrine, it is one that conveys a noble idea of Divinity, and summons men to a realization of their own highest nature and final destination" (206–7). Carlyle shared this evolutionary notion of the triumph of Islam: "I care little about the sword: I will allow a thing to struggle for itself in this world, with any sword or tongue or implement it has, or can lay hold of. . . . In this great Duel, Nature herself is umpire, and can do no wrong: the thing which is deepest-rooted in Nature, what we call *truest,* that thing and not the other will be found growing at last" (*Heroes* 65). The later opponent of Darwin had arrived at a quasi-Darwinian conception of might and right in the way that truth vanquished falsity in the spread of Islam.[3]

Sacy's admonitions about the impenetrable and confusing content of the Koran were also helpful to Carlyle, who struggled mightily with Sale's translation of it, a "wearisome confused jumble, crude, incondite; endless itera-

tions, long-windedness, entanglement; most crude, incondite; — insupportable stupidity, in short!" (*Heroes* 67). Sacy understood these frustrations:
"One only has to open the Koran to be overwhelmed by its incoherence, lack
of unity, repetitiveness, vaguenesses, not to mention the contradictions that
seem to occur on every page" (209). But the haphazard manner in which the
book was composed did not undermine its unique merits: "We can assure
our readers that there is much that is good, beautiful, profound, and graceful
in this book of Mahomet's teachings; and that the errors are largely attributable to the manner in which it was composed" (210). Carlyle overcame
"discrepancies of national taste" far enough to admit that "natural stupidity
is by no means the character of Mahomet's Book; it is natural uncultivation
rather. The man has not studied speaking; in the haste and pressure of
continual fighting, has not time to mature himself into fit speech. . . . The
panting breathless haste and vehemence of a man struggling in the thick of
battle for life and salvation . . . this is the Koran." Carlyle regards the book
as a reflex of the Prophet's own predicament, which places him at "the
centre of a world wholly in conflict" (*Heroes* 67–68). Sacy repeatedly
stresses Mahomet's reluctance to identify himself with miracles. For Carlyle, the Koran explains why. Mahomet's vision rests on the miraculousness
of the natural world, and the awe, wonder, and worship that it inspires:
"That this so solid-looking material world is, at bottom, in very deed,
Nothing; is a visual and tactual Manifestation of God's power and presence;
— a shadow hung out by Him on the bosom of the void Infinite." The
Prophet's response to those who demand miracles of him conveniently
affirms Carlyle's notion of natural supernaturalism at the same time it ma-
jestically illustrates his authority: "Mahomet can work no miracles; he often
answers impatiently: I can work no miracles. I? 'I am a Public Preacher';
appointed to preach this doctrine to all creatures. Yet the world, as we can
see, had really from of old been all one great miracle to him" (70). The
natural world marks both the finite limits of human knowledge and the
infinite possibilities of God's wisdom. In turn, for Carlyle, the Koran defines
the boundaries of Mahomet's vision, and in its exasperating intricacy ex-
emplifies the eternal truth that "to get into the truth of anything, is ever a
mystic act" (62). It may be that Carlyle himself had reached the boundaries
of his own faith in trying to comprehend Islam.

It is Sacy, rather than Sale or Gibbon, who persuaded Carlyle that Mahomet's religion "is a kind of Christianity; has a genuine element of what is
spiritually highest looking through it, not to be hidden by its imperfections"
(*Heroes* 75). Through the confining lens of postcolonial theory, this remark
can easily be construed as symptomatic of Carlyle's "Orientalist" blinders.

But it, and the subsequent discussion of Mahomet's "quackery" in the
essay on Shakespeare, cannot be separated from the central issue of Carlyle's own spiritual evolution. Islam intrigued and repelled him in the same
manner as the Scottish Calvinism of his parents. Both creeds were distinguished by the bedrock piety of their adherents: "Above all things, it has
been a religion heartily *believed.* These Arabs believe their religion, and try
to live by it! No Christians, since the early ages, or only perhaps the English
Puritans in modern times, have ever stood by their Faith as the Moslems do
by theirs, — believing it wholly, fronting Time with it, and Eternity with it"
(76). But the constrictive side of this austere devotion was the latent possibility of fanaticism and the enervation of rational judgment. The barriers
that separated the private and public realms of thought and action seemed
fragile and tenuous in both religions. Their "naked formlessness" (168)
simultaneously attracted and disturbed Carlyle. Having witnessed the de-
mise of his close friend and mentor Edward Irving (1792–1834), he was
suspicious of zealots, even those with "the life-guidance now of one hundred and eighty millions of men these twelve hundred years" (52). His
abrupt condemnation of the Koran in the essay on Shakespeare as "a stupid
piece of prolix absurdity" (102) forms part of the volcanic ebb and flow
of his skepticism. Conversely, it is Shakespeare's stubborn resistance to
prophecy that consoles Carlyle in periods of doubt: "Was it not perhaps far
better that this Shakspeare, every way an unconscious man, was *conscious*
of no Heavenly message? He did not feel, like Mahomet, because he saw
into those internal Splendours, that he specially was the 'Prophet of God:'
. . . was he not greater than Mahomet in that?" (101).

The Arabian prophet was not alone in being relegated beneath Shakespeare. Cromwell, "a Christian heroic man," falls short of the Bard's perfection: "We will not assert that Cromwell was an immaculate man; that he
fell into no faults, no insincerities among the rest" (*Heroes* 185). In the
retrospect of the 1850s, Carlyle's denunciation of Mahomet the "Babbler"
(101) was consistent with his vitriolic attacks against the "rubbishing Puritanism" of dissenters and the "beggarly Twaddle" (Wilson, *Zenith* 372) of
Victorian Christianity. More pertinently, in his later reflection on "Spiritual
Optics" (1852), Carlyle denounced the Old Testament and declared, "If we
had any veracity of soul and could get the old Hebrew spectacles off our
nose, should we run to Judæa or Houndsditch to look at the doings of the
Supreme? Who conquered anarchy and chained it everywhere under their
feet? Not the *Jews,* with their morbid imagination and foolish sheepskin
Targums" (Fielding, "Spiritual Optics" 232). The liberal theologian John
Tulloch rightly argued in *Movements of Religious Thought in the Nine-*

teenth Century (1884) that Carlyle's refusal "to look steadily at spiritual as distinct from natural life" vitiated his outlook. In Tulloch's view, the result of this fatal schism was that he could not imagine being created "save by a being who had a moral sense like his own. . . . He refused to acknowledge a Personal Life above his own life, a Life pitiful as well as just, Love as well as Law. And so his idea of the Divine reality sank into the idea of Supreme Force" (203–4). This explanation is a simplification, but Tulloch's charge cannot be dismissed entirely. In the essay on Mahomet, Carlyle found this "Divine reality" by imaginatively intersecting with the Prophet's spiritual awakening. The catalyst for this convergence was Sacy's essay in the *Biographie Universelle,* which allowed Carlyle to glean what he perceived as the "natural supernatural" essence of Islam and to unlock the secrets of its enduring sway. It allowed him to relive his own earlier spiritual struggle through the travails of the great Arabian prophet. With his customary astuteness, Kenneth J. Fielding has commented that "perhaps, at best Carlyle held to a religion of humanity" ("Skeptical Elegy" 255), and the essay on Mahomet amply supports this judgment. The spirit that Carlyle brings to his life of the Prophet is the antithesis of that embodied by radical Islamism in the twenty-first century, one that violates the sacred distinction between the will of the finite and of the infinite. Such an "idolatrous Idolatry" contradicts the teachings of Mahomet, who enjoins his faithful to "love one another freely; for each of you, in the eyes of his brothers, there will be Heaven enough!" (*Heroes* 108, 74).

NOTES

1. Said had faulted Carlyle for "overlooking the Prophet's own time and place" but acknowledged that his "attitude is salutary: Mohammed is no legend, no shameful sensualist, no laughable petty sorcerer" (152). Oddly, the most severe attack against Carlyle's essay on Mahomet came from outside the ranks of academic postcolonialism. In an essay delivered at the National Gallery of Art in Washington in 1965, Isaiah Berlin declared, "[Carlyle] does not begin to suppose that the Koran contains anything which he, Carlyle, could be expected to believe. What he admires Muhammed for is that he is an elemental force, that he lives an intense life. . . . The question of whether what Muhammed believed was true or false would have appeared to Carlyle perfectly irrelevant" (11).

2. For an analysis of Carlyle's use of the source, see my article, " 'Une Religion plus digne de la Divinité,' " and the digital facsimile of Sacy's essay that follows it as an appendix. Translations of Sacy are my own.

3. Carlyle always denied that he confused "might" with "right." In the margins

of a German biography of himself that he received in July 1866 he wrote, "What floods of nonsense have been and are spoken & thought (what they call thinking) about this poor maxim of Carlyle's! C. had discovered for himself, not without a satisfaction of religious kind, that no man who is not in the right, were he even a Napoleon I at the head of armed Europe, has any real *might* whatever, but will at last be found *might*less, and to have *done,* or settled as a fixity, nothing at all, except precisely so far as he was *not* in the wrong. Abolition and erosion awaits all 'doings' of his, except just what part of them *was right*" (Clubbe 98–99). For Carlyle and Darwin, see my article "Transcendent Wonder or Moral Putrefaction?"

"The First of the Moderns"

Carlyle's Goethe and the Consequences

TERENCE JAMES REED

I

Goethe was a revelation for Carlyle, and Carlyle was a fulfillment for Goethe. The warmth of appreciation was mutual, though the substance of the relationship was asymmetrical. A still developing young mind was drawing on the work — above all, as he saw it, the wisdom — of the established central figure in what gradually came to be seen as the richest literary and intellectual culture of contemporary Europe. The old poet was seeing his ideal of communication between cultures realized. The growing recognition of German culture in Britain was in good measure Carlyle's own doing. His advocacy as essayist and translator of "that strange literature" ("State of German Literature" [1827], *Works* 26:28), and of Goethe's work in particular, helped turn the tide of a cultural opinion that had long been uncomprehending, indeed hostile, toward all things German. Conservativism in taste had caricatured German drama as all wild excess. A matching narrow-mindedness in thought had rejected German philosophy as all obscure abstraction, even mysticism, mistaking Kant's term "transcendental" for "transcendent."

That is not altogether surprising, given Kant's bizarre choice of label for his central concept; though the confusion could have been avoided by reading Kant instead of relying on hearsay. Only Coleridge in this time had seriously read Kant and understood what he was driving at in his epistemological thinking. So with respect to both German literature and German philosophy there was a failure, indeed a total absence, of the empiricism on which British culture prided itself. Such truth as there ever was in the accusation of "wild" drama related to a phase now long past, the short-lived *Sturm und Drang* movement of the 1770s, a group of young writers who had mostly burned themselves out within five years, or at latest by 1781, the date of Schiller's youthful play *The Robbers,* which was the most quoted and parodied exhibit for the prosecution against their heightened emotionalism. The rebellious impulse *The Robbers* undoubtedly contains, even though disowned by its protagonist at the close, was read as seriously subversive in a Britain made jumpy by events in France. The play had, it is true, brought Schiller honorary citizenship of the new French republic. As late as 1820, Schiller and his literary partner Goethe were still being described by William Hazlitt as "incorrigible jacobins," set on "radical reform."[1] That Schiller had matured, long before his death in 1805, into a very different kind of writer was not noticed. Any of his later dramas were read — if read at all — in the light, or darkness, of fixed British prejudice, including his monumental masterpiece *Wallenstein* (1798) in Coleridge's translation. Goethe fared no better. The first part of his *Faust* (1808) gave offence to narrow morality and religion. The archangels' praise and celebration of the universe in the Prologue in Heaven was not enough to offset the flippant tone Mephistopheles used toward the Lord. Just what tone orthodoxy expected would be used from Down Below to Up Above is not clear.

All this anti-German prejudice bore down on young writers who might otherwise have been freely open to foreign stimulus. Fear of guilt by association prevented Coleridge from completing a translation of *Faust* he was contracted to make, and from putting his name to a selection he finally did put together.[2] Shelley was bolder, choosing to translate precisely the Prologue in Heaven and the orgiastic Walpurgisnacht scene. But then Shelley, having been sent down from Oxford for his pamphlet "The Necessity of Atheism" (1811), had nothing to lose. Nor did the always scandalous Byron, who in the second edition of his drama *Sardanapulus* (1832) publicly addressed Goethe as the "first of existing writers" who had "created the literature of his own country and illustrated [i.e., rendered more lustrous] that of Europe" (13:57). Nor was *Faust* the only source of offence in Goethe. The novel *Wilhelm Meisters Lehrjahre* (1795–96) also contained episodes and figures enough, especially the amoral and erotic Philine, to shock the conventionally minded British. The negative image of Goethe was completed by reports of his private life. That he had since 1775 been a leading figure in Weimar court society, and Duke Carl August's right-hand man in the practical administration of the duchy, was not noted.

Philine and the rest disturbed Carlyle too as he worked at his translation of the novel. He would probably not have approved of Goethe's metaphor in *Maxims and Reflections* (1809–32; 1833) for the function he was performing: "Translators are to be seen as active procurers who cry up a half-veiled beauty as highly worthy of our love: they arouse an irresistible desire for the original" (No. 947, *Werke* 12:499).[3] In general, Carlyle's enthusiasm for Goethe was not without such very British reservations, but they were amply overridden by the positive moral force he found throughout the master's works. This quality for him represented the essential Goethe — essential in the first place to meet Carlyle's own existential needs. It was in a sense pure chance that Carlyle was able to benefit from direct access to Goethe at all. He had begun to learn German in 1819 in order to read the mineralogical writings of Abraham Gottlob Werner, and had then discovered, probably through Madame de Staël's *De l'Allemagne* (1813), "a mine, far different from any of the Freyberg ones!" (3 Nov. 1829; *CL* 5:28).[4] His first literary reading in German was of Schiller's works, sent to him as unbound sheets that generated his earliest response, the biography of Schiller first serialised in the *London Magazine* in 1823–24 and published in book form in 1825. By that time, Carlyle had already published his translation of Goethe's *Wilhelm Meister's Apprenticeship* (1824).

By a further lucky chance, in 1827 Francis Jeffrey of the *Edinburgh Review* gave Carlyle a more or less free hand to write up German literature, indeed to "germanise" the public — surprisingly, since Jeffrey had till now been foremost in the opposition, arguing in 1802 that British literary taste was "fundamentally different from that of our neighbours in Germany" (qtd. in Ashton 9). By 1828, Carlyle wrote to Goethe and declared that Jeffrey had "virtually recanted" (18 April; *CL* 4:364). It is surely not sufficient explanation of this volte-face that Jeffrey had taken a shine to Carlyle personally as a young man of potential genius. Perhaps as for Carlyle himself *De l'Allemagne* was decisive: a culture that was now so highly regarded, and by so imposing a French authority at that, demanded to be looked at afresh. Carlyle's essays in the years to 1832, some of them published elsewhere (in the *Foreign Review,* the *Foreign Quarterly, Fraser's Magazine*), ranged widely: they treated the general condition of German literature; the medieval Nibelungen epic; Luther; German Romance; the idiosyncratic novelist Jean Paul Richter; the poet, dramatist, and aesthetic thinker Schiller — but repeatedly and above all Goethe: "Goethe's Helena" (1828), "Goethe" (1828), "Goethe's Portrait" (1832), and "Death of Goethe" (1832). Yet Carlyle's most eloquent response was to be in a quite different genre.

II

From 1824, when he sent Goethe a copy of his *Wilhelm Meister* translation, until the poet's death in 1832, the two corresponded. Their exchanges had obvious limitations. An unknown was approaching his hero, his spiritual

guide and father figure, reverently, "the humblest pool   may reflect faithfully the image even of the Sun" (18 April 1828; *CL* 4:365) in a spirit of
service to the great man and the cause he represents. There is gratitude for his
wisdom, for his kindness and condescension; there is naturally no breath of
criticism. The style on Carlyle's side is effusive, on Goethe's part friendly.
Small gifts are exchanged, from Goethe to Thomas's wife, Jane, from the
Carlyles to Goethe's daughter-in-law, Ottilie. Goethe sends some *vers d'occasion*. There is sometimes talk of a hoped-for visit to Weimar — "The hope
of meeting you is still among my dreams," runs the very first letter (24 June
1824; *CL* 3:87) — which never happens. For the rest the correspondence is
largely a diplomatic exchange between the representatives, however unequal, of two cultures. Carlyle regularly announces welcome progress in the
acceptance of German writing, Goethe's in particular, by the public, and he
is especially glad to report, given the earlier moral objections to *Wilhelm
Meister,* that one of its "warmest admirers" is "a lady of rank, and intensely
religious" (15 April 1827; *CL* 4:210). By the next year, the approval has
spread to a much broader audience: "Within the last six years, I should
almost say that the readers of your language have increased tenfold; and with
the readers, the admirers" (18 April 1828; *CL* 4:365). The next year Carlyle
reports further expansion of German literature to English speakers across the
globe, to "New Holland [Australia] itself." Further, Carlyle has "heard
lately that even in Oxford and Cambridge, our two English Universities,
which have all along been regarded as the strongholds of Insular pride and
prejudice, there is a strange stir in this matter" (22 Dec. 1829; *CL* 5:49). Jane
Welsh Carlyle has done her bit having read *Die Wahlverwandtschaften*
(*Elective Affinities* [1809]): "Shallow censurers of the 'Morality' of the
Work, who are not quite wanting here, she withstands with true female
zeal" (3 Nov. 1829; *CL* 5:26–27). Some achievement this, for a respectable
nineteenth-century lady: the novel narrates a double partner swap and the
birth of a legitimate child that resembles the two absent lovers.

There are practical by-products of the relationship, too. Letter formula-
tions of Goethe's are taken over into his published notice of Carlyle's
Schiller biography (20 July 1827; *Correspondence* 14, 22).[5] Help is asked
for and given on both sides. Carlyle needs a testimonial when he applies for
a chair of moral philosophy at St. Andrews University. Goethe provides a
substantial one, something more like a general essay: "Not quite one leaf
belongs directly to me" (*CL* 4:360), writes Carlyle to his brother John on 16
April 1828 after Goethe's letter has arrived, alas, too late. In the letter
accompanying his testimonial Goethe asks for Carlyle's opinion of a translation of his play *Torquato Tasso* — "*sacrilegious*" is Carlyle's verdict (18

April 1828; *CL* 4:366). Goethe also gently suggests placing a notice of its recent publication in one of the journals he knew Carlyle wrote for. There was only a single point of emotional intimacy in the correspondence, but that one crucial. Answering a request for "some particulars of [his] previous history," Carlyle sends Goethe a sketch of the spiritual struggles that his mentor's work had been decisive in resolving:

> With what readiness could I speak to you of it, how often have I longed to pour out the whole history before you! As it is, your works have been a mirror to me; unasked and unhoped for, your wisdom has counselled me; and so peace and health of soul have visited me from afar. For I was once an Unbeliever, not in Religion only, but in all the Mercy and Beauty of which it is the symbol; storm-tossed in my own imaginations; a man divided from men; exasperated, wretched, driven almost to despair; so that Faust's wild *curse*[6] seemed the only fit greeting for human life, and his passionate *Fluch vor allen der Geduld!* was spoken from my very inmost heart. (20 Aug. 1827; *CL* 4:248)

These are perhaps not quite the sort of "particulars" Goethe was expecting, "But," Carlyle continues, "now, thank Heaven, all this is altered" (*CL* 4:248). He would later recall the thanks owed to Goethe for this alteration in 1826, when Carlyle "emerg[ed], free in spirit, into the eternal blue of ether, — where, blessed be Heaven, I have, for the spiritual part, ever since lived." He saw this "immense victory" as no less than a "Conversion": "I then felt, and still feel, endlessly indebted to *Goethe* in the business; he, in his fashion, I perceived, had travelled the steep rocky road before me, — the first of the moderns" (*Reminiscences* 321).

III

Carlyle's grand public statement of his indebtedness to Goethe was of course *Sartor Resartus,* a work his correspondent never knew. The letters to Goethe increasingly hint at a creative turn, at the conscious ambition of "an Essayist . . . longing more than ever to be a Writer in a far better sense" (3 Nov. 1829; *CL* 5:29), and at the deeper and somewhat anxious sense of his potential to achieve that goal: "When I look at the wonderful Chaos within me, full of natural Supernaturalism, . . . I see not well what is to come of it all; and only conjecture from the violence of the fermentation that something strange may come" (31 Aug. 1830; *CL* 5:153–54). So strange, in the event, that its outlandish style might well have proved as little to Goethe's taste as the extravagances of his native Romantics. The persona of a professor of clothing history who glories in the name Diogenes Teufelsdröckh and comes from *Weissnichtwo* (*Sartor* 6), a grotesque very much in the mode of Jean Paul Richter's creations, might have seemed less than respectful. It might not have been obvious that it was a self-ironizing medium for Carlyle's autobiographical revelations. The fictional German professor has had to go through a dark night of the soul, the "Everlasting No," in which "Doubt had darkened into Unbelief" in order to arrive at a new affirmation which the work of Goethe, "the Wisest of our time" has inspired (121, 142). In the balancing chapter "The Everlasting Yea," gloom and "Weltschmerz" are defeated by a forthright resolve to replace one emblematic writer with another: "Close thy *Byron;* open thy *Goethe*" (143). The work of the Enlightenment, represented by Voltaire, is also declared finished. Moral injunctions and aperçus from *Wilhelm Meister* are scattered about, as are other Goethean concepts and phrases, including "healing sleep," "Renunciation" (142), and *"the living visible Garment of God"* (139, 142, 43).[7] The reassuring sense of earthly security that Goethe imparts is well captured in the phrase "a felt indubitable certainty of Experience" (145).

For Carlyle that sensual connection meant not just a material earthliness but a firmly grounded new spirituality. In the history of German literature that he never completed, Goethe and Schiller were to be the heroes of "a period of new Spirituality and Belief; in the midst of Old Doubt and Denial; as it were, a new revelation of Nature, and the Freedom and Infinitude of Man, wherein Reverence is again rendered compatible with Knowledge, and Art and Religion are one" (23 May 1830; *CL* 5:106). This literary revelation was a more markedly moral vision — more a replacement for religion — than the fundamentally secular art that Goethe and Schiller consciously practiced. The religious tone of Carlyle's vision for intellectual endeavor continues in the fifth lecture of *On Heroes and Hero Worship* — "The Hero as Man of Letters" — in which Goethe is declared a prophet in a profoundly unprophetic age. For Carlyle, art in its own right takes very much a back seat to earnest morality, which serves as the basis for his account of heroism. In a conversation with Emerson in 1847, he actually asserts that Goethe and Schiller wasted a lot of time with the "great delusion" of *"Kunst"* (7 July; Emerson, *Works* 5:274) and that Goethe realized this error and changed his tone in his late work — a thesis massively contradicted by the flow of lyrical poetry that continued right up to Goethe's death and by the completion, in the nick of time, of his *Faust* (1808–32). From all Carlyle's writings one would indeed scarcely know that Goethe was a poet, let alone the greatest lyrical poet in German to that or any date. Carlyle concentrates on texts from which doctrine can be extracted — the novel, above all *Wilhelm Meister*, where as its translator he has the text at his fingertips, the autobiography *Dichtung und Wahrheit* [Poetry and Truth] (1808–31), and collections of epigrams. He gets closest to the essential Goethe when, in the lecture "The Hero as Poet," he emphasizes the primacy of seeing: "To the Poet . . . we say first of all, See!" And: Goethe "*saw* the object" (*Heroes* 96). But that then becomes the notion of a Seer, more visionary than vision. Overall Carlyle is a cultural, rather than a literary, critic. It takes George Henry Lewes's biography to display Goethe to the English-speaking public in all his literary richness, righting the balance from the — indeed powerfully present — moral element to the aesthetic in which Goethe's morality is grounded.

Carlyle's emphasis on the moral or the "spiritual" was a reaction to what he saw as the materialism inherent in British society and codified in Utilitarian philosophy. The negative side of the "British empiricism" coin was an imperviousness to *ideas*. Not even just to specific ideas, but to ideas as such. Goethe himself noted in conversation with Johann Peter Eckermann that, however "great" they may be "as practical people," the English "as such are without actual reflection!" ["Alle Engländer sind als solche ohne eigentliche Reflexion"] (24 Feb. 1825; Eckermann 19:35). The suspicion of ideas may itself be the dubious idea, or meta-idea, that England contributed to the culture of the nineteenth century. The protest against this anti-intellectualism echoed down the decades, from Coleridge via Carlyle to George Eliot to Matthew Arnold, and at every point it was Germany that provided the term of comparison and a positive alternative model to British insularity. Coleridge from early on had to defend himself against the charge of dealing in ideas brought back from Germany. His successors went over to the offensive. George Eliot showed up the backwardness of British theology and scholarship. The antiquarianism of Mr. Casaubon in *Middlemarch* (1871–72) is itself hopelessly antiquated beside Germany's systematic modern *Wissenschaft*. Will Ladislaw tells Dorothea Brooke that "the Germans have taken the lead in historical inquiries, and they laugh at results which are got by groping about in the woods with a pocket-compass while they have made good roads" (194–95). Arnold likewise contrasted the unsystematic British approach to education, rooted in a fear of concerted state action that might endanger their freedoms (but freedom, he asked, to do what?) with Prussia's enlightened reform of schools and universities (see *Schools and Universities* [1868], *Prose Works* 4:185–264). And in the public controversies of which *Culture and Anarchy* (1869) was part, Arnold poses in *Friendship's Garland* (1871) as the editor of an imaginary German, Baron

Arminius von Thunder-ten-Tronckh, much as Carlyle had "edited" his Diogenes Teufelsdröckh.[8]

From being denigrated aliens, Germans had now become vital allies for
much that was best in Victorian thinking and writing.[9] Goethe is always in
the forefront: through George Henry Lewes's *Life of Goethe* (1855), which
as the first biography of the writer in any language had for once stolen a
march on German *Wissenschaft*; in John Stuart Mill's celebration in *On
Liberty* (1859) of Goethe's age as one of the three phases in European history
— the Reformation and the Enlightenment are the other two — in which "the
yoke of authority was broken" (*CWM* 18:243); and in Arnold's eloquent
praise of Goethe as *the* model for modern intellectual independence. There is
no better or more succinct account than Arnold's of Goethe as a continuator
of the Enlightenment in his essay "Heinrich Heine" (1863):

> Goethe's profound, imperturbable naturalism is absolutely fatal to all
> routine thinking; he puts the standard, once for all, inside every man
> instead of outside him; when he is told, such a thing must be so, there is
> immense authority and custom in favour of it being so, it has been held
> to be so for a thousand years, he answers with Olympian politeness,
> "But is it so? is it so to *me*?" Nothing could be more really subversive of
> the foundations on which the old European order rested; and it may be
> remarked that no persons are so radically detached from this order, no
> persons so thoroughly modern, as those who have felt Goethe's influ-
> ence most deeply. (*Prose Works* 3:110)[10]

IV

None of this, it is fair to say, could have happened without Carlyle's pioneer-
ing work. It would have delighted Goethe had he lived to see its rich conse-
quences. As it was, even its beginnings were a fulfillment for him. Not
merely for reasons of personal vanity, but because he could see how, through
one man's devoted mediation, Germany was enriching English culture. It
was an example of what he meant by "world literature" ("Weltliteratur"):
not an inert canon of works everyone felt they should have read, but a
dynamic interaction between national literatures, with individual writers
initiating and fostering relations across frontiers. From his earliest years,
Goethe had done this comparative work in imagination, had been a reader of
the world in all its geographical breadth and historical depth.[11] His tireless
empathy makes nonsense of any "anxiety of influence."[12] His work was

nourished by an intuitive understanding of his great predecessors from many cultures — English, Greek, Latin, Persian, Chinese. They provided stimulus and outer forms to speak through, but more deeply still the relationship was felt as a personal affinity, a live presence, friendship even: with Homer, with Shakespeare, with Catullus and Ovid, with Hafiz. An unbroken line runs down from them to his relations with contemporaries — with Byron, whom, unlike Carlyle, Goethe most admired among living writers,[13] through Carlyle to Sir Walter Scott. Carlyle tells Goethe that Scott's first published work was a translation of Goethe's history play *Götz von Berlichingen,* "to which circumstance many of his critics attribute no small influence on his subsequent poetical procedure" (18 April 1828; *CL* 4:364).[14] More simply put, the English historical novel had grown out of the German drama, which itself had grown out of Goethe's reading of Shakespeare. Such creative to-and-fro really was "Weltliteratur" at work. Carlyle writes to Goethe that Britain and Germany are now growing together: they "will not always remain strangers; but rather like two Sisters that have been long divided by distance and evil tongues, will meet lovingly together, and find that they are near of kin" (23 May 1830; *CL* 5:104). Indeed, all "Europe," Carlyle would later write, "in the communion of . . . its chief writers" is to "become more and more one universal Commonwealth" (22 Jan. 1831; *CL* 5:220). The sentiment is closely paralleled in the peroration of Arnold's essay "The Function of Criticism" (1859): "The criticism which alone can much help us for the future . . . is a criticism which regards Europe as being, for intellectual and spiritual purposes, one great confederation, bound to a joint action and working to a common result" (*Prose Works* 3:284).

Britain's relationship to Goethe is crowned by the gift of a seal from "Fifteen English Friends" on his final birthday in 1831 (28 Aug.; *Correspondence* 292–94).[15] By this time there is a London group, what Carlyle calls "a little poetic *Tugendbund* [virtuous society] of Philo-Germans forming itself, whereof you are the centre. . . . [I]t may grow into a more lasting Union" to match the Berlin Gesellschaft für ausländische Literatur (Foreign Literature Society) of which Carlyle had become an honorary member.[16] As he rightly comments of the English version of the society: that "such an attempt was possible among us, would have seemed strange, some years ago" (10 June 1831; *CL* 5:287), and he modestly refrains from claiming the credit. Goethe was surely in no doubt about it. Never, he writes, "did one nation take such pains to understand another, and show so much sympathy with another, as Scotland now does in respect to Germany" (15 June 1828, *Correspondence* 98–99).[17] For "Scotland," as they both knew, read "Carlyle." By the account of Goethe's amanuensis Eckermann, Goethe specifically admired the way Carlyle's literary judgments went to a writer's "spiritual and moral core." He perceived in Carlyle a "moral force of great significance" (to Eckermann, 25 July 1827; 19:576); he was certain of Carlyle's future achievement and effect.

V

Carlyle never met Goethe. A visit that was variously "among my dreams" (24 June 1824; *CL* 3:87) and "among our settled wishes" (17 Jan. 1828; *CL* 4:303) became "distant" and "a *luxury*" if always "worth entertaining." Weimar is regularly lauded, with all the force of Carlyle's initial capitals, as the "spot on this Globe" such as "Lovers of Wisdom" would of old make pilgrimage to in order to set eyes on the "Teacher of Wisdom" (20 Mar. 1830; *CL* 5:83). In the end, Goethe's home remains "a familiar City of the Mind" (10 June 1831; *CL* 5:286). Carlyle did not go to Germany until 1852. Goethe had been dead twenty years. Goethe's letters, packed away under other papers and their location forgotten, were only rediscovered after Carlyle's death.

VI

Eighteenth-century German writers had based a national literary renaissance on the perceived affinity with English literature, with Shakespeare as the great liberator. Nineteenth-century English writers took stimulus and conviction from German literature, with Goethe as the great example. It was a nice balance of obligation. Two world wars destroyed cultural relations between Britain and Germany. Germany was seen as above all the culture that produced and followed Nietzsche — a crude perception of a thinker who was himself crudely instrumentalized in the run-up to the First World War by nationalists and militarists like General von Bernhardi,[18] and again in the 1930s by the Nazis.

Such distortions aside, Nietzsche's perspective on Carlyle reveals deep divergences between nineteenth-century English and German intellectual developments, beyond those harmonies apparent in Carlyle and Goethe's relationship. Nietzsche — unknown at the time he wrote (c. 1870–1890) but destined in the twentieth century to be one of the most influential thinkers in European history, in his own arrogant but accurate metaphor "dynamite" (*Ecce Homo* [1888], *Werke* 2:1152) — was a ruthless secular thinker, an existential analyst with no time for conventional illusions or quasi-religious consolations. Ignoring the regard his admired Goethe had entertained for Carlyle and for the value of Carlyle's cultural mediation, Nietzsche sees in him "a semi-actor and rhetor, a tasteless muddlehead" who lacked philosophical depth, "an English atheist who makes a point of honour of *not* being one" (*Götzendämmerung* [*Twilight of the Idols* (1889)], *Werke* 2:998). He recognizes Carlyle's central importance in Britain, labeling as "Carlylism" the felt need for absolute belief, which he reads as a sign of weakness: for "the 'believer' of every kind is necessarily a dependent being — one who cannot posit *himself* as a purpose. . . . The 'believer' does not belong to *himself*" (*Der Antichrist* [1895], *Werke* 2:1221). Nietzsche makes much the same point against George Eliot: "They have got rid of the Christian god and believe they must now hang on all the more to Christian morality; that is an English consistency, we won't hold it against those little moral women *à la* Eliot. In England, in return for every small emancipation from theology, you have to restore your credit again as a terrifying moral fanatic. That's the *penance* you do over there" (*Götzendämmerung, Werke* 2:993). The English generally, of whose intellect Nietzsche has no high opinion, are plainly suffering from what he called "religiöse Nachwehen [religious afterpains]" (*Menschliches, Allzumenschliches* [*Human, All Too Human*] (1878), *Werke* 1:530). Considering the travails and contortions of other British intellectuals of the period — Arnold, Arthur Hugh Clough, James Anthony Froude, Edmund William Gosse — Nietzsche certainly had a point. Germans had left much of this intellectual angst behind them in the eighteenth century. Goethe and Schiller certainly had.

On much the same lines, Nietzsche attacks Carlyle's conception of the hero in history. For Nietzsche, great men embodied the raw realities of life — "injustice, lies, exploitation" — writ largest. Once these people had overcome opposition, "their essence was misunderstood and interpreted as good" (*Nachlass* [1881–84], *Werke* 3:861). Carlyle was the type of such interpreters. Nietzsche was on the whole in favor of raw realities — in favor, to start with, of recognizing them unblinkingly for what they were, but also concerned to derive from them a more vital culture and morality. On the first point, he was in agreement with that other major nineteenth-century German figure whose thinking invites comparison with Carlyle's, Hegel. Strangely, there is no sign that Carlyle was even aware of this dominant German intellectual authority of the 1820s. Perhaps he was too fixated on Weimar to notice what was going on in Berlin. In his lectures on the philosophy of history, Hegel like Nietzsche accepts and even celebrates the ruthlessness of "world-historical figures," the Alexanders, Caesars, and Napoleons. He differs from Nietzsche in not even attempting to derive anything worth calling morality from historical ruthlessness. At best these great figures realized, in both senses of the word, what the mass of people in their day must have wanted deep down, but were not conscious of until led by the nose. (As might be, Napoleon: "Let us invade Russia." People: "Ah yes, of course, Emperor.") Conventional morality is declared irrelevant, even sneered at: "Such world-historical individuals have, it is true, in pursuit of their great interests treated other, in themselves reputable interests and sacred rights casually, ruthlessly, behaviour that is exposed to moral blame. A great figure in his onward march treads underfoot many an innocent flower, must wreck many things on the way" (*Vorlesungen* 105). The ultimate justification for such acceptance is the alleged fact that history is the embodiment of Reason — the only assumption, Hegel says, that the philosopher brings to the study of history (*Vorlesungen* 28, 32).[19] Quite enough too, since any rational substance to history would need to be proved, not assumed. Hegel's is a ruthlessness of a different order from Nietzsche's, and it is a remarkable fact of the history of ideas that where Nietzsche has been demonized for his amoralism, to the point of becoming a byword outside specialist circles, Hegel in the public eye has got off virtually scot-free. Both thinkers, at all events, inhabit a different world from Carlyle. German and English cultures have touched, parted, touched and parted once more. They have yet, in any significant way, to come together again.

NOTES

1. "On the German Drama" (1820), qtd. by Ashton. Her study remains fundamental.

2. See Burwick and McKusick's edition of Coleridge's translation. This is a partial translation, with much of the original paraphrased in prose, designed to accompany a cycle of illustrations by Moritz Retsch. Coleridge's authorship is thought sufficiently uncertain to need stylometric support (312–30).

3. To Carlyle, Goethe speaks more circumspectly of the translator as "a prophet to his people" (20 July 1827; *Correspondence* 26). All translations in this essay are mine unless otherwise indicated.

4. Freiberg in Thuringia was the home of Germany's principal mining academy and Werner a leading light there in eighteenth-century geology. Carlyle does not mention Madame de Staël; her influence is asserted by Norton (*Correspondence* viii).

5. The notice related to the English original, and was published in Goethe's own journal *Über Kunst und Altertum* (1928) 6:2; for the German text see *Werke* 12:350.

6. "A curse above all on patience"; *Faust* Pt. 1:1606

7. Respectively the motifs "Heilschlaf" (see, for example, the prison scene in *Egmont,* or the opening of *Faust* Part Two), "Entsagen" (the theme especially of *Wilhelm Meisters Years of Travel*), and the quotation "der Gottheit lebendiges Kleid" from the speech of the Earth Spirit, *Faust* Pt. 1:509.

8. Both invented names betray the felt need, even when publicly drawing on German authority, still for safety's sake to hold it ironically at arm's length. Arnold's invention combines the legendary victor over the Roman armies of Varus in the Teutoburg forest in A.D. 9 (Arminius = Hermann) with a name drawn from Voltaire's *Candide* (1759)

9. For a fuller account of this process, see my essay " 'Jene seltsame Literatur . . .': Wie im 19. Jahrhundert der deutsche Geist den englischen gerettet hat."

10. Regrettably, Arnold did not feel able to take on the whole Goethe in an essay — it would be "an alarming task" (to Fanny Arnold, Dec. 1877; *Letters* 2:165).

11. On this creative openness of Goethe's, see my essay "Goethe — der Weltbürger als Weltleser. Lektüre als Akzeptanz des Fremden."

12. The author of that not very felicitous phrase unaccountably calls Goethe "one of the great deniers of influence" (Bloom 56). On the contrary, no writer has more generously declared his manifold indebtedness.

13. See the poems "An Lord Byron," a fatherly admonitory word to the wild, and "Auf Lord Byron," celebrating Byron's Greek commitment and mourning his death (*Gedichte* 583, 703). Euphorion, the child of Faust and Helena in act 3 of *Faust* Part Two, is a symbolic representation of Byron. When the overbold child falls to his death, the stage direction reads "We seem to recognise a familiar figure." For an extensive conversational response to Byron, see Goethe to Eckermann, 24 Feb. 1825 (Eckermann 19:131).

14. See the letter from Scott that gave Goethe much pleasure, quoted in full by Eckermann, 25 July 1827 (Eckermann 19:572).

15. See Goethe's poem in reply, "Den fünfzehn englischen Freunden," and the augmented version, "An die neunzehn Freunde in England" (*Gedichte* 295, 709).

16. The Berlin Society's citation, dated 24 Sept. 1830, was enclosed in Goethe's letter of 5 Oct.; see *Correspondence* 222–24.

17. See also Goethe to Eckermann, 11 Oct. 1828 (Eckermann 19:265).

18. See Bernhardi, *Deutschland und der nächste Krieg* (1912).

19. The way great men's powerful drives generate some pattern or other, which Hegel is committed a priori to regarding as "rational," is what he calls the "cunning of Reason [die List der Vernunft]" (*Vorlesungen* 105).

Carlyle, Elizabeth Barrett Browning, and the Hero as Victorian Poet

BEVERLY TAYLOR

The Poet who could merely sit on a chair, and compose stanzas, would never make a stanza worth much. He could not sing the Heroic warrior, unless he himself were at least a Heroic warrior too.
> —Thomas Carlyle, "The Hero as Poet," *Heroes* 77

On 4 February 1842 Elizabeth Barrett — who had spent a great deal of time composing stanzas while reclining on a sofa — echoed "the philosopher" Carlyle by calling "literature a 'fire-proof pleasure,' " observing that writing had provided her "occupation & distraction" especially valuable during her invalidism (*BC* 5:230). That EBB recalled his metaphor more than a decade after Carlyle had used it in an 1830 review essay on the German philosopher and novelist Jean Paul Richter (see *Works* 27:140) suggests both the power of Carlyle's imaginative expression and the degree to which his thought resonated with her own.[1] It was not really this utilitarian view of writing as "occupation & distraction" that forcibly spoke to her, however, so much as Carlyle's celebration of the poet as *vates,* a prophetic revealer of the transcendent and a heroic leader of his society. Carlyle's view of the poet as both prophet and activist advanced in *On Heroes, Hero-Worship, and the Heroic in History* chimed perfectly with her girlhood longing to liberate Greece from the Ottoman empire by leading troops into battle with her songs (see *BC* 1:361). In another letter penned on 4 February 1842, she echoed Carlyle's representation of Samuel Johnson in *Heroes.* Confessing that she did not have "the least bit of real love" for Johnson ("this great lumbering bookcase of a man"), she accepted Carlyle's assertion that he was "a specimen-man" (*BC* 5:231) because she was immensely enthusiastic about Carlyle himself, the "noble-high-thinking man" (*BC* 5:281) whose work on the hero as poet brought us "nearer . . . to the *Immortals*" (*BC* 5:231). "I am an adorer of Carlyle," she avowed, for "he has done more to raise poetry to the throne of its rightful inheritance than any writer of the day" (*BC* 5:281). Though passages from his earlier work stuck in her memory (see also *BC* 4:191), her "Carlyleship" (*BC* 6:6) essentially traces to

Heroes, and she enacted her "Carlyleship" by becoming an increasingly activist hero-poet even as Carlyle, "that profound thinker" (*BC* 5:82), voiced skepticism about the poet's importance.[2]

Though the biographer David Masson recalled that Carlyle's name ran "like wildfire through the British Islands and through English-speaking America . . . especially among the young men" (67), the influence of *Heroes* on mid-Victorian feminist activists deserves fuller scrutiny than I have space to consider here. We know that many women active in the period's social and political campaigns on both sides of the Atlantic passed through the Carlyles' drawing room at Cheyne Row, some becoming lasting friends of Jane Welsh Carlyle. The list would include Harriet Martineau, Geraldine Jewsbury, Bessie Rayner Parkes, Barbara Leigh Smith Bodichon, Margaret Fuller, and American abolitionists Lydia Maria Child and Rebecca Spring, among others.[3] Attention to the influence of *Heroes* on EBB, in particular, is especially noteworthy, because of the degree to which she embraced the role of radical intellectual encouraged by Carlyle. Having long believed, like Carlyle, that the poet-prophet "penetrated . . . into the sacred mystery of the Universe" (*Heroes* 78), she began in the 1840s to strive self-consciously to be the hero as poet, a "committed," rather than "detached," intellectual of the sort represented by Carlyle.[4] While *Heroes* emphatically articulated ideas EBB had already embraced about the reality of what John Holloway would describe much later as a "cosmic spiritual life" and a conception of the world defined by "*anti-mechanism*" (23), the impact of Carlyle's work is most conspicuous in her increasing dedication to speaking out on contemporary issues. As the friendships of Carlyle and Robert Browning and of Browning and EBB developed in the next few years, Carlyle would urge both Browning and EBB to assume the mantle of the public intellectual by writing prose. She, in contrast, would increasingly insist that the "hero as poet" was every bit as important as the "hero as man of letters" — and perhaps even more crucial to revealing the cosmic spiritual life that should determine the course of political and economic affairs. Carlyle's *Heroes* helped convert her long-standing attachment to literary tradition and aesthetics, an emphasis she characterized as her "filial spirit" and "reverent love" of poet "grandfathers" (*BC* 10:14),[5] into a commitment to aggressively treat contemporary political topics such as abolition and Italian unification and independence. In the course of making that shift in her writing, she increasingly quarreled with Carlyle over the importance of the poet even as she invoked his writings as foundational to her beliefs.

In April 1842 EBB described Carlyle as "a great prose poet," both for his apprehension of transcendent truth and for his celebration of the hero as poet. Flattered that her writing had been compared to Carlyle's, she exclaimed, "My prose style like Carlyle! — To remind anyone in the world of Carlyle were praise enough & too much!" She explained that his prose is poetic not because of its formal characteristics but because of its transcendent inspiration and its transcendent Truth:

> He does not write pure English . . no, nor quite pure German — nor pure Greek, by any means. But he *writes thoughts*. . . . There is something wonderful in this struggling forth into sound of a contemplation bred high above dictionaries & talkers — in some silent Heavenly place for the mystic & true. The sounds do come — strangely indeed & in unwrought masses, but still with a certain confused music & violent eloquence, which prove the power of *thought* over *sound*. Carlyle seems to me a great prose poet. At any rate he is a man for the love & reverence of all poets, seeing that he, almost sole among the present world's critics, recognizes the greatness & the hopefulness of their art. (*BC* 5:301)

His writing is poetic in its "thought," it derives from "the mystic & true." He also serves poetry, she says, by recognizing its "hopefulness," its potential to effect good. If at the level of "dictionaries & talkers" and musical sound he remains in the realm of prose, he nonetheless discerns and expounds the importance of the poet. Three years later, in one of her early letters to Browning, EBB reiterated her sense that Carlyle was a poet: "The great teacher of the age, Carlyle, . . . fills the office of a poet . . . by analyzing humanity back into its elements, to the destruction of the conventions of the hour. That is — strictly speaking . . . the office of the poet" (*BC* 10:101).

Ironically, whereas EBB praised Carlyle's prose for its poetry, he admonished her to abandon poetry for prose. She was not the only one he so advised. In 1841 (several years before Browning began corresponding with EBB), Carlyle similarly counseled that after *Sordello* (1840) and *Pippa Passes* (1841), Browning's "next work" should be "written in prose!" In Browning's case, Carlyle recommended prose as an antidote to obscurity. He judged that Browning had "a rare spiritual gift, poetical, pictorial, intellectual, by whatever name we may prefer calling it." But Browning suffered from obscurity, and prose represented his best chance of cure: "to unfold" this gift "into articulate clearness is naturally the problem of all problems for you." Though Carlyle affirmed Browning's "poetic faculty," that faculty would go unheeded unless he could make himself understood: "Unless poetic faculty means a higher-power of common understanding, I know not what it means. One must first make a *true* intellectual representation of a thing, before any poetic interest that is true will supervene" (*BC* 5:64–65).

After EBB sent her two-volume 1844 collection *Poems* to Carlyle,[6] she reported on 1 September that in "kind letters" he had observed "that a person of my 'insight & veracity' ought to use 'speech' rather than 'song' in these days of crisis" — a recommendation that she did not find "exceedingly gratifying" (*BC* 9:122).[7] As she reported to Mary Russell Mitford, she refuted Carlyle's implication that writers should grapple with the challenges of the times in prose: "I wrote to defend the exercise of my art, — telling him that if the Tyrtæuses were made to fight, instead of singing, till the battle was done, the battle wd not probably be *won*" (*BC* 9:127). In alluding to the story of the Spartan poet whose songs inspired his countrymen in their battles with the Messenians (see *BC* 9:128n10), EBB effectively echoed her own childhood ambition to effect political change through song. As she reported in a witty autobiographical essay about "Beth," probably written in the early 1840s, as a girl she had aspired to lead Greek troops to win their independence from the Ottoman Empire. She planned at the age of fifteen to "arm herself in complete steel" and as "chief of a battalion she wd destroy the Turkish empire, & deliver 'Greece the glorious.'" Though "the flashing of swords was bright in the eyes of Beth," she would first gather her battalion with song: "She was to sing her own poetry all the way she went . . . attracting to her side many warriors" who would liberate Greece (*BC* 1:361). Conceiving of poetic song as a potent weapon for vanquishing oppression, EBB deployed the same metaphor in refuting Carlyle's judgment that she should write prose, describing Carlyle's own achievements as a triumph effected by poetry: "In fact he is a poet himself with a rhythm of his own, — & while he thinks he fights, he is often singing" (*BC* 9:128).

Despite her youthful aspirations to effect social change by song, by the early 1840s EBB keenly felt her own failure to address "these days of crisis." Her 1843 poem "The Cry of the Children" constituted an important foray into social criticism, rapidly becoming influential in industrial reform literature. Inspired by her correspondent R. H. Horne's extensive research and report to Parliament on working conditions in mines and factories, her poignant, powerful evocation of the immiseration of child laborers spurred Edgar Allan Poe to associate the poem with Dante (one of Carlyle's two illustrations of the hero as poet), remarking "a horror sublime in its simplicity — of which a far greater than Dante might have been proud" (*BC* 10: 352).[8] But when the Leeds Ladies Committee in January 1845 invited EBB to write a poem for their Anti–Corn Law Bazaar, she ultimately declined because of opposition from her father and brothers. Although she contrasted her own "liberalism"[9] with her father's "Whiggery" and described herself as "leagues before the rest" of her family "in essential radicalism," she yielded to their pressure, influenced by her friend and kinsman John Kenyon and by critic H. F. Chorley's opinion that writing against the Corn Laws would "ruin . . . for ever" her "poetical reputation" (see her account of these events in *BC* 10:60–65). She agonized: "I wd rather not narrow the sphere of my poetry by wearing a party badge either in politics or religion," but she also lamented, "to refuse to give or rather to refuse to attempt to give, a voice to a great public suffering, when I am asked to do it . . . & when I recognize the existence of the suffering . . . should THIS be refused?" (*BC* 10:61–62).

This missed opportunity to become the hero as poet coincided with her vexation that Carlyle's commitment to the gospel of work now seemed to exclude the poet from the leadership role his *Heroes* had authorized. She first reported the invitation to write for the Anti–Corn Law Bazaar in January 1845 (*BC* 10:34). Less than a month later, in her fourth letter to her new correspondent Robert Browning, she queried, "Does Mr Carlyle tell you that he has forbidden all 'singing' to this perverse & forward generation, which should work & not sing? And have you told Mr Carlyle that song is work, and also the condition of work? — I am a devout sitter at his feet — and it is an effort to me to think him wrong in anything — . . . . But for Carlyle to think of putting away even for a season, the poetry of the world, was wonderful, and has left me ruffled in my thoughts ever since" (*BC* 10:81).

While regarding herself as "his disciple," EBB had clearly struggled with the tension between her view that writing poetry was socially valuable work and Carlyle's assertions that poetry was not the serious pursuit needed in the "age of crisis." In December 1842 she had published two sonnets that staged the debate. Though not juxtaposed in her collected *Poems,* the two appeared side by side in a manuscript sequence entitled "Sonnets in the Night," there numbered VIII and IX, and their titles "Work" and "Work and Contemplation" set them in conversation with each other. "Work," beginning "What are we set on earth for? Say, to toil" (line 1, *WEBB* 2:94) affirms Carlyle's gospel of the sacredness of work[10] and combines it with a suggestion of democratic liberalism: "God did anoint thee with his odorous oil, / To wrestle, not to reign" (lines 5–6). Subtly, however, the final lines, focusing on the "work" performed by a flower, hint that by merely existing in an aesthetically pleasing way and offering what it has to others, an apparently unindustrious creation nevertheless contributes: "The least flower, with a brimming cup, may stand, / And share its dew-drop with another near" (lines 13–14). "Work and Contemplation" more conspicuously foregrounds the argument with Carlyle, challenging the view he would spell out in *Past and Present* (1843), that the English are "a silent people, whose epics are in action," not a nation of poets and singers (*BC* 7:100). "Work and Contemplation," while specifically addressing "the dear Christian Church" (line 9, *WEBB* 2:106), also argues that individuals — most important, women — can perform their mundane appointed labor while simultaneously singing: "Thus, apart from toil, our souls pursue / Some high, calm, spheric tune, and prove our work / The better for the sweetness of our song" (lines 12–14).

Her sonnet's gospel of *work elevated by song* anticipates EBB's hostility to Carlyle's assertion in *Past and Present* (1843) that the English lack song and poetry. Reporting to R. H. Horne in May 1843 that she had been reading *Past and Present,* she questioned Carlyle's characterization of the English as "a dumb people" who "can do great acts, but not describe them" and whose "Epic Poem is written on the Earth's surface" (*Past and Present* 159). Nor is Carlyle's conclusion palatable to EBB: "Of all the Nations in the world at present the English are the stupidest in speech, the wisest in action. As good as a 'dumb' Nation, I say, who cannot speak, and have never yet spoken, — spite of the Shakspeares and Miltons who show us what possibilities there are!" (161). Though she still proclaims herself "a devotee of Carlyle," she judges that this new work has "nothing new in it — even of Carlyleism," and though she acknowledges that "almost everything" in *Past and Present* is "true," she vigorously questions its characterization of the "dumb" English, focusing especially on the reference to Shakespeare and Milton, whom Carlyle implies "are mere accidents." She counters, "This English people, — has it not a nobler, a fuller, a more abounding & various literature, than all the peoples of the earth 'past or present' dead or living — all except . . . the Greek people." "I wish I knew Mr Carlyle," she concludes, "to look in his face & say . . . we are a most singing people . . . a most eloquent & speechful people . . . we are none of us silent, except the *mutes* — " (*BC* 7:100).

Having remained "mute" when invited to write against the Corn Laws — a failure to speak out against a social evil that haunted her — she from this point on adhered to Carlyle's portrayal of Shakespeare and Dante in *Heroes* as hero-poets, rather than to his suggestion in *Past and Present* that Shakespeare and Milton were "mere accidents of their condition." And she increasingly chose the path of hero for herself. In 1847 she embraced the opportunity to write the trenchant poem "The Runaway Slave at Pilgrim's Point" for the Boston Anti-Slavery Bazaar's volume *The Liberty Bell,* sending the American abolitionists a poem she believed even they would find "too ferocious, perhaps" to publish: "Nobody will print it," she wrote to

Mary Russell Mitford, "because I could not help making it bitter" (BC 14:86, 117).[11] This trajectory toward more outspoken engagement with social, economic, and political issues reached full flower in *Aurora Leigh* (1856), with its attention to class schism, the plight of seamstresses and fallen women, the immiseration of the laboring classes, and the pros and cons of social welfare experiments in phalansteries. In the central book of this novel in verse, EBB's fictional poet Aurora invokes the gospel of work while confessing she has grown weary of the aesthetically pleasing but unengaged poetry (ballads, sonnets, descriptive verse) she had written earlier (see bk. 5, lines 84–91):

> Measure not the work
> Until the day's out and the labour done,
> Then bring your gauges. If the day's work's scant,
> Why, call it scant.
> (*Aurora Leigh*, bk. 5, lines 77–80, WEBB 4:121–22)

Determining "to mark . . . intimate humanity / In this inferior nature" (bk. 5, lines 99–101), she in an often-quoted passage links her commitment to contemporary social causes to Carlyle:

> Ay, but every age
> Appears to souls who live in 't (ask Carlyle)
> Most unheroic. Ours, for instance, ours:
> The thinkers scout it, and the poets abound
> Who scorn to touch it with a finger-tip.
> (bk. 5, lines 155–59, WEBB 4:123)

Inspired to turn to modern life, she articulates a manifesto for socially involved poetry:

> Nay, if there's room for poets in this world
> A little overgrown, (I think there is)
> Their sole work is to represent the age,
> Their age, not Charlemagne's, — this live, throbbing age,
> That brawls, cheats, maddens, calculates, aspires,
> And spends more passion, more heroic heat,
> Betwixt the mirrors of its drawing-rooms,
> Than Roland with his knights at Roncesvalles. . . .
> This is living art,
> Which thus presents and thus records true life.
> (bk. 5, lines 200–222, *WEBB 4:125*)

In criticizing the contemporary "poet who discerns / No character or glory in his times, / And trundles back his soul five hundred years, / Past moat and drawbridge, into a castle-court, / To sing . . . / . . . poems made on . . . chivalric bones" (bk. 5, lines 189–98, *WEBB* 4:124), EBB not only referred to poets such as Alfred Tennyson, who had already published *The Princess* (1847) and several short Arthurian poems and was known to be working on what would eventually become *Idylls of the King,* but may also slyly refer to Carlyle himself, who in *Past and Present* examined the current "condition of England" through contrasts with an idealized religious community of the Middle Ages. Her reiteration of the word *heroic* throughout the passage directs attention back to the Carlyle text so seminal for her.[12]

Her own "living art" after *Aurora Leigh* focused increasingly on the fate of Italy's *Risorgimento,* as EBB not only embraced the issues of her adopted homeland but became increasingly cosmopolitan and transnational in her concerns. Earlier, in June 1846, as she and Browning were planning to travel to Italy, Browning had reported Carlyle's sense that modern Italy's fragmentation, its "abasement" under foreign domination, expressed "a direct judgment from God — 'Here is a nation in whose breast arise men who *could* doubt, examine the new problems of the Reformation &c — trim the balance at intervals, and throw overboard the accumulation of falsehood — all other nations around, less favoured, are doing it labouriously for themselves . . . now is the time for the acumen of the Bembos, the Bentivoglios and so forth . . . and these and their like, one and all, turn round, decline the trouble, say 'these things *may* be true, or they may not . . . meantime let us go on verse making, painting, music scoring' — to which all the nation accedes as if relieved of a trouble — upon which God bids the Germans go in and possess them, — pluck their fruits and feel their sun after their own hard work.' — Carlyle said the *sense* of this," Browning concluded, "between two huge pipe-whiffs, the other afternoon" (*BC* 13:90). But Carlyle's lecture "The Hero as Poet" had concluded with a view of Italy far more sympathetic, asserting modern Italy's need for "an articulate voice" on the order of Dante: "Yes, truly, it is a great thing for a Nation that it get an articulate voice; that it produce a man who will speak-forth melodiously what the heart of it means! Italy, for example, poor Italy lies dismembered, scattered asunder, not appearing in any protocol or treaty as a unity at all; yet the noble Italy is actually *one:* Italy produced its Dante; Italy can speak!" (*Heroes* 103). In *Casa Guidi Windows* (1851) and the collection *Poems before Congress* (1860), EBB became a woman who would "speak-forth melodiously what the heart" of the Risorgimento meant to Italy and the world.

EBB expressed the Risorgimento's need for a heroic leader in *Casa Guidi*

Windows, Part One (1851), where she calls for "God's light organized / In some high soul, crowned capable to lead / The conscious people" (lines 761–63, *WEBB* 2:513; see also lines 769–73) and summons "civic heroes" (line 795).[13] For years she believed that Louis Napoleon, the elected president of France who, through a coup d'état in late 1851, eventually had himself named Emperor Napoleon III, would be that hero. Because he ultimately betrayed Italian interests by signing the Treaty of Villafranca with Austria and abandoning the Italian cause (Nice and Savoy having been conveniently ceded to France), many critics and biographers have regarded EBB as unworldly, undemocratic, and even hysterical in her hero-worship.[14] However, she was scarcely blind, over the years, to the flaws of various leaders she hoped would advance the cause of Italian unification and independence. As the "Advertisement" to the first edition of *Casa Guidi Windows* revealed, for example, while she had hoped that Pope Pius IX, "Pio Nono," would support unification, she was not guilty of naïve hero-worship, not shocked when he eventually sacrificed the great cause to satisfy his own political ends: she explained that she "certainly escaped the epidemic 'falling sickness' of enthusiasm for Pio Nono" (*WEBB* 2:491). Her higher hopes for Napoleon III relate directly to Carlyle's representation of the hero in the figure of Samson in *Past and Present,* elected by his fellows at St. Edmundsbury to lead their monastic community. While EBB did not find much to praise in *Past and Present,* its elaboration of the role of the hero elected to lead resonates with her persistence in the 1850s regarding Napoleon III as the potential savior of Italy. As Philip Rosenberg explains:

> Electing a leader in Carlyle's sense is a matter of great moment and takes on some of the characteristics associated with a religious conversion, for it constitutes no less than a decision as to what one's own calling is to be; to be truly meaningful, an election must be not so much a choice *between* potential leaders as a choice *of* a leader. What is more, insofar as it is a true election it is in a very real sense an election of oneself into the role of charismatic followership as much as it is an election of the hero. Such an "election" is the beginning of action for the individual making the decision, for in casting one's lot with a hero one commits oneself to an active role in the cause the hero leads. (194)

While others regarded Louis Napoleon as a ruthless autocrat when he declared himself emperor, EBB continually emphasized the people's mandate, an overwhelming popular vote in the plebiscite endorsing his coup: a vote of nearly seven and a half million for, and just under 641,000 against. Identifying herself as "purer democrat" than his critics (*BC* 17:204), she stressed the French population's overwhelming response to a ballot that asked — not that they choose between candidates — but that they vote yes or no to the proposition that they desired "the maintenance of the authority of Louis Napoleon Bonaparte." EBB revealed both her realistic skepticism about the man and her recognition that the people had elected him overwhelmingly: "I do not bind myself for Louis Napoleon's purity of motive, nor do I pretend to say that he will not make improper uses of his unparalleled position at this moment. . . . The election expresses the most extraordinary unity of national will almost ever manifested" (*BC* 17:208–09, 214n2). While acknowledging that "in another month he may be unjustifiable. I cant pretend to answer for his abnegation & patriotism," she explained to Mary Russell Mitford, "it seems to me that I am a purer democrat in admitting of an appeal to the universal suffrage of the people." She astutely added, "He will not *stand* except through standing fast by the people as well as appealing to them" (*BC* 17:204).[15]

EBB subscribed to the Carlylean view, as explained by Rosenberg, that the hero does not originate his cause but steps up to achieve what the time demands: "The greatness of the hero derives from his ability to recognize an as yet unrealized truth and to assist as midwife at its birth." Carlyle's heroes "act in response to the social needs of the cultures which produced them" (Rosenberg 192). For Carlyle, the hero was not necessarily heroic because he had a unique vision or pure motives, he was heroic because he discerned and courageously championed what the age demanded: "What [the hero] says, all men were not far from saying, were longing to say" (*Heroes* 35; qtd. in Rosenberg 193). Already passionately committed to the cultural imperative for a unified Italy, EBB found in Napoleon III the leader that the time and the cause required.

After Napoleon III abrogated his role as hero, stepping back from leading the Italian independence movement, EBB in "Mother and Poet" (published posthumously in 1862) wrote as a hero-poet, portraying a woman poet who in a sense performed the role for Italy that young EBB as "Beth" had envisioned herself performing for Greece. The speaker of the dramatic monologue is based on the Italian poet Olimpia Rossi Savio (1815–89), who in real life was herself a hero-poet, in song exhorting Italians to rally to their own cause.[16] Like Savio, having urged self-sacrifice in her patriotic songs, the speaker has lost her two sons in battles for nationhood that her poetry extolled. In contrast to Napoleon III and Pio Nono, who betrayed the cause to gratify their personal ambitions, EBB's speaker painfully records the personal cost of heroic work:

> Dead! One of them shot by the sea in the east,
>> And one of them shot in the west by the sea.
> Both! both my boys! If in keeping the feast
>> You want a great song for your Italy free,
>> Let none look at *me!*
>> (lines 96–100, *WEBB* 5:107)

A selfless leader whose songs have promoted Italy's cause, this hero-poet in her powerful grief conveys the value of the goal even as she bleakly asserts she can give no more to achieve it.[17] Presumably the mother's desolation will challenge auditors to summon their own reserves for the cause.

Like her speaker in "Mother and Poet," EBB in such poems as "The Runaway Slave at Pilgrim's Point," "A Curse for a Nation," *Casa Guidi Windows, Aurora Leigh,* and the collection *Poems before Congress* — and "Mother and Poet" itself — demonstrated that despite Carlyle's later admonitions that the engaged intellectual should address the needs of his day in prose, the activist poet imagined in *Heroes* still spoke powerfully in the nineteenth century — in a woman's voice.

NOTES

1. Employing "EBB," a designation the poet regularly used to sign letters and manuscripts and sometimes affixed to published poems, avoids the confusion of identifying her as Elizabeth Barrett before her marriage and Elizabeth Barrett Browning afterward.

2. EBB's personal friendship with Carlyle did not develop for a decade after *Heroes* prompted her "Carlyleship." Though Robert Browning had been friendly with the Carlyles for several years before he began writing to EBB in January 1845, she did not meet Carlyle until 1851, during a visit by the Brownings to London (see *BC* 17:85–86 and *CL* 26:115–116n). She became very fond of him when he traveled with them on their return to Paris later that year (see *BC* 5:367 and *CL* 26:185–94).

3. On Spring, see Brent E. Kinser, "Rebecca Buffum Spring and the Carlyles."

4. See Philip Rosenberg, viii–x. For a contrasting argument, that EBB emulated Carlyle's hero-poet's "transcendentalist discourse" rather than his engagement with the contemporary world, see Bina Freiwald.

5. This passage of EBB's letter to H. F. Chorley on 7 January 1845 is usually cited to illustrate her sense of the dearth of women poets in English, women gifted with "the faculty of poetry, strictly so called" and "the divine breath": "I look

everywhere for Grandmothers & see none. It is not in the filial spirit I am deficient, . . . — witness my reverent love of the grandfathers!" (*BC* 10:14).

6. EBB described her timidity in sending the collection to her hero Carlyle in a typically witty pun: she inscribed a copy to him "after a great deal of ebbing and flowing" (*BC* 9:94).

7. Rebecca Buffum Spring witnessed and recorded Carlyle's account of the exchange: " 'I wrote to her, that if she had anything to say, she had better say it in plain prose, so that a body could understand it, and not trouble herself to put it into rhyme.' Then putting up his chin, in his way, he laughing said: 'The woman felt so badly about it that I had to write her again' " (qtd. in Kinser, "Spring" 162). See also EBB's mention of the exchange to Browning, *BC* 10:81.

8. For a discussion of the inception and reception of "The Cry of the Children," see *WEBB* 1:431–35.

9. See also her self-representation as "a sort of fossil republican" (*BC* 10:60).

10. EBB observed the power and influence of Carlyle's "gospel of work": How "the words 'soul,' 'work,' 'duty,' strike down upon the flashing anvils of the age, till the whole age vibrates,' EBB said of Carlyle's writings in her contributions to the collection of essays *A New Spirit of the Age* (1844), on which she collaborated with R. H. Horne (*BC* 8:355).

11. On the composition and publication of "The Runaway Slave at Pilgrim's Point," see *WEBB* 1:409–20.

12. For discerning discussion of Carlyle's influence on EBB, especially on the sage discourse in *Aurora Leigh,* see Brent E. Kinser, " 'A Very Beautiful Tempest in a Teapot' "; see also Margaret Morlier's treatment of Carlyle's influence on EBB's experimentation with sage discourse in her two sonnets "To George Sand."

13. On Carlyle's influence on *Casa Guidi Windows,* see Linda K. Hughes 218 ff. and also 272–75.

14. See Elizabeth Woodworth. For an example of complaints that she was irrational and incoherent on the subject of Italian politics, see William Irvine and Park Honan 253–54.

15. For other examples of her comments on the French disposition to "hero-worship," the people's will, Louis Napoleon's flaws, and her confidence in his potential, see *BC* 17:187–88, 214, 217, 222–23. Significantly, one of Louis Napoleon's first actions after his coup was to implement universal suffrage (*BC* 17:184n2).

16. For more on the biographical background for the poem, see *WEBB* 5:103–8.

17. According to Pam Morris, in this mother-patriot-poet EBB creates a hero-poet who contrasts strikingly with the virile hero who "embodies a specifically masculine national ideal" (288), one "opposed to the peril of national effeminacy" (290).

"Leading human souls to what is best"

Carlyle, Ruskin, and Hero-Worship

SARA ATWOOD

Writing to his editor W. H. Harrison from Geneva in June 1841, the twenty-two-year-old John Ruskin expressed skepticism about both the subject and the style of Carlyle's *On Heroes, Hero-Worship, and the Heroic in History* with which he was as yet familiar only from reviews:

> We feel excessively hermit-like and innocent with respect to all literary matters here, being only able to get an occasional *Athenæum* or *Atlas* to bring us up. What are these Carlyle lectures? People are making a fuss about them, and from what I see in the reviews, they seem absolute bombast — taking bombast, I suppose, making everybody think himself a hero, and deserving of "your wash-up," at least, from the reverential Mr. Carlyle. Do you remember the *Sketches by Boz* — there is a passage quoted by the *Atlas* as "brilliant," every sentence beginning with "What," between which and the dinner lecture of Horatio Sparkins, Esq., beginning "We feel — we know — that we exist — nothing more — what more" — there exists a very strong parallel. And what is Boz about himself? (*WJR* 36:25)[1]

Later that day, Ruskin made the following note in his diary: "Read some of Carlyle's lectures. Bombast, I think; altogether approves of Mahomet, and talks like a girl of his 'black eyes'" (*Diaries* 1:199). Ruskin's response, while it betrays the confidence, even arrogance, of youth, is not altogether unwarranted, given Carlyle's mannered and histrionic style. The carefully crafted prose that Ruskin was to become master of, though often vituperative, could not be more different from Carlyle's dramatic fulminations, even when inspired by the elder writer's rhetorical strategies and concerns. As George Allen Cate has observed, Ruskin and Carlyle differed markedly in personality and in social character as well (Cate 7–8), and on the face of it, they seemed unlikely to share much in common. But Ruskin's opinion of Carlyle was to change dramatically. He was impressed by Carlyle's denunciation of the condition of England and the plight of the working classes in

Past and Present (1843), and his interest in Carlyle's work intensified along with his own commitment to social reform in the 1850s.[2]

Ruskin first met Carlyle sometime between 1847 and 1850 (Cate 3), and by the early 1850s the two were corresponding with some regularity. Ruskin came to consider Carlyle his "master,"[3] and their friendship, though not entirely uncritical on either side, lasted until Carlyle's death in 1881. Ruskin shared with Carlyle a powerful sense of indignation about social problems, a willingness to speak out, and a disregard for public criticism. Carlyle undoubtedly influenced Ruskin, who often quoted and praised his mentor's work in his own books. *Fors Clavigera* (1871–84) in particular, Ruskin's series of letters to "the workmen and labourers of Great Britain," has been described as a Carlylean text. Ruskin also came to see Carlyle's emphasis on hero-worship as a good deal more than mere bombast; the habit of reverence — along with obedience, gentleness, and justice — was for Ruskin indispensable to the sort of social transformation he envisioned, and the figure of the great man occupies a central place in his teaching. He was concerned to understand the ineffable qualities of greatness early on; the second volume of *Modern Painters* (1846), with its analysis of Imagination Associative, Penetrative and Contemplative, is an attempt to understand the agency by which great artists, but by extension all great men, grasp and reveal ennobling inner truths. His own considerable capacity for reverence, of both the natural and the material, drove much of his work, in relation to both art and society. Ruskin maintained that his particular talent lay in identifying and revealing the greatness of others, and that his teaching was thus not his own but "that which Heaven has taught every true man's heart, and proved by every true man's work, from the beginning of time to this day" (*WJR* 29:383). He had his own bede-roll of great men as varied as Carlyle's, whom he took for his "masters" and whose life and work are held up as exemplary in his books. Foremost among these were J. M. W. Turner and Sir Walter Scott. Plato, Dante, Carpaccio, and others also held a personal significance for Ruskin, as did Carlyle himself.[4]

Significantly, Ruskin's great men are not flawless, nor are they necessarily models of authority, for Ruskin held that it is greatness of heart that makes great men: "I believe," he wrote, "that the power of the heart over the intellect is common to all great men" (*WJR* 34:290). Ruskin's heroes, both past and present, are men above all rather than "embodiments of greatness" (Cate 56), and their faults are as instructive as their virtues. Writing of Scott in *Fors*, Ruskin observes that his life and work are intended as an example "the more perfect . . . because he is not exempt from common failings, and has his appointed portion in common pain" (27:563). J. A.

Hobson found this aspect of Ruskin's hero-worship markedly different from Carlyle's, noting in 1898 that "Carlyle was so ridden by his hero-worship as to pardon almost anything, almost hypocrisy itself, to the forceful man of destiny. . . . Mr. Ruskin's hero-worship is more consciously ideal; when he confronts the great men of history at close quarters he has an uncommonly shrewd eye for their defects" (204).[5] Ruskin, whose own candor often troubled those closest to him, assured readers of *Fors* of his frankness. In language that recalls Carlyle's *Sartor Resartus,* a book he deeply admired, Ruskin declares: "It is the modern method, in order to give you more inviting pictures of people, to dress them — often very correctly — in the costume of the time, with such old clothes as the masquerade shops keep. But my own steady aim is to strip them for you, that you may see if they are of flesh, or dust" (27:397). Yet although Ruskin felt that failings should be acknowledged, he urged that they not be unnecessarily magnified. Writing in reference to Turner in 1856, Ruskin declared the denial of defects in heroes "one of the most baneful abuses of truth of which the world is guilty. But though the faults of a great or good man should never be extenuated, they should be much forgiven, and at times forgotten. It is wrong and unwise to expose defects in a time or place when they take away our power of feeling virtues" (13:157).[6]

Like Carlyle, Ruskin believed that the English had forgotten how to worship; God had been replaced by the Goddess of Getting-On, and great men by small-minded, wealth-seeking adventurers (Carlyle's "Quacks" and "Dilettantes"). Indeed, for Ruskin the hypocrisy and faithlessness of modern society had much to do with the flawed character of its greatest men, including Carlyle himself. "There never yet was a generation of men (savage or civilized) who, taken as a body, so wofully [*sic*] fulfilled the words 'having no hope, and without God in the world,' as the present civilized European race," Ruskin declared in *Modern Painters.* The impact of this spiritual impoverishment was evident among the leading literary figures of the day:

Hence, nearly all our powerful men in this age of the world are unbelievers; the best of them in doubt and misery; the worst in reckless defiance; the plurality, in plodding hesitation, doing, as well as they can, what practical work lies ready to their hands. Most of our scientific men are in this last class: our popular authors either set themselves definitely against all religious form, pleading for simple truth and benevolence, (Thackeray, Dickens,) or give themselves up to bitter and fruitless statement of facts, (De Balzac,) or surface-painting, (Scott,) or careless blasphemy, sad or smiling, (Byron, Beranger). Our earnest poets and deepest thinkers are doubtful and indignant, (Tennyson, Carlyle); one or two, anchored, indeed, but anxious or weeping, (Wordsworth, Mrs. Browning); and of these two, the first is not so sure of his anchor, but that now and then it drags with him. (*WJR* 5:322–23)

Ruskin suffered his own crises of faith, yet even after he had relinquished the strict Evangelicalism of his youth, Christianity remained at the foundation of his teaching. Whereas Carlyle was content to preach and fulminate, Ruskin acted. As an instructor and professor, a philanthropist, and ultimately as the Master of the Guild of St. George, Ruskin persistently, if not always successfully, strove to put his principles into action by making them a key element in his pedagogy. For him, education was primarily an ethical process, defined by "leading human souls to what is best, and making what is best out of them" (*WJR* 11:261). Institutional reform was simply not enough; rather, one had to begin with the sort of moral education designed to nurture "Souls of a good quality" (17:56). The stories of great men constituted a valuable teaching tool in this respect, for they might be used to point important lessons. "The History of the World," Carlyle had declared, is "the Biography of Great Men" (*Heroes* 30); Ruskin uses this history to admonish present failings and inspire future transformation.[7]

Believing that great men had important lessons to teach, Ruskin sought in his work to perpetuate "the wisdom which the Masters of all men . . . [have] left for the guidance of the ages yet to be" (*WJR* 29:401). In *The Elements of Drawing* (1857), he had warned that great drawing could never be produced by mere imitation of masterly work. Instead, students must "acquire [the master's] knowledge and share his feelings" (15:83), raising themselves to the level of the great men they study. This concept of "The Rule of the Greatest" is further developed in a chapter of the same name in volume 5 of *Modern Painters* (1860), in which Ruskin writes that in order to learn from the great artists a student must strive to achieve the same "habitually noble temper of mind" (7:235). In the lecture "Of Kings' Treasuries" (1865), he discusses the same notion in relation to the wisdom contained in books. The end of education, Ruskin declares, is not worldly privilege but rather advancement of a different sort, the best books forming a "company of the noble" (18:59). Here again is "The Rule of the Greatest," for a person must rise to the level of the great thinkers in order to understand them. "Do you ask to be the companion of nobles?" Ruskin asks. "Make yourself noble and you shall be. Do you long for the conversation of the wise? Learn to understand it, and you shall hear it. But on other terms? — no" (18:62).

This notion of the individual rising to the level of great men is a theme that runs through Ruskin's work — yet he does not mean by it that everyone can become a great man. On the contrary, Ruskin's firm belief in the natural inequality of men is central to his concept of an organic society regulated by what he calls the Law of Help: each individual contentedly and productively filling the place best suited to him according to his aptitude and ability. In holding great men up as exemplars, then, Ruskin is not suggesting that greatness on the same level is possible to all. Instead, he urges a continual striving to understand and embody what these figures represent: reverence, goodness, justice, and obedience. In *On Heroes,* Carlyle enthusiastically calls for "a whole World of Heroes," by which he means "a *believing* nation. There needs not a great soul to make a hero; there needs a god-created soul which will be true to its origin" (112, 125). It is in a similar spirit that Ruskin urges his readers to seek to honor "that which educates your children into living heroes, and binds down the flights and the fondnesses of the heart into practical duty and faithful devotion" (*WJR* 12:160). Writing about education in *Time and Tide* (1867), a book that can be seen as a rehearsal for *Fors,* he identifies reverence and compassion as necessary ends of education, indicating that they might be properly developed by studying the lives and actions of exemplary individuals: "To teach reverence rightly is to attach it to the right persons and things; first, by setting over your youth masters whom they cannot but love and respect; next, by gathering for them, out of past history, whatever has been most worthy in human deeds and human passion; and leading them continually to dwell upon such instances, making this the principle element of emotional excitement to them; and, lastly, by letting them justly feel, as far as may be, the smallness of their own powers and knowledge, as compared with the attainments of others" (17:398).

In gathering together the wisdom of great men, Ruskin aimed at uniting "the force of all good plans and wise schemes" (*WJR* 28:235) and at bringing them to bear on contemporary social questions. Throughout *Fors,* and recalling Carlyle's method in *Past and Present,* he does a great deal of teaching by contrast, moving seamlessly, as Dinah Birch observes, "between the timeless and the topical" ("Multiple Writing" 181). *Fors* includes deliberately didactic accounts of historical figures, such as Henry the Fowler of Germany, Charlemagne of France, Alfred of England, and Sir John Hawkwood and his White Company. In Letter 25, January 1873, an excerpt from Froissart intended to illustrate the true "captainship" and honor of Edward III is paired with a recent newspaper report of the brutal murder of a workingman by four Irish ruffians; what Ruskin calls "a piece of modern British fighting, done under no banner, and in no loyalty nor obedience, but in the independent spirit of freedom" (27:460, 465). The lives and stories of such figures, though related with characteristic aware-ness of their failings, are repeatedly used to underscore the modern failure of faith and conscience. Ruskin also requires that his readers learn the history of five cities — Athens, Rome, Florence, Venice, and London — and of five men — Plato, Virgil, Dante, Carpaccio, and Shakespeare — the study of both cities and men offering apposite lessons for modern England. "If," Ruskin writes in Letter 18, June 1872, "after knowing these five men's opinions on practical matters (these five, as you will find, being all of the same mind), you prefer to hold Mr. J. S. Mill's and Mr. Fawcett's opinions, you are welcome" (27:314).[8] These five are among the wise men of *Fors,* "who *know* the truths necessary to human life" (28:732). They are also of great personal significance to Ruskin, their work and ideas having become part of the fabric of his mind.

Also prominent among the great men of *Fors* are Jean-François Mar-montel, Jeremias Gotthelf, and Sir Walter Scott. In Ruskin's hands, their work and lives become teaching tools, each extract of literature or biogra-phy serving as a lesson in how to live. Ruskin juxtaposes Marmontel's accounts of a simple, innocent way of life in which both the land itself and the people who cultivate it are uncorrupted by modern materialism with the poverty and filth of England's industrial cities, the loathsome work of the "machine-gods" (*WJR* 27:256). Yet, characteristically, Ruskin finds value in Marmontel's weaknesses as well, translating a story that demonstrates "many of the false relations between the rich and poor" (27:367) in order to illustrate the error of its falsely romantic tendencies. Gotthelf, whom Rus-kin introduces in Letter 30, June 1873, as "the wisest man, take him for all in all, with whose writings I am acquainted" (27:545–46), receives similar treatment.[9] Ruskin devotes considerable space over the course of several letters to translating excerpts of a story called "The Broom-Merchant," in which the young peasant Hansli achieves success in both business and marriage by dint of honest hard work and fair dealing. At the conclusion of the first excerpt Ruskin sets Gotthelf's picture of Swiss country life against a correspondent's account of the hardships endured by the poor of Jersey as a result of recent trade. Both story and letter are included for what they might teach separately as well as in contrast, and are intended to underscore basic verities: "The two facts which I have to teach, or sign, though alone, as it seems, at present, in the signature, that food can only be got out of the ground, and happiness only out of honesty. . . . Two important pieces of information [that] are never, so far as I am aware, presented in any scheme of education either to the infantine or adult mind. And, unluckily, no other information whatever, without acquaintance with these facts, can produce either bread and butter, or felicity" (27:558). Scott, whose work had been an important influence upon Ruskin since childhood and with whom he felt so much sympathy, is a frequent presence in Ruskin's books. In *Fors,* Ruskin undertook to demonstrate "what good Scott has in him to do":

> His ideal of honour in men and women is inbred, indisputable; fresh as the air of his mountains; firm as their rocks. His conception of purity in woman is even higher than Dante's; his reverence for the filial relation, as deep as Virgil's; his sympathy universal; — there is no rank or condition of men of which he has not shown the loveliest aspect; his code of moral principle is entirely defined, yet taught with a reserved subtlety like Nature's own, so that none but the most earnest readers perceive the intention: and his opinions on all practical subjects are final; the consummate decisions of accurate and inevitable commonsense, tempered by the most graceful kindness. (27:563)

Scott has the potential to teach all this and more to readers of *Fors,* and Ruskin makes clear his intention of "abstracting and collating (with comment)" (*WJR* 27:564) such passages from Lockhart's life of Scott, along with pieces of Scott's work and Ruskin's own analysis that will prove most instructive. Ruskin urges his readers, "Read your 'Waverley' . . . with extreme care" (28:496), paying close attention to the lessons in it. Many readers urged Ruskin to write his own biography of Scott, a project that Ruskin never took up. Noting in Letter 32, August 1873, that readers "are always willing enough to *read* lives, but never willing to *lead* them," Ruskin remarks that "they must please to remember that I am only examining the conditions of the life of this wise man, that they may learn how to rule their own lives, or their children's, or their servants'; and, for the present, with this particular object, that they may be able to determine, for themselves, whether ancient sentiment, or modern common sense, is to be the rule of life, and of service" (27:607, 606).

Foremost among Ruskin's heroes, however, and the foundational influence upon his teaching, is that "greatest of all Heroes" (*Heroes* 28) whom Carlyle was reluctant to name. Although Ruskin had abandoned Evangelicalism and remained critical of the interpretation and practice of church doctrine, he had never taken issue with Christ's teaching. Ruskin's educational philosophy is bound up with the very personal, humanistic form of Christianity that he had developed in response to the loss of his Evangelical faith. As Michael Wheeler points out, "His visionary idealism . . . was grounded in the New Testament teaching on which he believed Catholic Christendom had been established, and to which the modern Church of England appeared to pay only lip-service" (211).

Despite human frailties, Ruskin's great men in some way all reflect the Christian virtues that are at the heart of his program of social reform.[10] Even those figures who are not Christian, such as Plato, acknowledge a natural moral law founded on the same virtues. Observes Birch, "Plato is seen [by Ruskin] as the most valuable ancient philosopher because he is closest to the Christian spirit" (*Ruskin's Myths* 25). Having forged a religious understanding centered on values rather than doctrine and creed, Ruskin was able to draw together otherwise disparate figures and traditions into the sort of "Sacred literature, — both classic and Christian" (*WJR* 33:119) that might guide his readers toward the apprehension of those eternal laws, common to all ages and traditions, which alone sustain and sanctify life. Ruskin did not want his readers simply to think *about* the noble figures whose teaching he advocates in *Fors,* but to think *like* them: "Make yourself noble and you shall be" (*WJR* 18:62). In urging the teaching of Plato, Dante, Carpaccio, Marmontel, Scott, and others Ruskin hoped (to adapt a phrase used by American philosopher Will Durant) to build up an audience fit to listen to good men, and therefore ready to produce them.[11]

The ability to recognize good men, of course, is also vital to good government, and in this sense Ruskin's teaching is directed at transforming men and women into the sort of people who will be able to discern and obey a great man. A detailed analysis of Carlyle's and Ruskin's politics would require more space than can be afforded here, yet it is important to recognize the centrality of hero-worship and the figure of the great man to their respective conceptions of good government. "The common insolences and petulances of the people," Ruskin asserts in *Munera Pulveris* (1872), "and their talk of equality, are not irreverence in them in the least, but mere blindness, stupefaction, and fog in the brains, the first sign of any cleansing away of which is, that they gain some power of discerning, and some patience in submitting to, their true counsellors and governors. In the mode of such discernment consists the real 'constitution' of the state, more than in the titles or offices of the discerned person; for it is no matter, save in degree of mischief, to what office a man is appointed, if he cannot fulfil it" (*WJR* 17:243–44). This notion of discernment in regard to identifying and choosing leaders is important to Carlyle as well.[12] Both Carlyle and Ruskin believed in a society governed by a noble, wise, and strong leader, the sort of man to whom obedience is naturally due and freely given. Carlyle declares in *On Heroes,* "No Time need have gone to ruin, could it have *found* a man great enough, a man wise and good enough; wisdom to discern truly what the Time wanted, valour to lead it on the right road thither" (29).

Ruskin shared Carlyle's aristocratic attitude, having felt since childhood "a most sincere love of kings, and dislike of everybody who attempted to disobey them" (*WJR* 35:14). Yet his notion of kingship was centered on right, not might. "I was taught strange ideas about kings, which I find for the present much obsolete," he wrote in *Praeterita* (1885–89): "I observed that they not only did more, but in proportion to their doings, *got* less than other people — nay, that the best of them were even ready to govern for nothing! and let their followers divide any quantity of spoil or profit. Of late it has seemed to me that the idea of a king has become exactly the contrary of this, and that it has been supposed the duty of superior persons generally to govern less, and get more, than anybody else" (35:14–15).[13]

Like Carlyle, Ruskin deplored the rise of "Sham-Heroes and Valets and gaslighted Histrios" and envisioned a society ruled by a just and worthy leader. He agreed as well with Carlyle's condemnation of modern notions of liberty and with his insistence that "Liberty requires new definitions" (*Past and Present* 218, 211). Carlyle protested against "the liberty especially which has to purchase itself by social isolation, and each man standing separate from the other, having 'no business with him' but a cash-account; this is such a liberty as the Earth seldom saw," arguing instead that "the true liberty of a man . . . consist[s] in finding out, or being forced to find out the right path, and to walk thereon" (*Past and Present* 216, 210–11).[14] Similarly, Ruskin declared true liberty is obedience, the principle to which "Polity owes its stability, Life its happiness, Faith its acceptance, Creation its continuance" (*WJR* 8:248).

It is not surprising, then, that both Carlyle and Ruskin should have rejected "the inexorable demand of these ages" for democracy, which Carlyle memorably describes as "despair of finding any Heroes to govern you, and contented putting up with the want of them" (*Past and Present* 213). In a chapter entitled "Government" in *Munera Pulveris,* Ruskin argues:

> No form of government, provided it be a government at all, is, as such, to be either condemned or praised, or contested for in anywise, but by fools. But all forms of government are good just so far as they attain this one vital necessity of policy — *that the wise and kind, few or many, shall govern the unwise and unkind;* and they are evil so far as they miss of

this, or reverse it. Nor does the form, in any case, signify one whit, but its *firmness* and adaptation to the need; for if there be many foolish persons in a state, and few wise, then it is good that the few govern; and if there be many wise, and few foolish, then it is good that the many govern; and if many be wise, yet one wiser, then it is good that one should govern; and so on. (*WJR* 17:248–49)

Modern attempts at democracy — both Carlyle and Ruskin cite America rather scathingly in evidence — too frequently ignore these requirements, with the result that only the demands of the foolish many are audible. In urging the virtues of hero-worship, Carlyle encourages the sort of discernment that will lead to good government and universal justice; Ruskin incorporates the stories of great men in his pedagogy in an attempt to teach this discernment. "It is beyond the scope of the most sanguine thought," he wrote in the penultimate letter of *Fors*, "to conceive how much misery and crime would be effaced from the world by persistence, even for a few years, of a system of education thus directed to raise the fittest into positions of influence, to give to every scale of intellect its natural sphere, and to every line of action its unquestioned principle. At present wise men, for the most part, are silent, and good men powerless; the senseless vociferate, and the heartless govern; while all social law and providence are dissolved by the enraged agitation of a multitude, among whom every villain has a chance of power, every simpleton of praise, and every scoundrel of fortune" (*WJR* 29:499–500).

George Allen Cate observes that although Ruskin shared many of Carlyle's beliefs about government and social problems, his views, "imbued with the spirit of the New Testament" (54), were never as excessive as Carlyle's. Whereas Carlyle's work became increasingly harsh and even unpalatable, Ruskin continued to urge compassion and gentleness. His idea of justice was essentially Christian, while Carlyle's drew upon an Old Testament severity. "As Carlyle saw it," Cate writes, "it was *philanthropos,* not Rhadamanthus, that governed Ruskin" (54).

Carlyle and Ruskin have been criticized, both in their own day and in ours, for their aristocratism and authoritarianism. Hobson observed that their rejection of democracy stemmed from a shared belief that it represented "the assertion of absolute equality, and the negation of all reverence" and argued that both men had failed to truly understand the "more rational modern conception" (222) of democracy, which for Hobson is not inconsistent with reverence. Moreover, Hobson identified a tension between Ruskin's belief in an organic conception of society and his authoritarian model of government, concluding that Ruskin's organicism demanded a sort of self-government "entirely inconsistent with the dumb submission which his ideal government would seem to impose upon the masses" (224). While Hobson's thoughtful discussion raises interesting questions, it is arguable that he had failed to understand Ruskin's position in depth. Dumb submission is far from Ruskin's goal; obedience is for him not slavery but restraint and the willingness in the citizen to submit "to every law that could advance the interest of the community" (*WJR* 8:260). For Ruskin true obedience has the potential to transform "national happiness and virtue" (8:259) and to produce "an increased sense of fellowship among ourselves . . . a proud and happy recognition of our affection for and sympathy with each other" (8:260). Obedience is powerful, and essential to a stable, compassionate society.[15]

And what of today? Can anything be learned from Carlyle's and Ruskin's notions of hero-worship and great men? Modern society is fascinated by heroes. There exists a chronic longing for heroes and a willingness to discover and reverence heroism. Media outlets routinely pay homage to "Heroes of the Week/Month/Year," and yet the public seems to have a very confused notion of what constitutes the heroic, the most fundamental acts of human kindness or generosity eliciting paeans of classical intensity. In an age in which the self-interest and the materialism of the nineteenth century persist in new forms, the popular definition of heroism has been broadened to include just about anything that falls under the heading of humane or ethical behavior. Often, those lauded as heroes are people whose actions seem to reject selfish social norms: the athlete who forgoes a hefty sports contract to join the military; the bystander who intervenes to help a stranger; the individual who returns a lost wallet. Such things, while certainly admirable, would once have been regarded as simply the right thing to do; that they are now regarded as heroic indicates the extent to which the social and moral dislocation that both Carlyle and Ruskin decried still persists. Yet the very doggedness of the public search for heroes points to the vitality of our innate impulse to reverence. It would appear that reverence remains, as Ruskin declared in 1863 "as instinctive as anger; — both of them instant on true vision" (*WJR* 17:243). Yet now, as then, it is this true vision — discernment — that is lacking. The words that follow this declaration deserve to be taken to heart, for as Ruskin reminds his readers, "it is sight and understanding we have to teach, and these *are* reverence" (17:243).

NOTES

1. In a footnote E. T. Cook and Alexander Wedderburn compare Ruskin's style here to a passage in the first lecture in *Heroes:* "Nature was to this man, what to the Thinker and Prophet it forever is, *preter*natural. . . . [W]hat *is* it? Ay, what? At bottom we do not yet know; we can never know at all . . . : but *what* is it? What made it? Whence comes it? Wither goes it?" (*Heroes* 26; *WJR* 36:25).

2. This shift did not constitute an abrupt "removal from art to society" (Alexander 159) but was instead a natural extension of Ruskin's moral aesthetic. Having maintained from the first that good art could only be produced by a good society, he began to focus his energy on teaching people how to create such a society.

3. In a December 1873 letter to Carlyle, Ruskin signed himself "Ever your loving disciple — son — I have almost now a right to say — in what is best of power in me" (Cate 177). Thereafter he frequently addresses Carlyle as "Papa" in his letters.

4. Ruskin's greatest and lasting regard was for the work of men with whom he felt some elemental connection, as this passage from a manuscript sheet of *Fors* demonstrates: "I should not venture to say anything to you of Scott, or of any other great man, unless I knew myself to be in closer sympathy with them than you can generally be yourselves; but observe, in claiming this sympathy I do not claim the least approach to any equality of power. I had sympathy with Tintoret, with Scott, with Turner, with Carlyle — as a child with its father or mother, not as friend with friend. What they feel, I, in a feeble and inferior way, feel also; what they are, I can tell you, because in a poor and weak way I am like them — of their race — but no match for them" (*WJR* 29:539).

5. Carlyle's assertion that "might is right" is more complex than Hobson here acknowledges, however. As David R. Sorensen has observed, although Carlyle compromised his achievement "by his cruel and perversely unhistorical attacks against West Indian and American slaves, and by his cynical paeans to Cromwell in Ireland and Frederick in Silesia," he nonetheless ultimately discerned that in "the endless interplay of 'might and right' in the world . . . brute force will never impose the truth, since such force implies a closure of the very attitudes that nourish the possibility of greater wisdom" ("Symbolic Mutation" 75–76, 74).

6. See Ruskin's letter of 1877 to Mary Aitken (Carlyle's niece), in which he adds the following postscript: "I do not mask or deny Turner's sins, — nor do I wish any one who understands Turner to be ignorant of them. But not to know the sins without the virtues" (Cate 237).

7. In an unpublished paper entitled "Ruskin, Mass Education and the Search for a Moral Curriculum," Peter Yeandle explores the ways in which Ruskin's use of history, including his emphasis on the lives and accomplishments of historical figures, influenced "the construction of a moral curriculum in the 1890s."

8. Mill and his ideas were a frequent target of censure in *Fors.* In Letter 31, July 1873, Ruskin inserted the following footnote: "People would not have me speak any more harm of Mr. Mill because he's dead, I suppose? Dead or alive, all's one to me, with mischievous persons" (*WJR* 27:567). Mill had died on 8 May 1873.

9. Gotthelf was the pseudonym of Albert Bitzius (1797–1854), a Swiss writer and clergyman whose moral tales reflect his active interest in the economic and educational improvement of the poor rural area of Bern canton where he acted as Protestant pastor.

10. Introducing the St. George's Creed in *Fors* Letter 58, Ruskin remarks that it contains nothing that a good and religious person, regardless of his personal beliefs, could fear or refuse to profess. Ruskin demanded only a determination to live according to Christian ethics and loyalty to the aims of the society.

11. Of teaching philosophy in America, Durant writes: "Between us we might build up in America an audience fit to listen to geniuses, and therefore ready to produce them" (x).

12. Discernment, for Ruskin, is also related to issues of perception and seeing clearly, which are central to Ruskin's life and career. As he famously declares in *Modern Painters:* "Hundreds of people can talk for one who can think, but thousands can think for one who can see. To see clearly is poetry, prophecy, and religion, — all in one" (*WJR* 5:333).

13. In the lecture "Traffic," delivered in April 1864 and later published in *The Crown of Wild Olive* (1866), Ruskin declares that "It does not follow, because you are general of an army, that you are to take all the treasure, or land, it wins . . . ; neither, because you are king of a nation, that you are to consume all the profits of the nation's work. Real kings, on the contrary, are known invariably by their doing quite the reverse of this, — by their taking the least possible quantity of the nation's work for themselves. There is no test of real kinghood so infallible as that" (*WJR* 18:454).

14. See *Munera Pulveris,* where Ruskin writes that the "essential thing for all creatures is to be made to do right; how they are made to do it — by pleasant promises, or hard necessities, pathetic oratory, or the whip — is comparatively immaterial" (*WJR* 17:255).

15. Ruskin's understanding of obedience was shaped in part by his early religious training but further enriched by his study of Greek philosophy and of Plato in particular, with his emphasis upon order and the danger attendant upon unchecked liberty. In *Fors* Letter 73 Ruskin illustrates the necessity of obedience with a passage from the *Laws* describing the social breakdown that follows a loss of order and restraint. For further discussion of Plato's influence on Ruskin's teaching see my "Ruskin, Plato and the Education of the Soul" and *Ruskin's Educational Ideals.*

"Wild Annandale Grapeshot"

Carlyle, Scotland, and the Heroic

CHRISTOPHER HARVIE

I am engaged deep in a miserable set of lectures and have had to make it a rule not to go out anywhere till these be over, — in the end of the present month.
— Thomas Carlyle to Anne Bourne Jervis, 9 May 1840; *CL* 12:138

Perhaps no Scottish writer requires revaluation now more than Carlyle does, and certainly none is more likely to repay it or prove more pertinent to the most crucial problems of our age.
— Hugh MacDiarmid, "Carlyle Letters," *The Raucle Tongue* 3:310.

"No gods and precious few heroes"

In 1948 the Scottish radical and folklorist Hamish Henderson (1919–2002) published *Elegies for the Dead in Cyrenaica,* one of the greatest poem sequences on the desert campaign that checked Rommel. Henderson's Communist friend E. P. Thompson, author of the epic *Making of the English Working Class* (1963), reminded the poet in a letter of 10 February 1949 that the *Elegies* had been written for "the people of Glasgow, of Halifax, of Dublin[,] . . . for the vanguard of the people, the most thoughtful ones." Thompson's claim that Henderson was "an instrument through which thousands of others can become articulate" (qtd. in Finlay 29) is confirmed in the Seventh Elegy, "Seven Good Germans," in which the poet describes his rifling through the pockets and wallets of the enemy dead. He discovers that their lives — replete with the concern of their parents, being parted from wives or girlfriends, worries about cash or children — resemble those of his own men. For Henderson, "the memory of this odd effect of mirage and looking-glass illusion persisted, and gradually became for me a symbol of our human civil war, in which the roles seem constantly to change and the objectives to shift" ("Foreword," *Cyrenaica* 11). I deliberately chose a line from the First Elegy, "End of a Campaign" — "There were no gods and precious few heroes, . . . / (They saw through that guff before the axe fell)" (19) — as the subtitle to my *History of Scotland since 1914* (part of the New History of Scotland series), which has gone through four editions since its first publication in 1981. The title was also used by the folk fiddler Brian MacNeill (b. 1950) of the Battlefield Band for a political rallying song, and popularized by the singer Dick Gaughan (b. 1948), making it a vital part of the Scottish folk canon that Henderson himself revived through his research and recording.

Henderson's line seemed appropriate as a subtitle because the "guff" had ended in the previous world war, in which the aura of Carlylean hero-worship had hovered over both Christian Daniel Rauch's huge equestrian monument of Frederick the Great in Berlin and the British "captains of industry" and their victorious Carlylean leaders Lloyd George and Bonar Law. Scottish tradition did seem more interpellated by theology and philosophy than empirical England, and these traces, far from disappearing in the early twentieth century, as in England, came to define and possess this tradition. The Covenanters and Bunyan had been as great a presence as the ballads in the Scottish borders of my youth. Another presence was Carlyle himself, who had been resurrected and interpreted for my generation by Raymond Williams in *Culture and Society* (1958). I can recall the mark Carlyle made on one particular historical case study of the transport revolution, which the new Open University ran in 1969. In "Signs of the Times" (1829) Carlyle wagged a finger at us apprentice "programmed learners" as we set about constructing our "Industrialisation and Culture" units. His words still resonate: "Instruction . . . is no longer an indefinable tentative process, requiring a study of individual aptitudes, and a perpetual variation of means and methods . . . but a secure, universal straightforward business, to be conducted in the gross, by proper mechanism, with such intellect as comes to hand" (*Works* 27:61).

The less adaptable of Carlyle's residues — his Saxonist racism and authoritarianism — seemed to burn to ashes in the Berlin bunker, with Joseph Goebbels trying to console Hitler by reading him Carlyle's *History of Frederick the Great*. Approaches to Carlyle in Germany remain scarred by the flames for decades. Only with German reunification in 1989 was Carlyle allowed on stage again, lugging such metaphorical themes as prophecy and recurrence, clothing and status, the north, the desert, the New World, nationalism, religious dogmatism, heroes and icons, icebergs, volcanoes, and portraits.

"The Man on Horseback"

From this Scottish perspective one could appreciate the ambition and momentum of Carlyle's *Gesamtkunstwerk* ("totality of his art") of the 1830s. This involved not only a critical initiative on a scale rare in Europe (though with American parallels) but also the evolution from the systematized fact-categorization of the "enlightenment in Scotland" — encyclopedias, stadial analysis, statistics and their appraisal — into what Max Weber might have called "*Weltliteratur als Verstehen*" [World literature as understanding]. Carlyle yawed in his personal career after his first articles in the early 1820s between praxis and theory: from the early encyclopedia work to the proto-sociology of *Sartor Resartus* (1833–34); from the history of *The French Revolution* (1837) to the social theory of *Chartism* (1839). *Heroes and Hero-Worship* (1841) would leave his most obvious calling card: "Universal History, the history of what man has accomplished in this world, is at bottom the History of the Great Men who have worked here" (*Heroes* 21). But the lectures themselves — and it was their éclat that transformed a modest audience growth, from 120 to 180, into a printed best seller — were written at great speed during a single month, April 1840, while Carlyle was occupied with London Library committees and with research into the lectures' climactic figure, Oliver Cromwell.

Carlyle always judged his timing well. His *French Revolution* anticipated the fiftieth anniversary of the event in 1839. *Heroes* with its Cromwellian climax pitched into the three hundredth anniversary of the breakdown in 1641 of Charles I's autocracy, as well as into the first mobilization of Chartism, 1838–42, and the urban reform movement that culminated with the 1841 census and the subsequent publication of Edwin Chadwick's *Report on the Sanitary Conditions of the Labouring Population* (1842). Surveyed from Chelsea in 1840, London presented a far from Wordsworthian spectacle to the new (and short-lived) urban horseman, who reported to his brother that he had been "galloping many a mile every day": "Next letter I hope to send you a printed *Prospectus* [of the lectures]. The subject is 'Great Men.' . . . Feeling clearly how indispensable health is towards that, I say always, 'It depends more on my *horse* than on me,' and so ride along with unabated alacrity! . . . The best view you have is that of London in the distance (if you be to windward, as I always ride to be); monstrous London, filling half your horizon, like an infinite ocean of smoke, with steeples, domes, and the ghosts of steeples and domes confusedly hanging in it, —

dim-black under the infinite deep of Blue" *(CL* 12:98; to Alexander Carlyle, 8 April 1840).

This heroic Carlyle phase anticipated "the man on horseback" of two notable later elite studies influenced by him, S. E. Finer's *The Man on Horseback: The Role of Military in Politics* (1962) and F. L. Carsten's *Reichswehr und Politik* (1964) on the links between militarism and Nazism. Its contemporary meaning would expand further in the aftermath of *Heroes and Hero-Worship.* Signs of the book's influence — a template for its age — would proliferate in countless directions, among them Macaulay's poem "How Horatius Kept the Bridge" (1842); innumerable "heroic" statues; the ambiguous "demotic-monarchic" personalization of war with the creation of the Victoria Cross (29 January 1856); the Valhalla-like reconstruction of Westminster Palace between 1837 and 1857; the relentless exploration of unknown territory; missionary activity; and the changing nature of political leadership.

The circumstances in which *Heroes and Hero-Worship* appeared are themselves replete with Carlyle's own heroic gestures. Prospectuses went out from *Fraser's Magazine,* and it initially looked as if the author would receive only £50 as well as the net gate receipts (*CL* 12:109; to John A. Carlyle, 13 April 1840). He wrote four typeset pages each day "from breakfast (about 8 or 9) till 2 o'clock," powered by large quantities of Scots tobacco and the occasional *"blue pill,"* intended to combat chronic dyspepsia (12:115; to Alexander Carlyle, 21 April; to John Carlyle, 18 April). He was pleased by the result and reported to his mother on 9 May: "I gave my second Lecture yesterday to a larger audience than ever, and with all the success, or more, that was necessary for me. It was on *Mahomet;* I had bishops and all kinds of people among my hearers; I gave them to know that the poor Arab had points about him which it were good for all of them to imitate. . . . The people seemed greatly astonished, and greatly pleased; I vomited it forth on them like wild Annandale grapeshot; they laughed, applauded &c., &c." (12:138).

Carlyle now realized that his earlier hope of getting up to £100 for articles was on the low side. Writing to John Forster, his confederate in the founding of the London Library and the organizing of pensions for "men of letters," Carlyle speculated about the final form of the lectures: "Some general description of the whole phenomenon of these Lectures and outline of the purport of them, given as an Article after they were over, would not be objectionable, so far as I can see: yet I never know of such things whether for myself they are good or evil in the long-run, and am in the fixed

habit of leaving them altogether to themselves" (*CL* 12:146; 16 May 1840).
But the increasingly large audiences and the "good sum" of earnings convinced him that the lectures deserved a better literary fate than they had thus
far received. He informed his brother Alexander, "I ought . . . to add that
there is a reporter there for me; I have seen his sketch of the First Lecture, —
a very poor affair: I think more and more, I shall make the thing up by
myself, and promulgate it as a Book" (12:143; 12 May).

Umwelt/Environment

Carlyle invariably locates his heroic in the context of tradition, environment, and narrative as well as in its "mechanics." In his essay "State of
German Literature" (1827), he had referred to "the three great elements of
modern civilisation [as] Gunpowder, Printing and the Protestant Religion"
(*Works* 26:28). The heroic could intervene to freeze, remold, transcend, and
disremember all of these "elements." Carlyle realized that the "myth-kitty"
could not be projected back. Its earlier state governed the way that myths
operated. His alertness to topography and scenery in his biographical and
historical analysis raises in the penumbra the issue of the intelligence of
early or "uncivilised" man. To the journalist and civil servant Henry Cole,
he wrote on 25 April 1840 of his new friend Giuseppe Mazzini, "an honourable, brave and gifted man" (*CL* 12:118). But for Carlyle, Mazzini also
exhibited preliterary as well as heroic qualities, though these qualities were
unrecognized by conventional English documentation. If evidence existed,
it was in Sardinian or Austrian police files on terrorism. And if Carlyle was
a Scottish historian — and he took the idea seriously in the 1830s — he
stopped just when the going got interesting. The 1850s would be important
for reappraising the Scottish past: significant excavations of prehistoric
sites, the founding of historical and antiquarian societies, studies of "baro-
nial" architecture, and the beginnings of a Scottish history that would
attempt to account for the country's deep-seeded political neuroses.

Not only in Scotland itself was this need for reenvisioning history apparent. The "Ten Years' Conflict" that climaxed in the "Disruption" of 1843
— the withdrawal of the "Wild Party" led by Carlyle's old friend Thomas
Chalmers (1780–1847) from the Church of Scotland — was recorded on
camera in the Hill-Adamson calotypes. It also awoke an interest in Scotland's religious past and directly influenced social interpretations of biblical antiquity that depended on sophisticated theism. Both history and theology were at the forefront of Chalmers's Disruption social theory of the

Godly Commonwealth, which was informed by theocratic anticentralism. More logically, to different stadia of development Carlyle added and popularized, from the Saint-Simonians, the concept of critical periods. The link looks robust enough if we return to "Characteristics" (1831) and think of Carlyle's visible debt to Professor Adam Ferguson (1723–1816), the Scottish pioneer of sociology whose own stadial notion of progress was borrowed by Walter Scott. Ferguson himself had also been a fierce folkloristic partisan in his defense of James Macpherson's *Ossian* (1761).

This Scots-crafted foundation myth is not, however, repeated by Carlyle. The Anglophone "national epic" begins, for him, with Shakespeare as poet of English hegemony. Carlyle recognized parallels with Shakespeare's own day in the flood of Baconian logic that enveloped British life in the 1830s and 1840s: railway expansion, 1838, linking London to Manchester; the public telegraph, 1839; practical photography, 1840; the first Atlantic steamers, 1836–38; Chartism, 1838; and the Penny Post, 1840. To this list might be added the advent of the weekly press and the expansion of educational opportunity, as well as Henry Reeves's translation of De Tocqueville's *Democracy in America* (1835, 1840), Charles MacKay's *Memoirs of Extraordinary Popular Delusions* (1841), Chadwick's *Sanitary Report* (1842), John Stuart Mill's *A System of Logic* (1843), and Robert Chambers's *Vestiges of Creation* (1844).

Gods, Poets, Priests

Into this crowded and contested space, the would-be champion, open to his market and wide in his reading, merged the Scots parameters of his earlier training. Vesting faith in cultural palimpsest — let alone MacPherson's energetic forgery — would have got Carlyle nowhere. Instead the role of "hero as God" alights on Odin/Wotan, the central, flawed figure of the *Nibelungenlied*. The cultural duty — God's and also the priest's — was to create a belief system that interpreted the experienced environment as a family saga in which the anthropomorphic element was always present. In *Heroes* Carlyle comes close to Richard Wagner in his interpretation of Nordic "Könning," ending with his own Scots version of *Twilight of the Gods*: "The old Universe with its Gods is sunk; but it is not final death: there is to be a new Heaven and a new Earth; a higher supreme God, and Justice to reign among men" (48).

Carlyle was more than just "musical." He translated the Luther chorales as Scots hymns. He disliked operas of the Rossini sort, but the argument of the first chapter of *Heroes and Hero-Worship* — "Justice to reign among men" — seems directly to lead to Bernard Shaw's socialist interpretation of Wagner, not just of the Ring cycle but of *Die Meistersinger von Nürnberg* as well, with Carlyle of the Edinburgh Rectorial address posing as Hans Sachs. Where are the Scottish roots of this connection? Perhaps in Ferguson's less overtly patriotic *History of Civil Society* (1767), basic to the social world of Dugald Stewart (1753–1828) and the "theoretical history" of the Ayrshire novelist and essayist John Galt (1779–1839). What Carlyle found distinctive about the Nordic phase, and the God-King, was the appearance in it of a "progressive" rather than cyclic history, in the *Heimskringla* narrative of Snorri Sturluson, which conformed both to the same nation-building process Britain was currently going through and to the new centrality of the written account.

The second lecture, "The Hero as Prophet," centers on monotheism, the quality of sincerity, and the economics of faith. While Carlyle is unforthcoming about the politics of the Viking commonwealth (he would return to it at the end of his life in *Early Kings of Norway* [1875]), he is vivid on Mahomet's transformation of a declining Arab "nation." Why Mahomet and not, say, Benedict or Columba? Mahomedism had, Carlyle argues, a greater world impact than Christianity — "these hundred and eighty millions were made by God as well as we" (*Heroes* 52) — which in Mahomet's own career was already riven by doctrinal nitpicking at the Council of Nicaea — "*Homoiusion*" versus "*Homoousion*," "the head full of worthless noise, the heart empty and dead!" (66) being combated by Mahomet's force of character and human qualities."

Carlyle concentrated on Mahomet, "an uncultured semi-barbarous Son of Nature" (*Heroes* 69), as an educator and a teacher because of contemporary events. After its scientific, military, and technical advance, the Moslem world seemed to be in crisis. France occupied northeastern Algeria in 1839 in a demonstration of military superiority, with the factory-built rifle blowing the musket away. Yet in the same year Britain invaded Afghanistan and subsequently suffered a shattering series of reverses that forced it to withdraw in 1842. In 1840 Britain, in alliance with Austria and Prussia, also began a conflict in Egypt with Mehmed Ali Pasha (1769–1849), an Albanian from the city of Kavala in Greek Macedonia, who had harnessed Western technology — warships, engineering, and cotton mills — to support his "nationalist" cause of modernization. His Scottish chief engineer, Thomas Galloway (d. 1836), just failed to build him an Alexandria-Suez railway line in 1834, only four years after the inauguration of the Liverpool-Manchester line.

There is a gap here, one that Carlyle would only return to at the end of his life, in *Early Kings of Norway*. Schools of regnal thought and internecine caste squabbles do not interest him (pretenders or family rivals *subtract* from the true hero). The luminaries of *Heroes and Hero-Worship* are all "of the people." If there is an antihero — later to be extensively dissected by Carlyle in *Past and Present* — he is not active devilment but the "poor old Pope" (*Heroes* 120), who has become an automaton, like Jeremy Bentham. Carlyle was disdainful of the icon mongering that dominated the Oxford Movement and Newman's *Lives of the Saints* (1844, 1845). Ironically, this latter project was to be responsible for converting Carlyle's future biographer James Anthony Froude from Tractarianism to Carlylism, thanks to the intellectual frustrations that he experienced while writing his essay "Saint Neot." Carlyle's "hero-worship" was not idolatry — as many skimmer critics have supposed — but its opposite. Useful at this point was the notion of the "Scots worthies" preserved by the ballads and the folk tradition, and enhanced rather than suppressed by printing, from Chapman and Miller's first Scottish press (1507) onward. This brand of Scots ascension was strengthened by Knox and the later Covenanters, by Jacobite disputants such as Sir Thomas Urquhart of Cromarty (1611–c. 1660) and Allan Ramsay Senior (1686–1758), and in Carlyle's own time by radical Whigs such as David Steuart Erskine, eleventh Earl of Buchan (1742–1829), whose gigantic Wallace statue (1814) at Dryburgh "commodified" Burns's poetic references as part of a distinctive medieval revival. The revolutionary aspects of the idea, with its Whig origins, migrates to Carlyle, but not its specific representation of Scottish nationality.

Wallace's contemporary Dante was not only a poet of universalized feeling but also one embroiled in transnational conflict on a European scale. His focus was on Italy, but it extended throughout Europe. In an important sense Dante provides the first recognizable lay portrait in the postclassical period. Portraits would be a continuing preoccupation of Carlyle's. In the 1850s he advocated, on heroic lines (see the historical output of the enthusiastic David Scott [1806–49], whose brother William Bell Scott [1811–90] was a frequent visitor to Chelsea), the establishment of a Scottish portrait gallery. As Carlyle recognized, the Ghibelline poet Dante represented locality and language (and their dynamism) rather than the rigidities of elective emperors bred into a noble caste. Locations were always important to Carlyle. Consider his birthplace and the Carlyle family tabernacle, Ecclefechan, literally "the small church" at the heart of the "Welsh" kingdom. Dante coincided with the beginning of recorded poetry in Carlyle's own Scotland, and the publication of Andrew Wyntoun's *Orygynale Cronykil,* which included a famous lament for King Alexander III (1241–86). The lines from the *Purgatorio* — "He seeketh Liberty, which is so dear, / As knoweth he who life for her refuses" (1:71–72; trans. Longfellow) — were possibly cited and translated into Latin in the Declaration of Arbroath of 1320. At the least, the manifesto concludes in Dantean fashion, "It is in truth not for glory, nor riches, nor honour, that we are fighting, but for freedom — for that alone, which no honest man gives up but with life itself" (Fergusson 9).

Carlyle extends himself in "The Hero as Poet." In simple formal terms, this section is forty-four pages in the first edition, while Mahomet himself only got thirty (and was cut down to size in the "Poet" lecture). Out of Dante came intensity and music, with poetry enduring essentially as song. Mahomet's achievement was less lyrical. As Carlyle points out, "Dante has given us the Faith or soul; Shakspeare, in a not less noble way, has given us the Practice or body" (*Heroes* 93). Carlyle commends the breadth of Shakespeare but also his self-conscious craftsmanship. Yet there is, oddly, at this stage, no discussion of contexts of communication that were still personal. Carlyle does not place Dante in the politics of Florence (he would not be printed for two hundred years), or of Shakespeare in the expansive, urban yet uncivil, and even piratical culture of Elizabethan London.

Here there is a central contradiction. Carlyle's praise of Shakespeare sits awkwardly with his praise of Cromwell, the opponent of the theatrical. He chooses to demonstrate the "national epic" with *Henry V*, which celebrates an impressive figure, but also a candidate for iconic ritual and an image that has ceased to inspire, like the automaton pope. Laurence Olivier's presentation of the triumphant English in his film version of *Henry V* in 1944 has now retreated to an embalmed, lifeless status. Cromwell himself, moreover, was the contemporary of another great writer, John Milton, one who in many ways anticipated the Keatsian "negative capability" of the flawed hero. Indeed, Milton's Satan was almost precisely the outcome of political and character conflict that defined Cromwell's rise and fall. This doppelganger effect also illuminates the postprophetic internalization of Carlyle that is remarked on by such critics as W. R. Greg (1801–81), whose own vision of the sage oscillates between journalistic "attack" and historical coherence.

In "The Hero as Priest" this contradiction between appearance and substance continues. Printing, a branch of the mechanism Carlyle will condemn in the "godless" eighteenth century, is emphatically the vehicle for history. The central figure is, of course, Luther, who used the new technology brilliantly, developing Dante's linguistic politics in the interests of a higher

power, one influenced by the broadcasting of his personality through portraits by Lucas Cranach the Elder and Albrecht Dürer. The Luther portrait is
repeated *in petto* for John Knox, retaining hagiographic elements as well as
his "authorial" *History of the Reformation in Scotland* (1559–66), at literally face value in Adrian Vanson's portrait. Neglecting the moderating theology of Andrew Melville (1545–1622) or George Buchanan (1506–82), Carlyle also ignores their readers — the "bonnet lairds" or middling gentry, the
townspeople — for a Knoxian *force majeure* bestowing a sort of collective
national heroism. And throughout the discussion of Knox, Carlyle plays
down the enervating sequel of a country divided for thirty years by aristocratic mayhem in defense of particularist rights.

Men of Letters: Print Capitalism and the Ablemen

It is notable how in this lecture as in others, Carlyle leaves a tab — the hero as
autobiographer — that connects to the next phase of the heroic thesis but not
necessarily to the course of history. He had visited the Industrial Revolution
in "Signs of the Times" (1829) but did not warm to big business figures or to
their Samuel Smilesian portraits. In *Chartism* (1839) the "gross, bag-
cheeked, potbellied Lancashire man" (*Works* 29:182) Sir Richard Ark-
wright emerged as a counterfeiter rather than a technician. He is the pro-
totype of George Hudson (1800–1871) the Railway King, who is pilloried in
Latter-Day Pamphlets (1850) as a "paltry adventurer . . . worthy of no
worship . . . except from the soul consecrated to flunkeyism." Demeaned by
his popular sovereignty and ruling an unreal land that is frenetic with deceit,
Hudson is the very antithesis of an "Able Man . . . the born enemy of Falsity
and Anarchy" (*Works* 20:262, 107).

The drive of the essay series can, as Robert Burns would have said,
"gang aft agley." "The Hero as Man of Letters" seems in fact more ironic
than celebratory. It might be that Carlyle's intent can be summarized if not
bowdlerized in the alternate title, "The Hero as Bohemian." His statement
that "I many a time say, the writers of Newspapers, Pamphlets, Poems,
Books, these *are* the real working, effective Church of a modern country"
(*Heroes* 138) implies less an advance than the old saw that journalists'
troubles start when they become the story of their own reports. It is difficult
if not impossible to discern whether this moment of self-revelation occurred as a result of his reading the off–Fleet Street symposia of Samuel
Johnson, to whom Carlyle was the natural heir, or whether it was a rhetorical response to the similar sexual and economic problems of Rousseau and

Burns. Alternatively, it may have been rooted in Carlyle's consumption of German *Sturm und Drang* theory — particularly Schiller's *On the Aesthetic Education of Man* (1795) and Fichte's *On the Nature of the Literary Man* (1805) — themselves influenced by Adam Ferguson's vigorous strictures against commercial society. Whatever its origins, Carlyle's position in this lecture is unusually and explicitly democratic, or as close as he ever got to being so.

He insists that the hero can be collective, enacting in himself the universal desire to achieve a truthful identity. This possibility yields a Carlyle who is almost euphoric: "Literature is our Parliament too. Printing, which comes necessarily out of Writing, I say often, is equivalent to Democracy: invent Writing, Democracy is inevitable. . . . Add only that whatsoever power exists will have itself by and by organised; working secretly under bandages, obscurations, obstructions, it will never rest till it get to work free, unencumbered, visible to all. Democracy virtually extant will insist on becoming palpably extant" (*Heroes* 139).

Unfortunately, Carlyle's book heroes will always be diminished by their commercial position. Johnson is a "hard-struggling, weary-hearted man, or 'scholar' as he calls himself, trying hard to get some honest livelihood in the world, not to starve, but to live — without stealing!" (*Heroes* 151). Rousseau "sits at the tables of grandees; and has to copy music for his own living. He cannot even get his music copied: 'By dint of dining out,' says he, 'I run the risk of dying by starvation at home'" (160). And Burns the would-be "true" legislator "falls into discontents, into miseries, faults" as a result of the fatal "*Lionism*" (161, 160) of his commercial clientele.

The final lecture, "The Hero as King. Cromwell, Napoleon, Modern Revolutionism," at fifty-five pages in the first edition represents the longest of all the published lectures on heroes. The issue of revolution comes at the beginning, in which Carlyle proclaims the end of traditional authority and independent *gemeinschaft,* and foresees the volcanic destruction of pseudo-solutions and the literal "gigs" of the middle-classes. For him, the French Revolution confirms tendencies unleashed by the Reformation, but also reveals the thinness of the formulas that were supposed to replace them, the personal "gigs" of Voltaire and Rousseau. Carlyle acknowledges that the need for ideals to be united with political force and right had been given precedent, 150 years earlier, by the English Civil War. He identifies the English way with Oliver Cromwell, who as a patriot and a Christian had a duty to counsel and to lead to them truthfully and honorably. In a letter to Emerson on 26 September 1840, Carlyle remarked, "I have got, within the last twelvemonth, actually, as it were, to *see* that this Cromwell was one of the greatest souls ever born of the English kin: a great amorphous semi-articulate Baresark, very interesting to me." As a subject, the Protector formed one of Carlyle's most famous books, but in 1840 Carlyle was still struggling "to see if it be possible to get any credible face-to-face acquaintance with our English Puritan period; or whether it must be left forever a mere hearsay and echo to one?" (Slater 280). By *Cromwell's Letters and Speeches* (1845), the Scots for Carlyle will have moved from subject to object and indeed from friend to enemy: the personal "we" at the Battle of Dunbar is Carlyle-Cromwell-monarchical. A gey lang wey frae Annandale?

Cromwell is followed by a sharp jump in time and value to Napoleon, whose "compact, prompt, every-way articulate character is in itself perhaps small, compared with our great chaotic *in*articulate Cromwell's" (*Heroes* 191). The man was a measure of a uniquely postheroic age, and Carlyle was hard-pressed to find exemplars. The increasingly muscular and affluent United States had already been analyzed critically by de Tocqueville, and the work had been translated with a Whiggish antidemocratic bias by Reeve. It was much discussed in the light of parallels that had been drawn between Andrew Jackson's populism and the Chartist movement. Jackson demitted in 1837, followed by a succession of mediocrities — Van Buren, Harrison, Tyler, Taylor, Fillmore, Pierce, Buchanan — until Lincoln in 1861: another "semi-articulate *Baresark*" whom a much-altered Carlyle then deliberately spurned in favor of Frederick the Great. The engineer-hero should have filled this vacuum in 1840, but Carlyle had no inclination to include such a figure. This task would be left to Dr. Samuel Smiles, from Haddington like Jane Welsh, but farther from Carlyle than we might first imagine. For Smiles's idea of innovation was Utilitarian-rational, responsive to generalized social demands for "gross, bag-cheeked, potbellied" success stories. In Carlyle there is another more numinous desideratum. From the Scottish "common-sense" philosophy of the eighteenth century, he inherited an enduring sense of intuiting right conduct from conscience, a faculty that was not conditioned by the "*eyeless* Heroism" (*Heroes* 145) of Bentham and his British disciples.

Thomas Carlyle, Social Media, and the Digital Age of Revolution

BRENT E. KINSER

At the beginning of *On Heroes, Hero-Worship, and the Heroic in History,*
Carlyle identifies the heroic individual as the very source of all history:
"Universal History, the history of what man has accomplished in this world,
is at bottom the History of the Great Men who have worked here" (22). By
the conclusion of his series of lectures, after a considerable struggle with
identifying and justifying his conception of these "Great Men," Carlyle
seems to qualify his reliance upon individual, heroic worth in his vision of
the future: "I see the blessedest result preparing itself: not abolition of
Hero-worship, but rather what I would call a whole World of Heroes. If
Hero mean *sincere man,* why may not every one of us be a Hero? A world
all sincere, a believing world: the like has been; the like will again be, —
cannot help being" (112). In one sense, Carlyle's prophecy of a future
defined by universal heroism appears to rely on a reductive definition indeed — that the hero should be sincere, and that the hero should be a man.
From the perspective of twenty-first century readers, this view of heroes
seems restrictive, sexist, and obsolete. Regardless, the history of the 170
years since Carlyle delivered his lectures has only affirmed the importance
of and fascination with heroes and the heroic. Further, if sincerity and
maleness provide an inadequate definition, his idea of "a whole World of
Heroes" is not so easily dismissed, especially in a world in which the spread
of democracy has attained a religious status that transcends mere policy.
Recognizing, much less defining, the heroic and its representatives in such a
world has never been more important, or difficult, and Carlyle remains
central to the attempt.

At best, the problem of identifying heroes is a slippery one. For example, in seeking to trumpet the heroic characteristics of the computing guru
Steve Jobs, his biographer Walter Isaacson has remarked that his subject's
colleagues regarded him through the lens of a "hero/shithead dichotomy"
(34). Isaacson's paradoxical and crude assessment recalls Carlyle's characterization of Diogenes Teufelsdröckh [God-born devil's dung] in *Sartor
Resartus,* who looks down from his tower in Weissnichtwo [Know-not-

where] recording his impressions of the world in the bombastic language of a "Clothes-Philosophy" (58) that leaves the Editor and his readers mostly if not entirely bamboozled. Like Teufelsdröckh, albeit in a real-world setting, Jobs seems to have seen the world in a way that not quite anyone else could understand. But Carlyle did not confine his view of the paradoxical nature of mortals to fiction; contradiction also served as the nucleus of his real-life heroes. On this point Frederick the Great, or as Carlyle qualifies him in the subtitle of his biography, Frederick "called the Great," serves as exemplar: "To the last, a questionable hero; with much in him which one could have wished not there, and much wanting which one could have wished" (*Works* 12:14). Frederick is not alone, for none of Carlyle's heroes escapes his human inadequacies, from the oppressed complacency of Burns to the "berserker" mentality of Cromwell to the arrogant narcissism of Napoleon. Nor is Carlyle alone, for from his time to the present day, efforts to identify the qualities that define a hero have continued unabated. These attempts have invariably floundered on paradox. Carlyle's heroes, indeed all heroes, like the fictive Diogenes Teufelsdröckh, suffer from and become mysteriously elevated by being god-born devil's dung. It is this dualistic attribute, more than either sincerity or maleness, that serves as a universal characteristic of the Carlylean hero.

According to Isaacson, Jobs was a hero because he was sincere — obnoxiously so, if his colleagues are to be believed in their accounts of his insufferable micromanaging — and because he left the world a place much different from what it was when he arrived. His central role in creating and expanding the possibilities of the Information Age is indisputable. Whether or not this explosion in digital technology and communication that Jobs helped to bring about represents a positive step for the species, however, remains an open question. Almost certainly Carlyle would have seen the twenty-first century in much the same light as he saw the eighteenth: "The world's heart is palsied, sick: how can any limb of it be whole? Genuine Acting ceases in all departments of the world's work; dexterous Similitude of Acting begins. The world's wages are pocketed, the world's work is not done. Heroes have gone out; Quacks have come in" (*Heroes* 146). If he sought evidence of this pervasive "Quackery," Carlyle need only have cited *Time*'s "Person of the Year" recipient in 2006, which was "You." Unwittingly echoing the sage of Chelsea, Andrew Keen has remarked in *The Cult of the Amateur* (2007) that public opinion is now shaped by a "youth culture of digital narcissism" that reflects "the myopia of the digital mob." In his self-proclaimed "polemic against the Internet" (ix), Keen declares that there are "many thousands of people who, like me, are deeply

worried and confused about the economic, cultural, and ethical conse-
quences of our user-generated media revolution" (xv). It is true that the
inanities associated with the new social media, including Facebook, the
blogosphere, YouTube, and Twitter, represent a form of triviality that is
striking in its pervasive and sublunary influence. These new forms of communication do have the potential to be destructive, but in ways that Keen
neither imagines nor predicts. The new social media has become the engine
for a digital age of revolution, the priorities of which frequently intersect
with Carlyle's notions of the heroic.

To understand fully what Carlyle has to teach about this digital age of
revolution, it seems necessary to understand his own ambivalence toward
technology. Both he and his wife, Jane Welsh Carlyle, lived also in an era
that was marked by rapid and monumental technological advancement.
They saw the rise of travel by rail and by steamship, and they complained
incessantly about both modes of transportation. Nonetheless, they used
both forms when the need arose. When William Makepeace Thackeray
gave Carlyle two steel pens in 1859, Carlyle and his wife complained about
them, but they used them. They took advantage of the Penny Post, and there
are some ten thousand letters collected at the Carlyle Letters Office at Duke
University Press to prove it. And they reveled in the Graphic Revolution
mentioned by David Sorensen in the Introduction to this edition. Neither
Thomas nor Jane Carlyle turned down an opportunity to have their image
taken, whether in a painting or a photograph, nor did they miss an opportunity to complain about the inconveniences and distastefulness of the process. The point is that Carlyle may have been resistant to technological
advances, but he also showed a willingness to take advantage of them,
notwithstanding his continual complaints. As a young man, he even invented a horseshoe in which a short stob could be screwed to provide horses
with traction on icy roads. Were the Carlyles to be reincarnated today they
would certainly, like many Victorians, be horrified by displays of public
nakedness on warm days, but they would not be surprised or daunted by the
new technologies associated with the exchange of information. They would
complain about Facebook and Twitter, but they would likely do so on
Facebook and Twitter. More anxiety would be caused by the uncomfortable
shift to the digital form of the printed word that these technologies represent. Carlyle states this allegiance clearly in *Heroes:* "All that Mankind has
done, thought, gained or been: it is lying as in magic preservation in the
pages of Books. They are the chosen possession of men" (136). Carlyle
then extends the supremacy of the book to education: "The true University
of these days is a Collection of Books" (138). He would be astonished to

learn the number of books one may collect on a Nook or a Kindle. And he would, no doubt, use digital technologies such as Google Books and Internet Archive much as scholars use them today, or as they will use them as time retires the resistance to this new form of retrieving and making knowledge, just as the scroll makers and readers were retired by the codex those many aeons ago. And the question of whether or not the paradigm shift from analog to digital is a good thing or not reflects a central tenet of Carlyle's historical philosophy. Although the idea of "Progress of the Species" existed for Carlyle in "fact" as an "inevitable necessity" (106) that was ever extending the limits of human knowledge in an ever-expanding universe, the phenomenon was neither recognizable in the present nor a predictor for the future. For Carlyle, identifying "Progress" and the heroes who created it could only be revealed by historical distance. From a Carlylean perspective, history has not yet had sufficient time and distance to judge either Steve Jobs or his age.

Carlyle's valorization of books in *On Heroes,* however, is not limited to their power to educate or to invoke pleasure in readers, nor is it confined to ink and paper. In his judgment the true power of the published word exists in the ideas carried by books in the context of revolution:

> Writing, I say often, is equivalent to Democracy: invent Writing, Democracy is inevitable. Writing brings Printing; brings universal everyday extempore Printing, as we see at present. Whoever can speak, speaking now to the whole nation, becomes a power, a branch of government, with inalienable weight in law-making, in all acts of authority. It matters not what rank he has, what revenues or garnitures: the requisite thing is, that he have a tongue which others will listen to; this and nothing more is requisite. The nation is governed by all that has tongue in the nation: Democracy is virtually *there.* Add only that whatsoever power exists will have itself by and by organised; working secretly under bandages, obscurations, obstructions, it will never rest till it get to work free, unincumbered, visible to all. Democracy virtually extant will insist on becoming palpably extant. (*Heroes* 139)

As his critics have always enjoyed pointing out, Carlyle was no fan of democracy. Throughout his life, in his works, his letters, and his table talk, he continually professed his strong opposition to all things democratic, especially in the context of what he viewed as the impotency of the "ballot-box." At the heart of his argument for heroes, after all, is the contention that it is the Great Man, ultimately the benevolent king, who proves essential in the orderly construction of society, and for Carlyle, order was "the one thing needful" (43). Yet in this passage on the printed word, Carlyle recognizes the revolutionary power that transforms blots of ink into the ultimate instrument of human action: "Those poor bits of rag-paper with black ink on them; — from the Daily Newspaper to the sacred Hebrew Book . . . what are they not doing! . . . It is the *Thought* of man; the true thaumaturgic virtue; by which man works all things whatsoever. All that he does, and brings to pass, in the vesture of a Thought. . . . The thing we called 'bits of paper with traces of black ink,' is the *purest* embodiment a Thought of man can have" (139–40). If the ideas embodied figuratively by the black marks in books serve as the agent for human achievement, then the os and 1s that make up the digital word become an essential locus for consideration, for they also carry with them great, revolutionary power.

In the twenty-first century, an age that indeed has seen "Democracy" become not "virtually extant" but "palpably extant" (*Heroes* 139) in the world, the printed word has been translated into a digital realm defined by both speed and quantity. Carlyle's world of print has been subsumed by Jobs's world of bytes. And recently in this new world, a virtual revolution has erupted into historical reality in ways that could not have been conceived of just a few years ago. The Arab Spring of 2011 demonstrated the power of the digital realm in a massively destructive way to the status quo of self-styled cultural heroes, more accurately called dictators, who found themselves on the wrong side of history as forces of democracy manifested in the digital realm insisted on migrating, palpably, to the very real world of historical transformation.

On 17 December 2010 a young Tunisian vegetable merchant named Mohammed Bouazizi, frustrated by his treatment at the hands of local officials, set himself on fire in front of a municipal building in Tunis and helped to launch the Arab Spring, a series of revolutionary events that have caused the overthrow of dictatorial regimes in Tunisia, Egypt, and Libya. At the time of the writing of this essay, the revolutionary spirit that has driven the Arab Spring is still taking shape in Yemen, Syria, Bahrain, and elsewhere. A recent study conducted by Philip N. Howard and his colleagues at the University of Washington's Project on Information Technology and Political Islam (PITPI) includes what may seem an astonishing claim to people accustomed to viewing Facebook, Twitter, and YouTube through the lens of American cultural banality: "The Arab Spring had many causes. One of these sources was social media and its power to put a human face on political oppression" (Howard et al. 2). But Howard and his associates do not confine the personification of digital technology to the oppressors: "By using digital technologies, democracy advocates created a freedom meme that took on a life of its own and spread ideas about liberty and revolution to a surprisingly large number of people" (3). This strange personification — a kind of heroic avatar, or in Carlylean terms a "Thought" — made it impossible for the regimes in power to suppress the revolutions as they gained momentum. According to Howard, "The political uprising was leaderless so there was no long-standing revolutionary figurehead, traditional opposition leader, or charismatic speechmaker who could be arrested" (9). The activist Van Jones, who is attempting to align the Occupy Wall Street movement with extant liberal groups in the United States, provides a succinct parallel to Howard's analysis of Tunisia: "We don't want leader-centric movements. We want leader-full movements" (qtd. in Scherer 44). Revolutions in the digital age are not being guided by inspiring individual heroes whose survival determines the success of a particular political cause; instead, as Carlyle hoped and predicted, in these new circumstances, "every one of us [is to] be a Hero" (*Heroes* 112).

The revolutionaries of the Arab Spring who have thus far succeeded find themselves in a precarious position now that the regimes under which they suffered have been eliminated and dismantled. Carlyle viewed Napoleon in the aftermath of the French Revolution in a similar context: "[Napoleon] feels, and has a right to feel, how necessary a strong Authority is; how the Revolution cannot prosper or last without such. To bridle in that great devouring, self-devouring French Revolution; to *tame* it, so that its intrinsic purpose can be made good, that it may become *organic,* and be able to live among other organisms and *formed* things, not as a wasting destruction alone" (*Heroes* 193). The French "earthquake" had become a natural force with a life of its own. Similarly, the Arab Spring has been identified with a pervasive spirit rather than with a transcendent leader, which has made it impossible to predict just how this revolutionary spirit will or will not be transformed from a destructive to a creative force. Although the individual power manifested in Napoleon was able to keep the destructive element of the Revolution in abeyance for a time, he failed in the end to transform the Revolution from destructive to creatively organic ends. The reason, according to Carlyle, was Napoleon's great fault, which was his self-consuming arrogance: "The world was not disposed to be trodden down underfoot; to be bound into masses, and built together as *he* liked, for a pedestal to France and him" (195). One result of its apparent leaderless identity is that the Arab Spring has not yet created a Napoleon figure, a person able to conjure up the kind of mass support required to shape the chaotic aftermath of the revolutions into a creative cosmos for governance. Further, the potential return of dictatorial regimes that could result from such an investment of individual power causes much strife, especially among the revolutionaries, and perhaps rightly so. Still, the lack of an identifiable center to the revolutions of the Arab Spring has caused much anxiety in the nations looking forward to the creation of either new business partners or new enemies in the "War on Terror." As in the case of Jobs and his age, history has not yet judged.

The dangers of predicting the future aside, the role of the new social media in the revolutionary events of the Arab Spring offer a compelling new way to explore the concept of heroes and heroism. The naysayers of the digital age deny the import of the new social media by pointing to its over-whelming tendency to elevate the trivial, especially in the United States. Indeed, digital forms of communication and entertainment are ready-made for such abuse. Alexis Madrigal has recently reported that humans expend the equivalent of sixteen years worth of time every hour playing the digital game "Angry Birds," to the tune of an annual loss of $1.5 billion in wage-hour productivity. Similar hours wasted on Facebook and Twitter and YouTube would no doubt produce even more staggering statistics, pointing to the creation of a truly worldwide "opiate of the masses." In this respect, observers such as Keen are right to decry the anti-social and anti-democratic aspects of the new social media. Yet these media have also served as a catalyst for democratic revolution, demonstrating an unprecedented ability to resist oppressive authority. Carlyle conceived of London as "millions of Thoughts made into One; — a huge immeasurable Spirit of a THOUGHT, em-bodied in brick, in iron, smoke, dust, Palaces, Parliaments, Hackney Coaches, Katherine Docks, and the rest of it!" (*Heroes* 139–40). The new social media during the Arab Spring have demonstrated their ability to function in a similar way by channeling popular energies toward the objectives of demo-cratic change. According to Howard and his colleagues, as events unfolded in Tunisia "people increasingly Tweeted about events that were occurring in their neighborhood. Stories of success and difficulty spread widely and cre-ated a kind of 'freedom meme' " (13). In other words, the Tweets themselves — in the metaphorical guise of the unit of cultural evolution defined by Richard Dawkins as a "meme" in his *The Selfish Gene* (1976) — became the incarnation of the people's thoughts, or as Carlyle expressed it, "a huge immeasurable Spirit of a THOUGHT" (*Heroes* 139). What observers are left to wonder about and to document is whether or not these same forces will be equally effective in creating an Arab Summer that will transform the destruc-tive forces of the revolution into a creative agent of cultural re-creation. Hopes for this phoenix-like rebirth run high, but as Teufelsdröckh rhetori-cally asks in *Sartor Resartus,* "When the Phœnix is fanning her funeral pyre, will there not be sparks flying?" (175). The victims of the "sparks" from the Arab Spring are as yet uncounted, the victors unidentified.

But, as Teufelsdröckh also teaches, "this world . . . is emphatically the Place of Hope" (121). The metaphorical relationship between Tweet and meme is also fascinating because of the traditionally opposed qualities of machine and biological entity. It is because of the organic nature of the freedom memes created by Tweets in Tunisia that Howard turns to communication rather than to communicators: "Here we study Tweets, rather than simply Twitter users, because they represent a sense of conversation and active dialogue about freedom that transcended national boundaries." Howard goes on to include the Egyptian blogger Gigi Ibrahim's reaction to the ignominious departure on 14 January 2011 of the Tunisian president Zine El Abidine Ben Ali: "The Tunisian revolution is being twitterized . . . history is being written by the people." Howard then reports that the Egyptian blogger Tarek Shalaby responded to Ibrahim with a simple exclamation: "We will follow it!" (13). The memes created by the Tunisians, their Twitterized "it," had become worthy of followers, not only in Tunisia but also in Egypt. The virus was spreading, and in less than two months, on 11 February 2011, it was the Egyptian president Hosni Mubarak's turn to be removed from power. A new age of digital revolution, with the hero as Tweet at its center, had arrived, and given an entire nation hope. But there is good reason to retain a measure of Carlylean skepticism at this juncture of revolutionary events in the Arab world. The technology that has served the revolution also has the rather frightening potential for new forms of oppression and control, although as of yet the regimes of the Middle East have not been able effectively to utilize social media for their purposes. History has not yet adjudicated events, and no one can predict how long technology in the context of the Arab Spring will remain a vehicle for heroic change. It is indeed possible that the digital age of revolution will go the way of Carlyle's Napoleon: "For an hour the whole Universe seems wrapt in smoke and flame; but only for an hour. It goes out: the Universe with its old mountains and streams, its stars above and kind soil beneath, is still there" (*Heroes* 194). But it is equally possible that "self-devourment" (*Works* 4:243) will leave the Arab Spring defined as simply another manifestation of Thermidor.

As in the case of all Carlylean heroes, a paradox lies at the center of this digital force become living entity, the Tweet known as a "freedom meme," for it is created with a technology that can serve as a vehicle for and an emblem of both the highest and the lowest in human achievement. This binary once again recalls the metaphorical representation of the human conundrum Carlyle imbeds in the paradoxical name of Diogenes Teufels-dröckh. The figurative work that results from the name of Carlyle's fictive hero functions just as well in the "hero/shithead dichotomy" that defined Steve Jobs's life and career. The same species that produces a Mozart also produces a Hitler. If the new social media create the environment for ac-complishing the best that humans can achieve, then at the same time they provides an all too convenient escape platform for the worst possibility, a place for humans to excuse themselves from any achievement whatsoever. If the new media have the power to blur the boundary between mechanical and biological reality, and in doing so ascend to the status of hero, then they do so in the same paradoxical way that all human heroes do. Perhaps this parallel between machine and human can be explained by the fact that these remarkable machines are the self-reflective creation of humans. But as the Arab Spring continues, the Tweets themselves, as metaphorical vehicles of human thought, continue to take on lives of their own. Perceiving the new social media in this way creates a grand irony in the context of Carlyle's concerns about the mechanical nature of his own age: "The living TREE Igdrasil, with the melodious prophetic waving of its world-wide boughs, deep-rooted as Hela, has died out into the clanking of a World-MACHINE" (*Heroes* 144). Carlyle's contrast of the organic sacred tree with the mechan-ically destructive machine finds new relevance in the context of technolo-gies that are quickly eliminating the barrier between human thought and action. Implementations of brain-computer interfaces are years, not de-cades, away, and the applications of these technologies that unite the human and the machine will no doubt run the gamut from divine to evil.

The same Facebook and Twitter and YouTube and Blogosphere that allow colleagues and friends to complain about how busy they are also exists as a collective, palpable entity, one with the power to achieve a brand of revolutionary intervention that was inconceivable not long ago. There is no reason to believe that the causes of revolution have changed in any way, but the speed at which revolutionary ideas are exchanged via the new social media make these technologies enormously powerful. They have increased the likelihood of revolution, if not changed its underlying causes. And on this point, it is important to heed Carlyle once again: "Whoever can speak, speaking now to the whole nation, becomes a power, a branch of govern-ment, with inalienable weight in law-making, in all acts of authority" (*He-roes* 139). The revolutionary vehicle of choice is no longer books but social media, and the Arab Spring has shown that even a simple Tweet can be-come the voice of a nation, one demanding some brand of justice, change, and freedom. Oppressive regimes have attempted to shut down access to these technologies, with as much success as the book burners of history, which is to say very little, if any. Attempts to use social media against revolutionaries have similarly failed. It is possible to stop people by imprisonment or by death; ideas are another matter. Open elections have been held both in Tunisia and in Egypt, with apparent success. Other countries in the Arab world and elsewhere, it may be hoped, will be next. But these hopeful developments do not entail new governments and regimes in these countries that will align themselves with the forces of progress as defined by Western, democratic modernity.

For if Carlyle teaches anything in his lectures on heroes and the view of history that shaped them, it is to be wary of considering recent events, especially elections, as somehow predictive of human progress. Continuing violence and unrest aside, however, it remains arguable that the face of the hero and the nature of the heroic and hero-worship have changed forever, miraculously, in the guise of a 140-character-or-less meme. A statue to commemorate Mohammed Bouazizi's role in the Tunisian revolution was installed in December 2011. Emblazoned with the phrase "For those who yearn to be free," the sculpture depicts not Bouazizi but his vegetable cart, not the man but the idea. The age of the Tweet has come in, for better and worse. Like all digital technologies, the Tweet's lifespan will be short, but because of it the world will never be the same, and who knows what new miracles will present themselves along the digital way. No doubt, quacks will use them for nonsense and for ill, but still others will utilize their revolutionary, heroic potential to advance the cause of human liberty and freedom and to change the world yet again. Carlyle both asks and answers correctly: "The Age of Miracles past? The Age of Miracles is forever here!" (*Heroes* 113). Heroes also will be forever here, as long as humans never grow weary of embracing the true source of the heroic — the power to transform thought into action.

Abdallah: Abd Allah (545–570), the father of Muḥammad. He died during a caravan trip from Medina to Mecca before his son was born.

Abelard: Peter Abelard (1079–1142), preeminent French philosopher and theologian. His philosophical work made him a hero of the enlightenment, and his love affair with the French nun Héloïse d'Argenteuil (1090?–1164) made them both the stuff of Romantic legend.

Abu Thaleb: Abū Ṭālib (549–619), the elder brother of Muḥammad's father and the prophet's protector after the death of his mother, Aminah, in 577.

Addison: Joseph Addison (1672–1719), writer and politician, whose work with fellow writer Richard Steele (bap. 1672–1729) on the early eighteenth-century journals the *Tatler* and the *Spectator* transformed British periodical literature.

Aegir: The giant *Ægir,* similar to Poseidon in Greek mythology, was the king of the sea. In Old Norse the name means "sea ocean."

Æolian harps: The Aeolian harp, named for the Greek god of wind, Aeolius, was commonly used as a metaphor for the human imagination by the English Romantic poets. The harp, often placed near an open window, was a wooden box that played as the wind passed over strings strung across two bridges upon a sounding board.

Æschylus: The Greek tragic poet Aeschylus (525?–456? B.C.E.), was the first of the three great tragedians of Greek drama. He was followed by Sophocles (496?–405? B.C.E.) and Euripides (480–406 B.C.E.).

Agamemnon: King of Mycenae in Greek mythology, leader of the Greek armies during the Trojan War. He sacrificed his daughter Iphigenia on the way to Troy, and for this act, his wife Clytemnestra later murdered him.

Agincourt: See *Henry V.*

Al Amin: The young Muḥammad was called Al Amin, "The Faithful," because of his resistance to the temptations of Mecca.

Alexis: According to his early biographers, Luther unexpectedly joined the Augustinian monastery at Erfurt on 17 July 1505 because of the overwhelming fear of death that he experienced after witnessing the death of his friend Alexis, or Alexius, by either lightning strike or stabbing.

Ali, Cousin: The son of Muḥammad's uncle Abū Ṭālib (see Abu Thaleb) and also the prophet's son-in-law. Ali was ten years old when he accepted his cousin's revelation and became a Muslim. He ruled the Islamic caliphate from 656 until his assassination in 661. A dispute between followers of Ali, a blood relative of the prophet, and those of Abū Bakr, the prophet's father-in-law and close companion, created the rift that led to the formation of the Shi'a (Ali) and Sunni (Abū Bakr) branches of Islam.

Allegory: Carlyle alludes to the theory that ancient myths allegorize the world. He rejected this theory in favor of a euhemeristic view that gods and myths were created by traditional accounts of actual persons and events.

Alti guai: Italian for "deep groans or wails," found in *Inferno* (3.22–23).

Anabaptists: Radical reformists in sixteenth-century Europe who rejected infant baptism and other Christian practices. They are the ancestors of later movements such as the Amish and the Mennonites.

Antæus: A giant in Greek mythology, Antaeus was the son of Poseidon (Neptune), the god of the sea, and Gē, the earth.

Antoinette: Marie Antoinette (1755–93), archduchess of Austria and queen of France, convicted of treason and guillotined on 16 October 1793, nine months after her husband, Louis XVI (1754–93), king of France, suffered the same fate.

Argyles: Archibald Campbell (1575/76–1661), eighth Earl of Argyll, leader of the Covenanters who opposed the imposition of the liturgy mandated by William Laud in 1637. On p. 185 Carlyle alludes to Argyll's wavering loyalty and lack of conviction.

Aristotelian logic: The Greek philosopher Aristotle (384–322 B.C.E.) established logic as the central component of Western philosophy in his six works known as the *Organon*.

Aristotle's fancy: Carlyle later could not recall the source of this faulty allusion to Plato's allegory of the cave, as he wrote to his amanuensis and translator Joseph Neuberg: "I read the thing, forty years ago, in some poor Book or other, neither Aristotle nor Plato; and have ignorantly but now irremediably, twisted it to my own uses a little" (*CLO:* TC to Joseph Neuberg, 31 May 1852; *CL* 27: 133). Later editions of *Heroes* were amended to "fancy of Plato's."

Ark of Testimony: Also known as the Ark of the Covenant, the wooden container in which Moses placed the tablets of law upon which the Ten Commandments were written; see also Shekinah.

Arundel-marble: A collection of Greek antiquities donated to the University of Oxford in 1668 by Henry Howard, sixth Duke of Norfolk (1628–84). The marbles had been collected by Howard's grandfather Thomas Howard, fourteenth Earl of Arundel (1585–1646). They are now held at the Ashmolean Museum, Oxford.

Asgard: Home of the Norse gods, or *Æsir*. Connected to the human world, or *Miðgarð*, by the bridge *Bifröst*, the *Æsir*'s dwelling in *Ásgarð* was doomed to ruin at the time of *Ragnarök*, or the "twilight of the gods."

Atahualpa: The last Incan ruler of Peru, Atahualpa (1497–1533) was imprisoned and then garroted after he submitted to Christian baptism by the Spanish conquistador Francisco Pizzaro (1471?–1541).

Athanasius: Athanasius (296?–373), early church father and bishop of Alexandria who opposed Arius (250?–336), presbyter of Alexandria, at the Council of Nicaea (325). Athanasius contended that the Son and the Father were of identical substance (expressed as "the *Homoousion*") against Arius's argument that the Son was of similar but not identical substance to the Father and therefore less divine (expressed as "the *Homoiousion*"). Although the Council adopted Athanasius's position, he was dismissed from his see on several occasions by emperors sympathetic to the Arian cause. Athanasius's teaching was not fully affirmed until the Council of Constantinople (381).

Augeas's stables: According to legend, Augeas, king of Elis in the western part of the Peloponnesian peninsula, owned a huge herd of cattle. The fifth of the mythological Greek hero Hercules's twelve labors was to clear in a single day the filth that had accumulated in Augeas's stables over thirty years. Hercules accomplished the task by diverting two nearby rivers.

Augereau: Pierre-François-Charles Augereau (1757–1816), first Duke of Castiglione and marshal of France. After crowning himself emperor in the cathedral of Notre Dame on 2 December 1804, Napoleon allegedly asked Augereau his opinion of the service, which Carlyle cites on p. 194.

Augustine Convent: On p. 114 Carlyle alludes to the Augustinian monastery at Erfurt, which Luther joined on 17 July 1505. The Augustinians, named for St. Augustine of Hippo (354–431), lived under the Augustinian rule, which dictated that they give away their earthly possession and live a life of prayer and study.

Austerlitz: The Battle of Austerlitz, fought on 2 December 1805 and also known as the Battle of the Three Emperors, was one of Napoleon's greatest victories.

Ayesha: Aisha (d. 678) was the last and perhaps the favorite of Muḥammad's eleven wives; see also Kadijah.

Bacon: Sir Francis Bacon (1561–1626), Viscount of St. Albans, Lord
Chancellor, politician, philosopher, sometimes credited with being the true
author of at least some of Shakespeare's works. In his major work of
philosophy, *Novum Organum* (1620), Bacon rejected syllogism in favor of
inductive reasoning as the fundamental method for scientific investigation.
In a letter to King James I (1566–1625), Bacon called this new approach
the "new logic."

Balder: Second son of Odin and Frigg. The fair and wise Balder was most
often compared to Christ because of his descent into Hela, the
Scandinavian version of hell, from which it was prophesized he would
return from death in apocalyptic fashion. His inadvertent death at the hands
of his brother, the blind god Höðr, was the initiating event of the Ragnarök.

Barbone: Praisegod Barbon [Barebone] (1598?–1679), lay preacher and
politician, named as one of seven members from London elected to serve in
Parliament in 1653. Barbon's pious first name, his low social standing, and
his unfortunate last name led the London press to refer to the parliament as
the Barebones Parliament.

Baresark: Legendary Scandinavian warriors known as berserkers were
immensely strong and fought in a kind of mad trance. They also, according
to legend, wore a kind of bear shirt, or *ber serkr* (Old Norse).

Beatrice Portinari: Beatrice Portinari (1266–90) was the inspiration for
Dante in *The Divine Comedy.*

Bedford Fens: The Bedford Fens, also known as the Great Level Fens, in the
east of England (north of London), named for Francis Russell, fourth Earl
of Bedford (bap. 1587–1641), who attempted for years to drain the fens in
order to create new lands for himself and for King Charles, who took over
the project in 1638. Cromwell tendered legal advice to the peasants of the
fenlands who opposed the drainage projects. After his victory as a cavalry
commander under Fairfax at the Battle of Winceby (1643), Royalists began
to refer to Cromwell sarcastically as the "Lord of the Fens."

Bedlam: Originally founded as a priory in 1247, the St. Mary of Bethlehem
Hospital began accepting mental patients in 1463. The name was later
changed to Bethlem Royal Hospital, from which the corruption Bedlam is
derived.

Bellarmine: St. Roberto Francesco Bellarmino (1542–1621), Jesuit
theologian, who defended the Catholic Church against the forces allied to
the Reformation.

Bentham: Jeremy Bentham (1748–1832), philosopher, jurist, and reformer.
His *Introduction to the Principles of Morals and Legislation* (1789) defines
the basic principles of Utilitarianism. Referring to the hedonistic, or

"felicific calculus," Bentham argued that it was possible to quantify happiness and pain. Political economists used this notion to explain human behavior and to promote social policy based on statistical analysis.

Bianchi-Neri: The Bianchi ("Whites") and the Neri ("Blacks") were factions within the party known as the Guelphs. The Neri took power in Florence in 1302 and banished Dante. In his exile in northern Italy, Dante switched to the cause of the Ghibellines, against papal resistance to imperial authority; see Guelf-Ghibelline.

Black stone: See Caabah.

Blake: Robert Blake (bap. 1598–1657), the commander of Oliver Cromwell's navy.

Boccaccio: Giovanni Boccaccio (1313–75), poet, author, and great friend of Petrarch, author of *The Decameron* (1350–53), a collection of stories that may have served as an influence on Chaucer's *Canterbury Tales.* Boccaccio was also a diplomat in the service of the city-state of Florence.

Boswell: James Boswell (1740–95), lawyer, diarist, and best known as the author of *The Life of Samuel Johnson, LL.D.* (1791).

Bourdeaux: see Pipe of Bourdeaux.

Bourrienne: Louis-Antoine Fauvelet de Bourrienne (1769–1834), private secretary to Napoleon in Egypt and during the Consulate. He is best remembered for the account of these positions in his *Mémoires* (1829–31).

Bozzy: See Boswell.

Brobdignagian: Gulliver encounters the giants of Brobdingnag in part 2 of *Gulliver's Travels* (1726), by Jonathan Swift (1667–1745). Carlyle uses a common alternate spelling.

Bull, Papal (fire-decree): The *Exsurge Domine* was a papal bull, or formal decree, issued in response to Luther's *Ninety-Five Theses* by Pope Leo X, on 15 June 1520. Luther burned his copy on 10 December 1520 along with some copies of the canon law.

Bunyan, *Pilgrim's Progress:* John Bunyan (bap. 1628, d. 1688), author of the influential Christian allegory, *The Pilgrim's Progress* (1678).

Burke: Edmund Burke (1729/30–97), politician, philosopher, and author of the influential *Reflections on the Revolution in France* (1790), in which he expressed his conservative opposition to the Revolution.

Burns: Robert Burns (1759–96), known as the "plowman poet," Scottish poet and lyricist, celebrated worldwide for such songs as "Auld Lang Syne."

Burns's Schoolmaster: John Murdoch (1747–1824), Robert Burns's teacher and later his schoolmaster at Ayr Academy. According to the *ODNB,* "Murdoch described Burns as 'very apt,' although his 'ear' was 'remarkably dull,' and his voice 'untuneable.' "

Byron/Byronism: George Gordon Noel, sixth Baron Byron (1788–1824), known as Lord Byron, Romantic poet. Carlyle uses "Byronism" to refer to the sentimental attitudes promoted by poets who celebrated heroes exhibiting deep intelligence and morose anxiety about the human condition. For Carlyle, "Byronism" came to represent an egoistic worldview. In *Sartor Resartus* (1833–34) Diogenes Teufelsdröckh famously declares, "Close thy Byron; Open thy Goethe" (143), or in other words, reject the self and work faithfully and diligently.

Caabah: The Caabah, or Ka'bah, the most revered site in Islam, located in Mecca (in what is now Saudi Arabia). Muslims believe the temple to have been built by Adam and then rebuilt by Abraham and his son Ishmael. Muslims also believe that the Black Stone now serving as the eastern cornerstone originally fell from heaven to reveal to Adam and Eve the location for humanity's first building. After it was lost in the deluge, Abraham was shown the location of the stone by an angel, and he directed his son Ishmael to use it in the rebuilt temple. The daily prayers of Muslims are directed five times daily toward the Ka'bah.

Cagliostro: Giuseppe Balsamo (1743–95), shopkeeper's son, occultist, forger, adventurer. Carlyle called him the "King of Quacks" (Froude, *First Forty Years* 2:339). He was imprisoned in the Bastille for his alleged role in the infamous affair of the "Diamond Necklace," which involved Marie Antoinette and played a role in moving France toward revolution. He died a prisoner of the Inquisition in the fortress of St. Leo, Italy.

Calases: Jean Calas (1698–1762), French Huguenot tortured to death because he was accused of killing his son for attempting to convert to Catholicism.

Camille Desmoulins: Camille Desmoulins (1760–94), journalist and politician whose pamphlets "La Philosophie du peuple de français" (1788) and "La France libre" (1789) announced the coming revolution. He served as secretary general to the minister of justice, his good friend Georges Danton (1759–94). They were both guillotined on 5 April 1794.

Can della Scala: Can Francesco della Scala (1291–1329), known as Can Grande, became Lord of Verona in 1311. Dante dedicated the *Paradiso* to him.

Canopus: A star in the constellation of Argo that served Arab travelers as a southern pole star.

Caput mortuum: Latin phrase meaning literally "dead head"; i.e., a skull, or a worthless residue.

Cato: Marcus Porcius Cato (234–149 B.C.E.), famed Roman jurist, who according to Plutarch asserted that he would rather have people ask why he did not have a statue than why he had one.

Cavalcante: Cavalcante de' Cavalcanti was a Guelph leader noted for his Epicurean sensibility. His son Guido (1255?–1300) was a poet and a friend to Dante.

Cavaliers: Royalist supporters of King Charles I were known as Cavaliers.

Celia: Carlyle uses the name as a typical example of popular novels of the day, such as *Cecilia* (1782), by Frances "Fanny" Burney (1752–1840); see also Clifford.

Cestus of Venus: The girdle, or belt of Venus, was decorated with all objects that could elicit amorous desire. The magic sash compelled whomever the wearer met to fall in love; see the *Iliad* (14.213–45), in which the belt is given to Hera by Aphrodite.

Charles Fifth: Charles V (1500–1558), Holy Roman emperor, ruler of extensive lands in central, south, and western Europe, called Martin Luther to the Diet of Worms in 1521. A year after Luther's death, Charles ordered his troops to refrain from despoiling Luther's effigy and from digging up his remains to defile them: "I have nothing further to do with Luther; he has henceforth another judge, whose jurisdiction it is not lawful for me to usurp" (qtd. in Chalmers xc).

Charles I: Charles I (1600–1649), king of England, Scotland, and Ireland, whose struggles with Parliament ended with his execution, 30 January 1649.

Charles II: Charles II (1630–85), king of England after the Restoration in 1660. On the eve of his death in 1685, Charles II was received into the Roman Catholic Church. Three years later, his Catholic son, James II, was replaced by Parliament in favor of the Protestant William of Orange and his wife, Mary, James's daughter.

Charles Stuart: See Charles II.

Chartisms: The Chartist Movement was defined by its charter, which delineated six demands for institutional reform: universal male suffrage, annual parliaments, abolition of the property requirement for members of Parliament, paid members of the House of Commons, equal electoral districts, and secret voting by ballot. Carlyle wrote of the potentially violent aspects of the movement in *Chartism* (1839), but by 1848 the movement had reached its peak and eventually dissolved.

Chatham: William Pitt (1708–78), known as "the Elder," first Earl of Chatham, prime minister, known also as "the great commoner" for his opposition to his rival Sir Robert Walpole (1676–1745), first Earl of Orford and also prime minister, as well as for his resistance to the policies of King George III (1738–1820); see also Pitt.

Childe Etin: Carlyle refers to a ballad about a giant in Scottish folklore, but as he later found out from the publisher and writer Robert Chambers (1802–

71), "There is no ballad called Childe Etin, but there is one called Hynde
Etin" (*CLO:* TC to Robert Chambers, 27 May 1852; *CL* 27:124n). Later
editions of *Heroes* refer to the ballads the *Hynde Etin* and the *Red Etin of
Ireland.* Chambers published *Hynde Etin* in his collection *The Scottish
Ballads* (1829), 217–25.

Chillingworth: William Chillingworth (1602–44), theologian, author of *The
Religion of the Protestants: A Safe Way to Salvation* (1638). Chillingworth
converted to Catholicism in 1630 but reverted to the Church of England
four years later. During the English Civil War, Chillingworth was a staunch
Royalist.

Choiseul: Étienne François, Duc de Choiseul (1719–1785), powerful French
foreign minister, arranged the marriage between Marie Antoinette and the
future King Louis XVI.

Chosroes: Chosroes I, Persian emperor during whose reign (531–79) the arts
and sciences flourished.

Clarendon: Edward Hyde, first Earl of Clarendon (1609–74), politician and
historian, adviser to Charles I, Lord Chancellor and chief minister to
Charles II (1658–67). In 1667 Hyde was impeached and fled to France. He
was the author of *History of the Rebellion and Civil Wars in England*
(1702–4), chancellor of the University of Oxford (1660–67), and founding
benefactor of the Clarendon Press.

Clifford: Carlyle uses the name as a typical example of popular novels of the
day, including *Paul Clifford* (1830), by Edward Bulwer Lytton (1803–73);
see also Celia.

Coleridge: Samuel Taylor Coleridge (1772–1834), Romantic poet, critic, and
philosopher. Carlyle on p. 86 conflates remarks found in Coleridge's *Table
Talk,* where Coleridge writes, "To please me, a Poem must be either music
or sense — if it is neither, I confess I cannot interest myself in it" (350), and
in *Biographia Literaria,* where he paraphrases Shakespeare's *Merchant of
Venice* (5.1.83): " 'The man that hath not music in his soul' can indeed
never be a genuine poet" (20).

Columbian Republics: Formally organized in 1821, the Republic of Gran
Columbia consisted of what are now Venezuela, Columbia, Panama, and
Ecuador. The region was wracked by incessant revolution and civil war,
and had fallen apart by the end of 1830.

Confessions of Faith: The Westminster Confession of Faith, established in
1646 by the Westminster Assembly, a group of divines brought together by
the Long Parliament in order to reform the Church of England. The
Confession would eventually become the standard doctrine of the Church
of Scotland; see Long Parliament.

Conscript Fathers: Carlyle alludes to the Roman Senate. Its members were referred to as the *patres conscripti,* or "enlisted fathers."

Constance Council: The Council of Constance (1414–17) was convened to confirm the election of Martin V (1368–1431) as sole pope. It was remembered for its denunciations of John Wyclif (d. 1384) and his followers Jan Hus (see Huss) and Jerome of Prague (see Jerome).

Contrat-social [Social Contract]: See Rousseau.

Convocation of the Notables: The Assembly of Notables, unlike the elected Estates General, was a council of advisors chosen for their loyalty and fidelity to the French monarchy. They were periodically called to lend support from 1470. The convocation to which Carlyle refers was convened in 1787 by the controller general, Charles Alexander, Viscount de Calonne (1734–1802), who summoned the Notables to enlist their support for reform measures, including the approval of new taxes. The measures, though supported by King Louis XVI, were rejected, and Calonne was soon after dismissed and exiled.

Coriolanus: Shakespeare's tragedy *Coriolanus* was composed between 1605 and 1608. The play is based upon the life of the legendary Roman emperor of the fifth century B.C.E., Gaius Marcius Coriolanus.

Covenanters: With the first group in 1557 known as the "first band," the Covenanters were a group of Scottish Presbyterians who bound themselves to a series of covenants that sought to establish their independence from first the Catholic Church and then the Church of England. The most important of these covenants was the National Covenant of 1581. The adoption of the National Covenant in 1640 by the Scottish Parliament represented the power of the Covenanters and anticipated their significant role in the Scottish and English Civil Wars, as well as in the Irish Confederate Wars.

Cow Adumbla: Auðumbla, or Auðhumla, the primeval cow in Norse mythology whose milk nourished the first being, the giant Ymir.

Cowper: William Cowper (1731–1800), English poet and hymnodist who in seeking relief from intermittent attacks of depression turned to evangelical Christianity. Cowper lived in continual terror of becoming totally insane.

Cranmer: Thomas Cranmer (1489–1556), first Anglican archbishop of Canterbury, who played a significant role in seeking the annulment of the marriage between King Henry VIII (1491–1547) and his wife Katherine of Aragon (1485–1536) and in legitimizing the king's subsequent marriage to Anne Boleyn (1500?–1536).

Cromwell, Oliver: Oliver Cromwell (1599–1658), Lord Protector of England, Scotland, and Ireland. Carlyle was fascinated by Cromwell's rise to power first in the army and then in the arena of politics, his role in the regicide of King Charles I, and his attempts to transform Britain into a kind of republican theocracy; he published *Oliver Cromwell's Letters and Speeches* (1845).

Dante: Dante Alighieri (1265–1321), medieval Italian poet, author of *Commedia* (1321), or *The Divine Comedy,* an epic poem in three parts describing the allegorical journey of Dante through Hell (*Inferno*), Purgatory (*Purgatorio*), and Paradise (*Paradiso*).

David Hume: David Hume (1711–76), Scottish empirical philosopher and historian, author of *A Treatise on Human Nature* (1739), in which he claimed that a scientific study of human nature, or a "science of man," should serve as the basis for all other sciences, including religion.

David: Second king of the Israelites, who was just but flawed, credited with composing many of the Psalms, his story is told in the Hebrew Bible; see the books of 1 and 2 Samuel, 1 Chronicles, and 1 Kings.

Diet of Worms: A general assembly of the church convened on 6 January 1521 in the German town of Worms by the newly crowned Holy Roman emperor Charles V. Luther was called to appear before the Diet on 17 April 1521 and famously refused to recant any of his works unless it could be proven they were scripturally inaccurate. The assembly denounced Luther as a heretic.

Diocletian: Proclaimed emperor of Rome in 284, Diocletian (245?–313?) abdicated his throne in 295 to grow cabbages.

Diodorus Siculus: Sicilian historian of the first century B.C.E. According to Edward Gibbon, Siculus was among the first to write of the Ka'bah as a temple universally worshipped by the Arabians.

Dite, Hall of: "Dite" is French for "Dis," the city of the dead referred to in Dante's *Inferno* as having "vermillion mosques" (8.28), or as Carlyle translates, a "red pinnacle" (87).

Divine right of Kings: The doctrine that sovereigns rule as direct representatives of God on Earth, and that their authority is derived solely from Him. The doctrine did not survive the executions of Charles I of England (1649) and of Louis XVI of France (1793).

Doctrine of Motives: Jeremy Bentham claimed in his *Principles of Moral Legislation* that "a motive is substantially nothing more than pleasure or pain, operating in a certain manner" (100).

Dogberry: Dogberry and Verges are the legendarily foolish constables in Shakespeare's comedy *Much Ado about Nothing* (1600).

Dominic: St. Dominic, born Domingo de Guzman (1170–1221), founder of the monastic group the Dominican Order, known as the Black Friars in England because of the black capes they wore over white habits.

Douanier: An officer of the French customs. In writing of "the Dounaier at the Porte St. Denis" (30), Carlyle refers to a story he had recounted in his essay "Voltaire" (1829; *Works* 26:396–468). Voltaire apparently was stopped at the gates of Paris by customs officials, whom he told, "I believe there is nothing contraband here except myself." One of the guards recognized Voltaire, and in awe they allowed him to "pass on whither he pleased" (*Works* 26:438).

Duke of Weimar: Karl Augustus (1757–1828), patron of Goethe and of Schiller.

Dunbar: At the Battle of Dunbar, 2 September 1650, Cromwell's army defeated a Scottish force led by Sir David Leslie (1601–82), first Lord Newark, who commanded in support of the newly recognized king of Scotland, Charles II. After the victory at Dunbar, Cromwell was able to march unopposed on the Scottish capital, Edinburgh, which he captured.

Earl of Southampton: Henry Wriothesley (1573–1624), third Earl of Southampton, to whom Shakespeare dedicated his poems *Venus and Adonis* (1593) and *The Rape of Lucrece* (1594).

Eck: Johann Eck (1486–1543), professor of divinity and vice-chancellor of the University of Ingolstadt, in upper Bavaria, who attacked Luther because of his disagreement with Tetzel; see also Hogsatraten.

Edda, Elder (Poetic): The *Elder* or *Poetic Edda* is a collection of Icelandic tales and songs once attributed to be written or compiled by Sæmund Sigfússon (see Sæmund). The codex containing the *Elder Edda* was discovered in 1643 by the Icelandic bishop Brynjólf Sveinsson (1605–75).

Edda, Prose (Younger): The *Prose* or *Younger Edda* is a treatise on Icelandic poetics attributed to the Icelandic historian and statesman Snorri Sturluson (1179–1241). In addition to rules for versification the *Prose Edda* contains summaries of the Scandinavian myths.

Eidolon: The word for "phantom" in Greek, used in the New Testament to refer to an idol; see 2 Kings 17.2 and 1 Corinthians 12.2.

Eliot: Sir John Eliot (1592–1632). Eliot played a major role in the creation of the Petition of Right (1628), which limited the ability of the king to infringe on the rights of Parliament and of the people. For his involvement in the controversies surrounding the petition, Eliot was imprisoned in the Tower of London, where he died.

Essay on Language: See Smith.

Falkland: Lucius Cary, second Viscount Falkland (1609/10–43), leading Royalist and close associate of Chillingworth (see above), known for the circle of learned men who gathered at his house. Corroborating Carlyle's description of him as "dainty" (177), the biographer John Aubrey (1626–97) described Falkland as "but a little man, and of no great strength of body" (*Brief Lives* 1:152). Severely depressed because of the war, Falklands killed himself by purposefully riding into parliamentary fire at the Battle of Newbury (1643).

Farinata: Farinata degli Uberti (d. 1264), a Ghibelline noble who took part in the massacre of Guelphs at Montaperti in 1260; see also Guelf-Ghibelline.

Fichte: Johann Gottlieb Fichte (1762–1814), German philosopher, founder of the movement known as German Idealism, based upon the work of Immanuel Kant; see Kant.

Fond gaillard: A French phrase meaning "basis of gayety," used by Mirabeau to describe his son; see Carlyle, "Mirabeau" [1837], *Works* 28:447.

Fontenelle: Bernard Le Bovier de Fontenelle (1657–1757), French philosopher, poet, and advocate; nephew of the French dramatist Pierre Corneille (1606–84).

"Forked radish": One of Carlyle's favorite allusions to Shakespeare: "When 'a was naked, he was for all the world like a fork'd redish, with a head fantastically carv'd upon it with a knife" (*2 Henry IV* 3.2.332–35); see also *Sartor* 48.

Francesca: Francesca da Rimini (d. 1285), daughter of Guido da Polenta, Lord of Ravenna. She was married by proxy to Gianciotto Malatesta ("the Lame"), but she fell in love with the proxy, his younger brother Paolo. Soon after the wedding Francesca and Paolo were discovered and murdered by the jealous Gianciotto. Francesa was the aunt of Guido Novello da Polenta (d. 1330), Dante's host during the last years of his life. The story of Francesa and Paolo's adultery is told in Canto 5 of the *Inferno*.

French Philosophes: A group of late eighteenth-century French thinkers who influenced revolutionary thought in France, including the encyclopedists Denis Diderot (1713–84), Jean d'Alembert (1717–83), Claude Helvétius (1715–71), the Marquis de Condorcet (1743–94); and the Baron d'Holbach (1723–89).

Friedrich, Elector of Saxony: Frederick III (1463–1525), Elector of Saxony, also known as Frederick the Wise, saved Luther in 1521 from the Diet of Worms by abducting and taking him to the castle at Wartburg.

Frigga: Wife of Odin and Queen of Ásgarð.

Gauger: A "gauger" was a kind of tax official, or exciseman, who measured or gauged the capacity and usage of casks of ale in public houses. In 1789

the poet Robert Burns was appointed to the position of gauger for the
Dumfries area.

Gehenna: A name for hell used in the Vulgate, the fourth-century Latin Bible created in large part by church father St. Jerome (347?–420).

Genlis: Stéphanie Félicité, Comtesse de Sillery-Genlis (1746–1830), French writer and educator. The event to which Carlyle refers (154) can be found in her *Mémoires inédits* (2:13–16).

George, Duke: George, Duke of Saxony (1471–1539), known as "the Bearded," became duke in 1500, received a broad theological education when young, and was a cousin of Frederick, Elector of Saxony.

Gibbon: Edward Gibbon (1737–94), historian, author of the immensely influential *The History of the Decline and Fall of the Roman Empire* (1776–88).

Gilbert: Gilbert Burns (1760–1827), the younger brother of the poet Robert Burns, as well as a student of John Murdoch (see Burns's Schoolmaster). Gilbert Burns, whom Thomas Carlyle had met in 1821 (see *CLO:* TC to Alexander Carlyle, 6 June 1821; *CL* 1:363), was much admired by both Carlyles.

Giotto: Giotto di Bondone (1266–1337), known as Giotto, Florentine painter and architect. The work that Carlyle describes on p. 82 was not Giotto's portrait, but an engraving made not later than 1795 by the Neapolitan engraver and etcher Raphael Morghen (1758–1833) from a painting or drawing prepared for him by Stefano Tofanelli (1752–1812), who used as his model an oil painting on wood. See Holbrook Thayer, 182–83.

Globe Playhouse: Built in 1598–99 on the south side of the river Thames, with Shakespeare listed as one of the investors. It was destroyed by fire in 1613 and rebuilt a year later.

Glorious Revolution: The Glorious Revolution occurred in 1688, when Parliament rejected the Catholic James II (1633–1701) in favor of his Protestant daughter Mary Stuart (1662–94) and her husband William of Orange (1650–1702). William landed in England in November 1688, James fled to France, and Parliament recognized William and Mary as joint sovereigns.

Godwin: William Godwin (1756–1836), radical philosopher and writer. During the months that Carlyle was delivering his lectures on heroes, he was reading Godwin's *History of the Commonwealth* (1824–28), which he called "faithful, but dead as iron" (*CLO:* TC to John Forster, 11 December 1840; *CL* 12:361).

Goethe: Johann Wolfgang von Goethe (1749–1832), one of the most significant writers and thinkers in German history. He corresponded with Carlyle.

Grand Lamaism: A common nineteenth-century name for Tibetan Buddhism, the monks of which are known as lamas, or "superior ones."

Gray's fragments: Thomas Gray (1716–71) adapted two Norse poems from Latin versions: "The Fatal Sisters" and "The Descent of Odin," both composed in 1761; see *Complete Poems of Gray* 25–34, 211–20; see also *The Thomas Gray Archive* (http://www.thomasgray.org/).

Great Man Theory: Carlyle is often associated with this idea, that history is best explained through the lens of the individual personalities, or heroes, who shape and influence events.

Grimm: Jacob Grimm (1785–1863), German lexicographer, jurist, and mythologist, author of the influential *Deutsche Mythologie,* or *Teutonic Mythology* (1835). He and his brother Wilhelm (1786–1859), the Brothers Grimm, later became famous for their collections of folk and fairy tales.

Grotius: Hugo Grotius (1583–1645), Dutch jurist, author of *De Veritate Religionis Christianæ* (1627), in which he dismisses the quality of the miracles attributed to Muḥammad as "none but such as might easily be the effects of human art; as that of the dove flying to his ear" (235). Grotius allegedly told Edward Pococke that the story of the pigeon was taken from only Christian writers; see Twells 1:57.

Guelf-Ghibelline: The Guelphs, initially supported by Dante, were a political faction in medieval Italy that supported the papacy in its struggle against imperial authority, as opposed to the Ghibellines, who supported the emperor; see Bianchi-Neri.

Guises: The Guises were an aristocratic French family, founded by Claude de Lorraine, first Duc de Guise (1496–1550). Claude's daughter Mary of Guise was the mother of Mary, Queen of Scots. Both demonstrated openly their ambitions to the English throne via marriage and plots, and Mary, Queen of Scots was eventually executed for her ambitions; see Mary, Queen.

Gustavus-Adolphus: Gustav II Adolf, known as Gustavus Adolphus (1594–1632), king of Sweden, Protestant champion in the Thirty Tears' War, killed at the battle of Lützen while leading a cavalry charge.

Habeas-Corpus **Act:** The writ of habeas corpus, that persons may not be held unless they are charged with a crime, had been in effect from the late sixteenth century. The Habeas Corpus Act, passed by Parliament in 1679, imposed severe penalties on judges who failed without good cause to issue a writ.

Hackney Coaches: A hackney coach is a carriage for hire. They were established in London in the early seventeenth century.

Hagar: The handmaid of Abraham's barren wife Sarah, Hagar became his concubine and gave birth to Ishmael. In Islamic tradition Ishmael (the ancestor of Muhammad) and not Isaac was the favored son of Abraham, just as Hagar and not Sarah was his true wife.

Hall of Odin: Valhalla (Valhöll) was the chief hall in Ásgarð. There were 640 portals to Valhalla, where every Norseman who suffered a brave death was entitled to a seat.

Hamilton: Francis Hamilton of Buchanan (1762–1829), East India Company surgeon and botanist, author of *An Account of the Kingdom of Nepal and of the Territories Annexed to This Dominion by the House of Ghorka* (1819), in which Hamilton describes the Nepalese Hindus as "a deceitful and treacherous people, cruel and arrogant towards those in their power, and abjectly mean toward those from whom they expect favour" (22). His opinion of the Hindu religion is similarly "candid" and "sceptical" (*Heroes* 23), as suggested by Carlyle.

Hampden: John Hampden (1595–1643), politician, member of the anti-Royalist faction in Parliament that opposed Charles I and his attempts to diminish the power of Parliament. He was tried in 1637 for his refusal to pay "ship money," and the king attempted to have him and four others arrested in 1642. This act precipitated the English Civil War (1642–51). Hampden died after being shot in the shoulder during the Battle of Chalgrove Field (1643).

Hampton-Court negotiations: King Charles I was held under house arrest at Hampton Court Palace (24 August–11 November 1647), where he was allowed to receive commissioners and to negotiate various attempts at reconciliation. In November, Charles fled to the Isle of Wight, thinking that a disaffected army officer there, Colonel Robert Hammond (1620/21–54), would assist him in his escape. Charles and his advisers were wrong, and Hammond imprisoned the king in Carisbrooke Castle on the Isle of Wight.

Hans Luther: Hans Luther (d. 1530), the pious father of Martin Luther, is variously described as a farmer, a miner, a slate cutter, and a smelt owner; his wife was Margarethe (b. Lindemann). They moved from the German city of Eisenach to Eisleben just before Martin Luther's birth in 1483.

Harz-rock: The Harz Mountains are the highest range in northern Germany. Brocken, their highest peak, is featured in Goethe's *Faust*. In his 1838 lectures on the history of literature, Carlyle had alluded to the creation myth of the Saxons, who claimed to be formed "out of the Saxa or rock of the Hartz Mountains" (*Lectures* 148).

Hashem: Hāshim, the family name of Muhammad's father.

Havamal: The *Hávamál,* a poem in the *Elder Edda,* contains a series of wise sayings attributed to Odin. In March 1852, Joseph Neuberg pointed out the error in Carlyle's description of the poem's "rapt, earnest, sibylline" qualities (see *CLO:* TC to Joseph Neuberg, 31 May 1852; *CL* 27:132n). Later editions of *Heroes* more accurately refer to the *"Völuspa"*; see below.

Heathenism: Religions that do not accept the god of Judaism, Christianity, or Islam.

Hegira: Hijrah is the Arabic word for "flight." The hijrah for Muslims refers specifically to the flight of Muḥammad in 622 from Mecca to Medina after he was warned about a plot against his life.

Heimskringla: The first of the sagas of the kings of Norway by Snorri Sturluson (see *Edda, Prose*). *Heimskringla* derived from the first two words of the saga, *kringla heimsins,* "the circle of the world." The first section of the saga, *Ýnglingasaga,* contains an account of Odin as a human.

Hela: The Norse goddess of death and of rebirth, and queen of the underworld.

Henry V: Henry V (1386–1422), king of England. Carlyle refers to Shakespeare's history, composed circa 1599. The play focuses on the events surrounding the immensely significant Battle of Agincourt (1415), which was a major English victory during the long series of conflicts between England and France known as the Hundred Years' War.

Heraclius: (575?–641), Byzantine emperor known for adopting Greek as the official language of the empire and for his military campaigns against the Persians.

Hercules: Roman name for the Greek heroic mythological figure Heracles, the demigod son of Zeus and the mortal Alcmena.

Hermode: Hermóðr (Old Norse for "war spirit"), the son of Odin who traveled to Hel in order to negotiate the return of his dead brother Baldr. Hermode was changed to Hermoder in later editions of *Heroes.*

Hildebrand: Gregory VII (1020?–85), born Hildebrand Bonizi. After becoming pope in 1073, Gregory worked to assert the papal authority to appoint Church officials, which led to conflict with the German Holy Roman emperor Henry IV (1050–1106), who declared Gregory deposed in a diet at Worms (1076). The emperor was forced to yield after Gregory excommunicated him. With the issue of investiture unresolved, hostilities resumed in 1080 and resulted in a second round of mutual depositions. Henry took possession of Rome in 1084, after which Gregory again excommunicated him. Rome was liberated by Norman troops, but Gregory was forced subsequently to withdraw to Salerno, where he died.

Hindoos: Followers of the Hindu religion.

Hogstraten: Jacobus van Hogstraten (1460?–1527), Dominican monk and inquisitor, who defended Tetzel by attacking Luther; see also Eck.

Homer: (circa 9th century ~~B.C.E.~~), ~~Greek epic poet, author of the~~ *Iliad* and the *Odyssey*.

Homoiousion: Theological doctrine of Arius; see Athanasius.

Homoousion: Theological doctrine of Athanasius.

Hrolf: Hrolf the Ganger (860?–932), first Duke of Normandy, whose descendent William the Conqueror defeated the Anglo-Saxons at the Battle of Hastings (1066).

Hud: Hūd, An ancient prophet of Islam, said to have lived circa 600–300 B.C.E. The eleventh chapter, or sura, of the Qur'ān is named for him.

Huss: Jan Hus (1369?–1415), a follower of the doctrines of the English theologian and reformist John Wyclif, who translated the Vulgate Bible into English. Hus was excommunicated in 1411, denounced as a heretic at the Council of Constance in 1414, and burned at the stake in 1415 as a heretic.

Hustings-speeches: Before the Ballot Act of 1872, parliamentary elections were held and speeches related to them were delivered on temporary platforms known as hustings.

Hutcheson: John Hutchinson (bap. 1615–1664), parliamentary officer and regicide. Like Ludlow, Hutchinson served as a judge in the trial of King Charles I and signed his death warrant. His opposition to Cromwell and his plea to Parliament after the Restoration in 1660 caused him to be expelled from the legislature, but he was allowed to keep his estates.

Igdrasil: The immense ash tree Yggdrasill stood at the center of Norse cosmology. Its branches extended to the Scandinavian heaven and its roots to its hell.

Indulgences: An "indulgence" is a remission of an ecclesiastical penalty for a sin that has been forgiven by the Church. The practice of selling these indulgences in the early sixteenth century led to the strong opposition of Luther, which resulted in the Protestant Reformation; see Leo X and Tetzel.

Instrument of Government: The constitution framed by the Army Council on 16 December 1653. The Instrument named Cromwell as Protector without hereditary succession and established a triennial parliament that excluded Catholics permanently and Royalists temporarily; see *Works* 8:181–82.

Ironsides: The name given to Cromwell and his troops by the English press following their triumphant cavalry charge at the Battle of Marston Moor (1644).

Ishmael: According to Islamic tradition, the favored son of Abraham and Hagar and the ancestor of Muḥammad.

Isle of Oleron: The Île d'Oléron, off the central eastern coast of France, is the second-largest French island (after Corsica, Napoleon's birthplace).

Italian Campaigns: Military campaigns of Napoleon in Italy that led to the Peace of Loeben, 18 April 1797.

Jack the Giant Killer: A British fairy tale set in the Arthurian period; it first appeared in the early eighteenth century. Jack's magic shoes, cap, sword, and cape link him to Norse mythology.

James Watt: James Watt (1736–1819), engineer and scientist who patented the steam engine in 1769.

Jean Paul: Jean Paul, born Johann Paul Friedrich Richter (1763–1825), a writer of the German Romantic period best known for humorous stories and novels.

Jena: Although Fichte had lectured in Jena in 1794, the series to which Carlyle refers on p. 133 was delivered in Erlangen in 1805. The mistake was corrected in later editions of *Heroes*.

Jerome: Jerome of Prague (1365?–1416), friend and collaborator of Jan Hus, also condemned as a heretic and burnt at the stake.

Johnson: Dr. Samuel Johnson (1709–84), author and lexicographer, best known for his *Dictionary of the English Language* (1755), which he completed with only minimal clerical assistance in nine years. It remained the preeminent dictionary of the English language until the publication of the *Oxford English Dictionary* (1928).

Jonson, Ben: Ben Jonson (1572–1637), poet and playwright, friend and rival of William Shakespeare, who acted in many of Jonson's plays.

Jötun: The Norse word for "Giant." The *jötun* were a group of nature spirits often in conflict with the gods, although they also were known to marry and intermingle with them.

Jötunheim: The home of the *jötun,* from which they were able to menace both the gods in *Ásgarð* and the humans in *Miðgard.* The Jotenheimen is a mountainous region in the southern part of Norway.

Julius the Second: Pope Julius II, Guilliano della Rovere (1443–1513), known for his political and military ambitions. He commissioned Michelangelo to paint the ceiling of the Sistine Chapel and Raphael to paint the frescoes in his private library, the Stanza della Segnatura.

Kadijah: Kadījah (d. 619) was Muḥammad's first wife. They married when she was forty and he was twenty-five. She was a wealthy, twice-divorced woman who at critical junctures encouraged him to purse his mission as a prophet.

Karlstadt: Andreas Bodenstein von Karlstadt (1480?–1541), German theologian who attempted to apply radical reforms, such as the abolition of

Mass and Confession and the removal of images from the Castle Church in Wittenberg, during Luther's ten-month confinement in the Wartburg Castle beginning in May 1521. Luther subsequently rebuked Karlstadt for his iconoclastic zeal.

Katherine Docks: The St. Katherine Docks, just east of the Tower of London, were opened to traffic in 1828.

Keblah: Qiblah, "direction of prayer." The original quiblah for Muḥammad was the Temple Mount in Jerusalem, but further revelation led him to change it to the Kaʿbah, which remains the quiblah of Islam.

Keeper, The: Móðguðr, the maiden-keeper of the bridge Gjöll, on the way to Hel. In the *Prose Edda,* she confronts Hermóðr as he travels to find Baldr.

Knox: John Knox (1514?–72), religious reformer who was born in Haddington, Scotland, the birthplace of Jane Welsh Carlyle. The Carlyles mistakenly thought that Welsh Carlyle was a descendant of Knox.

Koreish: The tribe of Quraysh, to which Muḥammad belonged. The family claimed direct descendancy from Ishmael.

Kranach: Lucas Cranach the Elder (1472–1553), painter of the German Renaissance, court painter to the electors of Saxony, supporter of the Reformation, and close friend of Martin Luther, whose portrait he executed in 1529.

Ladrones Islands: The Mariana Islands, "discovered" in 1521 by the Portuguese explorer Ferdinand Magellan (1480?–1521), who was killed fifty-two days later by natives in the Philippines.

Laud: William Laud (1573–1645), archbishop of Canterbury, strong supporter of King Charles I. He was convicted and executed on charges of treason and of increasing popery. Carlyle found Laud's devotion to the ceremonial aspects of the church particularly distasteful.

Leo Tenth: Giovanni de Medici (1475–1521), elected Pope Leo X (1513), a patron of learning and art. His extensive plans for the rebuilding of St. Peter's Basilica, and his permission to sell indulgences in order to pay for the project, provoked Luther's Reformation.

Leyden jar: A device that stores electrical charges, invented in the eighteenth century at the University of Leyden, the oldest university in the Netherlands, founded in 1575.

Literature of Desperation: A phrase of Goethe's that Carlyle used to describe the state of French literature.

Lockhart: John Gibson Lockhart (1794–1854), son-in-law and biographer of Walter Scott, editor of the *Quarterly Review,* and occasional correspondent with Carlyle, who reviewed his *Life of Robert Burns* (1828) and his

Memoirs of the Life of Sir Walter Scott, Bart. (1837) in the *Edinburgh Review*.

Loke: According to Snorri Sturluson (see *Edda, Prose*), Loki was the son of the giant Fárbauti and the giantess Luafey. Loki was evil and fickle, the counterpart of Lucifer in Christian symbology.

Long Parliament: The parliament convened by Charles I on 3 November 1640. According to Carlyle, "the *Rump* or Fag-end of it did not finally vanish till 16th March 1659–60" (*Works* 6:107).

Lope: Frey Lope Félix de Vega y Carpio, most often referred to as Lope de Vega (1562–1635), prolific Spanish playwright, novelist, and poet.

Louis XIV ("Quatorze"): Louis XIV (1638–1715), the "Sun King" of France, the supreme power in Europe during his reign of seventy-two years, the longest documented of any European monarch.

Lucy, Sir Thomas: Sir Thomas Lucy (1532?–1600), gentleman, who lived at the family estate Charlecote, in Warwickshire. A nondescript member of the gentry were it not for the legendary story that a young Shakespeare, fallen in with bad company, had stolen deer from the park at Charlecote; see Shakespeare.

Ludlow: Edmund Ludlow (1616/17–92), Puritan general and regicide. He served as a judge in the trial of King Charles I and was the fortieth person to sign his death warrant. He was forced into exile after the Restoration (1660) and died in Vevey, Switzerland.

Luther: Martin Luther (1483–1546), German priest and professor whose rejection of Catholic doctrine, especially the practice of selling and granting indulgences, helped to cause the Protestant Reformation.

Luther's mother: Margarethe, b. Lindemann (d. 1531), the mother of Luther; his father was Hans; they were living at Mansfeld at the time of her death.

Madame de Staël: Anne Louise Germaine, Baronne de Staël-Holstein (1766–1817), writer, born in Paris, the daughter of the financier Jacques Necker (see below, Necker). She wrote novels, plays, historical and critical works, and political memoirs, becoming known with her *Lettres* (1788) on Rousseau, and achieving European fame with her romantic novel, *Corinne* (1807). She was admired by both Thomas and Jane Welsh Carlyle.

Mahomet: Mohammed, or Muḥammad (570?–632?), the founder of Islam, regarded by Muslims as the messenger and the prophet of God, the last and the greatest in a series of lawgivers from Adam to Jesus.

Malebogos/Malebolge pool: The eighth circle of Dante's Hell, where fraudulent abusers of reason are punished. Carlyle sometimes referred to London as the pool of Malebolge.

Margaret Luther: Luther's eldest daughter, Margaret was born in 1534. The passages related to Margaret in the first edition of *Heroes*, however, incorrectly refer to the elder daughter. It was Magdalena (1529–42) who became ill and died in her father's arms. The error is corrected in later editions of *Heroes*.

Marlborough: John Churchill, first Duke of Marlborough (1650–1722), politician and military officer, whose victory at the Battle of Blenheim (1704), during the War of Spanish Succession (1701–13), was historically significant because it thwarted French attempts to achieve continental dominance.

Mary, Queen: Mary Stewart, known as "Mary, Queen of Scots" (1542–87), the only daughter of James V, king of Scotland (1512–42), and Mary of Guise (1515–60). She was beheaded for treason after failing in several plots to replace Queen Elizabeth I on the English throne.

Meister: Carlyle alludes on p. 50 to Goethe's novel *Wilhelm Meister's Wanderjahre,* or *Journeyman Years* (1821–29), in which religious instruction is divided into three stages: the Ethnic, the Philosophical, and the Christian (see *Works* 24:267–68).

Mendicant Orders: The mendicant orders — Dominican, Franciscan, Carmelite, and Augustinian — are religious groups who depend upon charity for their livelihood. In principle the mendicant orders do not own property, either individually or collectively.

Midgard-snake: Miðgarðsormr, or Jörmungandr, the serpent surrounding Miðgarð, the realm of men. Thor attempted to kill Miðgarðormr and failed, although his eventual success at the Ragnarök is prophesized in the *Völuspá.*

Midianitish herds: As he was fleeing Pharaoh, who wished to kill him because he had murdered an Egyptian, Moses sought shelter in the land of Midian, where he tended sheep until ordered by God to return to Egypt; see Exodus 2.15–31 and 4.19.

Milton: John Milton (1608–74), poet and polemicist, author of *Paradise Lost* (1667).

Mimer-stithy: The forge of Mimir, a Norse god known for wisdom. He was beheaded during the wars between the gods. Odin carried his head with him and recited secret wisdom to it. Carlyle utilizes the image as an allegorical metaphor for the source of the Norse tales.

Mirabeau: Honoré Gabriel, Comte de Mirabeau (1749–91), moderate French revolutionary, writer, diplomat, and politician, whom Carlyle held up as the heroic figure of revolutionary France. Carlyle reviewed *Mémoires biographique, littéraires, et politiques, de Mirabeau* (1834–36) in the *Westminster Review* (1837); see *Historical Essays* 153–217.

Monarchies of Man: During his imprisonment in the Tower of London (1629–32), Sir John Eliot wrote a political treatise entitled *The Monarchie of Man,* which defends the concept of the "chain of being" and proclaims the king as the rightful head of state, ordained by God.

Montrose: James Graham (1612–50), first Marquess and fifth Earl of Montrose, he served in the Covenanter army in 1640 but transferred his allegiance to Charles I and led the Royalist army to victory at Tippermuir (1644). After the Royalist defeat at Naseby (1645), his army became disaffected and he fled to Europe, returning to Scotland after Charles's execution to avenge his death. His army was largely lost by shipwreck, and he was later taken prisoner and hanged in Edinburgh.

Morton, Earl of: James Douglas, fourth Earl of Morton (1516?–81), regent and chancellor of Scotland. A Protestant, he was made Lord High Chancellor by Mary, Queen of Scots, yet he was involved in the murders of her secretary David Rizzio in 1566 and of her husband Henry Stewart, Lord Darnley in 1567. He later played an important part in her overthrow. Morton joined the hostile noble confederacy and succeeded Moray (see below, Murray) as regent, but was later undone by his high-handed treatment of the nobles and the Presbyterian clergy. He was arraigned for his part in Darnley's murder and executed in Edinburgh.

Mount Hara: During Ramaḍān (see Ramadhan), Muḥammad often went to a cave on Mount Ḥirāʾ, near Mecca, to meditate. It is here that he received his first revelations from Allah.

Mount Sinai: The mountain in the Sinai Peninsula (between the gulfs of Suez and Aqaba), upon which Moses encountered God and received the Ten Commandments.

Murray, Regent: James Stewart (1531/32–70), first Earl of Murray, or Moray, illegitimate son of James V of Scotland, and half-brother of Mary, Queen of Scots. He served as Mary's chief adviser (1560), but supported John Knox and opposed her marriage to Darnley. After an attempted coup, he was outlawed and took refuge in England in 1565, but he was pardoned the following year and became Regent for Mary's son James VI in 1567, when she abdicated. He defeated her army at Langside in 1568. His Protestant and pro-English policies antagonized some Scottish nobles, and he was killed at Linlithgow by one of Mary's supporters.

Nanna: Wife of Baldr. She dies of grief after her husband's death, and they are reunited in Hel. When Hermóðr enters Hel to negotiate the return of his brother, Nanna gives him gifts for Frigga (a thimble according to Carlyle, but linen in most accounts) and for her servant Fulla.

Napoleon: Napoléon Bonaparte (1769–1821), began his career as a corporal of artillery in the French artillery, and in the aftermath of the French Revolution rose through the ranks to become emperor of France (1804). At his empire's high-water mark, Bonaparte controlled most of Europe, but his ill-advised invasion of Russia in 1812 doomed his army and his imperial ambitions. After the Battle of Waterloo (1815), where he was defeated by allied forces under the command of the British field marshal the Duke of Wellington (1769–1852) and the Prussian field marshal Gebhard Leberecht von Blücher (1742–1819), Bonaparte was exiled permanently to the island of St. Helena in the southern Atlantic.

Neale's History of the Puritans: Daniel Neal (1678–1743), independent minister and historian, author of the four-volume *History of the Puritans* (1732–38). Later editions of *Heroes* included this reference as a footnote.

Necker: Jacques Necker (1732–1804), Swiss-born banker, controller-general of France (1771–81). He attempted some administrative reforms, but his effort to finance French involvement in the War of American independence obliged him to borrow heavily and to conceal the deficit. Dismissed in 1781, he was recalled in 1788 to deal with the looming financial crisis. He summoned the States General, but his proposals for social and constitutional change aroused royal opposition and he was again dismissed. On this occasion his dismissal provoked widespread public disorder, which resulted in the storming of the Bastille. He was hastily recalled in 1789, but resigned the following year.

Nelson: Admiral Horatio Nelson (1758–1805), the hero of the Battle of Trafalgar, during which he lost his life but defeated Napoleon's navy and secured British naval supremacy for the next century.

Nemean Games: One of the four Panhellenic games of ancient Greece. The others were the Isthmian, the Pythian, and the Olympic Games. The Nemean Games, founded in 573 B.C.E., were held every two years originally in the valley of Nemea, near the small town of Cleônae in Argos. They were immortalized by the poet Pindar in his eleven poems to the victors known as the *Nemean Odes.*

Neptune: Neptune, or Poseidon, the Greek god of the sea, came often to the Greek isthmus to witness the games held there, according to Pindar (*Nemean* 5.35–40). The Isthmian games were in fact dedicated to Poseidon, although Carlyle writes that he was "seen once at the Nemean Games" (49), which were dedicated to Zeus; see Nemean Games.

Nescience: Meaning ignorance or lack of knowledge and often used by Carlyle as an antonym for science and that which is known.

Nessus'-shirt: The shirt of Nessus in Greek mythology was the blood-stained tunic of the centaur Nessus, which Deianeira gave as a gift to her husband Herakles (Hercules), thinking it would protect him. Instead, when he attempted to remove the shirt it burned him to the point that he threw himself on a funeral pyre for relief.

Nestorian Monk: See Sergius.

New Holland: Name of a Dutch colony in northwest Australia, and by extension the early name for the continent itself.

Niebuhr: Barthold Georg Niebuhr (1776–1831), German historian, Prussian ambassador to the Vatican (1816–23). Carlyle's description of his death (165) is recorded in Karl Josias Bunsen's *Life and Letters of Barthold George Niebuhr* (1852; 486–87).

Nornas: The collective name for the three female deities — Urðr, Verðandi, and Skuld — responsible for fixing the lifetimes of men.

Novalis: Friedrich Leopold, Baron von Hardenberg (1772–1801), wrote under the pseudonym "Novalis." He was an early poet and novelist in the German Romantic movement.

Novum Organum: See Bacon.

Ocadh: Okadh, or 'Ukāẓ, an annual gathering in modern-day Yemen, where the great poets of Arabia would gather for a month to emulate each other's poetry and to compete for a prize, according to Sale, "whence the place, it is said, took its name" (*Preliminary Discourse* 28).

Odin: The central deity of Scandinavian and Teutonic religions.

Olaf, King: Óláfr II Haraldsson (995?–1030), saint and king of Norway (1014–1030). He was largely responsible for Christianizing Norway, but when his reign was challenged by the powerful Danish king Cnut (985/995?–1035), Óláf's people revolted, and he spent the next two years in exile. When he returned, he fought the Danes at the Battle of Stiklestad (29 July 1030) and was killed; he was canonized in 1031.

"Open secret": Carlyle's translation from Goethe's *Wilhelm Meister's Travels,* "das öffentliche Gehemis" (*Works* 24:305). Carlyle's interpretation of Goethe conflates with Fichte's idea of the "Divine Idea." Carlyle intimates that the natural world is in essence the divine garment of the divine, or God; see Fichte and Goethe.

Orpheus: Venerated in Greek mythology as the first of the poets, Orpheus's singing was so powerful that he was able to follow his dead wife, Eurydice, to the underworld, where through his singing he convinced Hades and Persephone, the Lord and Lady of the realm, to release them both on the condition that neither would look back. Before they could reach the land of the living, Eurydice did look back and was lost to Orpheus forever.

Orson: A character from the French Romance *History of Two Valentyne Brethren, Valentyne and Orson* (1550?), by Henry Watson (flourished 1500–1518). As a child Orson is carried off by a bear and raised as a Wildman; Valentyne is raised as a knight.

Osborne, Bookseller: According to Johnson's report to Boswell, he once knocked down the bookseller Osborne for his impertinent behavior in "my own chamber" (*Life of Johnson* 112).

Paganism: Similar to heathenism, the term "paganism" describes religions that do not accept the god of Judaic, Christian, and Islamic tradition. Unlike heathenism, paganism often alludes specifically to Greco-Roman religion.

Paley: William Paley (1743–1805), the main proponent of theological utilitarianism. In *Evidences of Christianity* (1794) he claims that proof of God's existence resides in natural phenomena.

Palm: Johann Philipp Palm (1766–1806), bookseller of Nuremberg court-martialed and executed on Napoleon's orders for selling a pamphlet critical of the French.

Pandora's Box: In Greek mythology, Pandora was the first woman. Each of the gods gave her gifts. One of these was a large jar that contained the evils of the world. Although instructed not to do so, Pandora opened the box and unleashed evil on the world.

Paramatta: Paramatta is a city in New South Wales, Australia, founded as a British colony in 1788.

Parliamentary Army: The general term for the forces that served Parliament during the English Civil War. At the outbreak of the war in 1641, Parliament raised an army composed mainly of servants of large landholders. In 1645, Parliament formed an army of professional soldiers in three different divisions under the overall command of Lord Thomas Fairfax (1612–71), with Oliver Cromwell in command of the cavalry. This force was called the New Model Army. Instead of men being promoted on the basis of family connection, in the New Model Army they were rewarded for demonstrating military skill. The result was a highly trained and effective military force.

Patmos: While in exile at the castle of Wartburg, after the Diet of Worms, Luther signed his letters "From the Isle of Patmos," a small Greek island in the Aegean Sea, where in Christian tradition John the Evangelist was banished by the Romans and where he composed the book of Revelation (see Rev. 1.9).

Peace of Lœben: Peace negotiations after Napoleon's Italian Campaigns led to the signing of the Treaty of Leoben (18 April 1797), a preliminary document that ceded Austrian Netherlands (Belgium) to France and extended French influence into other territories.

Peasants' War: An uprising in central Europe (1524–25) influenced by Luther's defiance of the Church, but condemned by Luther himself. Historians have attributed the cause of the revolt to economic conditions and to a general rejection of authoritarian feudal practices.

Pericles: General and statesman (495?–429 B.C.E.) who presided over the "Golden Age" of Athens. Renowned for his oratory, his "Funeral Speech" (431/430 B.C.E.) as recorded by Thucydides, was an impassioned apologia for Athens' democratic principles and system of government.

Personification: A metaphorical construction in which a thing, an abstraction, or an animal is represented as having human qualities.

Petrarch: Francesco Petrarca (1304–74), known in English as Petrarch, a poet, a scholar, and an early humanist, who also travelled widely in service of the church; see Boccaccio.

Phalaris' Bull: Phalaris (d. 554 B.C.E.), tyrant of Agrigentum, in Sicily, who invented a brazen bull in which he would enclose his victims and burn them alive. The bull's last victim was Phalaris himself.

Phenician Alphabet: The twenty-two letter Phoenician script, which had become stabilized by circa 1050 B.C.E., was the probable source used by the Greeks for their adoption of the alphabet.

Philistine Mill: The Philistines, a seagoing people who came originally from Crete but, after defeat by the Egyptians, settled along the sea border of southern Palestine, where they became neighbors and enemies of the Israelites, whose King David claimed final victory over them (see 2 Sam. 8:1). In the Victorian period the term was used to denote cultural insensitivity and indifference to beauty. Carlyle links the term to the Benthamite philosopher James Mill (1773–1836) and regards its baneful influence as the consequence of Utilitarianism and industrialism.

Pillar of Fire: The story of the pillar of fire (Exodus 13.21), placed by God in the desert at night to guide Moses and the Israelites through the desert wilderness after their escape from Egypt.

Pindar: Ancient Greek lyric poet; see Nemean Games and Neptune.

Pipe of Bourdeaux: A pipe is a unit of wine measurement equivalent to a butt, or approximately 126 U.S. gallons. Bourdeaux, or Bordeaux, in southwestern France was and remains an important wine-making area.

Pitt: William Pitt (1759–1806), known as "the Younger," prime minister whom Carlyle accused of neglecting the arts and of condemning the poet Robert Burns to poverty.

Plutus: Guardian-symbol of the fourth circle of Hell in Dante's *Inferno*. He was a hybrid of the mythological god of the underworld and god of wealth.

Pocock: Edward Pococke (1604–91), oriental scholar, author of *Specimen Historiæ Arab...* (1650), in which Carlyle found Pococke's inquiry of Grotius (191ff.); see Grotius.

Podestà: The *podestà* were outsiders of an Italian city-state brought in to maintain public order; they fell under the authority of the priors.

Pombal: Sebastião José de Carvalho (1699–1782), Marquis de Pombal, de facto head of the Portuguese government who introduced several administrative and financial reforms. As his power increased he became more ruthless and dictatorial. He reduced the power of the Inquisition in Portugal by expelling the Jesuits.

Pope's-*Concordat:* In July 1801, Napoleon negotiated an agreement with Pope Pius VII (1742–1823). The Concordat recognized Roman Catholicism as the religion of most French people, while leaving Church appointments, salaries, and property at the disposition of the State.

Pride's Purges: On 6 December 1648, Colonel Thomas Pride (d. 1658), parliamentary army officer and regicide, signer of the death warrant of Charles I, purged the pro-Royalist members of Parliament from the House of Commons, the act that created the Rump Parliament (December 1648).

Prideaux: Humphrey Prideaux (1648–1724), dean of Norwich, author of *The True Nature of Imposture Fully Display'd in the Life of Mahomet* (1697), in which Prideaux delineated faults of Islam based not on original research but on the accounts of earlier Christian writers, including Pococke.

Printer Cave: Edward Cave (1691–1754), printer and magazine proprietor, founding editor of the *Gentleman's Magazine,* to which Samuel Johnson contributed.

Prior: Dante served as one of the six priors of Florence, 15 June–15 August 1300. The *Priore* were the executive committee of the city council; see also Podestà.

Protectorship: Cromwell was named Lord Protector of the Commonwealth of England, Scotland, and Ireland in December 1653. He reigned as such until his death, 3 September 1658, after which his son and designated successor Richard Cromwell (1626–1712) took power and ruled what is known as the Protectorate, at which time the Rump Parliament regained power and held it until the Restoration of Charles II (1660).

Punctum saliens: Latin phrase meaning a salient, or starting, point.

Pym: John Pym (1584–1643), politician. Pym took a leading part in helping to draw up the petition of grievances against Charles I known as the Grand Remonstrance (1 December 1641) and was one of the five members whom the king singled out to be impeached for treason in 1642.

Racine: Jean Baptiste Racine (1639–99), French dramatist of classical tragedies during the reign of Louis XIV. In "The Diamond Necklace"

(1837; *Historical Essays* 103), Carlyle blamed Racine's death on the king's 1689 rejection of him in favor of his rival Pierre Corneille (1606–84).

Ragnarök: The Ragnarök ("Doom of the Reigners"), known as "the twilight of the gods," was the apocalyptic end of the world, when Asgarð and Miðgarð would be destroyed and the gods slain by monsters.

Raleigh, Walter: Sir Walter Ralegh (1554–1618), courtier, explorer, and author, sometime favorite of Queen Elizabeth I (1533–1603). According to legend, Ralegh once placed his cloak in the path of the Queen so she would not have to walk through a mud hole, but he also spent time in the Tower of London in August 1592 for secretly marrying Elizabeth Throckmorton, one of her maids of honor.

Ramadhan: Ramaḍān, the ninth month of the Muslim year, features a month of fasting and is the month in which the opening passages of the Qur'ān were revealed to Muḥammad.

Raphael: Raffaello Sanzio da Urbino (1483–1520), known as Raphael, one of the great masters of the Italian Renaissance.

Red and White Roses: On p. 168 Carlyle alludes to the Wars of the Roses (1455–85), the dynastic struggle between the families of Lancaster (red rose) and York (white rose). The wars ended with the defeat and death of the Yorkist King Richard III (1452–85) at the hands of Henry Tudor, afterward Henry VII (1457–1509), at the Battle of Bosworth Field (22 August 1485).

Red Etin: Giant in Scottish folklore.

Redgauntlet: Sir Walter Scott (1771–1832), poet and novelist, author of the Waverley novels, including *Redgauntlet* (1824), a family mystery set in the context of the Jacobite rebellions in Scotland.In the novel, Alberick, the first of the Redgauntlets, rides over his disobedient son in pursuit of Edward Baliol, usurper of the Scottish crown, only to have his horse's hoof accidentally crush his son's head and kill him. Alberick returns to his castle and discovers that his wife has died giving birth to another son, "whose brow was distinctly marked by the miniature resemblance of a horse-shoe" (191). Afterward, most members of the Redgauntlet carry this "singular indenture of the forehead" (192).

Reform Bills: After two parliamentary reform bills failed to pass in 1831, a third attempt succeeded. This bill, the Reform Act of 1832, also known as the "Great Reform," extended the franchise to all males in possession of at least £10 of property, and eliminated several underpopulated and hence unrepresentative "rotten" boroughs.

Reformation: Religious movement, clearly visible at the end of the fifteenth century and driven by popular disgust at the decadence of the Church and the clergy, given more definite shape by Luther's nailing of ninety-five theses, or arguments against indulgences, to the door of Wittenberg's Castle Church (31 October 1517). The religious wars that followed were not concluded until the Treaty of Westphalia (1648).

Regiment La Fère: In 1785 Napoleon Bonaparte was commissioned as a second lieutenant of artillery to the regiment La Fère, then stationed at Valence, the nearest garrison town to Corsica.

Reynard: Reynard the Fox, legendary animal hero and trickster in several allegorical medieval stories known as "bestiaries."

Rochester: John Wilmot (1647–80), second Earl of Rochester, poet, courtier, patron of the arts, and notorious libertine.

Rollo: See Hrolf.

Rousseau: Jean-Jacques Rousseau (1712–78), Genevese political philosopher, educationist, and essayist, whose writings, especially the *Discourse on the Origin and Foundations of Equality* (1755) and *The Social Contract* (1762), exerted a profound influence on the French Revolution.

Rump Parliament: The Rump Parliament was the remnant of the Long Parliament after the Pride's Purges. It was the Rump Parliament that condemned Charles I to death, 20 April 1653.

Sabean: Ancient, pre-Islamic people who inhabited the kingdom of Saba, or Sheba. The Sabeans' religion was based upon a triad of deities, the Venus star, the moon god, and the sun goddess.

Sacy, Silvestre de: Antoine Isaac Silvestre de Sacy (1758–1838), orientalist, translator, commentator, and the primary author of an entry on Mahomet in the *Biographie Universelle* (1820; 26:186–213), which served as an important source for Carlyle's lecture on the Prophet; see David R. Sorensen, "Une religion" 25–32.

Sæmund: Sæmund Sigfússon (1056–1133), medieval priest, poet, and historian formerly linked as either the author or the compiler to the collection of tales and songs known as the *Elder* or the *Poetic Edda.*

Saint Helena: Volcanic island in the South Atlantic, where Napoleon was exiled in 1815 and where he died in 1821.

Sale: George Sale (1696?–1736), translator of the Qur'ān into English (1734); his edition was considered by most scholars as definitive throughout the nineteenth century.

Samson: Biblical, heroic figure, who after being granted enormous powers by God, loses them when he tells the woman Delilah that the secret of his power is his hair (see Judges 16.1–31).

Sansculottism: Derived from the French word "sansculotte," meaning "without breaches," a pejorative term used by aristocrats to describe the peasants in the French revolutionary army who wore long pants because they could not afford knee breeches, the style of the day.

Saxo Grammaticus: (1140?–1206), Danish historian, author of the first history of Denmark, *Historia Danica*, or *Gesta Danorum*, which he completed circa 1187.

Scepticism [Skepticism]: The rejection of unobservable phenomena was a central tenet of philosophical skepticism. Carlyle believed that skepticism was necessary for the destruction of "shams," but temporary because it lacked any constructive genius.

Schiller: Johann Christoph Friedrich von Schiller (1759–1805), German philosopher, poet, playwright, and historian. The work to which Carlyle refers on p. 39 is Schiller's essay "Über Anmuth und Wurde" ("On Grace and Dignity") (1793), in which he distinguishes between charm and beauty.

Schlegel: August Wilhelm Schlegel (1767–1845), German playwright, historian, and prodigious translator of Shakespeare's works into German. By 1801 he had published sixteen of the plays, which he described as the national epic of England.

Schweidnitz Fort: A fort captured from the Prussian king Frederick the Great (1712–86) on 1 October 1761 by the Austrian field marshal Gideon Ernst von Laudon (1717–90). The story of the Russian soldiers marched into a chasm to form a bridge is likely apocryphal.

Seid: Zayd, or Seid (588?–629), was originally given to Muḥammad's wife Kadījah (see Kadijah) as a slave. She and Muḥammad accepted and raised him as their adopted son. Zayd was one of the first to accept Muḥammad's revelation and one of the first Muslims. He later became a military leader and was killed leading a raid on the Byzantine city of Bosra.

Senatus Academicus: The Academic Senate, governing authority at Edinburgh University, where Carlyle had been an undergraduate.

Sergius: Known as Baḥīrā in the Arabic East and Sergius the Monk in the Latin West, said to have revealed to Muḥammad's uncle Abū Ṭālib (see Abu Thaleb) that the young boy was to be a prophet. Sergius also was imputed to have helped Muḥammad with the writing of the sections of the Qur'ān devoted to Christianity. Sergius was a member of the Nestorian Church, or the Church of the East, based upon the teachings of Nestorius, patriarch of Constantinople (d. 451). The Nestorians believed in the disunity of Christ's divine and human natures, a heretical view in the West. Baḥīrā was revered in the East but reviled in the West because he helped to inspire the Qur'ān.

Shakspeare: William Shakespeare (1564–1616), English poet and playwright.

Shekinah: The divine presence that surrounded the Ark of Testimony, also known as the Ark of the Covenant; see also St. Chrysostom.

Ship-money: Traditionally levied on seaports and trading towns to maintain the English fleet, the ship money tax was extended by Charles I to all counties in 1634 and 1635 without parliamentary consent. Many leading figures in Parliament refused to pay the tax, including Hampden, who was tried, convicted, and forced to pay in 1636. The tax was repealed by the Long Parliament in 1640 (see *Works* 6:74–75).

Simon de Montfort: Simon de Montfort (1208?–65), eighth Earl of Leicester. Montfort played a leading role in establishing the Provisions of Oxford (1258), which provided the barons a share of governance by establishing a King's Council. When King Henry III rejected the Provisions in 1261, Montfort and his fellow barons prepared for war, which was averted by the signing of the Treaty of Kingston in November 1261. The long-brewing hostilities between the followers of Montford and the king erupted into civil war in 1264. Montfort defeated and captured the king at the Battle of Lewes (14 May 1264). During Henry's house imprisonment a new council was established and met (January–March 1265). It was the forerunner of Parliament.

Sir Philip Warwick: Sir Philip Warwick (1609–83), politician and historian, knighted in 1660 by the restored King Charles II, whom Warwick served as clerk of the signet, and secretary to the treasurer. In his *Memoires of the Reign of King Charles I* (1701), Warwick recounts the story of a Dr. Simcott, who treated Cromwell's "hypochandriac maladies," which included the frequent "thought he was just about to die" (qtd. in *Works* 6:50).

Skalds: *Skáld* is the Old Norse word for "bard" or "court singer."

Skepsis: Σκέψις, Greek word meaning "inquiry, hesitation, doubt," particularly, for Carlyle, in the context of a skeptical brand of philosophy.

Skrymir: A giant fought, unsuccessfully because of his immense size, by Thor. Skrýmir turns out to be the earth itself.

Smith, Adam: The Scottish moral philosopher and political economist Adam Smith (bap. 1723–90), author of the seminal work on political economy *The Wealth of Nations* (1776). In his earlier work *Essay on Language: Considerations Concerning the First Formation of Languages* (1761), Smith explored the relationship between language acquisition and the history of human progress in the context of four distinct modes of communication: poetical, oratorical, historical, and didactic.

Snorro Sturleson: Snorri Sturluson; see *Edda, Prose*.

Snow-jokul: *Jökull* is the Icelandic word for "glacier."

Solomon: Biblical king of Israel, son of King David, builder of the first temple in Jerusalem. On p. 182 Carlyle quotes Ecclesiastes 3.7.

Sordello: In the first edition of *Heroes*, Carlyle mistakenly refers to the Italian poet and troubadour Sordello da Goito (1210?–69), who appears in cantos 6–9 of Dante's *Purgatorio*. Later editions of *Heroes* refer correctly to Brunetto Latini (1220?–94), Italian philosopher, scholar, statesman, and Dante's guardian/tutor, who appears depicted with "face *baked*" in the *Inferno* (15.26–27).

Southey, Robert: Robert Southey (1774–1843), radical poet, reviewer, and poet laureate after 1813.

St. Andrews Castle: Begun in the late twelfth century, St. Andrews Castle, now a ruin, overlooks the North Sea in the borough of St. Andrews in Fife. It served as the ecclesiastical center of Scotland before the Protestant Reformation in the sixteenth century.

St. Catherine Creed: St. Katherine Creed is a church on Leadenhall St. in the Aldgate section of London that was consecrated in 1631 by the then bishop of London, William Laud. The ceremonies were of such an elevated nature that they were used later as evidence of Laud's Catholic sensibility, for which he was convicted and executed in 1645.

St. Chrysostom: St. John Chrysostom (347?–407), named posthumously as Chrystomos, or "golden-mouthed," was an influential preacher in the early Greek church known for his speaking ability and for his resistance to ecclesiastical authority. He was an active participant in the destruction of pagan relics and places of worship. The writer Laurence Sterne in *Tristram Shandy* attributed the phrase "The true Shekinah is Man" to Chrysostom. The phrase also appears in Carlyle's *Sartor Resartus* (51).

St. Clement Danes: A church in Westminster, London, near Gough Square, the residence of Samuel Johnson. The church was completed in 1682 under the supervision of Sir Christopher Wren; see St. Paul's Cathedral.

St. Paul's Cathedral: Located on Ludgate Hill, the highest point in the City of London, a church has existed on the site of the current St. Paul's Cathedral since the seventh century. The current domed structure was designed by Sir Christopher Wren (1632–1723) and completed in 1711.

St. Pierre: Jacques-Henri Bernardin de St. Pierre (1737–1814), a follower of Rousseau and author of *Études de la Nature* (1784), *Paul et Virginie* (1787), and *La Chaumière Indienne* (1790). Of *Paul et Virginie*, Carlyle wrote in *The French Revolution:* "On the whole, our good Saint-Pierre is musical, poetical though most morbid: we will call his Book the swan-song of old dying France" (*Works* 2:60).

Star-chamber: A tribunal created in 1487 that took its name from the room in the royal palace of Westminster where it met. The Star Chamber was concerned with covert crimes, such as defamation, perjury, forgery, fraud, and sedition, and under the Stuart sovereigns, it was employed extensively to suppress political opposition and to punish dissent.

Stewart: Dugald Stewart (1753–1828), philosopher and professor of mathematics at the University of Edinburgh. Stewart was one of the first persons to recognize the genius of Robert Burns and to seek his acquaintance.

Tacitus: Gaius Cornelius Tacitus (55?–120), Roman senator and historian known for the concision of his Latin.

Tartuffe: Tartuffe is a celebrated literary hypocrite in *Le Tartuffe, ou l'Imposteur* (1669), by the French dramatist Molière (1622–73).

Tenth of August: On 10 August 1792 a French mob massacred a unit of the Swiss Guard at the Tuileries. The event was witnessed by Napoleon.

Terza rima: The rhyme scheme of Dante's *Divine Comedy.* Terza rima features a series of interlocked, three-line stanzas (tercets) in which the second line of each tercet rhymes with the first and third lines of the next stanza, e.g., aba, bcb, cdc, and so on; see also Dante.

Tetzel: Johann Tetzel (1465?–1519), Dominican monk appointed in 1516 to preach an indulgence in favor of contributors to the building fund of St. Peter's in Rome, which provoked Luther's Wittenberg theses.

Thebaid Eremites: A Thebaid is a person from Thebes, a popular location for hermits (Eremites) in the third and fourth centuries.

Thialfi: Þjálfi (Old Norse for delver, digger), servant whom Thor retained on his journey to Jötunheim.

Thor: Thor (Þór) ranks second only to Odin in the Scandinavian pantheon of gods. The most valiant of Odin's sons, Thor was revered as the god of thunder and lightning, which he shot from his hammer Mjöllner; see also *Thrym.*

Three Days of July, 1830: On 25 July 1830, the Bourbon king Charles X (1757–1836) and his chief advisor, Jules de Polignac (1780–1847), issued four ordinances, which suspended the liberty of the press, dissolved the Chamber of Deputies, reduced the electoral roll, and ordered new elections. On 27 July Parisian crowds erected barricades and next day laid siege to the Hotel de Ville. The king's troops mutinied and joined the protestors, forcing Charles X to abdicate. On 30 July Louis-Philippe (1773–1850) was invested with the title of lieutenant general and subsequently proclaimed king of the French.

Thrym, Hrym, Rime: A *jötun* slain by Thor in Jötunheim for stealing his hammer, Mjöllner. The story appears in "The Lay of Thrym" (*Þrymskviða*), in the *Elder Edda*.

Tieck: Ludwig Tieck (1773–1853), German poet, translator, editor, novelist, one of the founders of the German Romantic movement.

Tophet: A place in Jerusalem where children were sacrificed by being burned alive.

Torfæus: Þormóður Torfason, or Thormodus Torfæus (1636–1719), Icelandic historian and scholar, author of the *Orcades* (1697), in which he claims that Odin was a historical figure who arrived in Scandinavia from Asia approximately seventy years before the birth of Christ. Carlyle's source may have been Paul Henri Mallet's *Northern Antiquities* (1770; 1:21–22).

Transcendental Philosophy: On p. 133 Carlyle loosely and somewhat inaccurately summarizes the philosophy of Fichte and of Immanuel Kant (1724–1804), who in his *Critique of Pure Reason* (1781) distinguished between the observable manifestation of a phenomenon and its unobservable counterpart, the noumenon, or the thing-in-itself. For Kant, human understanding serves as a transcendental, categorizing bridge between the observable world and the unobservable reality that exists beyond reason. Carlyle refers specifically to Kant's *Critique* in his essay "Novalis" (1829; *Works* 27:26); see Sorensen, "Instinctive Kantian."

Treadmill: Sometime between 1812 and 1817, the civil engineer William Cubitt (1785–1861) adapted the treadmill for use by humans. They had been used previously with animals walking on a wheel to grind corn (wheat). The treadmill quickly became popular in jails as an instrument of punishment for prisoners sentenced to hard labor. The first prison treadmill was built at Bury St. Edmunds in 1819.

Trebisond, Council of: Trebisond, or Trebizond, or Trabzon, was an important Byzantine political, religious, and economic center on the southern coast of the Black Sea. No council has been known to have occurred there.

Trent, Council of: The nineteenth ecumenical council, held at Trent (now in northeastern Italy), sat from 1545 to 1563. The council was convened as a response to the Protestant heresies that resulted from Luther's Reformation.

Tuileries Palace: French Royal Palace, on the right bank of the Seine River, adjacent to the Louvre. It was destroyed in 1871.

Turenne: Henri de la Tour d'Auvergne, Vicomte de Turenne, known as Turenne (1611–75), marshal of France and commander of the armies during the reign of Louis XIV.

Twentieth of June (1792): On the anniversary of the "Tennis Court Oath" that initiated the French Revolution, crowds invaded the Tuileries in protest against the king's use of the royal veto. They encountered Louis XVI in person, and one of the protesters put a red cap of liberty on his head. Napoleon witnessed the scene and was outraged by it.

Uhland: Johann Ludwig Uhland (1787–1862), German poet, professor of German literature at the University of Tübingen (1830–35), author of *Der Mythus von Thor nach nordischen Quellen* (1836).

Ulfila the Mœsogoth: Bishop of the Arian Visigoths, Ulfilas, or Wulfila (311?–81?) translated the Bible into the Gothic language in 369.

Universal History: On p. 21 Carlyle refers to theories that compress all human history into developmental schemes, such as those speculated upon by Kant and by Schiller.

Universitas: Latin for "the whole," a founding principle of medieval universities, suggesting a community of scholars rather than a combination of disciplines.

University of Paris: Carlyle on p. 137 erroneously identifies the University of Paris, founded between 1150 and 1170, as the first institution founded upon the principle of *universitas*. Later in the nineteenth century, a team of Italian historians determined that the University of Bologna, founded in 1088, preceded Paris.

University of Wittenberg: Founded in 1502 by Frederick III. Luther earned his doctoral degree from Wittenberg in October 1512, and afterward the university became a focal point for the Protestant Reformation.

Usher de Brézé: Henri Evrard, Marquis de Dreux-Brézé (1762–1829), master of ceremonies to Louis XVI, who attempted unsuccessfully to deliver royal orders to the deputies of the Third Estate in June 1789; see Carlyle's *French Revolution* (*Works* 2:163–65).

Utgard: Útgarð (Old Norse for "Outyards"), the home of the giants, connected by the sacred tree Yggdrasil to the other two worlds in the Norse cosmos, Asgarð (home of the gods) and Miðgarð (home of the humans).

Utilitarianism: The philosophy of Utilitarianism establishes morality on the foundation of Bentham's theory that humans will naturally behave in ways that secure "the greatest happiness of the greatest number." Carlyle attacked the Utilitarians because he believed their fundamental principle subverted both individual responsibility and social order.

Valkyrs: The maidens who served Odin in Valhalla. They rode to battles, selected those who were to die, and then escorted them to Valhalla.

Vane: Sir Henry Vane, "the Younger" (1613–62), supporter of the parliamentary cause in the civil war who then opposed Cromwell's elevation to Lord Protector in 1653, after which he retired from politics. On Cromwell's death he returned to public life in 1659, opposed the Restoration, after which he was imprisoned and executed for treason in spite of assurances from Parliament and Charles II that his life would be spared.

Vates: Latin for "prophet," "seer," or "bard."

Vauxhall: Popular pleasure garden on the south bank of the Thames River in London form the mid-seventeenth century until its closing in 1859.

Verges: See Dogberry.

Virgil: Publius Vergilius Maro, known as Virgil, or Vergil (70–19 B.C.E.), Roman poet, author of the epic poem *Aeneid,* the pastoral poems the *Eclogues (Bucolics)*, and the agriculturally themed poem the *Georgics*

Voltaire: François-Marie Arouet (1694–1778), known by the pen name Voltaire, was a wit, a philosopher, and a leading figure of the French Enlightenment.

Völuspa: *Völuspá,* the first and best known song in the *Elder Edda,* prophetically expresses the system of Scandinavian mythology; see also Havamal.

Wagrams: Carlyle (???) alludes to the Battle of Wagram (6 July 1809). At Wagram, Napoleon defeated forces led by the Austrian emperor decisively.

Walpole: Horace Walpole (1717–97), fourth Earl of Orford, author, politician, patron of the arts, son of the prime minister Robert Walpole (see Chatham). Walpole's novel *The Castle of Otranto* (1764) is often referred to as the first Gothic novel.

War of Tabûc: The first of the wars against the Greeks is recounted in chapter 9 of the Qur'an, including the expedition to Tabūk, which occurred in the ninth year of the Hijrah (630), the year after the death of Muhammad's adopted son Seid at the Battle of Mu'tah.

Washington: George Washington (1732–99), victorious commander in chief of the Continental Army in the American Revolutionary War (1775–83), first president of the United States (1789–97).

Westminster Abbey: Ancient church in London, known officially since 1560 as the Collegiate Church of St. Peter at Westminster. The Abbey serves as a coronation church, a royal mausoleum, a memorial for tombs of the great, a national shrine, and the site of the Tomb of the Unknown Soldier. A memorial statue of Shakespeare was erected in 1741 in the "Poets' Corner" of the Abbey, near what legend holds to be the grave of Chaucer. The statue of Shakespeare points to a scroll that contains variant lines from the *Tempest* (4.1.152–56); see *Heroes* 100.

Westminster Confession of Faith: See Confessions of Faith.

Whitehall: The Palace of Whitehall, in Westminster, was the main residence of British monarchs in London from 1650 until 1698, when all but the Banqueting House, designed by Inigo Jones (1573–1652) in 1622, was destroyed by fire.

Wilhelm Meister: See Meister and "Open secret."

Witenagemote: The Anglo-Saxon council of king and nobles was known as *witena-gemot,* literally the "assembly of wise-men."

Worcester Fight: Cromwell's defeat of a Scottish army at the Battle of Worcester (3 September 1651) marked the end of the Civil War, which had been raging since 1642.

Wünsch: According to Jacob Grimm, *wünsch* for the ancients meant "the sum total of well-being and blessedness, the fulness of all graces" (*Teutonic Mythology* 1:138).

Zemzem: The well of Zamzam is located approximately twenty meters east of the Ka'bah (see Caabah) in the Al-Masjid al-Ḥarām, or the Sacred Mosque, the world's largest.

Works Cited

Al-Da'mi, Muhammed A. *Arabian Mirrors and Western Soothsayers: Nineteenth-Century Literary Approaches to Arab-Islamic History.* New York: Lang, 2002.

Alexander, Edward. *Matthew Arnold, John Ruskin, and the Modern Temper.* Columbia: Ohio State University Press, 1973.

Alighieri, Dante. *Purgatorio.* Trans. Henry Wadsworth Longfellow. Vol. 10. *Complete Writings of Henry Wadsworth Longfellow.* Craigie Edition. Boston: Houghton, Mifflin, 1904.

[Anon.]. "Carlyle's Lectures on Heroes." *Monthly Review* 2 (May 1841): 1–21.

[Anon.]. "Carlyle's Lectures on Heroes and Hero-Worship." *Tait's Edinburgh Magazine* 8 (June 1841): 379–83.

[Anon.]. "Islamism." *The Leader and Saturday Analyst* (18 Feb. 1860): 165.

apRoberts, Ruth. *The Ancient Dialect: Thomas Carlyle and Comparative Religion.* Berkeley: University of California Press, 1988.

———. "Carlyle's Religion: The New Evangel." *Literature and Belief* 25.1–2 (2005): 103–22.

Arnold, Matthew. *Complete Prose Works.* Ed. R. H. Super. 11 vols. Ann Arbor: University of Michigan Press, 1960–77.

———. *Letters of Matthew Arnold 1848–88.* Ed. George W. E. Russell. 2 vols. London: Macmillan, 1895.

Ashton, Rosemary. *The German Idea: Four English Writers and the Reception of German Thought, 1800–1860.* Cambridge: Cambridge University Press, 1980.

Atwood, Sara. *Ruskin's Educational Ideals.* Farnham, Surrey: Ashgate, 2011.

———. "Ruskin, Plato and the Education of the Soul." *Ruskin Review and Bulletin* 7.1 (Spring 2011): 6–14.

Aubrey, John. *"Brief Lives," Chiefly of Contemporaries.* Ed. Andrew Clark. 2 vols. Oxford: Clarendon Press, 1898.

Bentham, Jeremy. *Deontology; or the Science of Morality.* Ed. John Bowring. 2 vols. London: Rees, Orme, Browne, and Longman; Edinburgh: Tait, 1834.

——. *Introduction to the Principles of Morals and Legislation*. Ed. J. H. Burns and H. L. A. Hart. London: Athlone Press, 1970.

Berlin, Isaiah. *The Roots of Romanticism*. Ed. Henry Hardy. Princeton: Princeton University Press, 1999.

Bernhardi, Friedrich von. *Deutschland und der nächste Krieg*. Stuttgart: Cotta, 1912.

Birch, Dinah. "Ruskin's Multiple Writing: *Fors Clavigera*." *Ruskin and the Dawn of the Modern*. Ed. Dinah Birch. Oxford: Oxford University Press, 1999. 175–87.

Birch, Dinah. *Ruskin's Myths*. Oxford: Oxford University Press, 1988.

Bloom, Harold. *The Anxiety of Influence: A Theory of Poetry*. Oxford: Oxford University Press, 1973.

Boswell, James. *Life of Johnson*. Ed. Pat Rogers. Oxford World's Classics Edition. Oxford and New York: Oxford University Press, 1980.

Boorstin, Daniel. *Hidden History*. New York: Harper, 1987.

Browning, Elizabeth Barrett. *The Works of Elizabeth Barrett Browning* [*WEBB*]. Ed. Sandra Donaldson, Rita Humphrey, Marjorie Stone, and Beverly Taylor. 5 vols. London: Pickering and Chatto, 2010.

Browning, Robert, and Elizabeth Barrett. *The Brownings' Correspondence* [*BC*]. Ed. Philip Kelley, Ronald Hudson, Scott Lewis, and Edward Hagan. 18 vols. Winfield: Wedgestone Press, 1984–.

Burke, Edmund. *Reflections on the Revolution in France, 1790–94*. In *The Writings and Speeches of Edmund Burke*. Ed. L. G. Mitchell. Vol. 8. Oxford: Clarendon Press, 1989. 53–293.

Burleigh, Michael. *Sacred Causes: Religion and Politics from the European Dictators to Al Qaeda*. London: Harper, 2006.

Burwick, Frederick, and James C. McKusick, eds. *Faustus: From the German of Goethe*. Trans. Samuel Taylor Coleridge. Oxford: Oxford University Press, 2007.

[Byron, George Gordon]. *Sardanapulus, A Tragedy. Works. With His Letters and Journals and His Life by Thomas Moore*. Vol. 13. London: John Murray, 1836. 55–196.

Campbell, Ian, and Kenneth J. Fielding, eds. *Reminiscences. By Thomas Carlyle*. World's Classics Edition. Oxford: Oxford University Press, 1997.

Carlyle, Thomas. *Carlyle's Unpublished Lectures: Lectures on the History of Literature or the Successive Periods of European Culture*. Ed. R. P. Karkaria. Bombay: Curwen and Kane, 1892.

——. *Historical Essays*. Ed. Chris R. Vanden Bossche. Strouse Edition. Berkeley: University of California Press, 2002.

——. *Lectures on the History of Literature Delivered by Thomas Carlyle*,

April to July 1838. Ed. J. Reay Greene. London: Ellis and Elwey, 1892,
New York: Scribners, 1982.

———. *The Life of Friedrich Schiller. Comprehending an Examination of His Works*. London: Taylor and Hessey, 1825.

———. *Past and Present*. Ed. Chris R. Vanden Bossche. Strouse Edition. Berkeley: University of California Press, 2005.

———. *Reminiscences*. Ed. K. J. Fielding and Ian Campbell. World's Classics Edition. Oxford and New York: Oxford University Press, 2007.

———. *Sartor Resartus*. Ed. Rodger L. Tarr. Strouse Edition. Berkeley: University of California Press, 2000.

———. *The Works of Thomas Carlyle [Works]*. Ed. H. D. Traill. Centenary Edition. 30 vols. London: Chapman and Hall, 1896–99.

Carlyle, Thomas, and Jane Welsh Carlyle. *The Collected Letters of Thomas and Jane Welsh Carlyle [CL]*. Ed. Ian Campbell, Aileen Christianson, David R. Sorensen, et al. 40 vols. Durham: Duke University Press, 1970–.

———. *The Carlyle Letters Online*. Ed. Brent E. Kinser. Durham: Duke University Press, 2007–. http://carlyleletters.org.

Casey, John. "Do You Admire Thomas Carlyle?" *Spectator*. No. 278, 3 May 1997, 17–19.

Cate, George Allan, ed. *The Correspondence of Thomas Carlyle and John Ruskin*. Stanford: Stanford University Press, 1982.

Chalmers, Alexander. "Life of Luther." *The Table Talk of Martin Luther*. Trans. and ed. William Hazlitt. London: H. G. Bohn, 1857. xxv–xcvii.

Chambers, Robert. *The Scottish Ballads*. Edinburgh: William Tait, 1829.

Chesterton, G. K. *The Victorian Age in Literature. Collected Works*. Vol. 15. San Francisco: Ignatius Press, 1989.

Clubbe, John, ed. *Two Reminiscences of Thomas Carlyle*. Durham: Duke University Press, 1974.

Coleridge, Samuel Taylor. *Biographia Literaria II. The Collected Works of Samuel Taylor Coleridge*. Ed. James Engell and W. Jackson Bate. Vol. 7. Princeton: Princeton University Press, 1983.

———. *Table Talk I. The Collected Works of Samuel Taylor Coleridge*. Ed. Carl Woodring. Vol. 14.1. Princeton: Princeton University Press, 1990.

Dawkins, Richard. *The Selfish Gene*. Oxford: Oxford University Press, 1976.

DeLaura, David J. "Ishamael as Prophet: Heroes and Hero-Worship and the Self-Expressive Basis of Carlyle's Art." *Texas Studies in Literature and Language* 11 (1969–70): 705–32.

Durant, Will. *The Story of Philosophy*. 1926. New York: Simon and Schuster, 2005.

Eckermann, Johann Peter. *Gespräche mit Goethe in den letzten Jahren seines*

Lebens. Ed. Heinz Schlaffer. Münchener Ausgabe. Vol. 19. Munich: Hanser, 1986.

Eliot, George. *Middlemarch.* Ed. David Carroll. World's Classics Edition. Oxford: Oxford University Press, 1996.

Emerson, Ralph Waldo. *Complete Works.* Ed. Edward Waldo Emerson. Centenary Edition. 12 vols. Boston: Houghton and Mifflin, 1903–04.

Faulkner, Robert. *The Case for Greatness: Honorable Ambition and Its Critics.* New Haven: Yale University Press, 2007.

Fergusson, Sir James. *The Declaration of Arbroath, 1320.* Edinburgh: Edinburgh University Press, 1970.

Fielding, Kenneth J., ed. " 'Spiritual Optics?' or Carlyle's Gospel: A Revised Version." *Literature and Belief* 25.1–2 (2005): 219–38.

———. "A Skeptical Elegy as in Auchtertool Church." *Literature and Belief* 25.1–2 (2005): 239–58.

Finlay, Alec, ed. *The Armstrong Nose: Selected Letters of Hamish Hamilton.* Edinburgh: Polygon, 1996.

Flescher, Andrew Michael. *Heroes, Saints, and Ordinary Mortality.* Washington: Georgetown University Press, 2003.

Freiwald, Bina. " 'The World of Books Is Still the World': Elizabeth Barrett Browning's Critical Prose 1842–1844." *Newsletter of the Victorian Studies Association of Western Canada* 12 (1986): 1–24.

Froude, James Anthony. *Thomas Carlyle. A History of the First Forty Years of His Life, 1795–1835.* 2 vols. London: Longmans, Green, 1882.

———. *Thomas Carlyle. A History of His Life in London 1834–1881.* 2 vols. London: Longmans, Green, 1884.

Fukuyama, Francis. *The End of History and the Last Man.* New York: Free Press, 1992.

[Fuller, Margaret]. Review of *On Heroes, Hero-Worship, and the Heroic in History. Dial* 2.1 (1842): 131–33.

Fussell, Paul. *The Great War and Modern Memory.* New York: Oxford University Press, 1975.

Genlis, Stéphanie Félicité. *Mémoires inédits de Madame la comtesse de Genlis sur le dix-huitième siècle et la Révolution française.* 10 vols. Paris: Ladvocat, 1825.

Geyl, Pieter. "Carlyle; His Significance and Reputation." *Debates with Historians.* The Hague: Nijhoff; Groningen: Wolters, 1955. 35–55.

Gibbon, Edward. *The History of the Decline and Fall of the Roman Empire.* Ed. J. B. Bury. 7 vols. London: Metheun, 1901–02.

Gibbon, Peter H. *A Call to Heroism: Reviewing America's Vision of Greatness.* New York: Grove Press, 2002.

Gilfillan, George. *A First Gallery of Literary Portraits.* Second edition. Edinburgh: James Hogg, 1851.

Goethe, Johann Wolfgang von. *Werke.* Ed. Erich Trunz. Hamburger Ausgabe. 14 vols. Hamburg: Wegner, 1948–64.

———. *Gedichte 1800–1832.* Ed. Karl Eibl. *Sämtliche Werke.* Vol. 2. Frankfurt: Deutscher Klassiker, 1988.

Grant, James. *Portraits of Public Characters.* 2 vols. London: Saunders and Otley, 1841.

Gray, Thomas. *The Complete Poems of Thomas Gray: English, Latin and Greek.* Ed. Herbert W. Starr and J. R. Hendrickson. Oxford: Oxford University Press, 1966.

Grimm, Jacob. *Teutonic Mythology.* Trans. and ed. James Steven Stallybrass. 4 vols. London: George Bell, 1882–88.

Grotius, Hugo. *The Truth of the Christian Religion.* [*De Veritate Religionis Christianæ*]. Trans. John Clarke. Ed. Jean Le Clerc. New edition. London: William Baynes, 1829.

Hamilton, Francis. *An Account of the Kingdom of Nepal and of the Territories Annexed to This Dominion by the House of Ghorka.* Edinburgh: Archibald Constable, 1819.

Hegel, Georg Wilhelm Friedrich. *Vorlesungen über die Philosophie der Weltgeschichte.* Ed. Johannes Hoffmeister. Hamburg: Felix Meiner, 1968.

Henderson, Hamish. *Elegies for the Dead in Cyrenaica.* London: John Lehmann, 1948.

[Heraud, John Abraham]. "T. Carlyle on Hero-Worship." *Monthly Magazine* 5 (April 1841): 391–412.

Hobson, J. A. *John Ruskin, Social Reformer.* Boston: Dana Estes, 1898.

Holloway, John. *The Victorian Sage: Studies in Argument.* 1953. New York: Norton, 1965.

Howard, Philip N., Aiden Duffy, Deen Freelon, Muzammil Hussain, Will Mari, and Marwa Mazaid. "Opening Closed Regimes: What Was the Role of Social Media during the Arab Spring?" Working paper 2011.1. *The Project on Information Technology and Political Islam,* University of Washington. Web. 3 Nov. 2011.

Hughes, Linda K. *The Cambridge Introduction to Victorian Poetry.* Cambridge: Cambridge University Press, 2010.

Hughes-Hallett, Lucy. *Heroes, Saviours, Traitors and Supermen.* London: Harper Perennial, 2005.

Huxley, Aldous. *Brave New World.* New York: Harper and Row, 1932.

Huxley, Thomas Henry. *Life and Letters.* Ed. Leonard Huxley. 2 vols. New York: Appleton, 1900.

Irvine, William, and Park Honan. *The Book, the Ring, and the Poet: A Biography of Robert Browning*. New York: McGraw-Hill, 1974.

Irwin, Robert. *For Lust of Knowing: The Orientalists and Their Enemies*. London: Allen Lane, 2006.

Isaacson, Walter. "American Icon." *Time,* 17 Oct. 2011, 35–36.

Keen, Andrew. The Cult of the Amateur: How Blogs, MySpace, YouTube, and the Rest of Today's User-Generated Media Are Destroying Our Economy, Our Culture, and Our Values. New York: Doubleday, 2007.

Kinser, Brent E. "Rebecca Buffum Spring and the Carlyles." *Carlyle Studies Annual* 23 (2007): 157–68.

———. " 'A Very Beautiful Tempest in a Teapot': Elizabeth Barrett Browning, Thomas Carlyle, and the Annotation of *Aurora Leigh.*" *Browning Society Notes* 33 (2008): 21–39.

Leask, Nigel. *Robert Burns and Pastoral: Poetry and Improvement in Eighteenth-Century Scotland.* Oxford: Oxford University Press, 2010.

MacDiarmid, Hugh. *The Raucle Tongue: Hitherto Uncollected Prose.* Ed. Angus Calder, Glen Murray, and Alan Riach. Vol. 3. Manchester: Carcanet, 1998.

MacMechan, Archibald. Introduction. *On Heroes, Hero-Worship, and the Heroic in History. By Thomas Carlyle.* London: Ginn, 1901.

Madrigal, Alexis. "Estimating the Damage to the U.S. Economy Caused by Angry Birds." *Atlantic,* 13 Sept. 2011. Web. 16 Nov. 2011.

Mallet, Paul Henri. *Northern Antiquities; or a Description of the Manners, Customs, Religion and Laws of the Ancient Danes, and Other Northern Nations; including those of our Saxon Ancestors. With a Translation of the Edda, or System of Runic Mythology.* 2 vols. London: T. Carnan, 1770.

Masson, David. *Carlyle: Personally and in His Writings.* London: Macmillan, 1885.

Mill, John Stuart. *The Collected Works of John Stuart Mill* [*CWM*]. Gen. ed. John Robson. 33 vols. Toronto: University of Toronto Press, 1963–91.

Morlier, Margaret. "The Hero and the Sage: Elizabeth Barrett's Sonnets 'To George Sand' in Victorian Context." *Victorian Poetry* 41 (2003): 319–32.

Morris, Pam. "Heroes and Hero-Worship in Charlotte Brontë's *Shirley.*" *Nineteenth-Century Literature* 54.3 (1999): 285–307.

Niebuhr, B. G. *The Life and Letters of Barthold George Niebuhr.* 2 vols. London: Chapman and Hall, 1852.

Nietzsche, Friedrich. *Werke in Drei Bänden.* Ed. Karl Schlechta. 3 vols. Munich: Carl Hanser, 1960.

Norton, Charles Eliot, ed. *Correspondence between Goethe and Carlyle.* London: Macmillan, 1887.

Orwell, George. *Dickens, Dali and Others.* New York: Harcourt, 1946.

Oxford Dictionary of National Biography [ODNB]. Oxford. Oxford University Press, 2004–12. http://www.oxforddnb.com.

Pierce, Edward L., ed. *Memoirs and Letters of Charles Sumner.* 4 vols. Boston: Roberts Brothers, 1877–93.

Pionke, Albert D. "Beyond 'The Hero as Prophet': A Survey of Images of Islam in Carlyle's Works." *Literature and Belief* 25.1–2 (2005): 497–512.

Pococke, Edward. *Specimen Historiæ Arabum.* Oxford: H. Hall and Humphrey Robinson, 1650.

Reed, Jim. "Goethe — der Weltbürger als Weltleser: Lektüre als Akzeptanz des Fremden." *Goethe-Jahrbuch* 126 (2009): 161–73.

———. " 'Jene seltsame Literatur . . .': Wie im 19. Jahrhundert der deutsche Geist den englischen gerettet hat." *Ereignis Jena-Weimar: Gesellschaft und Kultur um 1800 im internationalen Kontext.* Ed. Lothar Ehrlich and Georg Schmidt. Weimar: Böhlau, 2008. 233–45.

Reeves, Minou. *Muhammad in Europe.* New York: New York University Press, 2000.

Reid, T. Wemyss, ed. *Life, Letters, and Friendships of Richard Monckton Milnes, First Lord Houghton.* 2 vols. London: Cassell, 1890.

Rose, John Holland, ed. *The French Revolution. A History. By Thomas Carlyle.* 3 vols. London: Bell, 1902.

Rosenberg, Philip. *The Seventh Hero: Thomas Carlyle and the Theory of Radical Activism* Cambridge, Mass.: Harvard University Press, 1974.

Ruskin, John. *The Diaries of John Ruskin.* Ed. Joan Evans and J. H. Whitehouse. Oxford: Clarendon Press, 1956.

———. *The Works of John Ruskin [WJR].* Ed. E. T. Cook and Alexander Wedderburn. Library Edition. 39 vols. London: George Allen, 1903–12.

Russell, George W. E., ed. *Letters of Matthew Arnold: 1848–1888.* 2 vols. London: Macmillan, 1895.

Sacy, Silvestre de (with Henri d'Audiffret). "Mahomet." *Biographie Universelle.* Vol. 26. Paris: Michaud, 1820–28. 186–213. Facsimile in *Carlyle Studies Annual* 23 (2007): 45–73.

Said, Edward. *Orientalism.* London: Routledge and Kegan Paul, 1978.

Sale, George. *The Koran, Commonly Called the Alcoran of Mohammed . . . to which is Prefixed a Preliminary Discourse.* London: Wilcox, 1734.

Scherer, Michael. "The Return of the Rabble Rouser." *Time,* 21 Nov. 2011, 44–47.

Scott, Walter. *Redgauntlet.* Ed. G. A. M. Wood and David Hewitt. Edinburgh Edition. Edinburgh: Edinburgh University Press, 1997.

Shepherd, Richard Herne, ed. *Memoirs of the Life and Writings of Thomas Carlyle.* 2 vols. London: Allen, 1881.

Slater, Joseph, ed. *The Correspondence of Emerson and Carlyle*. New York: Columbia University Press, 1964.

Sorensen, David R. "Instinctive Kantian: Carlyle, Kant, and the 'Vital Interests of Men.'" *Carlyle Studies Annual* 18 (1998): 53–64.

———. "'Symbolic Mutation': Thomas Carlyle and the Legacy of Charles Darwin in England." *Carlyle Studies Annual* 25 (2009): 61–81.

———. "'Transcendent Wonder or Moral Putrefaction?': Thomas Carlyle and the Legacy of Charles Darwin in England." *L'Héritage de Charles Darwin dans les Cultures Européennes*. Ed. Georges Letissier and Michel Prum. Paris: L'Harmattan, 2011. 19–26.

———. "'Une Religion plus digne de la Divinité': A New Source for Carlyle's Essay on Mahomet." *Carlyle Studies Annual* 23 (2007): 13–77.

Stephen, Leslie. "Thomas Carlyle." *The New Volumes of the Encyclopædia Britannica*. Tenth edition. Edinburgh: Adam and Charles Black; London: The Times, 1902. 26:593–99.

Tarr, Rodger L. *Thomas Carlyle: A Descriptive Bibliography*. Pittsburgh: University of Pittsburgh Press, 1989.

Thayer, Richard Holbrook. *Portraits of Dante from Giotto to Raffael. A Critical Study. With a Concise Iconography*. London: Warner; New York: Houghton Mifflin, 1911.

Thoreau, Henry David. "Thomas Carlyle and His Works." *Complete Writings*. Vol. 10. Riverside Edition. Boston: Houghton, Mifflin, 1898. 81–130.

Tillotson, Geoffrey. *A View of Victorian Literature*. Oxford: Clarendon Press, 1978.

Tulloch, John. *Movements of Religious Thought in the Nineteenth Century*. New York: Scribners, 1885.

Twells, Leonard. *The Theological Works of the Learned Dr. Pocock*. 2 vols. London: R. Gosling, 1740.

Watt, Montgomery. "Carlyle on Muhammad." *Hibbert Journal* 53 (1954–55): 247–54.

Westerlund, David. "Ahmed Deedat's Theology of Religion: Apologetics through Polemics." *Journal of Religion in Africa* 33 (2003): 263–78.

Wheeler, Michael. *Ruskin's God*. Cambridge: Cambridge University Press, 1999.

Williams, Raymond. *Culture and Society: Coleridge to Orwell*. London: Hogarth Press, 1987.

Wilson, David Alec. *Carlyle at His Zenith (1848–53)*. Vol. 4. London: Trench, Trubner; New York: Dutton, 1927.

———. *Carlyle on Cromwell and Others (1837–48)*. Vol. 3. London: Kegan Paul, Trench, and Trubner; New York: Dutton, 1925.

Woodworth, Elizabeth. "Elizabeth Barrett Browning, Coventry Patmore, and Alfred Tennyson on Napoleon III: The Hero-Poet and Carlylean Heroics." *Victorian Poetry* 44 (2006): 543–60.

Worden, Blair. "Thomas Carlyle and Oliver Cromwell." *Proceedings of the British Academy* 105 (2000): 131–70.

Yeandle, Peter. "Ruskin, Mass Education and the Search for a Moral Curriculum." Unpublished lecture delivered to the Ruskin Polygon Colloquium, Lancaster University, March 2007.

Contributors

Sara Atwood is the author of *Ruskin's Educational Ideas* (Ashgate, 2011) and guest editor of a special issue on Ruskin of *Nineteenth-Century Prose* (2011). Other recent publications include essays on *Fors Clavigera*, Ruskin and Darwinism, and the Platonic aspects of Ruskin's educational philosophy. She is a Companion of the Guild of St. George.

Owen Dudley Edwards, FRSE, renowned author, editor, broadcaster, and lecturer, is honorary fellow in the School of History, Classics, and Archaeology at the University of Edinburgh. He has written studies of T. B. Macaulay, Arthur Conan Doyle, P. G. Wodehouse, James Connolly, Burke and Hare, and Oscar Wilde. His most recent book is *British Children's Fiction in the Second World War* (Edinburgh University Press, 2007).

Christopher Harvie was a member of the Scottish Parliament for Mid Scotland and Fife from 2007 to 2011, when he retired as an MSP at the election. He was formerly professor of British and Irish Studies at the University of Tübingen. His publications include *A Floating Commonwealth: Politics, Culture, and Technology on Britain's Atlantic Coast, 1860–1930* (Oxford University Press, 2008), *Scotland: A Short History* (Oxford University Press, 2002), *Scotland and Nationalism: Scottish Society and Politics, 1707–1994*, fourth edition (London University Press, 2004), *No Gods and Precious Few Heroes: Twentieth-Century Scotland*, fourth edition (Edinburgh University Press, 2000), and *Cultural Weapons: Scotland in a New Europe* (London University Press, 1992).

Brent E. Kinser is associate professor of English at Western Carolina University. He is the author (with David R. Sorensen) of "Thomas Carlyle," *Oxford Bibliographies in Victorian Literature*, ed. Juliet John (Oxford University Press, 2012), and of *The American Civil War in the Shaping of British Democracy* (Ashgate, 2011), editor of *The Collected Letters of Thomas and Jane Welsh Carlyle* (Duke University Press, 1970–), coordinating editor of *The Carlyle Letters Online* (Duke University Press,

2007–), coeditor (with David R. Sorensen) of *Carlyle Studies Annual*, and coeditor (with Rodger L. Tarr) of *Marjorie Kinnan Rawlings's Cross Creek Sampler* (University Press of Florida, 2011) and *The Uncollected Writings of Marjorie Kinnan Rawlings* (University Press of Florida, 2007).

Terence James Reed, FBA, is Taylor Professor of German Language and Literature and emeritus fellow of Queen's College, Oxford. His publications include "Goethe's Alliance with Schiller" in *The Cambridge Companion to Goethe* (Cambridge University Press, 2002), as editor (with Martin Swales and Jeremy Atler), *Goethe at 250: London Symposium* (Ludicium, 2002), as translator, *Goethe, The Flight to Italy: Diary and Selected Letters* (Oxford University Press World's Classics, 1999), *Thomas Mann: The Uses of Tradition*, third edition (Oxford University Press, 1996), *Death in Venice: Making and Unmaking a Master* (New York University Press, 1994), *Schiller* (Oxford University Press, 1991), *The Classical Centre: Goethe and Weimar 1775–1832* (Oxford University Press, 1986), and *Goethe* (Oxford University Press, 1984).

David R. Sorensen is professor of English at Saint Joseph's University, Philadelphia. Since 1999, he has been an editor of *The Collected Letters of Thomas and Jane Welsh Carlyle* (Duke University Press, 1970–). His publications include (with Brent E. Kinser) "Thomas Carlyle," *Oxford Bibliographies in Victorian Literature*, ed. Juliet John (Oxford University Press, 2012), (with Kenneth J. Fielding) *Jane Carlyle: Newly Selected Letters* (Ashgate, 2004), (with Rodger L. Tarr) *The Carlyles at Home and Abroad* (Ashgate, 2004), and (with K. J. Fielding) an edition of Carlyle's *French Revolution* (Oxford University Press World's Classics, 1989). He is currently collaborating with Mark Engel and Mark Cumming on the Strouse Edition of *The French Revolution*. He is coeditor (with Brent E. Kinser) of *Carlyle Studies Annual*, and he is a Companion of the Guild of St. George.

Beverly Taylor is professor of English at the University of North Carolina, Chapel Hill, where at present she serves as chair of the Department of English and Comparative Literature. She is an editor of the five-volume *Works of Elizabeth Barrett Browning* (Pickering and Chatto, 2010) and coeditor (with Marjorie Stone) of *Elizabeth Barrett Browning: Selected Poems* (Broadview Press, 2009), and is completing a critical study of Barrett Browning. She has also published on nineteenth-century Arthurian literature and on, among others, Shelley, Byron, Carlyle, Tennyson, the Brownings, Arnold, and Siddal.

Index

Rethinking the Western Tradition

Groundwork for the Metaphysics of Morals
By Immanuel Kant
EDITED BY ALLEN W. WOOD

Sesame and Lilies
By John Ruskin
EDITED BY DEBORAH EPSTEIN NORD

"The Social Contract" and "The First and Second Discourses"
By Jean-Jacques Rousseau
EDITED BY SUSAN DUNN

Discourse on Method and Meditations on First Philosophy
By René Descartes
EDITED BY DAVID WEISSMAN

Culture and Anarchy
By Matthew Arnold
EDITED BY SAMUEL LIPMAN

The Idea of a University
By John Henry Newman
EDITED BY FRANK M. TURNER

The Prince
By Niccolò Machiavelli
TRANSLATED BY ANGELO CODEVILLA